VIKINGS ACROSS THE ATLANTIC

AUSTIN PUBLIC LIBRARY

Vikings across the Atlantic

. . . .

Emigration and the Building of
a Greater Norway, 1860–1945

Daron W. Olson

University of Minnesota Press
Minneapolis
London

Portions of chapter 2 were published in Daron W. Olson, "Norwegian-American Historians and the Creation of an Ethnic Identity," *Scandinavian Studies* 79, no. 1 (Spring 2007): 41–56.

Copyright 2013 by the Regents of the University of Minnesota

All rights reserved. No part of this publication may be reproduced, stored in a retrieval system, or transmitted, in any form or by any means, electronic, mechanical, photocopying, recording, or otherwise, without the prior written permission of the publisher.

Published by the University of Minnesota Press
111 Third Avenue South, Suite 290
Minneapolis, MN 55401-2520
http://www.upress.umn.edu

Library of Congress Cataloging-in-Publication Data

Olson, Daron W.
    Vikings across the Atlantic : emigration and the building of a greater Norway, 1860–1945 / Daron W. Olson.
    Includes bibliographical references and index.
    ISBN 978-0-8166-5141-2 (hc: acid-free paper)
    ISBN 978-0-8166-5142-9 (pb: acid-free paper)
    1. Norwegian Americans—History. 2. Norwegian Americans—Ethnic identity. 3. Norwegians—United States. 4. Norway—Emigration and immigration. I. Title.
E184.S2O44 2013
305.893'982073—dc23   2012029388

Printed in the United States of America on acid-free paper

The University of Minnesota is an equal-opportunity educator and employer.

20 19 18 17 16 15 14 13   10 9 8 7 6 5 4 3 2 1

Contents

Introduction: Mythmaking and Identity	vii
1. Creating Home: The Roots of Norwegian Emigration	1
2. Belonging to the Nation: Origin Myths and the Argument to Be American, 1860–1890	25
3. Modern Vikings: The Challenge to Anglo-American Superiority, 1890–1917	69
4. Backlash: Xenophobia and the Pressure to Assimilate, 1917–1929	115
5. A Shared Homeland: Celebrating Norwegian Identity across the Atlantic, 1929–1945	159
Conclusion: Building a Greater Norway	211
Acknowledgments	225
Notes	229
Index	265

· INTRODUCTION ·

Mythmaking and Identity

AROUND THE YEAR 1000 a Viking ship entered previously unexplored waters of the Atlantic Ocean to the south and west of Greenland. Its crew was composed of Icelanders whose ancestors had come from the western shores of Norway. They called their propitious captain Leif the Lucky, although his formal name was Leif Erikson, son of Erik the Red.[1] It was considered good luck to be aboard a ship piloted by Leif because his expeditions were nearly always profitable and his men returned safely to their homes. Leif had heard stories about a new land and was eager to explore it in the hope of finding great riches. The first time the crew went ashore, they found a landscape consisting mainly of rocks, and the second time one of forests and sandy beaches. Leif's luck proved good on the third try: they found dew on the grass; bringing the moisture to their mouths, "it seemed the sweetest thing they had ever tasted." Since it was late in the season, they decided to winter there, and they built houses along a riverbank a short distance from the coast. They noted that the river contained salmon bigger than any they had ever seen, and they discovered grapevines growing in the surrounding land. In the spring they loaded the ship with grapes and timber and prepared to return home. Impressed by the bounty of the new land, Leif decided to call it Vínland, meaning Wine Land.[2]

Nearly a millennium later, on June 7, 1945, King Haakon VII returned to Norway for the first time after being exiled by the German invasion of 1940. On that day in the capital of Oslo, thousands of Norwegians stood in the rain to see and listen to their king, who during the war had become a symbol of the nation's heroic resistance to Nazi tyranny. The honor guard was composed of British and American soldiers, in particular the soldiers of the American Ninety-ninth Battalion. The remaining members of the battalion served as security guards along the route of the king's procession on the way to the Royal Castle. The Ninety-ninth Battalion also represented an important symbol in the story of Norway's liberation. Better known as the Viking Battalion—its unit insignia depicted a Viking ship—the Ninety-ninth Battalion had specifically recruited men of Norwegian ancestry to fight for the liberation of Norway. Although Germany surrendered before the invasion could take place, the battalion was sent to Norway to process the German prisoners and to serve as a reminder of the close ties between America and Norway, allies for freedom in World War II.[3] More important, the presence of these modern Vikings, many of them "sons of Norway," validated the idea that those whose ancestors had emigrated from Norway to America still belonged to the nation of Norway.

These two moments formed narrative poles, so to speak, for the vision of a greater Norway. The essence of being Norwegian in this maritime nation has historically been tied to seafaring activities, which involves movement and strength. The Vikings served as the dynamic embodiment of Norway, a nation often manifested through its encounters with new lands. The idea that Leif Erikson and his Viking cohorts had been in the New World connected Norway with America through participation in the historical process of transatlantic migration. The nineteenth-century movement of Norwegians was envisioned as a continuation of that historical Viking exploration even though the large-scale migration of Norwegians to the United States did not occur for another eight centuries. When the ancestral homeland faced peril during World War II, the nation of Norway once again became articulated through movement across the Atlantic, albeit in a reverse direction. Moreover, the soldiers of the Viking Battalion reflected the resilience of Norway, a strength based on Norwegian ideals of freedom and democracy, which the Nazi occupiers ultimately could not vanquish.

This book argues that the vision of a greater Norway created a transnational and extraterritorial space that expanded the boundaries of the Norwegian nation. Forming the intersection between Norway's national identity and the Norwegian-American ethnic identity, the greater Norway existed as a nation whose occupants resided both within and outside Norway. While based on a shared Norwegian ethnicity, membership in the greater Norway was not limited to those residing within the physical borders of Norway; it was primarily determined by loyalty to Norway and her cultural traditions. In other words, the essence of belonging to Norway involved a sacred allegiance to a transcendent and imagined nation that was carried within the hearts and minds of Norwegians wherever they might roam. In an ideological sense, members of the greater Norway symbolized eternal Vikings who brandished their Norwegian identity—mobility and strength—in their encounters with new lands or fighting foreign oppressors, particularly those that threatened ancestral Norway. But in a larger sense the greater Norway stood for more than mere symbolism; it represented something so real to its members that many of them were willing to die to save it.

As with the birth of many nations, the genesis of the greater Norway was linked to a dramatic and transformative event, the June 7, 1905, declaration by the Norwegian national assembly, the Storting, of the dissolution of the Swedish–Norwegian dynastic union, which led to Norway's complete independence. Serving what Bernhard Giesen has termed a "triumphant myth,"[4] it symbolized the rebirth of the modern nation of Norway. Patriotic fervor gripped both sides of the Atlantic as Norwegian Americans offered their enthusiastic support for the homeland, including a petition to President Theodore Roosevelt urging the United States to recognize Norway; countless telegrams of support to Christian Michelsen, the Norwegian prime minister who guided efforts to win Norwegian independence; and even offers of military service to Norway.[5] Thus, through solidarity with homeland Norwegians, Norwegian Americans participated in what would become a foundation myth for the greater Norway.[6]

In the aftermath of the nationalist euphoria of 1905, leaders in Norway sought to harness the spirit of the times and give a voice to these transatlantic impulses. On June 21, 1907, Nordmands-Forbundet (Norsemen's Federation, or League) was founded in Norway's capital of Kristiania (renamed Oslo in 1925). The organization's first president, Carl Berner, had been the president of the Storting when it made its dramatic declaration on June 7, 1905, and his association with the organization legitimated the nationalist credentials of Nordmands-Forbundet. In the first issue of its monthly publication with the same name, in October 1907, its editor F. G. Gade and the folklorist and professor Moltke Moe articulated its mission to foster greater Norwegian nationalism in the homeland and to make all Norwegians, both at home and abroad, more interconnected. It also appealed to all Norwegians around the globe to feel bounded "by blood to Norwegian nationality." Through this articulation of *vor egen stamme* (our own race or nation), Nordmands-Forbundet proposed that Norwegians living outside Norway, including Norwegian Americans, were part of *et større Norge*—"a greater Norway."[7]

With the creation of the greater Norway concept, the Norwegian-American identity subsequently became bound to Norway's national identity. Previously, the development of the Norwegian-American identity had resembled the ethnic identity process of other immigrant groups.[8] The birth of that identity coincided with the decade of the American Civil War, a time when intense competition among various ethnic groups to demonstrate their loyalty to the United States was manifest. All immigrant groups competed to promote their image as good Americans in both deed and word, which in turn prompted Norwegians to attempt to show that they were the best immigrant group. A common strategy involved the use of myths of sacrifice, which argued that members of the immigrant group had died in military service to the United States or experienced other types of hardship. The dedication of Norwegians to military service in America won them the respect of their new country, allowing Norwegian-American immigrant leaders to construct the appropriate sacrifice myths showing that their group had shed blood for the United States. A second category of construction, origin myths, sometimes called foundation myths, highlighted how the immigrant group had played an important and historic role in the founding of the United States, including the involvement of people from the immigrants' homeland with the New World prior to the era of mass migration to the United States in the nineteenth century. Norwegian-American origin myths pointed to the lineage of Norwegians in the New World, arguing that since the time of the Vikings Norwegians had maintained a long association with the Western Hemisphere, or *Vesterheim,* an old Norse word first used by Rasmus Bjørn Anderson in 1875 to convey this long-standing relationship between Norway and its emigrated kin.[9] The construction of these two myths, prevalent among Norwegian-American identity-makers until about 1890, allowed Norwegians to claim that they were a valuable addition to America owing to their shared racial and civil virtues with Anglo-Americans.

Bolstered by heavy immigration rates—only Ireland sent a higher percentage of its population to America than did Norway—the Norwegian community in America grew and prospered, reaching its heyday from 1890 to 1917. Often referring to the community of Norwegian immigrants and their American-born descendents as "Norway in America," Norwegian Americans became increasingly confident in their ethnic identity. During this period, Norwegian-American leaders promoted hegemony myths to demonstrate that Norwegians were superior to all Americans, including Anglo-Americans. During these decades emigrated Norwegians made a concerted effort to proclaim their loyalty to their ancestral homeland, which raised awareness of the Norwegian-American image in Norway.

In the years immediately after World War I, the American political system waged a concerted effort against ethnic activity in the United States, especially any activities involving the use of the language of the immigrants' old homelands. Reacting to this new reality, and realizing that a viable Norwegian-language-based culture could not be maintained, Norwegian-American leaders shifted their strategy to the promotion of legacy myths in which they argued that Norwegian culture and history should be recognized and celebrated by the dominant Anglo-American culture. Although a shift in tactics, the construction of the Norwegian-American identity still developed on the assumption that loyalty and ties to Norway could be maintained by successive generations of Norwegian Americans.

That sense of optimism seemed warranted during the 1925 Norse-American Centennial, which observed the hundredth anniversary of the first large-scale Norwegian immigration to America, the arrival of the sloop *Restaurationen*. President Calvin Coolidge attended, and his speech seemed to validate the Norwegian-American identity when he spoke of their inclination for democracy and their solid citizenship, and he endorsed Leif Erikson, not Columbus, as the true discoverer of America. Yet scarcely two years later the U.S. Congress deliberated on the Origins Proviso to the 1924 Johnson-Reed Immigration Act. The proviso severely limited the numbers of Norwegians and other non-British Europeans who could legally enter the United States, and many Norwegian Americans as well as homeland Norwegians viewed it as an affront. The Origins Proviso went into law in 1929.

At this time the greater Norway project began to flex its proverbial muscles. Through the efforts of Nordmands-Forbundet (renamed Nordmanns-Forbundet in 1932 owing to official spelling changes), Norwegian government officials, and Norway's royal family, Norway made a concerted effort to include Norwegian Americans in the celebration of *norskhet*, Norwegianness. Prior to 1925, its most prominent effort had been at the 1914 Eidsvold Celebration in Kristiania, designed to honor the centennial of the creation of Norway's constitution. As part of its national exhibition, Nordmands-Forbundet had its own pavilion with an exhibit depicting Norwegians around the world, including Norwegians in America. Norway participated in the 1925 Norse-American Centennial by sending official representatives and a telegram from King Haakon. In Norway that same year, a statue was dedicated to Colonel Hans Christian Heg, the Norwegian-American Civil War hero whose legacy was a chief component of the celebration in the United States, as well as a smaller but corresponding celebration of Norwegian America held in Stavanger on July 4.

In fact, the Norse-American Centennial marked the beginning of a fifteen-year period leading up to the eve of World War II in which the promoters of the greater Norway staged a series of transatlantic celebrations of the Norwegian heritage. These celebrations showcased a transnational, shared identity between Norway and Norwegian America and were designed to foster closer ties between the homeland and its emigrated population in the United States. As a result the homeland included Norwegian-American heroes such as Colonel Heg and Leif Erikson within the pantheon of Norway's heroes. These celebrations often featured dual and simultaneous ceremonies in both Norway and America. Many of these events were broadcast via radio so that citizens of both nations could participate as members of the audience, augmenting a sense of shared experience. By tying Norway to the success of Norwegian Americans, these transnational celebrations located Norway's identity within a larger international framework. The celebrations emphasized the shared values between Norway and America, and by linking Norway ideologically to the United States they provided greater recognition of Norway on the world stage.

Without the advent of World War II, the bonds between Norwegians living on both sides of the Atlantic might have remained only an ideological formulation. However, the German occupation of Norway tested the greater Norway. Though an occupied nation, Norway remained an active combatant as its government and king went into exile in Britain. Meanwhile, prominent Norwegians including Crown Prince Olav and exiles like Sigrid Undset and Halvdan Koht spoke tirelessly in the United States about how Norway represented the values of democracy and freedom that both nations were striving to save. Norwegian Americans contributed money to the relief of Norway, and many fought for the Allied cause, including those modern Vikings of the Ninety-ninth Battalion that ended up in Norway. Ultimately, the ordeal of World War II validated the greater Norway concept through the shedding of blood by Norwegians on both sides of the Atlantic.

Studies of immigrant groups traditionally have focused on either the extent to which the immigrants assimilated (and integrated) or the extent to which they retained their ethnic heritage within a milieu of cultural pluralism. In either case, the emphasis is on the receiving country. More recent theoretical approaches, however, have argued that immigrants engage in networks and patterns of life that encompass both their host and home societies.[10] The theory of transnationalism identifies the cultural hybridity of immigrant groups and their long-term attachment to their homeland. As the intersection of the ethnic Norwegian-American identity and Norway's national identity, the greater Norway created a transnational social space. As defined by Thomas Faist, such a space spans at least two or more places, yet it is imbued with a social meaning that extends beyond simple territoriality. For that space to have true meaning, moreover, it must have concrete social and symbolic ties for potential migrants. In other words, the greater Norway occupied a social space that transcended the mere physical boundaries of either Norway or America and existed in what Faist terms "a metaphorical alternative."[11] And by extension, the greater Norway had social and symbolic ties for the inhabitants of the homeland, a concept that John W. Meyer et al. refer to as "global associational processes."[12]

Many transnational theorists, though, imply that only contemporary immigrants are capable of building and maintaining ties with the homeland, which requires modern technological advances such as the Internet, telephones and new cellular phone technologies, jet airplanes, satellite dishes, and faxes.[13] Scholars of industrial-era immigration, particularly historians, take exception to this qualitative distinction. Peter Kivisto and Eva Morawska, among many, argue that many immigrant groups continued to maintain an active interest and involvement in their homeland and sought to selectively transplant aspects of their cultural heritage, something akin to Herbert Gans's idea of "symbolic ethnicity." Nancy Foner further contends that many historians have long documented the existence of transnational ties in the past even if they did not use the term "transnationalism."[14] The existence of strong ties between Norway and emigrated Norwegians in America during the early to mid-twentieth century owed much to the technologies of the time including telegrams, radio broadcasts, and faster ships and airplanes.

As a concept shared by the citizens of two nations, the idea of a greater Norway likewise raises questions about the nature of nationalism. As Richard Handler points out, nations are thought to be bounded by both physical space, as indicated by their boundaries, and time, since they have defined origins that are usually located in the distant past. Nationalism, as an ideology, places boundaries on its citizens by constructing them as a homogeneous population whether the population is actually homogeneous or not. However, he notes that the construction of national cultures is a fairly recent phenomenon occurring in Western thought. He argues that other worldviews do not place boundaries on collective identities and that identities, including ethnic ones, can exist outside the assumed "boundedness" of the nation.[15] Hence, the authors of the greater Norway transcended the boundedness of Norwegian nationalism by placing it in a transnational context.

Benedict Anderson's concept of the nation as an imagined community likewise reinforces the validity of the greater Norway concept. Although Anderson's formulation speaks of the nation being imagined as both *limited* and *sovereign*, the concept is flexible enough to account for the greater Norway. Elite image-makers on both sides of the Atlantic could imagine the Norwegian nation existing in both a European and an American homeland, a *Heimland* (homeland) and a *Vesterheim*. Indeed, the concept also embraced Norwegian communities in Canada, South America, Africa, and Asia. Thus, in the sense of a limited imagined community, the greater Norway, despite existing beyond the territorial boundaries of Norway, did not encompass all members of the human race. The issue of sovereignty is more problematic, but Anderson differentiates between the concept of national freedom and actual practice. For instance, he acknowledges that regardless of the degree of inequality or exploitation—the idea that all members of a nation might not be on equal footing—the nation is conceived as a fraternity, or what Anderson terms "a deep, horizontal comradeship," and the creators of the greater Norway envisioned it from this perspective.[16]

Collective memories, especially migration memories, also point to the relationship between emigration and nationalism. Felicia Medved has written that since modern nations are invented, they must have homeland myths whose mystique provides legitimacy to the nation. Moreover, she notes that migration and homeland are bound together and that almost all nations "find migration memories in their histories." In effect, migration memories form an integral part of a nation's myths. "People involved in settlements abroad engrafted their prior history onto subsequent events of the place." She stresses that emigration epics are often described as attempts to seek freedom in the everyday world by escaping the restrictions of the old society, including its past and its memories. Paradoxically, however, they represent a spiritual return to the homeland for the emigrant who carries an abstract image of that homeland.[17] The great migration of Norwegians to America therefore formed a migration memory of the newly emergent Norwegian nation. And given that Norway's nationalist fervor was fairly recent, and thus more intense than that of other nations, the greater Norway concept was more eagerly adopted in the homeland than, for example, a similar concept concerning Swedish emigrants and Sweden.

Nationalism takes form in many contexts, and John Hutchinson has argued that nations are developed through a political dimension and a cultural dimension. The goal of political nationalism is to secure an independent state for the nation, which Norway achieved in 1905. The goal of cultural nationalism, meanwhile, is "the moral regeneration of the historic community" and "the re-creation of a distinctive national civilization." He further observes that cultural nationalism often is not tied to statehood, which helps explain why Norwegian Americans, as citizens of the United States, could belong to the greater Norway because their nationalism was manifested through cultural discourse. Øystein Sørensen notes that although Norway was an "old nation" historically, it was a new nation in the modern sense, and thus there was great need to not only achieve political independence but to define what was culturally unique about Norway.[18] Through their participation in the greater Norway, Norwegian Americans, although having a limited role in Norway's political nationalism, did contribute to Norway's cultural nationalism by demonstrating their loyalty to Norwegian values and preservation of its cultural traditions. In addition, homeland advocates of the concept could point to the success of the Norwegian immigrants in America to buttress their contention that Norway was a great nation.

As Eric Hobsbawm and Terrence Ranger have observed, the process of constructing the modern nation relied on invented traditions: the establishment of secular nationalist institutions such as public schools, the introduction of public ceremonies, and the mass production of public monuments.[19] In America, Norwegian Americans engaged in all three types of invented traditions. They built a series of Norwegian-American institutions including churches, secular organizations, and educational institutions designed to maintain Norwegian traditions. They routinely participated in public ceremonies honoring Norway including May 17 and Leif Erikson Day celebrations. Norwegian Americans erected numerous monuments to honor their heroes from Norway, including Leif Erikson, Ole Bull, Henrik Wergeland, Bjørnstjerne Bjørnson, and Henrik Ibsen.

In Norway these same types of invented traditions enabled the inclusion of Norwegian Americans within Norwegian nationalism. The Norwegian school system introduced instruction on *Norge i Amerika* (Norway in America) in the public school curriculum, while the Norwegian government participated in transnational celebrations such as the centennial of Norway's constitution in 1914, the centennial celebrating Norwegian immigration to America in 1925, and the visit by the crown prince and his wife to the United States in 1939. By the 1920s, homeland Norwegians were participating in celebrating Leif Erikson Day and America's Fourth of July. They raised monuments to Norwegian-American heroes such as Leif Erikson and Colonel Hans Christian Heg. These commemorations allowed homeland Norwegians and emigrated Norwegians to share in a common national identity. The sense among Norwegian Americans that they belonged to the nation of Norway—the greater Norway—and their encouragement in this way of thinking by leaders in Norway reflect Anthony D. Smith's concept of "a felt reality of the nation."[20]

Belonging to a nation, therefore, is not limited to living within the boundaries of the homeland. Rogers Brubaker defines nations as "substantial, enduring collectives," and he urges scholars to "think about nationalism without nations" and to see "nation as a category of practice, nationhood as an institutionalised cultural and political form and nationness as a contingent event or happening." In a similar vein, Smith relates that nationalism should not be viewed as just a belief system but also as a species of religion.[21] If one views the greater Norway as a form of religion, then to promote it, its practitioners and creators needed only to sell it to the potential members of the congregation, both in Norway and America.

Of course the ethnic connection between Norwegian Americans and homeland Norwegians provided the most obvious reason for including immigrants within the greater Norway. Smith emphasizes that ethnic communities form the basis for the emergence of nations, and he places limits on "the nation as invention." Instead, he argues that modern nationalists borrow and reinterpret existing ethnic symbols that are used to promote the "new nation." Only cultural symbols with legitimacy or authenticity for the core ethnic group (in this study, the Norwegians) work to effectively create the modern nation.[22] Seen from this perspective, Norwegian Americans could claim valid membership within the nation of Norway.

It is also possible that the identity-forming activities of Norwegian immigrants in America more accurately reflect the activities of a diaspora group. Diaspora has often been used to denote religious or national groups living outside an (imagined) homeland, while transnationalism, by contrast, is used both in a more narrow sense of migrants' durable ties across countries and also more broadly to encompass social formations, including transnational networks, groups, and organizations.[23]

The term "diaspora" has been recast in the academic literature and public discourses of recent years. The traditional usage of "diaspora" referred to a forced dispersal of a national or ethnic group, often into several new homelands. Furthermore, a traditional diaspora meant that one intrinsically resisted the cultural encroachment of the temporary host country while remaining tied in spirit and usually practice to the norms and cultural traditions of the homeland, even if it had to be imagined. More recently, however, nationalist groups or governments have often used the term to pursue agendas of nation-state building or mobilizing populations abroad for a group identity or some political project in the service of an external homeland. In terms of scholarly usage, "diaspora" no longer refers exclusively to forced dispersal but to any kind of dispersal, including voluntary migration diasporas. Migrants no longer view returning to the homeland as the ultimate goal but are instead motivated by strategies intended to maintain lateral ties with the homeland. Diaspora theory also focuses almost exclusively on the community or group, which contrasts with transnational theory's emphasis on individuals, families, and kin networks.[24]

A question that therefore arises is whether the construction of a Norwegian-American identity represented a transnational or a diaspora experience. In many ways, the Norwegian-American efforts to remain loyal to Norway represented a diaspora, or at least the dynamic of a diaspora. As Thomas Faist notes, "Concepts of diaspora deal with dispersal, whether traumatic or not, and the resulting emergence and reproduction of some sort of collective identity, with varying intensities of ties to the country of emigration and the countries of immigration."[25]

Furthermore, the Norwegian-American experience does seem to conform to the definitional criteria defined by Roben Cohen and Gabriel Sheffer.[26] One criterion, which Michael Bruneau refers to as "choice of destination" diaspora, is carried out in the structure of migratory chains across oceans that link migrants with those already installed in the host countries. Another criterion is "identity awareness" diaspora in with the migrant community retains a strong recollection of the society of origin, which is linked to the memory of its territory. It also implies a strong sense of community, and in the case of the homeland nation it relies on a collective narrative linked to the homeland territory and to a memory that is transmitted across migrant generations.[27]

A key weakness to the argument for diaspora is the resistance among the group to assimilation. Since diaspora communities most often are situated with reference to a sometimes imagined, if indeed unobtainable, homeland, the preservation of their national identity within the borders of host countries takes on a degree of urgency, a need to retain their distinctiveness.[28] In the case of Norwegian immigrants, however, the degree of resistance to their adopted American home was not of this extent; in fact, most Norwegian Americans adopted American practices, including the use of English at the expense of Norwegian. Yet, as Kachig Tölölyan observes, the postmodern refining of the concept of diaspora that views it as "resistance to the hegemonic, discriminatory, and culturally homogenizing" efforts of the host nation and "the celebration of multiplicity and mobility" might allow the Norwegian-American encounter with the United States to be viewed as something akin to a diaspora migration.[29] Although this study will refer to the transnationalism of the greater Norway project, it must be noted that the occupation of Norway during World War II and the subsequent reaction to the occupation was highly reflective of a diaspora dynamic.

To understand how the greater Norway became realized, it is necessary to trace the formative years prior to its intellectual conception. Chapter 1, "Creating Home: The Roots of Norwegian Emigration," looks at how conditions in Norway influenced Norwegian immigration to America. It shows how national romanticism played a significant role in influencing Norway's nineteenth-century identity. Having been under Danish rule for over four hundred years, Norwegian intellectuals desired to re-create a purely Norwegian nation. They turned to the Norwegian peasantry who they believed had preserved pure Norwegian culture and traditions. The chapter also looks at how the change in Norway from subsistence to commercial farming threatened the traditional way of life in Norway; some sought to preserve that lifestyle by leaving for America. In the United States, Norwegians engaged in preservationist strategies, such as living in ethnically Norwegian enclaves and establishing Norwegian-language churches. A related argument is that Norwegian emigrants were tied into a world economic system, and their immigration to America must be viewed as part of large-scale labor migration.

These impulses from Norway would in turn be modified to fit the Norwegian experience in America. In chapter 2, "Belonging to the Nation: Origin Myths and the Argument to Be American, 1860–1890," the genesis of an early Norwegian-American identity is explored. Through duty to the Union in the American Civil War, Norwegian leaders argued that Norwegians had shown their loyalty to their new homeland by shedding their blood for it. The construction of myths of sacrifice served notice that Norwegians had proven their worth as an immigrant group. The second type of myths, origin myths, owed much to Rasmus B. Anderson's work in promoting the legacy of Leif Erikson. By highlighting the role of the intrepid Old Norse explorer, Anderson promoted the idea that Norwegians were the first Europeans to be associated with the New World. He further noted that through their colonization efforts in England and Normandy during the Viking Age, Norwegians first introduced into the English-speaking world the values of love for democracy and freedom, hard work, and respect for law and order. In constructing these origin myths, Anderson and other Norwegian-American image-makers contended that the Norwegians were the best immigrant group in America. Moreover, their construction of a Norwegian-American identity sought to place Norwegians in a position that showed they were loyal to both America and Norway, thereby crafting a hybrid or complementary identity.

Not satisfied with merely being among the best immigrants, Norwegian-American leaders advanced a step further and proclaimed their superiority over old-stock Americans. Chapter 3, "Modern Vikings: The Challenge to Anglo-American Superiority, 1890–1917," identifies the strategies used by Norwegian-American leaders, including Waldemar Ager and Ole E. Rølvaag, to claim that Norwegian Americans were superior to Anglo-Americans on their own terms. In effect, Norwegian-American identity-makers argued that Norwegians were more racially pure, more "Nordic" than Anglo-Americans, that they were more religiously Protestant than Anglo-Americans, and that they were the true source of American values as a result of their Viking heritage. Moreover, Norwegian-American leaders contended that Norwegians were eminently suited to the progressive lifestyle of the modern era because of traits first revealed in their Viking ancestors, such as the ability to solve problems, embrace education, and support political reforms. This chapter also examines how increasing connections between Norway and Norwegian America enhanced the immigrants' sense of loyalty to Norway.

Such boastful claims would not pass unchallenged, and chapter 4, "Backlash: Xenophobia and the Pressure to Assimilate, 1917–1929," views how societal pressures during World War I and the following years led Anglo-Americans to enact political limits on immigration and foreign-language usage in the United States. The onslaught against hyphenated Americans meant that Norwegian-American leaders had to devise a strategy that would emphasize the loyalty of Norwegians to America. With the resulting legacy myths, they argued that Norwegians had been the best and most loyal immigrant group, although they no longer openly challenged Anglo-Americans as the hegemony myths had. In addition, creators of legacy myths, such as Rølvaag, advanced the idea that the history and culture of the Norwegians should be promoted and remembered as part of the American cultural curriculum. This strategy developed against the reality that the pool of new Norwegian immigrants had virtually dried up and that the Norwegian language was dying out among immigrants. The culmination of this phase was the 1925 Norse-American Centennial in which Norwegian-Americans showcased the values they shared with their American home. Norwegian-American leaders hoped that American political leaders would grant Norwegians an exemption from harsh immigration quotas, but the failure to achieve special dispensation seemed to spell the end of an active Norwegian America.

At this point, when the Norwegian-American identity seemed moribund, it was the homeland that came to the rescue. Chapter 5, "A Shared Homeland: Celebrating Norwegian Identity across the Atlantic, 1929–1945," details how Norway took the lead in advancing the Norwegian-American identity. Leaders in Norway, a peripheral nation, sought to increase Norway's global position by tying its success to that of America (a core nation), especially by emphasizing the success of Norwegians in America. During this stage, the Norwegian-American identity intersected Norway's national identity, creating the transnational greater Norway identity. It was an identity promoted through the celebration of a series of shared celebrations in both Norway and America. The validity of the greater Norway concept faced its greatest challenge with the foreign occupation of Norway during World War II, testing the concept with the need for real sacrifice.

The book concludes by confirming that the greater Norway concept succeeded and that Norwegians on both sides of the Atlantic, in Norway and America, had participated as members in the nation of Norway. The greater Norway's aim had been to make Norwegians living outside Norway feel fully welcomed as members in the nation of Norway, and the willingness of Norwegians abroad to sacrifice their lives in order to free Norway proved how loyal they had always been to Norway and that they would continue to show their love of Norway. The restoration of an independent and free Norway in 1945 therefore represented a great, tangible, and most satisfying victory for the greater Norway.

· CHAPTER 1 ·

Creating Home

The Roots of Norwegian Emigration

HILDA STEGNER, the daughter of Norwegian immigrants and the mother of the novelist Wallace Stegner, grew up in Iowa and gave birth to her son at Lake Mills in 1909. Married at an early age, she led a roving lifestyle, moving frequently from place to place. The wanderlust of her husband, George, meant that she never had the "nest" that she wanted, a permanent home and a neighborhood with friends and family nearby.[1]

Years later, Wallace Stegner visited relatives in Norway. He told of meeting an elderly relative there who had once lived in America for five or six years. Stegner's relative worked for sixteen different farmers in Minnesota, North Dakota, and Iowa, all of whom came from his home community of Ulvik, Norway.[2]

Although Stegner's relative also led a roving life, the connections he enjoyed with relatives and friends from his home community meant that the context of his American experience differed essentially from that of Hilda Stegner. The fact that he lived and worked in a familiar cultural environment, and most likely spoke Norwegian almost exclusively, ensconced him within an environment that came far closer to achieving the "nest-like" quality of life that Hilda never attained.

The tale of Wallace Stegner's Norwegian relative highlights the character of the Norwegian migration to America. Forces within Norway, largely economic but some political, and forces outside the homeland (the attraction of America) combined to lure Norwegians to the New World during the nineteenth century and into the twentieth. This push-pull dichotomy anchors much of the explanation for the Norwegian exodus.

Yet, it is more appropriate to view the Norwegian migration experience as part of a larger narrative involving the development of capitalism and the alteration of the world labor market. Viewed from this perspective, the Norwegian migration expressed the collective actions and decisions of numerous individuals coping with radical changes to their traditional way of life. Those individuals, moreover, normally made their decisions in the context of family and larger kin-network considerations, and they plotted what they perceived to be the most effective strategies in allowing them to survive, adapt, and succeed in a rapidly changing world.

Norwegian immigrants to America adapted to their new homeland by referencing that which they knew best: their family and community ties in Norway. Those ties granted them a sense of security and continuity that made America not totally unfamiliar. Norwegians in America formed ethnic enclaves or colonies in which their Norwegian customs and cultural traditions could be preserved as much as possible. Subsequent waves of Norwegians joined these ethnic enclaves or struck out to form new enclaves, thereby replicating the pattern. This pattern of chain migration, though not limited to Norwegians, created the conditions in which Norwegians could live in ways that referenced their ancestral homeland.

As Linda Basch et al. have observed, transmigrants use the world "home" for their society of origin even when they have clearly made a home in their country of settlement.[3] This chapter therefore discusses how Norwegian transmigrants to America created *ethnoscapes* in which they re-created and reproduced their Norwegian customs in the context of their American experience.[4] It also introduces the context against which the creation of a Norwegian-American identity was ultimately produced.

Conditions in Norway and the Norwegian Emigration

In the years between 1820 and 1930, some 33 million persons emigrated from Europe to the United States. In absolute numbers the groups that contributed the most were the Germans, the Italians, the Irish, and the British. Although the emigration from Norway does not compare in numbers, it was significant. Between 1825 and 1930 almost 880,000 Norwegians immigrated to America. During this same period Norway's population increased from 1.0 million in 1825 to 2.8 million in 1930. Norway had one of the highest rates of emigration in Europe, surpassed only by Ireland.[5]

Clearly something must have been lacking in Norway for such a sizable percentage of Norwegians to make the often risky and uncertain exodus to the New World. To a large degree Norway's physical setting, its geography and climate, set harsh limits on the productivity of its agriculture. In a nation where an industrial economy would not become a driving force until the first decades of the twentieth century, the overwhelming majority of Norwegians derived their livelihood from farming and related occupations throughout the nineteenth century. In 1845, 88 percent of Norway's population was rural, and by 1875 the rural population still amounted to nearly as much, 82 percent.[6]

That rural population, however, was not homogeneous. A class of relatively independent yeoman farmers known as the *bønder* occupied the top position of the rural hierarchy. In 1845, the *bønder* numbered 77,780 out of a population of 1,328,471, about 6 percent. In addition to the *bønder*, the rural population of Norway in 1845 included 58,049 cotters, or *husmenn*; 25,047 renters and laborers; and 146,000 hired hands. The *bønder*'s rise to preeminence during the nineteenth and twentieth centuries impacted Norway's development. From the *bondestand*, or freeholder class, came a large number of Norway's political leaders, writers, poets, musicians, and professional men. This same class also contributed a large proportion of the leaders among the Norwegians who immigrated to America.[7]

During this same time national romanticism played an especially significant role in influencing the development of Norway's national identity. From 1397 until 1814, Norway had been not an independent nation but a colony ruled by the Danish throne. During the Napoleonic wars, Denmark's alliance with France cost her Norway. At first, Norwegian nationalists aspired for Norwegian independence, but the country was awarded to Sweden to compensate for its loss of Finland to Russia in 1809. Sweden had switched sides, ironically, after the Swedish crown was offered to France's marshal Jean-Baptiste Bernadotte, who became crown prince, then King Karl XIV Johan. As a compromise, Norway reluctantly joined into dynastic union with Sweden but with its own constitution, administration, and laws. After centuries of Danish rule, many Norwegian intellectuals, who did not belong to the peasant class, nonetheless desired to "re-create" a purely Norwegian nation, and they turned for their inspiration to the peasantry, whom they believed had been largely uncorrupted by foreign influences. True Norwegian culture, it was believed, resided in the pristine traditions of the peasantry, and leading nineteenth-century intellectuals, including the poet Henrik Wergeland and the writer Bjørnstjern Bjørnson, argued that authentic Norwegian culture could only be realized if it were based on rural traditions.[8]

Norwegian society did not remain pure and untouched during the early to mid-nineteenth century. Agrarian society underwent a profound structural shift that originated early in the century and became appreciable around 1850. Known as *den store hamskiftet,* the great transformation, it marked the large-scale conversion from communal subsistence agriculture to individual commercial farming. The transformation likewise affected the social structure of Norway's rural communities. The breakdown of the traditional communal lifestyle opened the way for the emergence of a new class of commercial, freeholding farmers. Changes to Norway's economic system further exacerbated class tensions. Between 1801 and 1855 the number of freeholders in Norway increased by 25.9 percent, while during the same period the number of cotters increased by 81.7 percent, the number of day laborers by 225.3 percent, and hired hands by 34 percent. These lower-class members of rural society lacked suffrage since they could not meet property qualifications. Poverty, an often grueling work schedule, and a lack of status made for enmity between them and their landlord rivals. It is not surprising, therefore, that many Norwegian emigrants were from these lower classes.[9]

The era of mass migration from Norway to America began in 1825 when, in October of that year, fifty-three Norwegians arrived at New York from the sloop *Restaurationen.* The sloopers, as they have become known—among them were some Quakers—came to America seeking religious freedom, although economic reasons also may have influenced their decision. Between 1825 and 1855 Norwegian emigration was sporadic, but thereafter its pace quickened, and by 1865 nearly 80,000 Norwegians had crossed the Atlantic. In absolute numbers, the first forty years of Norwegian emigration to America represented a mere trickle.[10]

The appeal of American religious toleration was one of the more important reasons for Norwegian emigration during this early period. Among the Norwegian peasantry, there was a strong reaction to the austere formalism of the Norwegian State Lutheran Church. A lay movement known as Haugeanism, named after its founder, the lay preacher Hans Nielsen Hauge (1771–1824), offered a fundamentalist and pietist alternative. Moreover, the overwhelmingly rural followers of Hauge viewed his struggle with the clergy of the state church as extending beyond, to one between them and the urban elite. By the 1830s, rural areas of Norway began to elect increasing numbers of *bønder* to the Storting, the Norwegian national assembly, and these legislators formed a regular opposition group to the urban elite. The Haugeans also viewed emigration to America as part of an overall strategy designed to combat the influence of the urban elite.[11]

Restaurationen (*The Restoration*), the ship that transported the original Norwegian immigrants to America in 1825. Courtesy of the Norwegian Emigrant Museum, U00651.

Another factor that cannot be overlooked was the increasing sense of self-worth among the agrarian classes in Norway. As noted previously, the national romantic movement of the early nineteenth century glorified the folk culture of the agrarian classes, and it gave them a new feeling of self-importance and dignity. Norway's rural citizens responded by demanding full appreciation and recognition of their way of life, their ethical values, and their culture. In effect, Norwegian peasant customs, values, and culture became what sociologist Peter Munch termed the "sacred symbols of loyalty and group identification."[12]

As the political consciousness of Norway's peasants became more pronounced, many, especially among the poor, unenfranchised class, embraced the radical ideas of Marcus Thrane, a one-time schoolmaster and newspaper editor who founded the nation's first labor associations. Through his articles and speeches, Thrane encouraged workers, rural laborers, and cotters to organize into cooperative societies, calling for the establishment of cooperative methods at all levels of production. He also railed against the exploitation of the rural and urban workers, singling out the clergy of the state church, whom he regarded as among the worst oppressors of the common man. Although Thrane's influence in Norway was short-lived (he was jailed and ultimately left for America), his ideas were influential, and he too advocated emigration as a potential solution to the plight of Norway's lower classes.[13]

The connection between these protest movements and emigration shows the complicated factors that stimulated emigration. While the decision to emigrate as an individual or even family choice cannot be discounted, emigration had its roots in the larger historical forces affecting Norway and the world at this time. In effect, emigration must be viewed as one possible strategy in the struggle to come to grips with the increasingly accelerated changes of the modern world.

Structural changes affecting Norway during this period were paramount. Population increases were characteristically tied to increased rates of Norwegian emigration, and the country witnessed rapid rises in the number of young adults from 1835 to 1845, in the late 1860s, and again in the early years of the twentieth century. The shift to commercial agriculture plus the introduction of the potato were significant factors in explaining these population increases. When economic conditions were bad, there was a similar spike in emigration.[14] According to more recent scholarship, however, economic hardship alone does not adequately explain the high rates of emigration between 1865 and 1914. Increasingly, scholars have emphasized how a changing economic system coincided with changing social conditions.

In his study of migration from Balestrand, Norway, Jon Gjerde has stressed this set of mutually interconnected factors in explaining the causes of Norwegian emigration to America. He observes that the transformation of the Norwegian economy provided greater work opportunities and more certain food sources, which resulted in lower ages of marriage among landless youths. The combination of a growing population, ever-limited inheritance of land, and improved conditions for these couples meant that fewer immediate landed positions were available for their children. With diminished future prospects, marriage might have to be delayed. At the same time, changes in social behavior led to an increasing number of prenuptial births that were not followed by marriage. Finally, Gjerde notes how this change in behavior created social cleavages that resulted in attempts by the landed to reduce night courting (evening dates by couples, often without a chaperone) and to encourage pietistic religious movements. These pietistic impulses, which were designed to reconcile the community's moral teaching with present realities, divided the landless, the group most affected by the ambiguities of the changing society.[15]

To a large degree, Gjerde's scholarship confirms that emigration from Norway to America was not an act of desperation but a rational approach to a set of possible opportunities. In fact, his study shows that the initial migrants from Balestrand represented the wealthier elements of the community. There was an element of prestige to take into account for many younger sons and daughters of the landholding *bønder.* It was considered disgraceful for the son of a landholding farmer to become an industrial worker; it was better to emigrate to America and become a farmer there. A sizable number of Norway's farmers, cotters, and laborers found the allure of large tracts of open American land too hard to resist as well.[16] Gjerde maintains that these land-hungry emigrants, whether wealthy or poor, were not seeking a completely new life but instead were attempting to preserve their cultural patterns of life in the vast, isolated expanses of the American prairie. His findings resonate with those of Ingrid Semmingsen, Norway's eminent emigration scholar, who identifies the same conservative motivation as Gjerde, noting that Norwegian emigrants chose America because it allowed them to preserve their traditional culture, language, and social relationships.[17]

It must be acknowledged that the impulse for social reform likewise attracted many immigrant communities to America. Attempts at founding model or utopian communities usually failed, but the motivation for such societies nonetheless attracted many Norwegians. Cleng Peerson, the man who helped found many early Norwegian communities in America, favored the idea of communal religious fellowship, and he joined the Swedish utopian Bishop Hill colony in Illinois for roughly a year. Another example was Ole Rynning, a Norwegian who wrote the first travel guide for prospective Norwegian emigrants in 1838, who wanted all Norwegians in America to unite and live in just one community. Perhaps the most famous enterprise of this type was the Oleana colony in Pennsylvania, founded by the famous Norwegian violinist Ole Bull. Although the utopian settlement failed after only a few years in the 1850s, it demonstrated again the impulse among Norwegian social reformers to establish an alternative community in America.

In the half century from 1865 to 1915, the pace of emigration quickened, and these years were a time of mass migration from Norway to America. As mentioned earlier, although Norwegian migration did not compare in absolute numbers with the number of German, Irish, Italian, or Polish immigrants, it was substantial for such a small country. The bulk of Norwegian emigration occurred in three successive major waves. The first lasted from 1866 to 1873, the second from 1880 to 1893, and the last took place during the first decade of the twentieth century. During these peak years an average of 18,900 Norwegians left annually.

Norway's economy in the latter half of the nineteenth century was still overwhelmingly rural, although becoming increasingly commercialized, and the country was overpopulated, with a labor surplus in many areas. By contrast, America during this same period was precisely the opposite. Manpower was scarce. The economy was rapidly industrializing, and the interior of a vast continent was being settled. In America immigrants were welcomed. Midwestern states such as Minnesota and Wisconsin established state government agencies charged with recruiting European immigrants. Railroad companies needed people to settle near the lines, and they undertook similar campaigns designed to draw people from distant shores into these underpopulated areas so as to create a sufficient number of customers. States, steamship lines, and railroads recruited men of influence within various immigrant groups to entice their compatriots to settle in the desired areas. Many prominent Norwegian Americans, such as Paul Hjelm-Hansen and Ole C. Johnson, worked as agents whose job was to lure Norwegians to settle America's vast prairies.[18]

The changing world economy in the latter half of the nineteenth century provided impetus for further Norwegian emigration. The transformation to a commercialized and industrialized world economy affected predominantly agricultural nations like Norway. In particular, the importation of cheap grain from abroad forced many Norwegian farmers to switch from grain production to animal husbandry, which required less labor. As a result of this trend, between 1865 and 1900 the agricultural labor force in Norway dropped by fifty thousand. Furthermore, the emphasis on commercialized, specialized agriculture made it difficult for many Norwegian farmers to adapt, and many had to sell their farms. In some areas newer methods were not feasible. Marginal farms in particular were steadily abandoned, and cotters' dwellings were especially vulnerable.

Economic transformation was not limited to agriculture. In the 1880s the transition from sailing ships to steamships impacted Norway's shipping industry because a steamship required only a fraction of the crew employed on a sailing ship in order to carry the same amount of cargo, and consequently, fewer sailors were employed in 1900 than in 1875. Livelihoods related to the shipping industry also declined, and the cities and towns of Norway's south coast, the center of its shipping industry, experienced a precipitous decline. The inland farmers who supplied timber likewise felt the hardship associated with the new realities of the shipping business.

Changes in the workplace sometimes impacted settlement patterns as well. One striking example brought on by changes in the shipping industry was the largely transient Norwegian-American community in Brooklyn, New York. As foreign steamships replaced native sailing vessels, large numbers of seamen and boatyard workers would periodically leave their families in southernmost Norway to seek employment in America, often repeating this pattern over the course of several years.[19]

This rapid economic transformation further served to erode Norway's old social bonds. Solidarity in the trades between masters and journeymen was replaced by mutual suspicion as many craft workers instead opted to join labor unions. A similar phenomenon occurred in the countryside where commercialized agriculture led to a division between the owners of large farms and the laborers they employed. Rural workers, much like their urban counterparts, became increasingly likely to join workingmen's societies. The attraction of unions and workmen's associations to workers and rural proletarians reflected the social uncertainty created by a rapidly transforming world. A significant feature of the new world economy was increased mobility of the working population. Workers had to be readily available to meet the constantly changing laws of supply and demand, internationally as well as within nations. In the years between 1865 and 1925, America required agricultural workers to settle its vast interior and industrial workers to labor in its ever-expanding factory towns and cities. In its simplest sense, immigration merely echoed the changing nature of the workforce within the emerging system of industrial capitalism. For many workers and rural laborers, emigration offered a plausible and rational solution to their employment quandary.

Global structural economic changes impacted the nature of the immigrant experience itself. Steamships and railroads provided faster transportation than was previously available, and the relative cost of the transatlantic journey became cheaper in the latter years of the nineteenth century. The composition of the emigrants, including those from Norway, changed as well. Prior to the 1880s, Norwegians tended to emigrate as families, each typically consisting of a man and a wife between thirty and forty years of age with several children, often including one in the womb. By the 1890s individual emigration became the normative mode. Norwegian emigrants during this period tended to be young and unmarried in comparison to the generations that had preceded them.

These new emigrants were also less likely to come from rural areas of Norway. In 1870, 90 percent of the emigrants were rural, but by the eve of World War I less than half of them were. After 1875, Norway's cities produced the highest emigration rates. There was also a tendency for would-be emigrants to migrate first to Norway's large cities from its small towns and rural areas. After a period spent working in the larger cities, many would then book passage on a steamship to America. These emigrants came from all regions of Norway. While some still originated in the south and west of Norway (where the earliest emigrants had originated), large numbers now left from regions in the east and north of the country. The working classes still constituted the majority of the emigrants, but it was not uncommon for members of the middle classes to emigrate as well. In effect, the new emigration reflected the changing composition of modern society.

The phenomenon of return migration represented an additional strategy for migrants from Norway. Cheap transportation coupled with the availability of prepaid tickets sent by relatives in America made the journey far less difficult than during earlier decades. The 1920 U.S. federal census showed that nearly fifty thousand returned Norwegian Americans were living in Norway. After 1880, one-fourth of all emigrants returned to Norway, with about thirty thousand of them returning between 1911 and 1920, most of them after a stay of about seven to eight years. Many of these re-migrants were involved in the shipping and fishing industries. Semmingsen concludes that for these later emigrants going to America was a temporary strategy by which money could be accumulated to buy a farm or a house in Norway, an interpretation shared by David C. Mauk. Mark Wyman's study on return migration upholds these observations, and he argues that later emigration was more of a labor strategy than a lifestyle strategy like the earlier emigration, since it was often not permanent.[20]

The increased likelihood of re-migration reinforces the interpretation that Norwegians migrated for largely conservative reasons. The journey to America for re-migrants often had as its goal advancement to a higher station in Norway than otherwise would have been possible. Even those emigrants who stayed in America permanently often sent money back to Norway so that those that remained might prosper. Furthermore, those who emigrated permanently often did so for conservative reasons. For those sons of a Norwegian farmer who did not inherit land and faced the prospect of slipping into the life of a rural laborer or, worse, an industrial city dweller, emigration to America offered them the opportunity to purchase land for a farm and continue their existence as farmers, not as laborers. Because many, if not most, of these emigrants settled in areas populated by other Norwegians, it is easy to see why their aspirations tended toward preserving their traditional rural Norwegian way of life rather than surrendering it entirely to American customs.

From 1900 to 1914, 214,985 Norwegians emigrated to America. During the Great War, the rate of migration decreased to a trickle. When emigration resumed, 88,250 Norwegians emigrated during the decade of the 1920s. The average rate was only 8,852 as compared with 14,332 yearly in the prewar decade. The yearly rate would no doubt have been higher except that restrictions imposed by the Johnson-Reed Immigration Act of 1924 limited the number of Norwegian immigrants to an annual figure of 2,377.

Emigration from Norway tailed off dramatically as a result of the Great Depression. Moreover, 32,000 Norwegians in America returned to their homeland during this period. Norwegian statistics indicate that between 1891 and 1940 as many as a quarter of all emigrants to America returned to Norway, although historian Odd Lovoll thinks this figure is somewhat inflated.[21]

The emergence of a modern economy in Norway, the so-called take-off period, was achieved by the 1920s and 1930s. Industry, not agriculture, now dominated the Norwegian economy. Surplus rural workers no longer needed to travel overseas to find work. Norwegian society reflected this change. The Arbeider (Labor) party had replaced the Venstre (Liberal) party as the dominant left-wing party. The first long-lived Labor government came to power in 1934 (in 1927 the first Labor government lasted only a few days). Labor unions flexed their muscles as cities came to dominate the nation's life. By the 1930s, despite setbacks caused by the Great Depression, Norway had become a modern society. The Norway of the 1930s had more in common with America than during the nineteenth or even early twentieth century. And while America still offered opportunities for many, the pull of America was less pronounced than it had been in the previous century.

Norwegian Immigration and Settlement, 1825–1945

Although the first Norwegian immigrants to America arrived aboard the sloop *Restaurationen* in 1825, annual migration did not occur until 1836. Despite an increase during the 1840s, large-scale immigration did not begin until after the American Civil War. Of the total number that immigrated to America up to 1980, roughly 87 percent, about 780,000, arrived between 1865 and 1930. During the founding phase between 1825 and 1865, 77,873 Norwegians immigrated to America. Scholars of Norwegian immigration refer to these years as the pioneer era, and its characteristics differed in significant ways from the subsequent periods.

Prior to 1836 almost all the immigrants came from the western Norwegian counties of Hordaland and Rogaland. During the next decade, immigrants from nine of Norway's counties, including the cities of Christiania (Oslo) and Bergen, could be found in the New World communities. By 1860, on the eve of the Civil War, all nineteen of Norway's counties had experienced emigration to America. The Norwegian communities that experienced emigration during this forty-year period would have some of the highest rates of emigration in Norway during the later years of heavy emigration, from 1865 to 1930. These communities thus served as the initial bellwethers of later emigration to America.[22]

A number of push factors (in Norway) and pull factors (in America) influenced the decision to emigrate. Since the former have already been discussed, the American forces will be considered here.

The initial trickle of immigrants revealed to a large degree the importance of personal contacts in the migration experience. The migration of the sloopers would not have been possible without the stalwart efforts of Cleng Peerson, who has been called "the father of Norwegian emigration" or "Peer Gynt on the Prairie." Through Peerson's efforts, the sloopers established the first Norwegian-American colony in Kendall County, New York. Although it was a short-lived colony, the Kendall settlement did serve as a springboard for subsequent Norwegian immigration. By 1833, Peerson set his sights on western lands for further Norwegian immigrant settlements. After visiting several states, he selected a site along the Fox River in northern Illinois that would serve as a base for Norwegian immigration into the upper Midwest.[23]

Letters sent by immigrants back to relatives and friends in Norway were a significant factor in transmitting information about opportunities in America. Early accounts were for the most part highly enthusiastic,

Drawing of Cleng Peerson, the man known as the "Norwegian Pathfinder" for his efforts in helping early Norwegian immigrants find land in America. Courtesy of the Norwegian Emigrant Museum, U01162.

and their descriptions of America offer insights into how the immigrants viewed conditions in Norwegian society. One widely noted author of early American letters was Gjert G. Hovland, whose letters were copied and copied again until hundreds of copies existed in Norway. His letters emphasized how America offered the immigrant much greater opportunities for wealth and land. In addition, he noted that the common man had just as much influence as the rich and powerful because he could participate in American-style democracy. He also observed that American clothing did not reflect status differentiation.[24]

By 1837, the appeal of America and the rising level of interest in emigration among Norwegian farmers had made it relatively difficult for opponents of emigration to stem the tide. In that year, Jacob Neumann, bishop of the archdiocese of Bergen, published a pastoral letter titled "A Word of Admonition to the Peasants in the Diocese of Bergen Who Desire to Emigrate." Widely published, the letter used religious, patriotic, and economic arguments in urging Norwegian peasants to remain at home. Neumann offered an alternative to emigration by suggesting that the colonization of available lands in the Norwegian province of Finnmarken and other northern areas offered better possibilities than those to be found in America.[25]

Other writers used their experiences in America to author critiques of Norway. Perhaps the bitterest critic of the homeland was Hans Barlien, a one-time Storting member and member of the peasant class who emigrated to America in 1837. Barlien, who penned a treatise on the Norwegian constitution in 1836, contrasted the two countries and praised America for its religious freedom and freedom of occupation. In contrast, he viewed the Norwegian constitution as a document that largely served the interests of public officials and other members of the upper class.[26]

The most influential of the early Norwegian settlers was Ole Rynning, the son of a Lutheran minister and thus a member of the middle class. He emigrated to America in 1837, the leader of a group bound for the newly established Fox River settlement in Illinois. Although he died the next year, he authored an advice book written for prospective Norwegian emigrants. Widely read in Norway, his book concentrated on practical matters while providing a generally positive account of America, stressing that those willing to work hard would succeed. He observed that Norwegians in America had "a good reputation for their industry, trustworthiness, and the readiness with which the more well-to-do have helped the poor through the country."[27]

Norwegian immigrants themselves influenced emigration by their return visits to Norway. Ansten Nattestad emigrated to America in 1837 and returned the following year to recruit additional immigrants. Traveling through Numedal and Telemark, Norway, he attracted large crowds who came to hear him speak about America and its opportunities. That same year he published a book detailing his travels to America, and it was widely read for many years in the homeland. The next year he went back to America with a large group of immigrants, joining his brother Ole in Wisconsin.

Another example was Johan R. Reierson, editor of the Norwegian newspaper *Christiansandsposten* (Christiansand Post), who traveled to America in 1843–44 where he visited several Norwegian communities. In 1844 his account of his travels, *Veiviser for norske Emigranter til de forenede nordamerikanske Stater og Texas* (Pathfinder for Norwegian Emigrants to the United States and Texas), was published in Norway. Reierson subsequently recruited a party the following year that formed the Normandy settlement near Brownsboro in northeastern Texas.[28]

America's social freedoms attracted many immigrants who were dissatisfied with the Norwegian State Lutheran Church as well as the country's largely closed political system. America's religious toleration attracted Haugeans and Quakers, as well as a Moravian colony founded by Nils Otto Tank near Green Bay, Wisconsin, in 1851. American adult males—excluding slaves and Native Americans—had the right to vote, unlike in Norway. America's civil liberties, combined with its egalitarian society, appealed to many Norwegians. The observations of Reierson concerning immigration implied that there was widespread dissatisfaction among the Norwegian peasantry. Moreover, many Norwegian peasants sensed that the government was not doing enough to promote economic conditions and opportunities for land ownership, which likewise made America highly attractive.[29]

Norwegians settled primarily in the upper Midwest during this period. Inspired by Ole Rynning, Ole and Ansten Nattestad became the first Norwegian settlers in Wisconsin. The settlement they founded in 1838, Jefferson Prairie, served as a gateway for future Norwegian settlement into Wisconsin, Minnesota, and Iowa. Populated almost exclusively by Norwegians, early settlements like Jefferson Prairie typify what historian Odd Lovoll has termed the local community phase of Norwegian immigration. During this phase, immigrants from the same communities in Norway traveled to America in an attempt to re-create their old societies, to save a way of life that was no longer tenable in the Old World but eminently feasible in the new one. This view has been borne out by the settlement patterns of other immigrants such as the Swedes.[30]

Among the earliest Norwegian immigrants to America, Ole Nattestad and his brother Ansten were the first Norwegian settlers at Jefferson Prairie, Wisconsin, in 1837. Courtesy of the National Library of Norway, Norwegian-American Collection.

The phenomenon of chain, or stage, migration characterized Norwegian settlements. Once an immigrant colony had reached its natural limits, usually bounded by other ethnic communities, a small portion of the colony would often break away to form a new colony on the frontier. This process might be repeated several times. A community of Vossings, for example, might form their first colony in Illinois or southern Wisconsin, and subsequent colonies would then be established in western Wisconsin, Iowa, or southern Minnesota, and later in western Minnesota or the Dakotas. As the available land was claimed, newer colonies might be formed all the way out to the Pacific coast.

Other Norwegian communities, albeit smaller ones, were also established during these years. The Norwegian community of Chicago came into existence during the mid-1830s. Opportunities in the Great Lakes shipping industry attracted many of these early immigrants as well as employment in construction and crafts. Some worked just long enough to earn the money needed to purchase land for an American farmstead. In New York's Red Hook section of Brooklyn, a floating Norwegian community began in the 1850s, consisting mostly of transient seamen and dockworkers employed by the shipping industry. A small Norwegian community in Bosque County, Texas, was founded in 1853 and numbered around five hundred on the eve of the Civil War. The 1849 California gold rush lured a number of Norwegian fortune seekers, but the San Francisco area was also home to seamen, maritime workers, and a small community of businessmen.

During the pioneer era in America, most Norwegians earned their living from agriculture. Some immigrants owned their farms outright. Others worked as hired hands for established Norwegian-American or American farmers, often to pay the debt for a prepaid ticket to America. To supplement their income from agriculture, many Norwegians worked in lumber camps in Wisconsin or Michigan; some found employment as miners. Those residing in urban areas found employment in shipping or other industries. It is worth noting that farming in America differed from what it was in Norway. The farms tended to be larger, and additional crops, such as corn and potatoes, were more widely grown. Time was needed to clear the land before it could be brought into production, and the prairie soil required the use of heavy plows. Many immigrants pooled their resources and shared oxen and plows. As noted by Carlton C. Qualey, many Norwegians came to share the American conception that they were taming the frontier, thus serving as America's pioneers.[31]

The end of the Civil War led to a renewed interest in immigration, and Norwegians were no exception. Like other immigrant groups, Norwegian communities characteristically were not dispersed but rather clustered into islands of "little Norways." Rural areas of the upper Midwest were the favored destination. The states of Minnesota, Iowa, Wisconsin, the Dakotas, and Illinois all had sizable Norwegian communities. In addition, there were Norwegian enclaves in the Pacific Northwest and in the cities of Minneapolis–St. Paul, Chicago, New York, and Seattle. The result of this clustered settlement pattern was that Norwegian communities in America were well positioned for the preservation of Norwegian values. At the same time, there were continual pressures from mainstream American society to conform to its values. Thus, Norwegian Americans confronted a constant tug-of-war between two value systems, and this tension lay at the heart of the emerging Norwegian-American identity.

From 1865 to 1914, many of the most ethnically Norwegian communities were established. From initial settlements in Wisconsin and Illinois, Norwegians advanced into Iowa and Minnesota. The areas of northwestern Iowa, western Wisconsin, and southeastern Minnesota became early "little Norways." Norwegian immigrants who came primarily from Voss, Telemark, Sogn, and Valdres settled in the Iowa counties of Mitchell, Winneshiek, Winnebago, Clayton, and Worth. In southeastern Minnesota, too, the settlements had a strongly local flavor as the immigrants settled in tightly clustered communities that attempted to replicate the old regional communities back in Norway. Goodhue County, for example, had a settlement called Vang that had been populated by immigrants from Valdres. Other counties such as Houston, Fillmore, Mower, and Rice had a strong Norwegian presence as well, often reflecting a particular region of Norway.[32]

Norwegian expansion continued across Minnesota and into the Dakotas during the 1870s and successive decades. Their leapfrog pattern of settlement is evidence that many settlers left the older settlements in search of new lands and opportunities. From the Norwegian settlements in southeastern Minnesota, new Norwegian communities appeared first in the central Minnesota counties of Kandiyohi, Pope, and Douglas. These settlements in turn served as springboards for later settlements in the Red River region of western Minnesota and eastern North Dakota, as well as eastern South Dakota.

Moreover, these daughter colonies served to preserve ties to a specific *bygd*, or community, in the old country. Jon Gjerde has observed how emigrants from Balestrand, Norway, established a series of settlements in the Upper Midwest, creating a moving community that maintained personal family and kinship ties throughout the various communities. The network of personal contacts originating in the old *bygd* was not, however, always confined to such compact settlements. The ties, not only of national origin, but of *slekt* (family) and *bygd*, largely determined the geography and nature of Norwegian America. By the last two decades of the century, the Norwegian diaspora would extend into northern and northwestern North Dakota, the Pacific Northwest states of Washington and Oregon, and the Canadian prairie provinces.[33]

Despite this dispersal, the ties between Norway and the American frontier became stronger during this period. Both countries were undergoing rapid structural changes with the emergence of industrial capitalism. America's great advantage was the opportunity it offered to Norwegian emigrants, especially in land and employment. Norway's emergence as an industrial nation would not take place fully until the early decades of the twentieth century. For impatient Norwegian cotters and laborers who were unwilling to wait fifty to sixty years for homeland conditions to improve, America offered a more immediate solution. As one Norwegian newspaper noted as early as 1869, the American West was a Norwegian frontier.[34]

Technological change improved the journey for prospective immigrants in the post–Civil War decades. Steamships reduced the time needed to cross the Atlantic from two months or more to about two weeks. The cost of transportation declined by one-half between 1865 and 1890, and large numbers were able to travel from Norway to America using money or prepaid tickets. Within America, a vast program of railroad expansion meant that it required less time to reach frontier destinations.

New pull factors attracted large numbers of Norwegians. In 1862 Congress passed the Homestead Act, which granted 160 acres without cost in return for cultivation of the land. America letters from this period spread word of the large quantities of available land, and the desire among Norwegian peasants to own their own farm—a large one by Norwegian standards—resulted in heavy immigration.[35]

The entities involved in the business of immigration, including shipping companies, railroad companies, and state and private interests, employed various methods to attract immigrants. Shipping companies, for example, advertised heavily in Norwegian and Norwegian-American newspapers with ads that provided glowing accounts of opportunities in America as well as the costs of services. Throughout Norway they hired agents in those businesses that might cater to prospective immigrants, including storekeepers and innkeepers. A similar series of networks operated in America, and the agents of the companies maintained contacts with Norwegian Americans who knew of family and friends in Norway who were seeking to immigrate. One of the most effective means was the so-called Yankee system in which Norwegian Americans revisiting their homeland were employed as agents by steamship companies.

Newspapers in America, especially Norwegian-language ones, promoted settlement through favorable editorials and by running advertisements from railroad and shipping companies. They would feature letters from established Norwegian immigrants describing the advantages of potential settlements.

Rates of heavy emigration from Norway were tied to years of agricultural downturn in the home country, but from the 1880s on, mass migration from Norway was an indication of the serious structural crisis confronting European agriculture as a whole, owing to the development of a worldwide transportation network and increased competition from cheap imported grain, especially from the American Midwest. Like most European countries, Norway's population continued to increase, but domestic industry was not sufficiently developed to employ those forced off the land.[36]

Mass emigration from Norway between 1880 and 1917 must be viewed as part of a worldwide transformation in which emigration came to be one strategy utilized for economic advantage. The newer immigrants tended to be younger, unmarried, and male, and the heaviest proportion had emigrated from Norway's cities. Most of them were from the peasant class, but an increasing number were urban laborers, and a small but influential number of engineers, technicians, intellectuals, artists, and other professionals emigrated to America, primarily to the cities.

A number of smaller urban Norwegian communities developed in towns such as Decorah, Iowa; Northfield, Minnesota; and Fargo, North Dakota, to name but a few. Employment in industry and white-collar professions became more prevalent among Norwegians in America. Norwegians were especially prominent in the shipping industry, and large-scale urban communities coalesced in New York, Chicago, Seattle, and San Francisco as well as in cities such as Milwaukee and Superior, Wisconsin. In the Pacific Northwest, Norwegians found employment in fishing, logging, and construction. The Norwegian-American Andrew Furuseth in San Francisco became known as "the Abraham Lincoln of the Sea" for his efforts to improve the conditions of seamen through his labor activities along the West Coast.

Norwegian women immigrants, like the men, were mostly young and unmarried. The high rate of emigration from Norway of young males meant a decline of marriage prospects in the homeland for young women. Employment opportunities for young women in the homeland suffered as an oversupply of female labor kept wages low. A common American practice was for affluent and middle-class families to employ live-in housemaids, and Scandinavian girls were considered particularly desirable for such positions. According to the 1890 federal census, as many as 80 percent of all Norwegian immigrant women who worked outside the home were classified as "domestic and personal services."

Despite the increasing urbanization of Norwegian America, however, they remained a predominantly rural group. The 1910 federal census identified the percentage of urban-dwelling Norwegian-born as only 42 percent, which was significantly lower than the 46 percent among all native-born Americans. By comparison, the percentage among all foreign-born was 72 percent. In fact, Norwegians remained the most rural group among all European immigrants.[37] A significant divide remained, nonetheless, between rural, more conservative Norwegian Americans and their urban counterparts. This tension will be explored in detail in later chapters.

The large-scale exodus of Norwegians to America created a need to explain its causes back in Norway. One theory advanced in conservative circles suggested that those who emigrated to America represented the least desirable elements of Norwegian society, those whose presence would not be missed. This argument, however, could hardly be maintained as ever-larger numbers of Norwegians, including prosperous landowning farmers and even some professionals, continued to emigrate. A second theory implied that the American promise of riches was largely an illusion and that gullible Norwegians had fallen prey to highly embellished propaganda accounts coming from America. The popularity of America letters that argued otherwise, plus the observations of Norwegian travelers to America, negated this argument as well. Clearly something was wrong with Norwegian society.[38]

For Norwegian liberals, emigration offered proof that Norwegian society required drastic reforms. Ole G. Ueland, the early peasant political leader, argued that emigration confirmed the need for higher standards of living, freedom of occupation, and democratic laws. In fact, emigration played a major part in producing needed legislative reform in Norway, while the exodus itself relieved pressure on the soil and set limits to the advance of further division of the land. It also hastened the mechanization of Norwegian agriculture, specialized cash-crop agriculture, and improved farming methods in general.[39]

A conservative counter to the allure of emigration came in 1909 with the formation of the Society for the Restriction of Emigration, which advocated strategies to colonize Norway's unused lands and to promote return migration to Norway. In 1916, the society changed its name to New Soil: A Society for the Inner Colonization of the Country and for the Restriction of Emigration, a change that reflected the society's emphasis on these strategies. One of its leaders, Johan E. Melbye, authored a publication, *Mot emigration* (Against Emigration), that offered detailed explanations as to why America remained attractive to Norwegians. He argued that Norway needed to improve its own land as much as possible to make the country as independent as possible. With the aid of the central government and numerous private organizations, the society hoped to entice former emigrants to return to Norway. In 1917, Knut Takla, a prominent leader of the society, concluded that not the United States but Norway was "the land of the future for the Norwegian people."[40] A fairly significant number of Norwegian Americans did return to Norway. The 1910 Norwegian census indicates that more than nineteen thousand had come back, and more than 80 percent of them lived in rural districts.

The Norwegian government formed a commission in 1912 to investigate the emigration problem. The commission noted the economic conditions that made America an attractive destination. The commission praised the return of emigrants in a report on the Sørland region in southern Norway: "They bring home with them much practical experience and understanding, which redounds to the advantage of the whole region." On the whole, the commission concluded that Norwegians who had been in America and returned to Norway brought with them knowledge of better farming techniques, which in turn made them highly valuable to their homeland.[41] This verdict further eroded the old conservative view that those who had left for America constituted the dregs of Norwegian society.

With the exception of the early 1920s, Norwegian immigration largely dried up between 1917 and 1945. A combination of immigration restriction legislation, greater economic opportunities in Norway, the Great Depression of the 1930s, and World War II served to severely limit or even curtail emigration during these years. Urban environments were the favored destination of these newest Norwegian immigrants because opportunities for owning land had become quite remote by 1920. Within America's cities they found employment in various industries. Norwegian working-class male immigrants were especially prominent in the building trades. An increasing number of the new immigrants had university degrees and professional training, and there was significantly more Norwegian representation in white-collar professions. A large group was involved in commerce and clerical work, and the number of Norwegian-born engineers and architects continued to increase during this period. Many prominent Norwegian engineers were employed in the building of bridges, tunnels, subways, and skyscrapers, especially in cities like New York. Norwegians were likewise well represented in certain manufacturing sectors, including agricultural machinery and service industries such as banking, bookkeeping, and accounting. For example, Arthur Andersen, a Norwegian American from Illinois, founded the well-known accounting firm that bore his name until recent times.

Among Norwegian women, the later-arriving immigrants mostly located in cities, demonstrating the same pattern as their male counterparts. Norwegian immigrant women found employment in factories, although at a far lower rate than for immigrant women of other ethnic groups. Telephone and telegraph companies employed Norwegian women in large numbers, and increasing numbers of them entered professions such as teaching and nursing. Some were also employed in commerce and as office workers.

Of equal significance was the upward mobility experienced by the descendants of Norwegian immigrants. Second- and third-generation Norwegian Americans continued to be employed in agriculture, but increasing numbers of them turned to white-collar professions such as pastors, lawyers, and clerical workers. They entered the health professions as medical doctors, dentists, and other specialties. Likewise, Norwegian-American women achieved upward mobility as they entered professional and business life. A small but visible minority of Norwegian men and women entered academic life. Agnes Mathilde Wergeland served as professor of history at the University of Wyoming between 1902 and 1914, and perhaps the most famous Norwegian academic was

Thorsten Veblen, whose work *Theory of the Leisure Class* (1899) remained a classic for many years.[42]

These trends showed the extent to which Norwegians were being integrated into American life. Without an influx of large numbers of new immigrants, the Norwegian community in American gradually became more American and less Norwegian. However, as will be shown in later chapters, the tenacity with which a Norwegian-American identity persisted revealed the strength of ethnicity as a factor in American life.

In a similar vein, it must be noted that the entirety of the Norwegian immigrant experience in America involved a similar negotiation. Norwegians in America sought to create an identity that was transatlantic, one that satisfied the requirements of being loyal to American values, to homeland Norwegian ones, and most important, to those of Norwegian America. The building of that identity would involve a lengthy, often difficult process that would involve Norwegians giving their lives for both America and, ultimately, Norway.

· CHAPTER 2 ·

Belonging to the Nation

Origin Myths and the Argument to Be American,
1860–1890

IN AN APRIL 1866 LETTER, a Norwegian who fought for the Union wrote, "I have fought for America; its freedom. I have strengthened [America] with my blood, and just as America is so much freer and better than before, I shall be to the same extent and eat with officials and not just beggars."[1]

Like other immigrants in America at that time, this Norwegian war veteran craved the acceptance of his adopted land, and his service had earned him his place. Through his efforts, he had contributed to the building of America, making it "freer and better than before," and in the process he had likewise improved as an individual. Through war, the Norwegian immigrant had transformed into an American.

At another level, through the collective shedding of their blood, Norwegian immigrants who fought in the Civil War transformed their entire Norwegian immigrant community. It is important to realize that the blood sacrifice of this immigrant and his fellow Norwegian veterans had been Norwegian blood, a sacred symbol of their ancestral heritage. Their sacrifice had earned Norwegians the right to "eat with officials," a metaphor that conveyed their status as equals with native-stock Americans. According to this sentiment, being both American and Norwegian was not inherently contradictory but complementary since Norwegian blood had proven to be every bit as patriotic as native-stock blood.

During the second half of the nineteenth century, Norwegians in America negotiated an existence that allowed them to claim loyalty to both America and Norway. In constructing the Norwegian-American identity, its image-makers created origin myths designed to show how Norwegians had sacrificed for the American nation and how they had forged a long association with the New World. The end result of this mythmaking process would prove that Norwegian cultural values and American cultural values were highly compatible, even essentially the same.

The involvement of Norwegians in the Civil War, especially on the Union side, satisfied the requirement that they had sacrificed on behalf of their new home. In giving their lives, Norwegian soldiers became cultural martyrs for the Norwegian immigrant community and tangible proof in American eyes of their newly won status as authentic Americans. It meant that Norwegians now belonged to the American nation.

Beyond that, however, leaders of the Norwegian immigrant community aimed to show that being Norwegian also meant being a good American. Norwegian-American origin myths denoted how the Vikings had been the first Europeans to reach America and that it had been Norwegians, through their actions in the settlement of medieval England and the Norman Conquest, who had been the progenitors of basic values such as freedom and democracy that were then carried to the shores of the New World. Put more succinctly, Norwegian-American leaders claimed that Norwegians who immigrated to the United States during the nineteenth-century were already good Americans even before they set foot on its soil. Ergo, Norwegians were the best immigrant group.

The Proto-Norwegian-American Identity

Prior to the Civil War, the Norwegian self-image in America lacked a coherent synthesis. The reasons for this deficiency are rather obvious. For one, the Norwegians had not attained a sufficient population mass before 1860. Another factor was that although the first Norwegian immigration had occurred in 1825, the first permanent Norwegian settlements did not begin to coalesce until the 1840s. As a result, that initial generation, often struggling to survive in its new environment, was by default a collection of Norwegians who had located in America. Until a significantly large Norwegian community composed of additional generations had emerged, there was no incentive to produce a collective memory of their shared past.

A third reason was that a Norwegian elite did not really become an effective advocacy group until the 1860s. A fourth reason was that the Norwegians lacked certain raw historical material, including documented service to their new homeland. The sacrifice of numerous Norwegians in the Civil War provided that raw material.

Finally, the first synthesis of Norway's own national identity, which began in the 1840s, was not fully developed until the 1860s, and the leaders of the Norwegian-American community built on many of the characteristics of Norway's national identity.[2]

Despite this lack of a coherent Norwegian-American identity, there were elements of a proto-identity, developed in the late 1840s and 1850s, which focused on three aspects of the Norwegians' experiences in America: their role as pioneers, their role as sailors, and their role in religion. The Norwegian traveler Ole Munch Ræder observed during the 1840s the beginning of a common Norwegian-American identity grounded in the defense of their group in relation to Americans as well as other immigrant groups.[3]

The American Civil War represented the watershed event for the development of the Norwegian-American identity. Through sacrifice to their adopted land, Norwegian Americans could offer proof to the Anglo-American elite that they were a worthy immigrant group. That identity did not emerge overnight, although one can discern its components being articulated during the 1860s and 1870s. Rasmus B. Anderson synthesized the first coherent Norwegian-American ideology around 1874 and 1875. By participating in the Civil War, Norwegians became part of a collective experience in which they perceived themselves as part of the Union and in opposition to the Confederate South. The Confederate rebel as villain offered a foil, as the Other, in opposition to those values for which Norwegians stood.[4]

On the eve of the Civil War, one Norwegian immigrant wrote a letter to Norway comparing Norway's peasant struggle against an aristocratic elite to America's struggle to free itself from the slaveholding aristocracy of the Democratic party of the South.[5] Participation on the winning side of the Civil War meant that Norwegians had earned their stripes through defense and sacrifice to their adopted land. The war provided the raw material necessary for the construction of a Norwegian-American identity.

Four Norwegian authors from the late 1860s capitalized on the enhanced reputation that Norwegians now enjoyed as a result of their service in the Civil War. In 1869, John A. Johnson published his history on the Scandinavian Regiment. Although he used the term "Scandinavians" in his book, his characterization was especially pertinent to Norwegians. He comments on how Scandinavians were "more liberal and cosmopolitan in their thinking" than most of the other European nations. They were also among the "most willing to serve their country." Moreover, Scandinavians had a great "affection for freedom, and law and order," which "was so well known in their Nordic home."[6]

Another significant author from this decade was Svein Nilsson, who developed an early Norwegian-American identity through his articles in *Billed-Magazin*. He stressed that Leif Erikson, a Norwegian, had been the first European to discover America, and thus Norwegians had a long association with the New World. More important for Nilsson, however, was the role played by the sturdy Norwegian pioneers in America. He argued that the Norwegian was a superior type of immigrant, one who excelled at hard work and frugality. Nilsson made the stereotyped Irish immigrant the natural foil to the Norwegian immigrant, thereby adopting the prejudices of Anglo-Americans and incorporating them into the Norwegian-American identity. Moreover, he pointed out that Norwegians were better educated than other immigrants. He described them as law-abiding and moral citizens, robust frontier men and women who eschewed the decadent life of urban America.[7] In effect, Nilsson advanced the idea that Norwegians were a civilized and cultured immigrant group.

Meanwhile, during the summer and fall of 1867, Herman A. Preus, pastor and president of the Norwegian Synod, published a series of lectures on the condition of the church in America, *Syv Foredrag over de kirkelige Forholde blandt de Norske i Amerika* (Seven Lectures over the Religious Status of the Norwegians in America), which also presented a glimpse into some of the formative aspects of the Norwegian-American self-image. He mentioned that in America Norwegians had a good reputation for industry, frugality, and honesty, serving as tamers of the frontier. Yet he worried that the great prosperity of America and assimilationist pressure might lead the normally pious Norwegians to stray from their faith, especially since the transplanted church could not rely on the state to back its positions.[8]

An interest in Norwegian immigrants among homeland Norwegians also became more pronounced around this time. In an article published in the Norwegian journal *Norden* (The North) in 1868, Peter Hendrichson, a Norwegian immigrant who had returned to Norway for graduate study, described the Norwegian pioneer life in America. He shared many of the views presented by authors such as Nilsson, including the idea that the Norwegian pioneers in America were bringing civilization to the frontier, often while fighting the difficult conditions of plague and climate found on the American prairie. He likewise noted that Americans had a positive image of Norwegians, especially when compared to the typical Irish immigrant whom he described as "a filthy, ragged, foreboding, and apathetic figure." He viewed Norwegians as embodying the virtues of republicanism and love of freedom. However, he countered this positive image by stating that Norwegians had their flaws; they were especially intolerant of other perspectives with regard to their Lutheran orientation. At the end of his article, he urged Norwegians to become more like Americans and embrace a classless society, unlike Norway's, and become liberal and open-minded like the citizens of their new land.[9]

Henrichson's work underscores the tensions present in the negotiation over the Norwegian-American identity. While many elite Norwegian-American leaders wanted to transplant as much as possible of their homeland traditions to America, there was also a strong incentive for the immigrants to become more like Americans, a sentiment that came not just from Anglo-American leaders but also from many in the Norwegian-American community.

One sees a similar idea in David Monrad Schøyens's history of America, which was published by John Anderson's *Skandinaven* publishing house between 1874 and 1876. The author was an attorney from Norway who had served as an officer in the Scandinavian Regiment, becoming a newspaperman for *Skandinaven* after the war. Schøyen's history is largely concerned with the role of prominent Anglo-Americans in the development of the nation, and he devotes little space to the Norwegian element. He does point out that Norwegians had a long association with America, going back to the Viking age. He also describes the role of Norwegians in the Civil War, but with little fanfare. Like Henrichson, he implies that Norwegians should try to become more like Americans.[10]

Not everyone was in favor of Norwegians assimilating American ways. Fredrik M. Wallem, a correspondent for a newspaper in Bergen, Norway, traveled among the Norwegian settlements in Wisconsin in 1871 and had his travel letters published back in Norway. Overall, he paints a positive picture of his countrymen in America, whose prosperity was increasing. They served as agents of civilization in the middle of a sometimes hostile continent. In noting that the Norwegian peasants were fast becoming Americans, he found that they were "stout, strong, and perseverant workers" who compared favorably with American workers in "intelligence, capability, and experience." Moreover, the Norwegians had "adapted quickly to American ideas of equality." Yet their efforts came at a price, for they had abandoned their national dress, their language, and many of their customs. And owing to the cost of sea travel at that time, Wallem lamented that barely one in a thousand would ever again see "det gamle Land" (the old country).[11]

Jørgen Gjerdrum, a Norwegian businessman, wrote a series of letters back to Norway in which he commented on conditions among the Norwegians in America. Published by the liberal organ *Dagbladet* in 1874 and 1875, they painted a largely positive picture of his countrymen, although he was not always impressed by conditions in New York. He observed how life along the city's seafront was rife with debauchery, including prostitution and drink, which was having a deleterious effect on the sailors. He was condescending toward the city's Norwegian-American elite, noting that their churches did not measure up to the ones in Norway, although he did approve of the Norwegian Society because it knit the community together. In comparing the material prosperity of Norwegian-American tenant farmers to cotters in Norway, he acknowledged that those in America were more affluent, though not rich. He also poked fun at the newly affluent Norwegian who, despite his deep Norwegian roots, "was becoming a man of breeding" but alone with his children could "not speak about the customs of the old country, which he had long since forgotten."

Notwithstanding these shortcomings, he concluded that a cotter's situation in Norway could not compare with that of the mostly prosperous farmers in America. He came away favorably impressed with the status of Norwegian immigrants, whom he viewed as "independent and respected citizen[s] of the New World." The material prosperity of America even made them morally superior to their homeland.[12]

By the early to mid-1870s, one could detect the rudimentary outlines of a Norwegian-American identity. Its themes, however, were scattered and not effectively unified in a cohesive whole. What the Norwegian-American identity needed was someone to provide the spark, to synthesize these themes with extant Norwegian symbols, thereby creating a true Norwegian-American identity. Before venturing into that process, however, it is useful to step back and take note of the impulses from Norway that would play a pivotal role in the creation of the Norwegian-American ethnic identity.

Influences from Norway

Effective mythmaking remained central but elusive in the creation of the Norwegian-American identity. Orm Øverland locates the Norwegian-American identity and its creation of myths within a process that applied to nearly every immigrant group. His model accurately describes how the Norwegian-American identity evolved with regard to how that identity was negotiated between Norwegian-American leaders and Anglo-American leaders. Two other important aspects, however, should not be overlooked. Norwegian-American identity-makers also constructed their myths through negotiation between themselves and national myth-makers back in Norway. Historian David Mauk terms this part of a triangulation process in which Norwegian-American elites sought to locate their self-image within an ideological framework that would appeal to both American and Norwegian ideals. He notes that this resulted from the tension between what Werner Sollors has termed "descent" from a European homeland and "consent" to the new loyalty of American nationalism.[13] It is true, as Øverland observes, that elites in Norway often ignored the ideas surrounding the Norwegian-American self-image, although he also acknowledges that there was "a two-way traffic of ideological contributions."[14] What is important to understanding the construction of the Norwegian-American self-image is not the *degree* of acceptance by Norway's elites but that the *intent* of these ideas was to appeal to the image-makers back in Norway.

In addition to this triangulation process between American and Norwegian nationalisms, it is also important to remember that Norwegian-American image-makers crafted their ideology with regard to the larger Norwegian-American community. They sought to make its message acceptable to three target audiences: Americans, homeland Norwegians, and Norwegian Americans. H. Arnold Barton has shown how a similar tendency marked the development of the Swedish-American identity toward the end of the nineteenth century. He identifies how Swedes in America came to view themselves as being Swedish-Americans, a group neither purely Swedish nor purely American. In time, they viewed themselves as part of a distinct nation. For example, the Swedish-American author Carl Fredrik Peterson's 1898 survey articulated how Swedish Americans had created in America the "solid foundation for a great nation," which implied that immigrant Swedes had crafted an identity unique unto themselves. Johan Person, publisher of *Svensk-amerikansk studier* (Swedish-American Studies), articulated this viewpoint fully in a series of articles from 1912.[15] Through a similar process, Norwegians in America came to view their group as Norwegian-American, whose members represented a new, hybrid nation in America.[16]

One other aspect of the mythmaking process was the motivation behind the ideology. Øverland points out correctly that the myths were basically part of a "forward-looking argument for an American future." He further observes that the myths served to function as an argument for a right to a home in the new land.[17] During the years in question, 1860 to 1890, the Norwegian-American image-making process was motivated by the argument that Norwegian-Americans deserved their rightful place in American society. In this regard, the ideas of Rasmus Bjørn Anderson and the other Norwegian-American mythmakers served as *origin myths* because they argued that Norwegian Americans belonged in America.

As will be shown later in this study, however, the motivation behind the myths changed as circumstances in America and Norway changed. Thus, between 1890 and 1917, Norwegian-American leaders constructed what might be termed *hegemony myths,* which argued that Norwegians were at first the best immigrant group and later the best Americans. During the years from 1917 to 1945, as the pool of new immigrants dried up and Norwegian language usage rapidly decreased, Norwegian-American leaders constructed their ideology around the concept of *legacy myths,* which would gain a prominent place for the reputation of Norwegian-Americans both in America and Norway.

Familiar with the development of Norway's nineteenth-century nationalism, Norwegian-American leaders sought to create a self-image that would be satisfactory to a homeland Norwegian audience. Øystein Sørensen observes how Norway's nationalism during the century had components of modernization and political nation-building as practical goals. The third strain, cultural nationalism, or national romanticism, attempted to construct a Norwegian national identity that was free from the tinges of Danish or even Swedish influences. A group of elite leaders, including the national poet Henrik Wergeland, aimed to build Norwegian nationalism on the virtues of the peasantry.[18]

Viewed as part of "the National Breakthrough," a phrase scholars use to describe the articulation of a coherent Norwegian national identity, the ideological component of national romanticism was an elevation of the peasant culture of Norway, which was viewed as the true Norwegian culture. Those things associated with the peasant culture, including fairy tales, legends, songs, and dances, assumed national importance among Norway's cultural elite. The elite also extolled the greatness of Norway's ancient history, above all the Viking age. Romantic sentiment greatly influenced Norway's art. Painters such as J. C. Dahl and Adolph Tideman depicted the grandeur and rugged beauty of Norway's rural landscapes, and their peasant subjects were given a glorious luster. Meanwhile, the Norwegian ethnologists Peter Christen Asbjørnson and Jørgen Moe published their collection *Norske Folkeventyr* (Norwegian Folktales) from 1841 to 1844, which while often humorous nonetheless emphasized the innate, pre-Christian traits of Norwegians.[19]

At a popular level, schoolteachers played an important role in the second half of the nineteenth century as dispensers of the ideas of Norwegian nationalism. An alternative system of higher education, the so-called folk high schools, based on principles advanced by Grundtvig, were established during the 1860s. By the late 1870s they had become bastions of an ideology that viewed the Norwegian peasantry as both a cultural and religious bulwark against the perceived moral decadence of the European intelligentsia. The folk high schools played an especially important role in developing the idea that Norway's national identity was founded on the virtues of the peasantry, an outright rejection of the perceived Danish qualities of Norway's urban-based elite.[20]

The national romantic cause found a voice in many of Norway's nineteenth-century writers, especially Bjørnstjerne Bjørnson, who was influenced by the Norwegian historical school. In his early career he wrote on national romantic themes; his most famous work of this genre was *Synnøve Solbakken,* whose heroine was a Norwegian peasant girl. Although Bjørnson later directed his writings toward social realism, he remained an ardent Norwegian nationalist through his association with the Liberal party. His strident nationalism earned Bjørnson the title of "Father of Norwegian Nationalism."[21]

Norway's writers likewise explored the topic of emigration in their writings. The pros and cons of emigration certainly came to the fore during the 1840s and 1850s, and Wergeland, for instance, touched on the subject in many of his works. A common theme in the anti-emigration literature was the idea that while America was a land of potentially greater economic reward than Norway, it was also a crueler and more merciless place, an idea that became especially pronounced after the American Civil War. One finds these ideas especially prevalent in the novels of Kristofer Janson, who lived in Minneapolis as a Unitarian minister during the 1880s. A play of his titled *Amerikanske Fantasier* (American Fantasies) showcases a jurist from Norway who visits America in order to report back to the

Luther College in Decorah, Iowa (shown here in 1876), was among the colleges founded by Norwegians. Courtesy of the Wisconsin Historical Society, 27418.

homeland. During his three years there, however, this jurist finds little positive to write home about, for America is a land largely bereft of culture, with little respect for those in academia. He cannot understand how Norwegians can be so smitten with such an uncivilized land.[22]

In the early writings of Bjørnson an anti-emigration bias is sometimes present. In *Kongen* (The King) and *Det nye system* (The New System), the author presents characters who criticize America for its republicanism and godlessness. Such sentiments were naturally present among Norway's elites within the government; for them, America represented a lack of respect for authority and tradition. Other prominent Norwegian authors also played up this sentiment, such as Henrik Ibsen, albeit to a somewhat muted extent, and Alexander Kielland, in whose work *Fortuna* (Fortune) America is depicted as a land of crooks.[23]

Support for emigration in Norway was also tied to the political struggle between the officials and the peasantry. The early 1850s radical movement of Marcus Thrane had advanced emigration to America as a strategy to bring attention to the inequalities present within Norwegian society. The agrarian leader Søren Jaabæk published the poem *Udvandringen* (The Emigration) in 1866, in which he argued that America, with its wealth and abundant soil, would be like a magnet to people who lived in a land like Norway, which was plagued by burdensome laws and taxes. The struggle between the upper and lower classes even manifested itself in a clash over Norway's official language. Many who sided with the peasantry and the Liberal party, including the writer Arne Garborg, urged the adoption of Landsmaal, a rural-based synthetic language developed by Ivar Aasen, in place of the more conservative Riksmaal, the Dano-Norwegian language spoken by urban elites. After the Liberals achieved power in the 1880s, the two languages were given equal official status.[24]

Perhaps the strongest defender in Norway of emigration was Aasmund Olavson Vinje, a lyrical poet and product of the peasant class. Writing exclusively in Landsmaal, he authored several essays on the theme of emigration. In "Vaart Husstell og Gardsstell" (Our Domestic Work and Our Farm Work), he observed that as long as the Norwegian people were unaware that a better life existed, they were content, but once they learned of a land like America, they could not be stopped. He also countered the criticism that Norwegians who emigrated did so out of some irrational wanderlust; instead, Vinje argued that the urge to emigrate was the result of a rational acquisition of knowledge, that Norwegians understood that Norway did not offer them opportunities to improve their condition in life. He took exception to the idea that Norwegians who emigrated were unpatriotic and insisted that large-scale emigration to America reflected a critique of Norwegian society. "Should Norway become emptied of its population because Norwegians through this strategy [emigration] attempt to craft better lives for themselves, then it ought to be the way of nature."[25]

During his tenure as an editor for *Norsk Folkeblad* (Norwegian People's Paper), from 1866 to 1871, he had the opportunity to read letters from America that Norwegian immigrants had sent to the paper and gradually changed his views. He came to see America as being on the leading edge of modernization. To him America was a good land that supplied reactionary Norway with new ideas. Bjørnson's sentiments revealed his increasing dedication to liberalism, and the allure of America, with its relatively class-free system and economic opportunities, pointed to the direction that Norway must take in order to survive and prosper. The Norwegian government, he upheld, needed to take better care of its poorest citizens and to create better employment opportunities that would bind the would-be emigrants to Norway.[26]

During the 1880s, events in Norway and in Norwegian America pointed to closer cooperation in the future. In Norway, the Liberal party, under the stellar leadership of Johan Sverdrup, finally succeeded in establishing parliamentary democracy in 1884. During this decade important Norwegians, including Bjørnson, Janson, and the author Knut Hamsun, made visits to Norwegians in America. Norwegian-American leaders, meanwhile, honed the message of the Norwegian-American self-image, making their ideas available to both America and Norway. Two exemplars of this process were Hans A. Foss and Hjalmar Hjorth Boyesen, who published works that refined the Norwegian-American self-image and at the same time attempted to win acceptance of their ideas among a wider audience. Furthermore, the types of nationalist strategies being pursued in Norway impacted how Norwegian-American identity-makers presented their self-image.

Published in 1884, Hans A. Foss's novel *Husmandsgutten: En Fortælling fra Sigdal* (The Cotter's Son: A Story from Sigdal) was well received in both Norway and Norwegian America. Briefly, the story revolves around Ole Haugen, a cotter in Norway, who falls in love with the daughter of the farm owner for whom he works. Class differences in Norway prevent them from getting together, so Ole immigrates to America, and through his perseverance he becomes wealthy enough to return to Norway. Back in the old country, he buys the farm he once worked on, marries his sweetheart, and returns as the prodigal son. The novel is both a justification of the desire to emigrate—the American Dream—and a criticism of the class system then prevalent in Norway.[27]

A strong admirer of Bjørnson, Foss utilized peasant themes in all of his novels, although his works lacked the complexity often found in those of his hero. At a popular level the novel is a triumph of good over evil. Moreover, in *The Cotter's Son*, as in all his novels, good characters avoid drink, while evil ones often drink to excess. It is the social criticism of the novel, especially its attack on the exploitation of the cotter system, that makes its realistic portrayals of the cotters appealing to many of its readers. Thus, although the novel has its roots in national romanticism, it also reflected the growing social realism that would become the preferred genre of such authors as Bjørnson and Henrik Ibsen.[28]

The Cotter's Son also owed some of its popularity to the idealism represented by America. In America people can work to overcome poverty, and some even become rich. America offers hope, and there Norwegian immigrants can own their own farms, something unlikely to happen in Norway.[29]

The novel stressed the popular liberal ideas that shaped Norway during the 1880s and 1890s. Liberal poets such as Bjørnson and Ibsen often portrayed America positively in their poems and other works. They viewed America as progressive and tolerant, with little need for archaic class structures. Still, Foss's novel was a novelty in that it was the first to depict cotters as heroes and farmers as villains.[30]

Thus, one must view Foss's novel as a product of both American and Norwegian influences. It presented America in a positive light, as an environment in which Norwegians could succeed. More important, Ole Haugen's ultimate victory comes in Norway, when he marries his love and becomes a farmer. Foss drew on themes present in Norway's national identity, national romanticist ideas that glorified the peasant and liberal-nationalist ideas that sought to modernize Norway and strike down the country's outdated class structure. Through his novel *The Cotter's Son*, Foss was attempting to enter the discourse surrounding the nascent nationalisms in Norwegian America and Norway.

Another Norwegian-American writer who helped to negotiate the Norwegian-American identity with Norway was Hjalmar Hjorth Boyesen. Born in Norway in 1848, he immigrated to America in 1869, ultimately securing a position in 1881 as professor of German literature at Columbia University in New York. A. N. Rygg notes that while Boyesen was an enthusiastic American, he was also proud of his Norwegian ancestry. His works often dealt with subjects from Norway's history including *Gunnar, a Norseman's Pilgrimage* and *The Story of Norway*.[31]

Not only joyous family celebrations, weddings offered opportunities for ethnic celebrations, as shown in this photograph from a wedding at Norway Grove Church in Wisconsin in 1879. Courtesy of the Wisconsin Historical Society, 27787.

Clarence Glasrud has noted that Boyesen, as an intellectual living in New York, did not really fit in with his fellow Norwegian immigrants. Over time his writings moved away from his earlier romantic orientation toward one that stressed social realism. Yet Boyesen's most popular works remained his romantic ones, especially his early efforts. Glasrud argues that only in his early years did Boyesen capture the sense of longing and nostalgia for Norway, themes that resonated well with the immigrants on the plains. Despite his separation from the larger immigrant population, however, Boyesen understood the sense of the loss of old Norway among the immigrants, and most of his works take place in Norway.[32]

The concept that the Viking spirit endowed Norwegians with the necessary traits to succeed in modern society had become a component of the Norwegian-American self-image by the 1880s. The kernel of this concept can be found in Rasmus B. Anderson's 1875 speech and in Boyesen's *Gunnar*. Another source, obviously reflecting the spread of this concept among Norwegian Americans, was Boyesen's *Modern Vikings: Stories of Life and Sport in the Northland,* a children's book published in 1887. Written in English, it is obviously intended for a wider American audience, yet many of the ideas would doubtless be familiar with educated homeland Norwegians as well.

The book contains a series of short stories set primarily in Norway and a few in Iceland. Dedicated to the author's three male children, the stories repeat common themes concerning the importance of maintaining one's cultural traditions. "The Cooper and the Wolves" demonstrates these themes very well. Set in a small rural Norwegian valley, the central figure is a cooper named Tollef Kolstad. His son, Thor, is only a small boy, but he has a corner in his father's shop. Thor uses tools that are smaller replicas of his father's to build pails, buckets, and baskets that he sells to other boys in the neighborhood. Ever frugal, Thor gives his money to his mother who keeps the money in a small tin.

Tollef receives an order for a barrel from a rich peasant who wants him to deliver it just before Christmas. Tollef works arduously and completes the barrel the day it is due. He borrows a neighbor's horse and sleigh and takes his son Thor along with him to deliver the barrel later that evening. The young boy brings along his whip and small hatchet, which will prove fortuitous. Their journey requires them to cross a frozen lake, and at about the halfway point they are attacked by wolves. Their only recourse is to hide inside the barrel. The circling pack attempts to reach inside the barrel but Tollef uses Thor's little hatchet to cut off a paw of each wolf who attempts to gain entry. The two humans eventually make a run for it but not before they had gathered up the severed wolf paws. They eventually reach safety at the house of a nearby cotter. As a reward, Thor is allowed to sell the eleven wolf paws to the sheriff, which nets him a nice reward. The reward nearly bursts his old savings tin, so his mother buys him a new one. Thor is the hero. His father Tollef tells his wife, "If it had not been for him, you might have no husband to-day. It was his little whip and toy hatchet that saved our lives."[33]

This tale from *Modern Vikings* presents two themes. The first is that Thor represents true Norwegian virtue because he follows his father's ways. In his allegorical way, Boyesen stresses the importance of maintaining and observing Norwegian cultural traditions. The second theme is that Thor is thrifty; he is able to utilize his natural talents and prosper, even as a child, in a harsh environment. Again, this suggests the ability of hardy Norwegians to adapt to difficult conditions. Moreover, because Thor follows the old traditions, including martial prowess, he is able to save the day, and he is amply rewarded. The message to future Norwegians in America is that they can prosper in the modern world if they maintain those stout "Viking" virtues. As modern Vikings, Norwegians made excellent citizens.

During the decade of the 1880s, Norwegian-American image-makers sought inclusion for their group within Norway's national identity. They attempted to locate a Norwegian-American identity that would prove satisfactory to elite Anglo-American leaders yet also permit them to share in the ongoing development of Norway's evolving national identity. In attempting to negotiate between American and Norwegian national identities, Norwegian-American leaders were creating a new national hybrid identity, the Norwegian-American national identity. That process involved adapting to pressures within America while simultaneously adapting Norwegian forms of nationalism, thereby conserving as much of the Norwegian content as possible. It should also be noted that in crafting this hybrid identity, Norwegian-American leaders were being selective about which elements of the homeland Norwegian identity they desired to preserve. They had no intention, for instance, of retaining the class-based social differentiation prevalent in Norway at the time.

Thus, one sees that Hans A. Foss adopts the Norwegian glorification of peasant culture but adapts it to make a sharp social criticism of the treatment accorded the cotter class in Norway. As such, America serves as a counterweight to the problems inherent in Norway's archaic class structure. Meanwhile, Hjalmer Hjorth Boyesen takes the image of the Viking and makes it a metaphor for success in the modern world. The idea of Norwegians as modern Vikings, in a capacity that extended beyond seafaring, was thus entered as part of the negotiation between the two nationalisms, Norway and Norwegian America. In effect, the evolution of a Norwegian-American self-image must be seen as part of a changing discourse that was influenced by developments on both sides of the Atlantic Ocean.

Creating an Early Norwegian-American Identity: The Construction of a Norwegian-American History

Norwegians in America were thus being pressured from both the American and the Norwegian sides, and they still lacked a coherent ideology that would fulfill the conditions of their complementary identity as both Americans and Norwegians. The development of the Norwegian-American identity owed much to Norwegian-American historians who constructed a historical narrative of Norwegian immigration to the United States that sought to legitimate and advance their group's position within American society. They argued that Norwegians had a long and uninterrupted association with America since they were the first Europeans to "discover" the New World. Furthermore, Norwegian-American historians claimed that it had been Norwegians who had first introduced into the English-speaking world those values held so dear by Anglo-Americans, namely, a strong sense of individualism, love of freedom, and a desire for democratic institutions.

It should be noted that the concept of history employed by Norwegian-American historians, or other ethnic leaders for that matter, was a broad one. Those who authored the history of Norwegians in America would never have considered themselves historians, and many of those who did had dubious credentials by today's standards. Their constructed history must be primarily understood as an ideological exercise designed to promote a self-aggrandizing Norwegian-American identity with historical accuracy occupying second place.

The emergence of the Norwegian-American identity coincided with the nascence of the filiopietistic tradition among the largely amateur historians, from roughly 1865 to 1925, although it lingered on into the 1930s. Because the basic ideas of that tradition were developed in the formative decades following the Civil War, the treatment of the constructed Norwegian-American historical tradition will be covered in this chapter even though many of its later authors wrote in the years beyond 1890. By 1925, professional historians started to supplant this approach.[34] Although their history was not always accurate, the writings of the filiopietistic Norwegian-American historians formed the core of the Norwegian-American identity. Hence, the study of that historical construction tells much about the Norwegian-American self-image. They created a Norwegian-American history that claimed that the Vikings discovered

America, that their ancestors were among the first European colonists, that Norwegian-American heroes had contributed to the success of America through both service and sacrifice, and that Norwegian immigrants settled and tamed much of the American frontier.

The attempt to gain recognition was common to all immigrant groups. As Victor Greene has shown in his study on American immigrant leaders, every immigrant group had the need to impress Anglo-Americans and other immigrant groups. Greene points to two strategies used to accomplish these goals. First, the immigrant group had to demonstrate that it had a long involvement in American history. Second, it had to show that it shared similarities with Anglo-American culture and ideas.[35] Additionally, the immigrants, in this instance the Norwegians, needed to impress themselves with their own worth in a new and challenging environment and to make homeland Norwegian leaders aware of the significance of the immigrants' accomplishments.

A sense of history was basic to implementing these strategies. In his study of Swedish-American identity, Dag Blanck demonstrates how Swedish Americans of the Augustana Lutheran Synod combined elements of three historic traditions—those of Sweden, the United States, and Swedish America—to create a Swedish-American history that addressed the present-day needs of Swedish immigrants and their children in the United States.[36]

H. Arnold Barton observed a similar tendency in his study of the evolving Swedish-American identity. He notes how their principal spokesperson, Johan A. Enander, created a history that emphasized Swedish contributions to America's history. In it, the Swedes' Viking ancestors had been the real discoverers of America, and in the seventeenth century the Swedes had been one of the three northern European powers to colonize America. Enander noted that prominent Swedish Americans, including John Morton, were among the founders of the republic, and in an 1876 speech he declared that the seeds of American freedom had their origins in the "land beneath the North Star," a clear reference to Sweden. As Barton observes, the Swedish-American ideology proclaimed Swedes as steadfast allies of the American worldview, and it ensured that they would be viewed as a highly desirable immigrant group.[37]

Orm Øverland has shown that virtually all immigrant groups created homemaking myths in which their group made the most significant contributions to America's history. Studies by Wilbur Zelinsky and Jon Gjerde have shown how America's national identity was an ideological construct based on a universal set of values—liberty, equality, and republicanism—that were open to all Europeans. Gjerde and Lawrence Fuchs point out that another significant idea, especially to immigrant leaders, was that complete assimilation was not necessary as long as the immigrant group remained loyal to American civic culture.[38]

In creating their ethnic group's history, Norwegian-American image-makers turned to recognizable tropes, and the Viking age loomed large in their formulation. Enthusiasm for the Viking age was not limited to Norwegian Americans. In 1837 the Danish scholar Carl C. Rafn published his *Antiquitates Americannae*, which gave a detailed treatment of the Norse discoverers of America. An American translation by William Jackson, with the same title, appeared the following year. In 1839 American clergyman Joshua T. Smith published *Norsemen in New England, or America in the Tenth Century*. Two years later, *The Discovery of America in the Tenth Century*, by the Englishman North Ludlow Beamish, appeared and remained the standard work on the subject for over two decades. In 1844 the Scottsman Samuel Laing published an English translation of the *Heimskringla (Saga of the Norwegian Kings)*, which proved popular reading. These authors argued that the Old Norse sagas were historically accurate and that relics such as the Dighton Writing Rock, the Newport Tower, and the alleged remains of a Viking warrior found near Fall River, Massachusetts, were authentic examples of a Norse presence in America. These works stated that Columbus knew of the New World from the sagas before he sailed. American authors Henry Wadsworth Longfellow and John Greenleaf Whittier likewise glorified the Viking presence in America, and these speculations enjoyed widespread popularity among Americans.[39]

Drawing on these ideas, Norwegian-American identity-makers proceeded to advance their own historical construction about Norwegians in America. In a short article from 1869, the journalist Svein Nilsson penned a brief account of how Leif Erikson and his party of Viking explorers had established an early Norwegian presence in America. Although he described the Norsemen in America as Norwegians, they were in fact Greenland colonists from Iceland, where the population was of predominantly west Norwegian origin. To Norwegian-American historians of this period, they were simply labeled "Norwegians."[40]

The Norwegian-American leader who attempted to synthesize that ideology, to provide a self-image or identity that would argue for their success as both Americans and Norwegian, was Rasmus B. Anderson. Building on a combination of Norwegian and American ideas, his thesis was that owing to the discovery of America by Leif Erikson and the Vikings, Norwegians must be seen as the first Europeans to be associated with the New World. Furthermore, through their colonizing efforts in England and Normandy, it had been the Norwegians who had introduced to the English-speaking world its values of democracy, freedom, hard work, and respect for law and order.

Anderson owed much of his emphasis on the Viking age and the early Middle Ages in Norway to the work of Norway's national romanticist historians who saw this period as the country's golden age. University professors Rudolf Keyser and P. A. Munch, the founders of the Norwegian historical school, argued that the ancestors of Norwegians had migrated from the north and east, rather than from the south as the Swedes and Danes had done. Norway's historians were following the lead created by the Danish bishop Nikolai F. S. Grundtvig, an early nineteenth-century advocate of the Germanic rather than the Latin contributions to humanity. This school of thought contended that Norwegians were purer both racially and culturally than their Nordic and Germanic neighbors. In the 1870s the concept of the two Norways, advanced by the author Arne Garborg and the historian Ernst Sars, insisted that pure Norwegian culture had been preserved through the centuries in the peasantry, whom they depicted as stalwart, pure-blooded Norwegians, the descendants of the Vikings. In contrast, the largely urban upper classes, which descended from Danish and other foreign elements, were portrayed as effete and impure.[41] A second idea was that the literature and history of the period, especially the eddas and the sagas, were exclusively Norwegian and not the product of a shared Scandinavian culture. Moreover, Iceland, the source of most of the medieval material, was likewise Norwegian since it had been colonized by Norwegians.[42]

As professor at the University of Wisconsin, Anderson was familiar with the Norwegian school and adopted the glorification of the Viking age to serve as the cornerstone of his synthetic ideology. To the ideas of Keyser and Munch, he added an American component to the story by promoting Leif Erikson as both a Norwegian and an American hero. His most inventive concept was the idea that American values owed their origins to the activities of the Norwegians. For the Norwegian historians, the American connection was virtually nonexistent. Anderson's synthesized image of Norwegians in America, therefore, was intended to promote Norwegian immigrants as good Norwegians and good Americans, a process that sought to place Norwegian Americans within the framework of the two evolving national identities, Norwegian-American and Norwegian. Gaining acceptance for that self-image through a public discourse, however, was generally limited to individuals who could reach a relatively large audience, including non-Norwegian Americans, and thus during the years from roughly 1860 to 1890 the role of spokesperson for Norwegian Americans fell to Rasmus B. Anderson.

Beginning in 1868, he tirelessly promoted his thesis of the Norwegian discovery of America through his public lectures and publications. In his first published work in 1874, *America Not Discovered by Columbus,* he unabashedly proclaimed:

> The subject to which your attention is invited is, if properly presented, of equal interest to Americans and Norsemen. For those who are born and brought up on the fertile soil of Columbus, under the shady branches of the noble tree of American liberty, where the banner of progress and education is unfurled to the breeze, must naturally feel a deep interest in whatever facts may be presented in relation to the first discovery and early settlement of this their native land; while those who first saw the sunlight beaming among the rugged, snow-capped mountains of old Norway, and can still feel any of the heroic blood of their dauntless forefathers course its way through their veins, must, as a matter of course, feel an equally deep interest in learning that their own ancestors, the intrepid Norsemen, were the first pale-faced men who planted their feet on this gem of the ocean, and an interest, too, I dare say, in having the claims of their native country to this honor vindicated.[43]

At an Independence Day speech presented at Chicago on July 5, 1875, Anderson outlined the full text of his vision of the Norwegian-American identity. Speaking in Norwegian, he stated that America's birthday was also the birthday of Norwegian-American immigration "because the first large-scale immigration from Norway had occurred fifty years earlier with the arrival of the *Restaurationen.*" He then proceeded to outline how their destiny had led the Norwegians to return to the land, whose character owed much to the people of the Midnight Sun.[44]

Anderson compared the gift of liberty to a plant. He noted that the Norwegian plant of liberty had been brought to Normandy, reimported to England through William the Conqueror, and finally was transplanted to America by the Puritans. Another branch of the plant, the one that took root in Iceland, was also of Norwegian origin. In 872, the tyrannical King Harald Fairhair became the first to unify Norway. According to Norway's nationalist historians, the prospective loss of liberty under King Harald influenced many Norwegian freeholders to move to Iceland. Anderson used this interpretation to explain how Norwegian liberty became associated with a later descendant named Leif Erikson, the "Norwegian" discoverer of the New World.[45]

Anderson related to his audience that the seed matured in America until it sprouted on the Fourth of July 1776. The beauty of the blossom attracted the nations of the world, in particular Norway. When blight appeared on the more southerly leaves of the American plant of liberty, it was removed with "the blood of Lincoln." Here too Anderson made a connection, noting that Norwegians had risked their lives in the Civil War to protect the plant of liberty, just as the ancestors of the Norwegians had protected it back in Norway, shielding the plant during the centuries of foreign oppression.[46]

A strong racial argument runs throughout Anderson's speech. Citing many of the leading studies of the day, he noted that there was "Norwegian blood in the veins of three fourths of the populations of England and America." He further described how the Norwegian *bonde*, or peasant class, had preserved the purity of the Norwegian race and kept alive a love of freedom, which he contrasts with that of the official class, whose blood had long been tainted with foreign influences. It was, he added, the peasantry that led the struggle for political freedom in Norway. Of course, Anderson's mostly Norwegian audience would realize that they too were immigrants or descendants of those who had emigrated from the peasant class.[47]

The allusions to key American themes showed how Anderson sought to position Norwegians as an important immigrant group. As Orm Øverland notes, Anderson used the language of the Declaration of Independence to explain the debt the world owes to Norway, inasmuch as the great founding document of the United States was essentially Norwegian. In this regard, he was adapting the raw material of American history and using it to synthesize what Øverland terms "Norwegian-American homemaking myths."[48]

In rudimentary form, one sees the concept of latter-day Vikings present in Anderson's speech, even though he does not use that term. Throughout the lifespan of the Norwegian-American self-image, the metaphor of the Viking—stout, resolute, defender of freedom and liberty—would remain as one of the primary components. Anderson and other Norwegian identity-makers, both in America and Norway, would advance the notion that the blood of the Vikings still flowed in latter-day Norwegians and that those racial traits made the Norwegians especially well adapted to modern life, whether as farmers, business operators, engineers, politicians, or soldiers. The Viking thus served as a very flexible symbol for Norwegians, one whose attributes could change to fit changing circumstances. For homeland Norwegians, the Viking was primarily a symbol of their modern seamen; for immigrant Norwegians, he was often compared to the frontier colonist who "sailed his wagon" on a sea of prairie grass.

However, Anderson was not content with promoting his ideas solely in America; he aimed to win over the Norwegian homeland as well. During the 1880s, he served as America's ambassador to Denmark. In 1886, he published *Amerikas første Opdagelse* (America's First Discovery). Published in Copenhagen, the book largely rehashed his ideas concerning his interpretation of the Viking discovery of America, which he obviously wished to make available to a larger Norwegian, as well as Scandinavian, audience. Seeking to place his history within Norway's nationalist school, Anderson claimed that the North (Norway) had not received historical credit for either its influence on great nations such as England and Germany or its discovery of America. He was implying that Norwegian immigrants were merely returning to the land they, not Columbus, had discovered and so were not newcomers to America.[49]

By publishing his interpretation of the Norwegian discovery of America in Europe, Anderson was attempting to negotiate with Norwegian leaders a place for Norwegian Americans. In fact, Anderson carried on a long battle with the Norwegian historian Gustav Storm over the location of Leif Erikson's New World discovery. Storm maintained that Erikson landed in Newfoundland and had not reached farther south into what would later be the United States. Anderson insisted that Erikson had made it farther south, making landfall in the area around contemporary New England.[50]

Such new ideas were not automatically accepted, and there was often a period of delay before at least some Norwegian elites were convinced. When his book was first published, European critics were overwhelmingly negative. A leading Copenhagen paper attacked Anderson personally. The main conservative Norwegian papers, *Aftenposten* and *Morgenbladet*, were even harsher in their criticism. The former dismissed the book as "propaganda and fanaticism," and the latter termed it "worthless and superfluous." The liberal *Dagbladet* gave it a kinder reception, though it noted that the work would have benefited from an inclusion of later scholarship.[51]

Anderson's positions thus made him something of an embarrassment among his fellow Norwegian-American leaders, whose goal was to obtain respectability from homeland Norwegians. The acknowledgment of Leif Erikson within the Norwegian national identity did not make real headway until the onset of World War I, and it was not accepted on a popular level there until the mid-1920s. However, the attempt to make elements of the Norwegian-American identity accepted among homeland Norwegians continued to influence the development of that identity, and the construction of the Norwegian-American national identity must be seen in that context.

In his synthetic work on American immigrant groups, Orm Øverland observes that each immigrant group tried to show that it had been an early participant in the history of the New World. Through his emphasis on the Viking age, Anderson was creating what Øverland terms a "foundation myth" that was designed to prove that Norwegians had a long association with America and were not simply late arrivals in the New World.[52]

Likewise, Øverland notes how immigrant groups attempted to create myths of ideology showing that they had been the source of American civic virtues. Norwegian-American historians claimed that it was Norwegians who had first planted the seeds for those values most cherished by Americans. Thus, Anderson's idea that the freedom-loving values of the Norwegian Vikings had been planted in England via the Norman invasion, which he articulated in his 1875 speech, must be seen as the creation of a myth in which the immigrant Norwegian culture shares the same values as the dominant American culture.[53]

Depicting Norwegians as the Viking discovers of America and the source of American civic values would long dominate Norwegian-American history. Building on the work of Nilsson and Anderson, successive Norwegian-American historians like Martin Ulvestad, writing in 1907, and Hjalmar Rued Holand, in 1908, utilized the argument that Norwegians were responsible for a number of firsts in the New World. In addition to Leif Erikson being the first European discoverer of America, they noted that Norwegians had been the first European colonists in the New World and that the first white persons to be born and to have died in the New World were Norwegians.[54] The exploits of the Vikings therefore strongly supported a Norwegian-American claim of an early presence in America to which few other immigrant groups could lay claim.

Anderson's other dictum—that Norwegian traits developed during the Viking age ensured that Norwegians made good Americans—found favor among Norwegian-American identity-makers. Writing in 1905, the Norwegian-American author and essayist Waldemar Ager noted that the Viking blood of the Norwegians had imbued them with the traits of steadfastness, honesty, desire for action, and frugality. In a 1922 essay, author Ole E. Rølvaag expressed similar sentiments when he stressed how the Viking age had invested Norwegians with a passion for liberty, insistence on individual rights, the primacy of the law, and the right of democratic government.[55]

Competition with other immigrant groups meant that Norwegian-American historians often had to impugn the legacy, particularly the heroes, of other ethnic groups. An obvious example is Christopher Columbus, whose exploits as European discoverer of the New World made him a hero to both Italian and Spanish immigrant groups. Anderson went to great lengths to prove that Columbus had prior knowledge of a western continent prior to sailing in 1492. He listed five arguments to support this supposition, including the idea that Columbus had visited Iceland in 1477 and must have learned of the Norse voyages from the natives of the island. Lloyd Hustvedt, the leading authority on Anderson, noted that one of Anderson's major objectives was to reduce the figure of Columbus and thereby remove some of the traditional glory given to Italy and Spain.[56]

The strong Lutheran Protestantism of Norwegian Americans further exacerbated tensions between them and Catholic immigrant groups. In 1928, for instance, Ulvestad complained that in the United States the public schoolbooks contained a great amount of material on Columbus but comparatively little attention was accorded Leif Erikson. He claimed that the Catholics constituted a powerful political force and that their agitation had won favorable treatment for them and their religion. He lamented that this politicization had seriously distorted the historical facts, which prevented Norwegians from receiving the proper credit for their achievements.[57]

Writing in the filiopietistic tradition often meant that Norwegian-American historians supported contentious evidence. Anderson, for instance, gave his endorsement to the authenticity of the Dighton Writing

Rock, which allegedly contained Old Norse runic inscriptions, while he, Ulvestad, and Holand all upheld the authenticity of the Newport Tower, a seventeenth-century tower allegedly built by Vikings, and the supposed Viking warrior found near Fall River, Massachusetts.[58]

Anderson, Ulvestad, and Holand also argued for a continued Norwegian presence in the New World long after the eclipse of the Viking age. Anderson mentioned that a woman named Freydis—the wife of Thorfinn Karlsefni—led an expedition to Vinland in 1011, and he pointed out that Bishop Erik Upsi visited the thriving Vinland colony as a missionary in the year 1121. Although Johan A. Enander presented this idea as a "dream" in his historical account of the Swedes in America, he clearly believed it, and the idea was widespread at that time among Scandinavian Americans that their presence was long-lived after Leif's discovery. Holand, meanwhile, relied on evidence in the sagas and other medieval sources to document several Norse contacts with Vinland. In all he cites six references, dating from the years 1070 to 1347, that referred to Vinland, thereby allegedly confirming a continual Norwegian presence in the New World.[59]

The most enduring controversy surrounded the discovery in 1898 of the Kensington Rune Stone by a Swedish-American farmer near Alexandria, Minnesota. Its inscription purportedly described a mixed Norwegian and Swedish expedition to the area in 1362. Although most scholars dismissed it, Holand continued to defend its authenticity until his death in the 1960s. Anderson, perhaps out of professional jealousy, refuted the authenticity of the stone. While most present-day scholars see the Kensington Rune Stone as a hoax, the debate continues, and some scholars, mainly non-historians, still maintain that the inscription is authentic.[60]

Despite the pitfalls of bad history, the legacy of the Viking age remained an important component for Norwegian-American historians. In an age dominated by Social Darwinist theories of race, the Viking image of the robust and virile Nordic archetype enhanced the image of Norwegians in America. The theme of Norwegian racial affinity for freedom not only became solidly entrenched among amateur Norwegian-American historians, but its message found its way into the prose of normally circumspect scholars. For example, in his 1915 *History of the Norwegian People*, Knut Gjerset made similar observations concerning freedom and the Norwegians:

> The freedom of the Norwegian people is the result of a long development, and their struggle for liberty had been of the same conservative kind as that of the English nation. They did not win freedom

suddenly through a revolutionary uprising, but the struggle which lasted through centuries was waged for the sake of preserving freedom which was theirs from time immemorial.... In these long struggles the Norwegian people have not only had an experience in popular self-government which has proved most valuable in their new environment in America, but they have developed in the trials of these struggles a self-assertive social temperament, an austere spirit of liberty, a rigid adherence to established principles, and a conservatism of thought which is clearly noticeable in their political life in the New World ... of the spirit which has knit strong the fraternal ties between the Viking race of the North and the land of the freedom in the New World.[61]

The Viking legacy, therefore, served as a basic component of the Norwegian-American historical construction. Establishing an early Norwegian presence in the New World provided Norwegians in America with a proud pedigree that was unmatched by other immigrant groups. Furthermore, Norwegian-American historians used the Viking age to showcase Norwegian values. Independence, a love of freedom, determination, honesty, a willingness to work hard, and an affinity for democratic government were all characteristics of the Norwegian immigrants, whose Viking ancestors had first planted these ideals in the English consciousness. This myth of the Norse origins of British and American democracy thus became an important element in the Norwegian-American conception of history.[62]

Yet an immigrant group needed more than an early New World presence; it also required a close association with the founding years of the American republic. As part of this process, Dag Blanck observes that immigrant groups in America sought to be recognized as charter peoples rather than simply as off-the-boat immigrants trying to measure up against the original British cultural and political traditions of the New England colonists.[63]

Creating a Norwegian presence during America's colonial period was problematic for Norwegian-American historians because Norway was ruled by Denmark from 1397 until 1814. Unlike Sweden, for instance, which established the New Sweden colony on the Delaware River between 1638 and 1655, no similar state-sponsored Norwegian enterprise was historically available.

Undaunted, Norwegian-American historians nonetheless located the American colonial period within the Norwegian-American conception of history, further fulfilling the need for foundation myths. For the most part, this effort concentrated on the exploits of individuals. One exception was the settlement of Bergen, New Jersey, in 1624, which Norwegian-American historians cited as evidence of an early Norwegian presence in colonial America. The fact that the town's origins are Dutch, named after Bergen op Zoom, did not deter Norwegian-American historians from using this apocryphal myth.[64]

Norwegians played a significant role in the early Dutch settlement of New Amsterdam (later New York). For example, Holand noted that the first white child born in what became New York State, John Vinge in 1614, was Norwegian. He referred to Captain Jens Munk from Norway, who while in service to the King of Denmark led a mostly Norwegian expedition to explore Hudson's Bay, claiming the area as Nova Dania. An especially prominent Norwegian was Anne Hendricksdatter from Bergen, Norway, who in 1650 married Jan Arentszen Van der Bilt, ancestor of the famous Vanderbilts. Holand was especially fond of the exploits of Hans Hansen from Bergen, Norway, who in 1633 led a group of Dutch and Norwegians across the Hudson River and built a settlement from which Jersey City rose. He mentioned that the first Norwegian doctor to emigrate, Dr. Johan M. Kalberlahn (Calberlaine), died in 1758 while trying to treat sufferers in a typhus epidemic.[65]

The most detailed Norwegian-American accounts of the Norwegian role during the colonial period were offered by George T. Flom, professor of languages at the University of Iowa, and John O. Evjen, professor of church history at Augsburg Seminary in Minneapolis. Flom wrote about many of the early settlers already mentioned, the Norwegian role in the founding of early Protestant congregations in New Amsterdam, and Thomas Johnson, a Revolutionary War hero. Evjen's account contained detailed biographies of Scandinavians who lived during the early years of the New York colony.[66]

One of Flom's more interesting accounts dealt with the Societas Scandinaviensis, founded in Philadelphia in 1769, the oldest Scandinavian association in America. He noted that its first president, Abraham Markoe, was a Norwegian. The society's greatest moment occurred in 1782 at a farewell banquet honoring the Swede Count Axel von Fersen, a hero of the Battle of Yorktown. The highlight of the banquet was an appearance by General George Washington, who decorated Fersen with the prestigious Order of Cincinnati. During the course of the festivities, Washington explained his delight at being among the people of his forefathers. According to Flom, Washington explained that his family's origins were at Wass, Denmark, and that his ancestors had settled in England in 970. On account of his Scandinavian ancestry, the society elected Washington an honorary member in January 1783.[67]

American writers likewise idealized Washington's Scandinavian roots. In 1879, Albert Welles, president of the American College for Genealogical Registry and Heraldry, published a book on the pedigree of the first president to demonstrate his Scandinavian ancestry.[68] Some Norwegian-American writers went further and claimed that Washington's ancestry was ultimately Norwegian. For example, Martin Ulvestad referred to a similar account of the Fersen banquet in which Washington identified his ancestry as Norwegian. Simon Johnson, a prominent Norwegian-American novelist, also referred to the Norwegian ancestry of America's first president.[69]

As a final adaptation to the theme of Norwegian involvement in America's colonial era, some Norwegian-American leaders posited a strong connection between America's Puritan settlers and Norway. As noted earlier in this chapter, Rasmus Bjørn Anderson made this argument in 1875, and the widespread acceptance of this idea would eventually make its way into ideological Norwegian-American literature. A fine example is Ole E. Rølvaag's 1931 novel *Den signede dag (Their Fathers' God)*, which underscores the tension between assimilated English-speaking Norwegian youth, who are ignorant of their heritage, and culturally loyal Norwegians, who represent the best Americans. At a key moment in the novel, Reverend Kaldahl, who embodies the culturally loyal element, informs the novel's main character, Peder, that eastern England, where most of the Puritans had come from, was originally settled by Norwegians. The Reverend then stresses to young Peder that it was the Norwegian desire for liberty and individualism that had been brought over to America by the Puritans.[70]

Although Norwegian involvement during the American colonial period did not match that of the Viking age, it was important nonetheless because it allowed Norwegian-American historians to posit a continued Norwegian presence in America. By serving to bridge the gap between the Viking age and the period of large-scale Norwegian immigration that began in 1825, the Norwegian colonial era served as an important foundation myth.

The contributions of significant Norwegian Americans and Norwegians were of central importance in the construction of a Norwegian-American history. For an immigrant group, cultural heroes offer proof to society at large of its collective ability and contributions to American society. The lionization of these heroes for their service and sacrifice, most notably in America's wars, raises the status of the immigrant by demonstrating patriotic loyalty toward the United States and its democratic values.[71]

Norwegian Americans could point proudly to a number of heroes. Leif Erikson occupied a pivotal position; Boston (1887) and Chicago (1901) erected statues to him, and President Franklin D. Roosevelt proclaimed Leif Erikson Day on October 9, 1935. Another prominent hero was Cleng Peerson, the Norwegian trailblazer who helped organize the first voyage of Norwegian emigrants who sailed aboard the sloop *Restaurationen* that arrived in New York City in 1825. Peerson worked diligently to establish Norwegian colonies, including the short-lived one at Kendall, New York, and successive ones in Illinois and Texas. Elling Eielsen, an early Lutheran pastor, arrived in America from Norway in 1839 and toiled under difficult circumstances to spread the Gospel to the Norwegian immigrants of northern Illinois and southern Wisconsin. Knute Nelson, meanwhile, had a distinguished political career in Minnesota, serving as state senator and congressman, governor, and U.S. senator.[72]

Since it is not feasible to detail the treatment accorded Norwegian-American heroes fully, it will suffice to describe briefly the portrayal of perhaps the most famous of them, Colonel Hans Christian Heg. Born in Drammen, Norway, in 1829, he emigrated to America in 1840. Leading a colorful life, he participated in the 1849 California gold rush and later returned to his father's homestead at Norway, Wisconsin. By 1859, he operated a business in Waterford, Wisconsin, and that same year was elected the state prison commissioner, perhaps the first Norwegian elected to any state office in America. Two years later, he was appointed colonel of the Fifteenth Wisconsin, more commonly known as the Scandinavian Regiment.

The exploits of the regiment were the subject of John A. Johnson's *Det Skandinaviske Regiments historie* (The Scandinavian Regiment's History) in 1869. The author used the account to extol the virtues of Scandinavians, including Norwegians. The death of Colonel Heg at the Battle of Chickamauga in 1863 merited special praise: "He displayed an especially strong sense of heroism through his sacrifice." Johnson noted how Heg's death gave proof of the loyalty and bravery of Norwegians.[73]

Author Ole Amundsen Buslett published his history of the regiment in 1894, but he viewed it largely in terms of its Norwegian component. He too singled out Colonel Heg for praise, whose death was felt deeply, not only in the regiment but among the entire brigade. According to Buslett, Heg's sacrifice proved how all Norwegians had sacrificed in service to their adopted country.[74]

The legacy of Colonel Heg aided the Norwegian-American cause on the eve of America's entry into World War I. Nativist sentiment caused many Americans to question the loyalty of immigrant groups, including Norwegians. In 1916, Waldemar Ager, a leading Norwegian-American writer, published a history of Colonel Heg in defense of the Norwegian reputation in America. Praising the regiment for its service "during the long and bloody war," Ager stressed how it was "such an honorable chapter in the history of the Norwegian people." In effect, the regiment's conduct showed how Norwegian Americans had done their part to save the Union.[75]

According to Ager, the bravest of the brave was Colonel Heg. The author was fond of stating that Heg exemplified the virtues of the Viking blood of the Norwegian race. "He was above everything else a man bound by a strict sense of duty.... He forgot nothing and neglected nothing. He was a brave and intelligent officer." Ager further noted that Colonel Heg had died with sword and reins in his hands and that other Norwegians had carried his mortally wounded body from the battlefield.[76]

The image of Colonel Hans Christian Heg, the valiant leader of a loyal people, remained etched on the collective Norwegian-American consciousness. As noted by Øverland, the concept that Norwegians had saved the Union through the sacrifice of their soldiers, wedded to stories of foundation, and ideological and racial ties with Anglo-Americans established a comprehensive homemaking mythology.[77] The portrayal of Heg and other outstanding Norwegian Americans permitted Norwegian-American historians to demonstrate in dramatic fashion how well their compatriots embodied the positive characteristics held in high esteem by Anglo-Americans. Moreover, these myths ultimately served not only to promote the Norwegian-American self-image but also to defend Norwegian language and culture.

The importance of Norwegian-American settlements formed the fourth part of Norwegian-American identity. Norwegian-American historians lauded the efforts of their strong-backed compatriots in clearing and transforming the American prairies into bountiful fields and flourishing pastures. By viewing themselves as the vanguard of civilization, Norwegian

Americans could make their claim to being latter-day colonists from Norway. Earning the distinction of Midwestern trailblazers, however, was not easy. As Odd Lovoll has noted, Anglo-Americans usually claimed Anglo-Americans as the trailblazers, an image that Norwegian-American leaders worked hard to correct.[78]

Central to this viewpoint was the idea that Norwegian pioneers were the agents of civilization. Svein Nilsson authored an early example of this type of myth in an 1869 article. He emphasized how the industry and stamina of Norwegians had transformed the arid plains into productive regions. He elaborated on the character of Norwegians, noting that Yankee Americans valued them for their industry, frugality, and loyalty. He added that they willingly obeyed the nation's laws, and there were few criminals among them.[79]

More than sixty years later, Hjalmar Rued Holand echoed these claims and added a few others. He commented on the overall quality of Norwegian farm buildings and how they were operated. He observed that one of the best characteristics of Norwegians was their rugged honesty, which meant that criminals were rare among them. Norwegian Americans, he noted, placed particular emphasis on hospitality, a trait inherited from Viking times.[80] According to Norwegian-American historians, Norwegians represented the best immigrant group because they were willing to do the hard work that other immigrant groups often avoided. As a whole, they claimed, Norwegians did not reside in the decadent cities but rather were sons and daughters of the soil, embodying those values that made America great.[81]

By portraying their group as hardy yeoman farmers, Norwegian-American historians were playing to a long-held Anglo-American view that true American virtue was to be found among the ranks of America's rugged agrarians. In Holand's 1930 work on Norwegian immigration, he offered a resounding affirmation of the idea of Norwegians as resolute pioneers and agents of civilization:

> Norwegians were most often the first to cross the uncharted expanses of the West, and it was from their hearths that the first smoke columns ascended skyward, waving like banners of victory over the wilderness of the Northwest. Norwegians carved the first plow furrows in the western virgin plains. And it was Norwegians who built the first churches and schoolhouses. To others they left the

cramped confines of the cities and allowed those who desired it the tyranny of the factories. Instead, Norwegians preferred to head out—out into the open wilderness. This was the life yearned for by the Norwegian pioneers. Whether in forests or on the prairies, they were not afraid to confront Nature in all her power.[82]

Norwegians achieved in other fields of American life as well. They were more than simple farmers. In 1888, the Norwegian-American journalist Knud Langeland wrote about the diversity of Norwegian success in all aspects of American life, including business, industry, science, and religion. As American society became more complex, he reasoned, the intelligence and higher educational levels of Norwegians would enable them to supply increasing numbers of professionals.[83]

As previously noted, national romanticism in Norway had idealized the *bonde*, the landholding Norwegian peasant, as the caretaker of the nation's core values and traits, and it was not surprising that Norwegian-American historians made a similar connection when they developed a highly romanticized image of the Norwegian-American pioneer farmer. Their emphasis on the rural character of the Norwegian immigrants paralleled the old Anglo-American self-image of being a basically rural people. By the late nineteenth century, the rising distrust among the Anglo-American elite of the morally decadent cities (populated increasingly by eastern and southern European immigrants) made them view with fondness a predominantly rural immigrant people like the Norwegians.[84]

Thus, Norwegian-American history continued to depict Norwegians largely as pioneers. Norwegian-American historians could portray Norwegian Americans as the embodiment of American values, as salt-of-the-earth tillers of the soil, not land speculators or urban workers. In effect, they could claim that the basically conservative American values—love of freedom, respect for law, and devotion to God—were most prevalent among the Norwegian settlers on the prairie. Prominent Anglo-American leaders, such as Kendric Charles Babcock, shared this view about all Scandinavians, including the Norwegians.[85]

The year 1925 was a watershed year for Norwegian America. That summer, the Norse-American Centennial, held in Minneapolis–St. Paul, celebrated a century of modern Norwegian immigration. At the three-day celebration, the themes of filiopietistic Norwegian-American history were proudly displayed. The centennial offered ample portions of Vikings,

Norwegian Civil War heroes, and Norwegian pioneers. It reiterated the themes of Norwegian-American history: the Norwegians had a long and successful association with the New World; and through their love of freedom, individualism, and hard work, they had prospered in America. In the official history affiliated with the centennial, Olaf M. Norlie authored perhaps the most complete manifestation of filiopietistic Norwegian-American history. In his final remarks, he noted of the Norwegians: "They are staunch defenders of law and land, but feel no shame in loving the little land from which they sprang."[86]

The creation of the professionally oriented Norwegian-American Historical Association (NAHA) in 1925 sounded the death knell for the filiopietistic tradition. J. R. Christianson observed that the early members of the NAHA were not heroes or Vikings and that they desired a new myth of their collective path.[87] Yet many of the ideals of the filiopietistic tradition never died out completely. In constructing their ethnic past, Norwegian-American historians developed an identity that expressed support for Norwegian and Norwegian-American symbols while concomitantly remaining loyal to American values. This idealized history allowed Norwegian-American leaders to claim superiority over other immigrant groups, and by claiming that Norwegians were the source of American values, it allowed Norwegian Americans to claim superiority even over Anglo-Americans. Collectively, these various ethnic myths, their constructed history, served as the core of the Norwegian-American identity. While the Norwegian-American historical construction did not always make for good history, from a Norwegian-American point of view, it made for a most satisfying self-image.

Celebrations and Visitations, 1860–1890

Public celebrations such as Norway's May 17 Constitution Day were highly important in promoting a Norwegian-American self-image. At these public festivals the common people and the cultural elites came together and acted out the rituals associated with the Norwegian-American identity. The chance to participate in the celebrations also gave the common people a chance to reaffirm their allegiance to their ethnic culture while simultaneously displaying the compatibility between their cultural practices and American ideals. At another level, participation in these celebrations allowed the Norwegian-American community, particularly its leaders, to reaffirm their loyalty to the cultural traditions of the old country. The dual purpose of these celebrations revealed how the construction of a Norwegian-American identity involved a process in which the image-makers sought to promote an image that proved their membership within the American and Norwegian national traditions.

One of the earliest Norwegian Constitution Days celebrated in the United States was in Chicago on May 17, 1864. Organized by the Nora Lodge of the Order of the Knights of the White Cross, it marked the fiftieth anniversary of the proclamation of Norway's constitution. The costumes of the order, replete with Viking and medieval-age weaponry and ranks, affirmed the national identity of Norway as a nation founded by robust warriors. The celebration was overwhelmingly Norwegian in its emphasis; the date was Norway's great national holiday, the immigrants waved Norwegian flags, and the order's activities were conducted in Norwegian. Yet there were American overtures as well. The Norwegians also waved American flags, they honored Union dead in the American Civil War, and the president of the Nora Society proposed a toast to President Lincoln, which was met with three loud hurrahs.[88] Seen in this context, the celebration aimed for a position that reminded its participants of their mutual allegiances to Norway and America.

As historian Odd Lovoll has observed, these secular celebrations, often the product of an urban elite, competed for allegiance among the mass of Norwegian Americans. The Norwegian Lutheran clergy tended to view these occasions as too worldly and lacking the solemnity called for by more religiously oriented celebrations. Lovoll notes that by the 1870s most rural Norwegian-American communities had started to celebrate May 17, but these occasions differed greatly from the lodge-organized festivities of the cities. The rural celebrations centered on a church outing, usually a service, at which the Lutheran clergy reminded the faithful that Norwegians were a pious, God-fearing people whose Protestant ideals closely matched those of American society.[89]

In contrast to this churchly vision, the urban Norwegian-American celebrations became ever more elaborate. For example, another historic occasion for Chicago's Norwegian community was the July 1872 observance of the millennium of Norway's unification under the Viking King Harald Fairhair. A large throng of people gathered on North Peoria Street, and a procession was formed and marched to the railroad station to be transported to Haas Park in forty-three railway cars. The *Chicago Times* reported that "the descendants of Odin and Thor" were joining with the homeland in its observance of the milestone. At the celebration at Haas Park, the occasion was festive, marked by loud cannon fire and music, including the singing of the new Norwegian national anthem by Bjørnstjerne Bjørnson, "Ja, vi elsker dette landet" (Yes, We Love This Country). The event also paid homage to pan-Scandinavian ideals with speeches presented on behalf of Denmark and Sweden. The main address, delivered by Pastor C. J. P. Petersen of the First Norwegian Evangelical Lutheran Church, stressed the historical origins of Norway in the "thousand-year festival." The event was also significant because the organizers sent a congratulatory telegram to Haugesund, Norway, where the main homeland observance was held, which further "signified ethnic bonds across the Atlantic."[90]

Participation of homeland Norwegians in these American celebrations enhanced the sense of a shared national heritage. One example was Chicago's May 17 celebration in 1869 that featured the Norwegian National Theater. That same year, in Minneapolis, the violinist Ole Bull performed in concert in early May, thus providing the impetus for that city's first May 17 celebration. Later, in 1888, the May 17 celebration in Minnespolis–St. Paul featured a large parade in which important Norwegian dignitaries formed the lead element. And in the 1880s it was common practice to

Norwegian immigrants often gathered to celebrate Syttende mai (May 17), Norway's national day, as shown in this photograph taken at John Larsen's farm in New Richmond, Minnesota, in 1890. Courtesy of the Norwegian Emigrant Museum, U00091.

include children's processions as part of the ceremonies. At the suggestion of Bjørnson, this practice had been added to Norway's May 17 celebrations in the 1870s.[91]

These public celebrations afforded Norwegian Americans the opportunity to display their loyalty to Norway through the adoption of symbolic dress. The Order of the Knights of the White Cross strongly emphasized the greatness of Norway's Viking origins and early medieval kings. The members were known as knights and appeared at festive occasions wearing red capes adorned with a white cross over the left shoulder. A member's respective rank entitled him to wield a cross, a halberd, or a spear. The president was known as *drot* (monarch), the first vice president as *jarl* (earl), the second vice president as *lendemend* (feudal lord), and the treasurer as *skatmester* (tax master). Thus, Norwegian Americans, who had achieved material success in their adopted homeland, went to great lengths to promote their Norwegian self-image, albeit one based on a romantic interpretation of the past. It was during the middle decades of the nineteenth century that national romanticism reached its peak in Norway, suggesting a Norwegian worldview transplanted onto American soil.

Yet as studies by Odd S. Lovoll and Orm Øverland have shown, this was a selective transplantation because the immigrants were unwilling to preserve those features of Norwegian society that they disliked, including the more rigid class structure and the lack of economic opportunities; in effect, they were combining homeland traditions with American traditions.[92]

In addition to donning Viking-age clothing, the participants would often adopt more modern dress. One example was the 1888 May 17 parade in Minneapolis–St. Paul that featured a number of military costumes modeled on elite Norwegian military units. David Mauk notes that these costumes had an overt political message, for many Norwegian Americans had donated money, including some for the purpose of purchasing rifles, to support the Liberal party in Norway, which strove to make Norway less dependent on Sweden.[93]

Initially, many of the May 17 celebrations had a Scandinavian flavor, often featuring speeches by prominent Swedish or Danish Americans. However, as the population of the Norwegian urban communities increased, and aided by an aggressive self-image, the ceremonies took on a more nationalistic tone. Thus, by the 1880s a Norwegian model had replaced the Scandinavian one even in the emerging Norwegian enclaves in New York and the Pacific Northwest.[94]

Visits by important Norwegians presented opportunities for Norwegian Americans to reaffirm their old country heritage. In April 1872, a few months after the devastation of Chicago's Great Fire, the Norsemen's Singing Society marched in a procession with flags, banners, and, in an ironic touch, torches to serenade the deeply moved Ole Bull at the Grand Central Hotel. The violinist also struck up a close friendship with Rasmus B. Anderson in February 1868, and it was shortly thereafter that he began his lectures on Leif Erikson and spoke of Norwegians as "cultural giants." Bull also cooperated with Anderson in an effort to have Leif Erikson recognized as the true discoverer of America. One of their first victories, although it occurred after Bull's death, was in 1887 when the city of Boston erected a statue of the Viking explorer.[95]

Out of a sense of obligation to Bull, the Norwegian author and national poet Bjørnstjerne Bjørnson decided to travel to America at the request of Sara Chapman Bull, the violinist's second wife and widow. A member of the Thorps, a Boston Brahmin family, she had cared for Bull during his final years despite some contentious earlier years. Bjørnson visited the Bull home in Cambridge, Massachusetts, which allowed him to meet with America's New England elite. During his more than two-month stay in Massachusetts during the winter of 1880–81, he spoke with important Americans including Henry Wadsworth Longfellow, ex-president Ulysses S. Grant, and Oliver Wendell Holmes.[96] In a letter that appeared in the Norwegian paper *Dagbladet* on November 16, 1880, Bjørnson spoke enthusiastically of the New World, noting "that 'the people' ruled in America" and that the United States had "a proportionately larger choice of excellent men" than any European country. The great author also repeated a favorite theme of Norwegian Americans: "We Norwegians have a right from olden times to be here 'in spirit,' because this was the old 'Vinland' of our forefathers."[97]

Bjørnson had not planned to visit the large Norwegian settlements in the upper Midwest because he had come to New England, the cradle of American freedom, in order to learn from its practices, and he initially saw little need to go west. In Bjørnson's mind the pernicious triple alliance of monarchy, church, and privilege worked together to prevent the attainment of republican ideals in Norway. However, the experience of his Norwegian-American countrymen, or for that matter the Anglo-Americans, suggested that membership in their American liberal Protestant churches did not hamper allegiance to republican ideals. Bjørnson, the religious freethinker, therefore felt compelled to show his countrymen in America the folly of their adherence to their dogmatic Lutheran churches.⁹⁸

During the previous year Bjørnson's Norwegian neighbor Kristofer Janson had ignited the flames of controversy with his lecture tour of Norwegian-American settlements. Like Bjørnson, Janson was a freethinker, a Unitarian with strongly democratic ideals. He shared with Bjørnson an admiration for America's republican government, which in his view stood in stark contrast to Norway's. Janson's speaking tour was highly successful for the most part; he extolled the virtues of Norwegian culture, urging greater ties between the immigrants and the homeland.⁹⁹

But at his final lecture, delivered at Chicago on April 8, 1880, he attacked the religious orthodoxy of the Norwegian Synod pastors, which he saw as failing to measure up to the true tenets of Christian charity and love. In retaliation many Norwegian-American pastors and some editors denounced Janson. To many, an attack on the Lutheran Church was an attack on Norwegian America. While still in Norway Bjørnson had defended Janson during the summer of 1880, noting that "a light of freedom dwelt within Janson; he loves the little man in the Fatherland and seeks his own merry path in the hope that others will follow." Bjørnson also wrote a spirited defense of Janson when he was in America, calling the speech "the best I have read in Norwegian in many years."¹⁰⁰

The crusade of the west, as one writer calls Bjørnson's speaking tour of the Norwegian settlements, owed much to his friends among the Norwegian-American elite. He gave his first speech to the Norwegian heartland at Chicago on December 26, 1880, a speech that focused on politics in the Scandinavian countries. Aware that his audience was composed of Scandinavians and not just Norwegians, Bjørnson delivered a rousing speech praising the Nordic race. At a second lecture he ventured into the realm of religion, invoking higher biblical criticisms to claim that the deity of Judeo-Christianity owed much to myths of solar deities. He raved against the false doctrines of modern religion, arguing that "the pastors and their teaching are humbug." His audience departed in a mixed mood—some confused, others irate; yet he received hearty applause and made several curtain calls.¹⁰¹

Proceeding to visit upper Midwestern Norwegian settlements, Bjørnson lectured for roughly two months, despite horrific snowstorms and brutally cold temperatures, to deliver his message of pride in the Norwegian race and its proclivity for freedom and democracy, alternating with his message of the evils of Lutheran ministers. He especially noted how in America Norwegians had become stronger, handsomer, and prouder than in Norway. His message clearly won more favor among the urban, secular elite found in Minneapolis and Chicago than in the more conservative rural settlements. At a speech in Minneapolis he defended his views on religion, claiming that he only wanted faith to be based on truth and not on legends.[102]

Budstikken gave a favorable review to the speech, observing how Bjørnson had inspired Norwegians in America because "he gave new value and esteem [to us], and his spreading message will help each and every one of us to more greatly respect that freedom we enjoy here. It is with open eyes for the father of that freedom that we aim to make us worthy of that freedom."[103] The reference to Bjørnson as the father of Norwegian-American freedom certainly paralleled his reputation in Norway where he was seen as the father of Norwegian nationalism. As a representative of Norway, Bjørnson thus participated in the negotiation between Norwegian nationalism and the emerging Norwegian-American nationalism, helping the latter to define itself as an aspect of Norway's national identity.

Not all Norwegian-American voices praised Bjørnson; the clergy were highly critical of him. After reading accounts of Bjørnson's speech "The Prophets," the Reverend H. Halvorsen of Coon Prairie, Wisconsin, wrote that the author's speech was "a crass attack on Christian faith as such" and that Bjørnson should declare himself a "Darwinist." He also attacked those who had applauded him: "It was a great forebearance of God that He did not let Hell open its jaws and devour you right during this laughing and clapping of yours."[104] The divided reception that Bjørnson received reflected the religious/secular split within Norwegian America between its urban elite and its mostly rural, conservative body and clergy.

Even Pastor Sven Oftedal, the liberal theologian of the Augsburg Conference at Minneapolis, took exception to Bjørnson's religious views. He attacked the famed Norwegian author for his anti-Christian bias. He further suggested that Bjørnson failed to appreciate the accomplishments of his countrymen in America who had tamed the prairie, prospered materially, and learned to take part in the governance of a great nation. In effect, whereas Bjørnson saw only material prosperity among the Norwegian immigrants, Oftedal saw both material and spiritual success.[105] Norwegian-Americans would have clearly favored the national-romanticist Bjørnson over the social realist whose religious views had become agnostic.[106]

In a March 1881 letter to *Dagbladet*, published on April 6, 1881, Bjørnson sums up how he viewed the Norwegian-American image. He worried that Norwegian Americans' adherence to the formal dogma of the Norwegian Synod would have deleterious consequences for their cultural development. He also defended those who had immigrated to America and those contemplating it. The availability of education and the right to vote in America was something sorely lacking, especially for the lower classes, in Norway. He further notes that Norwegians in America are known for their honesty and their frugality, although he observed that they had been criticized for uncleanliness and drunkenness. He added that Norwegian Americans tended to stay on the land and avoided speculating in land as their American counterparts were wont to do. Near the end of the letter, Bjørnson states that Norwegians adopt American practices more quickly than other immigrant groups:

> When I look at the speed with which comparatively many of our countrymen have acquired the view on institutions, education, trade, and customs that is based on nature, then this strengthens the conception that Norwegians have a more pronounced rationalistic strain than most people. They are positive, i.e. believers in the victory of the sensible and the just, and they have the energy, which such a faith gives. Therefore they are already zealous, particularly with their own candidates and their many newspapers. They Americanize their thinking much faster than any other people.[107]

In his encounter with Norwegian America, Bjørnson not only shaped the Norwegian-American self-image—that they were a good immigrant group whose values were compatible with American ones—but also Norway's national identity. The competition between European nationalities that provided a measuring stick of the greatness of a particular immigrant group and the success of Norwegians in America, the land of freedom and democracy, reinforced Bjørnson's idea that homeland Norwegians were well suited for a more liberal, more modern society. Through his close friendship with Norwegian-American elites, including Rasmus B. Anderson, he came to share many of their ideas. His support for Anderson's idea of the Norwegian origins of American freedom adumbrated a future period when the Norwegian-American self-image would serve as an addendum to Norway's national identity.

Other Norwegians commented on the reciprocal nature of the relationship between Norway and her immigrants in America. In an 1884 report titled *Det udflyttede Norge* (The Emigrated Norway), its author observed, "This Norwegian-American society in due time will exert considerable influence on the Motherland through those impulses, which this land will receive not only because of kinship ties, but it must also be assumed that such influence will develop due to a relatively lively relationship between Norway and the Norwegian-American society." The report noted that as Norwegian immigrants traveled from America back to Norway, they would bring with them the more advanced practices found in America.[108] One can add that as contact increased between the two communities, there would be a concomitant exchange of ideas as well, including those involving how the two emerging nationalisms would be defined.

Not all Norwegian travelers to America came away with positive descriptions. As a young writer, Knut Hamsun, the future Nobel Prize winner, visited America in the mid-1880s and, in 1889, published an account of his travels, *Fra det moderne Amerikas aandsliv* (The Cultural Life of Modern America). Unlike Bjørnson, Hamsun held a largely negative view, likely owing to the radical political views of the younger man. Hamsun wore a black ribbon in mourning for the anarchists executed in Chicago in 1887, and he was highly critical of the "aristocracy of money" that ruled America. Moreover, he saw Americans as extremely arrogant, for the Yankee recognized no superiority in any foreign nation. To Hamsun, this created a strange paradox. He saw American intellectual life as underdeveloped, yet "they demand unqualified recognition as the most advanced nation in every field, as the nation with the greatest cultural riches in the world." He found America even more insular than Norway. "Americans are fundamentally a *conservative* people who in many fields still cling to positions that even Norway, as behind the times as it is, has long since abandoned."[109] For Norwegian Americans, Hamsun's message is that they have not selected the best country in the world and that they would have fared better back in Norway.

By 1890 the Norwegian-American community had established a self-image as a good immigrant group. Their leaders crafted a national Norwegian-American identity that sought to place them within the acceptable boundaries of Norwegian and American modes of nationalist thought. The process involved a continual negotiation in which Norwegian-American image-makers sought to locate the Norwegian-American identity so that it would remain loyal to the notions of what it meant to be a true Norwegian, a true American, and a true Norwegian American. This effort was part of a process to establish and maintain what Jon Gjerde has termed "complementary identities."[110]

The range of that process, however, extended beyond America's borders, for Norwegian-American elites wished to have Norwegian elites validate their self-image. By 1890, a segment of the Norwegian elite had recognized the importance of the Norwegian-American self-image, but that recognition was not widespread throughout Norway. The academic and political elites of Norway had not yet noticed the contributions of Norwegian Americans. Winning acceptance among a wider homeland audience thus remained a goal of Norwegian-American image-makers.

· CHAPTER 3 ·

Modern Vikings

The Challenge to Anglo-American Superiority, 1890–1917

THE 1893 WORLD'S COLUMBIAN EXPOSITION in Chicago celebrated the twin themes of discovery and progress. As the name suggests, it was a tribute to Columbus's "discovery" of the New World. The theme of progress referred to the rapid expansion of America and, by extension, Chicago, which had grown from a sleepy town to the nation's second-largest city in a little over fifty years. Competition between nations was in abundance, and Spain sent replicas of Columbus's fleet; the three ships arrived on July 7.

Not to be outdone, a Norwegian crew sailed a Viking ship replica, the *Viking*, to Chicago, arriving on July 12. Its captain, Magnus Andersen, had served as a sailor aboard Norwegian vessels before he settled down in New York, where he became the first manager of the Norwegian's Seamen Home in 1887. Andersen conceived of the idea of sailing a replica Viking-age ship from Norway to Chicago as a dramatic way to promote Norway's national image. Norway's pavilion at the fair, modeled on a stave church design from the twelfth century, likewise reflected a historical affiliation with the Viking age. The Norwegian painter Christian Krogh produced a romanticized portrait of Leif Erikson discovering America, commemorating the Viking discovery. The overall effect implied to the fairgoers that Norway, not Spain, had the longest association with the New World.[1]

More than a month before the ship's arrival, the *Chicago Herald* proclaimed the forthcoming arrival of "the modern vikings." On July 12 the city welcomed Andersen and his eleven-man crew for "bringing this dragon ship" to Chicago. Mayor Harrison and Fair president Thomas W. Palmer both greeted the crew. At a ceremony held at Jackson Park, where the ship would be docked, Andersen gave a speech in which he told the audience that Norwegians "are a free and liberty-loving people." He emphasized

The arrival of the Viking *at the 1893 Columbian Exhibition in Chicago. Courtesy of the Norwegian Emigrant Museum, U02738.*

that the ship had been sent from Norway and was not a product of either Sweden or Denmark. Toward the end of his speech he reminded his American listeners, "It was the Viking blood in the old Anglo-Saxon race that has made this country [America] what it is."[2]

Both Norwegian-American and American newspapers stressed the parallel between the Vikings of old and their latter-day descendants. *Skandinaven* provided detailed coverage of the *Viking*'s journey, including profiles of the leading crew members. It pointed out that the replica was exact in every detail and that the claims of the sagas were correct; the dragon prows had proven their seaworthiness in modern times. The *Chicago Record* issued "the heartiest of welcomes to the countrymen of Leif, son of Eric.... Where else than among the children of the vikings are there men to go voyaging in a hollow ship?" The *Minneapolis Journal* emphasized that Captain Andersen and his men sailed in a duplicate of Erikson's ship, which justified the pride of the people of "Norseland" in their special achievement.[3]

Nearly a week later, on July 18, the official banquet honoring Andersen and his crew took place at Scandia Hall in Chicago. The captain and his officers received decorations for their efforts in the form of commemorative sketches of Leif Erikson. A prominent member of the Norwegian-American community, Ole Bendiren, read aloud his tribute to the *Viking* and her crew, which ended: "Above all this heroic deed honors ye Norwegian men who have shown by their triumph that the Viking blood lives on for the ages in the Viking descendants."[4]

The idea that Norwegians, and by association Norwegian Americans, were modern Vikings formed a central tenet of the Norwegian-American self-image. Its proponents argued that those racial traits that had made their ancestors such intrepid, hardy adventurers were also present in the latter-day descendents of the Vikings. Thus, modern Norwegians were a robust and virile race, capable of taming the American frontier or building its modern cities.

Latter-day Vikings

The modern Vikings concept became widely disseminated both in Norway and among Norwegians in America. The emphasis on the Viking heritage, and the invocation of the Leif Erikson cult, owed much to the burgeoning urban Norwegian-American leadership of the 1890s that spread these ideas from the cities to Norwegian farms and small cities. Andersen published his account in his 1893 book *Vikingefærden: En illustreret beskrivelse af "Vikings" reise* (The Viking Voyage: An Illustrated Description of the *Viking*'s Journey), and the Norwegian-American Lars A. Stenholt published his tribute *Moderne Vikinger* (Modern Vikings) a year later. Although his works were not considered great literature, Stenholt was one of the most widely read Norwegian-American authors, and his account would have made the idea of the modern Viking well known.

Stenholt used the opportunity to portray Andersen as a modern Leif Erikson and to stress that Norway was a modern, progressive nation whose sailors were the best in the world. Moreover, the Norwegian immigrants who embodied those modern Viking virtues could point to the crew of the *Viking* as heroes of their nation. Andersen's achievement, he added, had also contributed to greater ties between "the members of the great cultural world's family."[5] In an earlier 1893 work, *Nordmændenes opdagelse af Amerika* (The Norwegians' Discovery of America), the author had made a similar argument: "Every Norwegian farmer, craftsmen, or common laborer is a modern-day descendent of Leif [Erikson]."[6]

The modern Viking concept is still popular today, especially among rank-and-file Norwegian Americans and Scandinavian Americans. In his 1904 travel account of Norwegian America, the Norwegian author Thoralv Klaveness comments on how the Norwegian immigrants were like "Vikings on the Prairie" because they sailed their wagons on the endless seas of grass. Other Norwegian-American image-makers likewise employed the metaphor. In 1905, the Norwegian-American author Waldemar Ager noted the connection between the Viking blood of the Norwegians and their inherent American-style values. The placement of the Viking legacy in a purely Norwegian context must be viewed in the context of relations between the Scandinavian groups, especially the Norwegians and Swedes. Both immigrant groups had achieved populations in America that allowed for institutional self-sufficiency, while at the same time the worsening relations within the Norwegian–Swedish union, eventually leading to its dissolution in 1905, created growing bitterness between the two groups and their institutions.[7]

The modern Viking image also had a place in the major festivals of Norwegian Americans. In 1914 Norway celebrated the centennial of its constitution. The occasion was also celebrated among Norwegian Americans, and a large celebration took place in May of that year in Minneapolis–St. Paul, which stressed the shared Norwegian and American heritage; among the speakers was Norway's minister to the United States. To commemorate the celebration, the Minnesota–Norway 1914 Centennial Exposition Association published a volume titled *Minnesota*, which showcased the achievements of Norwegians in a number of fields including the economic, the social, and the religious.

The fullest expression of the latter-day Viking concept was in the chapter "The Nineteenth-Century Viking Expedition," whose main idea was that Norwegian immigration to America in the 1800s represented the latest large-scale Viking activity, albeit one of colonization rather than of plunder. The author, U.S. Senator Knute Nelson, noted how prominent Norwegian-American writers such as Rasmus B. Anderson, Hjalmar R. Holand, George T. Flom, and others had penned the sagas of these nineteenth-century Vikings. He even compared Cleng Peerson, the founder of many of the early Norwegian settlements in America, to Gange-Rolf (Rollo), the founder of Normandy.[8]

Nelson also praised the bravery of the Norwegian pioneers on the vast ocean prairie, comparing them to Daniel Defoe's character Robinson

Crusoe. Stranded on a Pacific island, Crusoe had faced the elements alone and triumphed, a metaphor not lost on his reading audience. Last, Nelson completed the transformation of the latter-day Vikings. The romantic version of the Vikings as sailors on the prairie seas of grass merged into a progressive vision in which the Norwegians were America's best citizens, striving to build the world's most modern nation. With great pride, he noted, "The Norwegian people have been highly successful as craftsmen, businessmen, and professionals in our cities and have participated in the great industrialization." Moreover, Norwegians had played a great role in the building of America in all fields:

> With their churches, schools, periodicals, and newspapers, and with their energy, their propensity for hard work, and their loyalty, they have been a considerable force in this land's great development. And they have not disgraced their old Mother Norway. Their saga is completely deserving of an honored place in the history of the Norwegian people during the nineteenth century.[9]

Nelson pitched his latter-day Viking analogy to a Norwegian audience as well. In the 1914 article "To Norway," which appeared in the Norwegian journal *Samtiden*, he offered congratulations to the country for its great triumphs in education, literature, the arts and sciences, and in the fields of exploration and discovery. He also expressed the idea that the success of the Norwegian immigrants owed much to the gifts they had inherited from the mother country:

> Like the children of many another mother with scant resources we felt that there was not room for all of us at home and being imbued with that spirit of adventure possessed by our viking ancestors, and yearning to see what was "beyond the lofty mountains," with sad but hopeful hearts, we bade her good by [sic], and turned our faces to the land of promise, to America, and she received us with open arms and treated us as though we were her own children by birth right. And this reception and this treatment was [sic] accorded to us, largely because we were the offspring of such a noble and worthy mother.[10]

A year later, in the same journal, Nelson published a short article titled "Norske vikinger i det 19de aarhundrede" (Norwegian Vikings in the

Nineteenth Century), which reprised most of the arguments he had stated in the *Minnesota* centennial publication, including a concise explanation of the latter-day Viking concept: "The Viking spirit persevered and overcame all obstacles. The Viking in our time has become a model for an American citizen."[11]

Norwegian authors also recognized the value of stalwart Viking blood. Writing in 1901, historian Alexander Bugge commented on how the Viking age revealed the best cultural characteristics of the Norwegian people. Through their wide travels and contacts with the other peoples of the world, the Vikings had experienced a rapid phase of cultural activity including the birth of the separate Scandinavian languages. He admitted that the Viking age had its dark, bloody side, but "it was a proud time, a time of strong independent people, a time full of emerging spiritual power, a time predisposed for fresh and deep impressions."[12]

Through the efforts of the folk-school teacher and writer Nordahl Rolfsen, the modern Viking concept of the immigrants reached a wide Norwegian audience. In fact, in Norway the Rolfsen series was second only to the Bible in the number of its readers. In 1915, Rolfsen added a volume on Norwegian Americans to his primary-school reader series. In the preface he observes that the spirit of the Vikings had been present in Norwegian immigrants, for they suffered the dangers of ocean travel and then faced the perils of the American frontier, from harsh weather and insects to attacks from Indians. He compared Cleng Peerson to Leif Erikson and added a Norwegian immigrant, Guri Endresen Rosseland, as a model of a Norwegian-American heroine. The latter courageously survived the 1862 Indian uprising that devastated the Norwegian settlement of Norway Lake, Minnesota. Rolfsen applauded the statue raised to Guri by the state of Minnesota in 1908, and her heroism, he maintained, reflected her true Viking heritage as "a Norwegian historical type" found in the sagas.[13]

In promoting their immigrant group as latter-day Vikings, Norwegian-American leaders sought to construct an identity that allowed them to gain maximum advantage as both Norwegians and Americans. Prior to this period, most homeland Norwegians tended to equate the concept of modern Vikings with the exploits of their sailors and explorers. The well-publicized adventures of Norwegian Arctic explorers such as Fridtjof Nansen and Roald Amundsen fit this definition, and their exploits contributed to the reputation of Norway as a nation of adventurers, if not modern Vikings. However, Norwegian-American leaders broadened the concept to include excellence in almost any number of endeavors, including business, professions, and industry. In this vein, Norwegian Americans also portrayed themselves as modern colonists for Norway. By colonizing America, Norwegians were simply returning to the land that their ancestors had discovered nearly a millennium earlier. One was reminded that it had been Norwegians during the Viking age and the early medieval period who had introduced into the Anglo-Saxon world those cherished values of freedom and love for democracy.

Orm Øverland has shown that similar ideas were present among all immigrant groups in America. The Norwegian-American self-image, however, underwent additional refinement in a process by which the basic concepts of the Norwegian-American identity were negotiated with cultural leaders in Norway. Thus, the Norwegian-American self-image became an addendum to Norway's national image. The successes of Norwegian Americans, owing to the unique traits they had brought with them from Norway, served as proof of the value of the Norwegian national character. Norwegian intellectual leaders in 1917 were not prepared to accept Rasmus B. Anderson's idea that Norwegians were the source of the American values of liberty and freedom. But they were willing to accept the idea that the success of modern Norwegian "Vikings" in America proved that the hardy racial traits of the Vikings still flowed in the veins of latter-day Norwegians.

Norway in America

To demonstrate how well Norwegian Americans had preserved the traditions of the homeland, Norwegian-American leaders advanced the idea that they were creating "Norway in America." Norwegian-American image-makers worked strenuously to promote this idea to elites in Norway, and the concept gained popularity from 1890 to 1917. The message of a transplanted Norway in the New World centered on three types of activities. The first involved those who published these ideas in popular form both in Norway and America, including Norwegian travelers who visited the Norwegian settlements. The second involved the efforts of an emerging professional and business elite and the organizations they developed to promote closer ties between Norway and its colonists in America. The third involved celebrations that included cooperation between elites on both sides of the Atlantic. Through these three paths, the Norway in America concept would be channeled toward its intended audience in Norway.

Norwegian Americans' efforts to define their own identity were two-sided: to the American public they sought (in English) to promote the idea of their invaluable place in the American nation, but they also emphasized to the homeland Norwegian public (in Norwegian) their creation of a true Norway in America. As will be seen later in this chapter, the strong assimilationist sentiment of World War I would strongly test the dual Norwegian-American identity. Norwegian America's cultural elite, especially Waldemar Ager, used this concept to reconcile both sides by arguing that Norwegian Americans could be the "best Americans" only if they resisted full assimilation and upheld their own uniquely valuable cultural milieu. In effect, Ager's argument consisted of thesis (American), antithesis (Norwegian), and synthesis (Norwegian American). Thus, Norway in America represented a strategy to satisfy the demands of the two competing nationalisms.

Once again, Lars A. Stenholt helped to popularize the idea in his short book *Norge i Amerika* (Norway in America), which appeared in 1897. He argued that Norwegians were prospering and had helped to build a flourishing civilization, yet they had preserved their traditions by building churches and schools and publishing Norwegian-language newspapers. Furthermore, he observed, a Norwegian could travel through vast stretches of the upper Midwest and never hear any language spoken but Norwegian. He also boasted that the Norwegians in America had retained many of the old-country dialects, although they learned English more quickly than most immigrants. Much of their success was due to "an inheritance from the old Fatherland" and because one could find "resolute nobility" in "these kings of the prairie."[14]

Travelers from Norway shared many of Stenholt's ideas. The Norwegian pastor A. Sollid visited America in 1893 to view the World Columbian Exposition and to visit Norwegian settlements. The vastness of the American Midwest was not lost on him, and he described the prairie with its colorful flowers as "a flowing sea," where one finds himself "at the lowest point" surrounded by "the horizon." Sollid also observed how in the more concentrated settlements the Norwegians "live in paradise" and they have their own Norwegian churches, pastors, schools, religious instructors, and their own democratic society. In Chicago, he contrasted his countrymen's dwellings, which were "cozy and pleasant," with those of Italians, which he described as overcrowded and dirty. At the World's Fair he noted that Norway was well represented, but its displays were too modest and did not adequately represent the nation's accomplishments, although the Viking ship was impressive.¹⁵

Writing in 1904, Hans Seland likewise noted how strongly the Norwegians had preserved their heritage in America. His countrymen had prospered in America, and they enjoyed greater freedom than they would have had in Norway. Norwegians had discovered America and tamed its frontier. Moreover, he mentioned how proud they were of the fatherland. An intelligent observer

> would tell how true it is that in "the Northwest" the Norwegians are among the best and most numerous farmers. And he will be made aware of this when he first finds a compatriot and learns that he outperforms the arrogant Yankee. To be a good sport about it he afterward may have to join a Norwegian association and sing loudly toward the sky: "I am proud of my fatherland."¹⁶

Christian Gierløff, a Norwegian journalist who penned his travel account in 1904, supported the concept that Norwegian Americans were preserving their culture. He titled one of the sections of his book "Norge i Amerika," in which he suggested that the immigrant community was a Norwegian colony. He noted how Minnesota, which was two-thirds the size of Norway, had "400,000 Norwegians, 500 Norwegian churches, 20 Norwegian schools, and 30 Norwegian newspapers." He went on to note how numerous Norwegians were in states such as Wisconsin, the Dakotas, Illinois, the "Mormon Lands," and the Pacific Coast states of California, Oregon, Washington, and the Alaska Territory. He also indicated that their prosperity represented a real economic opportunity for Norway. Gierløff gave special emphasis to how the Norwegian Americans represented an extension of Norway. "What a colony! A real part of Norway outside of Norway. A million, three hundred thousand actual Norwegians outside the boundaries of the Homeland."¹⁷

Norwegian travelers praised the extent to which the immigrants had maintained their Norwegian traditions. "The transplantation of our people on foreign soil," observed Thoralv Klaveness in 1904, "was necessary in every respect for an improvement in their condition." He chastised Norwegians back home who simply dismissed the immigrants as being "lost to Norway." Among all the citizens of America one could find no other group that "took part to as great an extent in its homeland's cultural and material life as the Norwegian citizens."[18] Thus, though the participation by Norwegian Americans in their ethnic organizations was part of the Americanization experience, Norwegian-American leaders capitalized on those activities to promote the idea to homeland Norwegians that the immigrants had largely transplanted their homeland culture to American soil.

Another factor that cannot be overlooked in contributing to increased Norwegian chauvinism was the increasing tension between Norway and Sweden over the nature of their dynastic union. At the heart of the crisis was the issue of a separate Norwegian consular service, which resulted in more strident rhetoric on both sides during the 1890s. The matter came to the forefront in 1904 and 1905 when Norwegians contended that Sweden had broken a 1903 promise to allow for the creation of a separate Norwegian consular service. Since Norway was only joined to Sweden dynastically and was considered an equal partner, many Norwegians thought that a separate consular service was a perfectly reasonable request. Many Swedes, including members of the government and royal house, considered the Norwegian position to be hardheaded as well as impractical. As negotiations between the two governments failed to reach a solution, nationalist impulses eventually led Norway's parliament to seek a more radical solution.[19]

Swedish Americans likewise expressed outrage at the impertinence of Norway, and many letter writers suggested solutions ranging from urging Sweden to invade Norway during the early stages of the crisis to the denunciation of Norway when it became apparent that the union would not last. Some Swedish Americans looked to the American Civil War for inspiration, comparing Norway's rebellion with that of the Southern states, and they suggested that Norway be dealt with in a similar fashion. A Swedish American with pro-Norway sentiments, however, suggested that the correct American model was the Revolutionary War, and that Norway was like the American colonies seeking independence. Shortly after the Norwegian declaration of independence on June 7, 1905, Norwegian immigrants circulated a petition asking President Theodore Roosevelt to mediate between Sweden and Norway in the same manner as he was engaged in to bring about an end to the Russo-Japanese War. This action promoted one Swedish immigrant to claim this as proof of "Norwegian hatred of Swedes." Despite their residence in the United States, both Norwegian and Swedish Americans participated in the nationalist fervor, offering bold proclamations of their respective loyalties to the Nordic homelands.[20]

The tumultuous year of 1905, in which Norway severed the bonds of union with Sweden, provided Norwegian Americans with the opportunity to affirm their allegiance to the homeland. That year a petition signed by twenty thousand people, many of them Norwegian-American, appeared in *Skandinaven* and urged American authorities to side with Norway in the dispute. In a similar attempt, Norwegian Americans mailed numerous letters and petitions to Washington encouraging support for the homeland against Sweden. A leading Norwegian American, A. Stahlberg of Chicago, offered to recruit five thousand able-bodied Norwegian men to fight against Sweden, while another Chicagoan, Dr. Charles Hornby, was willing to recruit Norwegian-American physicians to provide their services on the battlefield. On June 7 of that year, the Norwegian parliament declared the act of union void, and from that day onward Norway was an independent and sovereign state. The Norwegian-American press proudly announced this development. One example was *Minneapolis Daglig Tidende*'s headline the next day, which announced "The Independent Norway," and the day after it noted that Norway was now flying the traditional tricolor, a symbol of an independent Norway.[21]

In a long editorial on the events of early June in Norway, *Minneapolis Daglig Tidende* stated, "Norway's new Declaration of Independence was being greeted with overwhelming praise and enthusiasm by Norwegians and this expression reflected their innermost wishes and hopes." The editorial ended by noting that "Norwegians everywhere were sending the Norwegian people's representatives, Parliament, and government, their warm greetings and especially their sincere hopes that the events of the last few days will lead to the benefit of all of Scandinavia."[22]

The paper likewise devoted significant coverage to the official royal entrance of the new king, queen, and crown prince into Kristiania on November 24, 1905. It prominently featured photos of the new Norwegian royalty: King Haakon VII, Queen Maud, and Crown Prince Olav. The king, a Danish prince married to a member of English royalty, had changed his name from Carl to Haakon and renamed his son Olav, both names of respected Norwegian monarchs of the past. *Minneapolis Daglig Tidende* printed several pages in honor of Haakon's coronation in Trondhjem on June 22 of the following year. It reported that when William Jennings Bryan, head of the American delegation, moved to the speaker's position, American and Norwegian flags were unfurled behind him and the audience broke out in jubilant applause.[23]

Thus, the Norway in America concept not only posited that Norwegians in America had preserved their cultural traditions but also articulated the idea that emigrated Norwegians could still participate in celebrations of homeland Norwegian nationalism. Eventually, this second idea would evolve into a much larger concept of a transnational Norwegian identity in which emigrated Norwegians were members in good standing.

In his study of Irish, Polish, and Jewish immigrants, Matthew Frye Jacobson identifies a similar tendency, although it was framed in somewhat more negative terms. Jacobson notes how these immigrant groups perceived of themselves as exiles in America whose self-image was that of equal participants in the creation of an independent homeland or, in the case of the Jews, an imagined homeland. He further observes how these immigrants often disapproved of attempts by America to crush or limit nationalist aspirations, as in their criticism of America during the Spanish–American War of 1898 and subsequent treatment of Cuba and the Philippines.[24]

A sense of place formed an important and related component of the Norway in America concept. The Norwegian-American clergyman D. G. Ristad, for example, compared northern Minnesota to a new Normandy that had been colonized by nineteenth-century Norwegian immigrants. His account implied a further connection to the homeland because its landscape shared with Norway an abundance of lakes and forests. Moreover, these natural boundaries determined the shape of the communities, further enforcing bonds between land and people. Kristin Ann Risley observes how visions of an idealized landscape convey expressions of filial loyalty and the transfer of values from Norway to America.[25]

In the opening to his work *I et nyt Rige* (1914; *From Fjord to Prairie, or In the New Kingdom*), Simon Johnson's main character, Bernt Aasen, interprets the American landscape in Norwegian terms. He views the prairie as threatening and wild, "as if on a wide sea . . . to the very edge of the sky." It was a place where "the heavens seemed to grow paler and colder than elsewhere." Aasen's sanctuary comes to him on cold evenings when he looks at pictures of people and places in Norway. The picture of the woman he loves back in Norway comforts him, and he escapes by invoking the memory of the Norway he likewise loves. The dear old place in Norway where "the white snow covered the mountain slope . . . The young folks were out with skis and sleds. Glowing cheeks shone back to the laughter of merry lips. The heavens were clear and blue." He recalls the "happy homes, lights above the lights the hillside over. And away down in the valley boomed the waterfall with its fatherly old bass."²⁶ The imagined landscape of Norway thus formed an important part of the Norwegian-American self-image.

The organizations developed by Norwegian Americans between 1890 and 1917 reveal much about how the immigrant community viewed itself and the tensions inherent between different sets of its elite. One group consisted of an emerging business and professional class based in the large urban centers, and its members were active in the Norwegian clubs. A second group comprised the academic and professional elite found in the major urban centers and also in smaller communities such as Decorah, Iowa, or Fargo, North Dakota. A third group consisted of those who represented the Norwegian-American working and middle classes and were active in the Sons of Norway. Among these groups, there was often overlap of membership in the organizations.

In opposition to the business and professional elite were the more conservative, rural elite. They tended to promote the *bygdelag* movement. A

The Sons of Norway organization gave Norwegians opportunities to celebrate their ethnic heritage and create a system of mutual assistance. This photograph of the Tordenskjøld Lodge in Spokane, Washington, is from the early nineteenth century. Courtesy of the Norwegian Emigrant Museum, U01169.

fifth group consisted of Lutheran clergy, who often opposed most of the activities of the other elite groups. Although these differing groups frequently utilized similar symbols in promoting a Norwegian-American self-image, the emphasis placed on those symbols often differed significantly, and they presented competing visions of what Norway in America meant.

The influence of an imported Norwegian-born professional and business urban elite served to promote one version of Norway in America. Although numerically small, it enjoyed close ties with similar elites in Norway, and their activities often revolved around receptions for important dignitaries from Norway. During the 1893 World's Fair, for example, the Arne Garborg Club entertained several notable visitors, including Viggo Ullman, the president of the Norwegian parliament. At a 1912 banquet, the Chicago Norwegian Club welcomed as its guests Norway's delegation to the international convention of Chambers of Commerce. That same year, New York's Norwegian Club held a banquet to honor such Norwegian dignitaries as the minister of labor affairs and Johan Ludwig Mowinckel, a shipowner and future prime minister of Norway. The Norwegian Society of Minneapolis honored Bishop Anton C. Bang from Norway at its May 17 celebration in 1908. Three years later, it held a banquet that featured H. H. Bryn, Norway's minister in Washington and other prominent Norwegian visitors.[27] These activities show the strong ties that the Norwegian-American business elite had with a similar elite in Norway. In addition, as both were interested in promoting commercial activities between the two countries, they favored a self-image that would stress the success that Norwegian Americans had achieved in business, education, and the technical fields, which can be termed the progressive orientation of the Norwegian-American identity.

A complementary elite consisted of Norwegian-American professionals and intellectuals, many of whom were active in Norwegian societies in the major cities. For example, the Norwegian Society of America was involved in celebrations that featured shared representation with the homeland, such as the 1904 ceremony in Fargo, which featured the unveiling of a monument to Bjørnsterne Bjørnson, and the 1908 ceremonies for the dedication of a statue to the Norwegian poet Henrik Wergeland. This latter celebration had two parts, a festival at Minneapolis–St. Paul (Twin Cities) on May 17 that featured a speech by Bishop Bang and the actual unveiling of the statue at Fargo, North Dakota, later that summer. The society was also involved in a ceremony held at Wahpeton, North Dakota, where a bust of Henrik Ibsen was unveiled, and in a 1912 ceremony held at Fargo to dedicate a statue received from France in recognition of Rollo of Normandy.[28] The elite associated with the Norwegian societies promoted a self-image that stressed the high culture of Norway. Furthermore, many members of this group were also active in the Norwegian clubs, and they promoted a Norwegian-American self-image that shared many of the same features, although the two were not identical.

To ensure that the Norwegian heritage would receive its proper recognition, the Sons of Norway participated in celebrations that recognized Norway's cultural contributions. The order helped to raise much of the money necessary to dedicate a statue to Ole Bull at the Norwegian Constitution Day activities in Minneapolis in 1897. Drawing on its vast connections with the working- and middle-class Norwegian families, the Sons of Norway became highly active in generating large crowds for the annual Twin Cities' May 17 celebrations during the years leading up to World War I. Its most successful effort came in 1905, when it organized a unified May 17 celebration in Minneapolis–St. Paul that featured letters of greeting from President Theodore Roosevelt and King Oscar of Norway and Sweden (the celebration took place before the Storting renounced the union on June 7, 1905). In praise of the Norwegians and Swedes attending the event, Roosevelt wrote, "There are no better citizens in our land than those of Scandinavian birth or extraction." Through the Sons of Norway and its activities, nonelite Norwegian Americans could participate in affirming an elite-created Norwegian-American self-image.[29]

One other factor that must be acknowledged was the contributions of small-town Norwegian-American leaders in promoting that Norwegian-American self-image. Odd S. Lovoll's recent study has shown how they used their direct contacts with rural Norwegians to shape how their compatriots viewed themselves. Norwegians in the rural hinterlands tended to be segregated by concepts of *bygd,* or native place, kinship ties to Norway, and other traditions including differences in dialect. In contrast, he observes how the Norwegians in town were of more diverse old-country origins and were in favor of a more universal Norwegian identity, undoubtedly inspired by the ideas emanating from the Norwegian enclaves in the Twin Cities and Chicago. Small towns thus served to mediate between rural and urban Norwegian Americans, making it possible to articulate an identity that was mutually satisfactory.[30]

At times local Norwegian-American leaders would promote a regional Norwegian-American identity. Perhaps the best example occurred among Norwegian Americans of the Red River Valley region of North Dakota and Minnesota. Between 1904 and 1916 they dedicated seven statues to heroes of the Norwegian homeland. Bjørnstjerne Bjørnson, the famed Norwegian author and father of Norwegian nationalism, was honored in Fargo, North Dakota, in 1904 and at Mayville, North Dakota, in 1916. Fargo was the site for the celebration of Henrik Wergeland, Norway's nationalist poet, in 1908, and Rollo, Duke of Normandy (Gange-Rolf), in 1912. Henrik Ibsen, the Norwegian playwright and dramatist, was honored at Wahpeton, North Dakota, on May 17, 1912; and Hans Nielsen Hauge, the prominent lay preacher of the Low Church movement within Norwegian Lutheranism, was honored at Concordia College in Moorhead, Minnesota, on June 12, 1912. A year later, on June 7, the college hosted a ceremony in honor of Ivar Aasen, the Norwegian philologist who synthesized Landsmaal, an attempt to create a pure Norwegian language after centuries of Danish rule. Taken together, these celebrations formed what David Glassberg has termed a "central historical theme" common to all Progressive Era ceremonies. The historical oration at the ceremonies narrated local and national histories in a context that was both secular and religious.[31]

Statue dedications did not come cheaply, and the fact that Norwegians of the Red River Valley conducted seven in a twelve-year span is testimony to their organizational strength as well as the prosperity of the immigrants. This success owed much to the energetic elite among the Red River Valley Norwegians. In particular, Herman O. Fjelde, a physician who resided in the small town of Abercrombie, North Dakota, but practiced in Fargo, deserved the lion's share of the credit for making the various statue dedications a reality.

It was Fjelde who first suggested in 1903 that a monument be dedicated to Bjørnson in the Red River Valley, which resulted in the May 17, 1904, ceremony in Fargo. He played a leading role in getting successive statues, including the 1908 Wergeland statue and the 1912 Rollo statue, to be placed in Fargo. He used his influence abroad to contract for the sculptors as well, securing Sigvald Asbjørnson of Norway to create the Fargo Bjørnson statue and the Hauge statue, and Gustav Vigeland for the Wergeland statue. Fjelde's brother Jacob had sculpted the initial Ibsen bust in 1885, and the sculptor's son, Paul, crafted the Mayville Bjørnson. Fjelde was the most visible member of a small but active Norwegian-American elite. Other important leaders included A. A. Trovaten, the publisher of the newspaper *Fram* (published in Fargo), Professor John G. Halland of the North Dakota Agricultural College, Fargo attorney B. G. Tennyson, and Fargo businessmen H. H. Aaker and Lars Christianson, among others.[32]

This core of leaders capitalized on their connections with the immigrant community, the local business community, and Norway to secure funding for the statues. Often the Red River Valley Norwegians had to compete against other Norwegian-American communities to secure the placement of the statues. A good example involved the decision on where to locate the Wergeland statue. Det Norske Selskab (the Norwegian Society) took on the issue at its annual meeting in 1907. There, owing to the inspiration of Fjelde, it was decided to hold a ceremony in honor of the poet at Minneapolis, since the Twin Cities were generally acknowledged as the capital of Norwegian America. The ceremony would take place on May 17, 1908, on the centennial of Wergeland's birth, and would parallel a statue dedication to him at his birthplace of Christiansand, Norway. However, a number of competing cities vied for the location of the actual statue. That decision was finally reached at a later meeting when Fjelde led a successful lobbying committee sent by Fargo. The society, persuaded by Fjelde, chose Fargo as the site for the Wergeland statue.[33]

Despite the competition among Norwegian-American communities, what made the celebrations ultimately possible was the success of Norwegian Americans in working with the business, professional, and political elite of the cities of the valley. Fargo's mayor gave a speech at both the 1904 Bjørnson ceremony and the 1912 Rollo ceremony. The Fargo Commercial Club played a major role in the three Fargo statue dedications, especially their efforts to promote the events and to sponsor many of the activities. For example, it paid the costs of shipping and transporting the Wergeland statue to Fargo and hosted the evening banquet. The *Fargo Forum and Daily Republican*, in an account of the 1912 Rollo statue dedication, acknowledged that it was made possible because so many of North Dakota's prominent people "in business, professional, and political circles are descendants of the vikings."[34]

The seven statue dedications were all well attended: the Fargo celebrations ranged from about four thousand for the Wergeland ceremony to around ten thousand or more for the Bjørnson and Rollo celebrations, and the Hauge affair in Moorhead numbered close to ten thousand. The small town dedications in Wahpeton and Mayville both numbered about two thousand participants.

With such large audiences, the organizers wanted to emphasize that Norwegian Americans had remained loyal to Norway. Each celebration began with a lengthy parade, usually including local schoolchildren and featuring leading ethnic organizations such as the Sons of Norway lodges from various communities. The presence of the schoolchildren mirrored Norway's national holiday, May 17, in which Norwegian schoolchildren were an important element. Of similar prominence, the various Norwegian singing societies representing various Red River Valley communities marched in the parade and sang Norwegian songs during the dedication ceremonies that followed the parades. Norway's national anthem was a staple.[35]

Members of these organizations often wore traditional Norwegian costumes, or *bunader*, and many wore or waved Norwegian flags. The 1904 Bjørnson celebration featured a traditional Norwegian wedding, the couple in traditional costumes, on the evening of the dedication. At each dedication, a young local woman, usually of Norwegian ancestry and wearing a *bunad*, would remove the Norwegian and American flags, and in the case of Rollo, the French tricolor, to reveal the statue to the audience. In this role, the young women were "symbolic abstractions" in the construct of memory. Specifically, for the Norwegian-American celebrations, the young women represented the sacred feminine principle, the personification of energy that gives birth to forms. In removing the veil from the statue, each was symbolically giving birth to it, bringing forth a rebirth of the Norwegian nation in the New World.[36]

As John Bodnar has noted, celebrations of public memory were not just ceremonies honoring the past but were directed toward matters of power in society and questions of loyalty to both official and vernacular cultures. The organizers of the Red River Valley celebrations were careful to ensure that sponsorship was divided between the Norwegian-American elite and local American business and professional leaders. Thus, the statue in each ceremony was ritualistically "accepted" on behalf of the dominant power structure, such as the mayor of Fargo or the presidents of the North Dakota Agricultural College and the North Dakota State School of Science, as in the case of the 1904 Bjørnson and 1912 Ibsen dedications. It was usual for a prominent state official to be present, as when Governor John Burke of North Dakota gave a speech at the 1908 Wergeland dedication. The dedications also included prominent speakers from other interested groups. Thus, because Henrik Wergeland had fought for Jewish rights in Norway, his dedication featured a speech by Rabbi Dinhart from Minneapolis. At the 1912 Rollo ceremony, the secretary of the French embassy, G. Mauras, gave a speech. And Norway had a representative at all the dedications, usually a consular official or members of the state church.[37]

These performance rituals strongly expressed loyalty to the nationalisms of Norway and the United States, thus fulfilling a major objective of Norwegian-American leaders. When combined with the speeches given at the dedications, they proclaimed the basic outlines of a regional Norwegian-American identity.

Prominent Norwegian Americans, homeland Norwegians, and local American leaders delivered the speeches that focused on the basic ideas of the Red River Valley Norwegian-American identity. Its three components were the preservation of Norwegian traditions, including religious values, loyalty to American values, and a regional Norwegian-American identity that challenged the supremacy of the Twin Cities as the capital of Norwegian America.

In preserving their Norwegian traditions, Norwegian Americans were participating in the genesis of a transnational identity in which they were the vanguard of the spread of the Norwegian nation. A favored tactic was to draw parallels between the immigrant community and homeland heroes. At the 1904 Bjørnson ceremony, John G. Halland noted that like Norwegians of the valley, Bjørnson was descended from Norwegian farming stock, while J. H. Worst, president of the North Dakota Agricultural College, stated that "its educational work was in harmony with Bjørnson's ideals." At the Wergeland dedication, B. G. Tennyson proclaimed that the statue was like "a lamp of liberty" that is still reflected in the minds and hearts of the Norwegian race.[38]

The speakers observed how Norwegian Americans preserved their basic values. The featured speaker at the Wergeland dedication, Pastor J. O. Hougen of Tacoma, Washington, contended that Wergeland personified "Norwegian character—honest, faithful, unbiased, fearless, and yet modest and resigned," and that Norway was presenting the statue "as a token of friendship and love to their sons and daughters in this country—the freest and greatest republic in the world." At the 1912 Rollo ceremony, Professor Julius E. Olson of the University of Wisconsin offered a more bombastic interpretation when he claimed that the Teutonic spirit of freedom "was found in its highest potency among the tribes of the Scandinavian North; for the mountain fastness and the salt sea of a bracing northern clime fostered an unquenchable love of liberty, of which the poets Wergeland, Ibsen, and Bjørnson are the modern embodiment." He later remarked that Norwegian Americans had proven this quality by building a statue to Rollo in America.[39]

The ceremonies reflected on the religious character of Norwegian immigrants. During his speech at the 1912 Hauge ceremony, President J. A. Aasgaard of Concordia College stated that it was appropriate to locate the monument on a Norwegian Lutheran school's grounds and asked almost rhetorically of the audience if "one could be a legitimate Norwegian without being a Norwegian Lutheran?" Pastor Hans Nielsen Hauge (the grandson of the lay preacher of the same name, the founder of Haugeanism) was present at the dedication. In his speech he observed that in America one could find more Norwegian Lutheran congregations than in Norway, and that for Norwegian Americans a living Christendom was the most important aspect of life. The elder Hans Nielsen Hauge had been imprisoned by Norwegian authorities for his illegal, low-church activities, but his teachings greatly influenced Norway's peasant class, and the appearance at the Hauge dedication of his grandson and Bishop M. O. Bøckman of Trondheim, Norway, offered validation of the religious character of Norwegian America.[40]

Visiting dignitaries from Norway stressed the need for Norwegian-American youth to preserve their language and customs in America. As the closing speaker at the Aasen dedication, Hulda Garborg, inventor of the modern national Norwegian *bunad* and wife of the late Norwegian nationalist author Arne Garborg, directed her comments to the young people in the audience. Ivar Aasen's life work had been to champion the cause of a Norwegian national language, and by honoring Aasen, Norwegian Americans were affirming their loyalty to homeland culture.[41]

Yet the speakers as a rule were quick to point out how Norwegian Americans had embraced American values while still remaining loyal to Norwegian ones. At the Hauge ceremony, Bishop Bøckman offered them lavish praise:

> You have prospered in this new country, which you have made your home. You have adapted to this nation's customs. You are obedient to this nation's laws and honor this nation's flag. This is as it should

Monument to Hans Nielsen Hauge on the campus of Concordia College, Moorhead, Minnesota. The Norwegian community of the Fargo–Moorhead area dedicated the monument in 1912. Author's photograph.

be. You should be true citizens of this nation for it is your nation, but I hope the time may never come in America when a child having the blood of the Norsemen in his veins will fail to remember the land of his ancestors and be ashamed to let it be known that his fathers came from that small country across the waters.[42]

Moreover, in upholding those American values, Norwegian Americans had sacrificed for their nation, a fact made forcefully at the 1916 Bjørnson ceremony by A. L. Kraabel, a candidate for lieutenant governor of North Dakota. Against the nativist backdrop of World War I, he spoke of

> the way in which the Norwegian emigrant has displayed the flag both in daily work and in the battlefields. Norwegian immigrants fought and fell as heroes for the Union, when native-born Americans found reasons not to fight. They died for the Stars and Stripes while so-called Americans would trample it into the dust. When Americans, therefore, tell us that we are poor Americans, we should tell them to study Norwegian literature... when they remind us to be good Americans.[43]

Ever eager to defend themselves, Norwegian-American leaders in the valley promoted the idea that the upper Midwest, especially the Red River Valley, was the most Norwegian part of America, an idea often shared by prominent Americans. In giving his speech to accept the Bjørnson statue on behalf of the North Dakota Agricultural College, President J. H. Worst compared the heartland of Norwegian America to a new Normandy:

> Through Normandy the Norsemen have left their mark of human civilization in England and her colonies for all time to come. Through millions of Norwegians today holding and occupying large portions of Illinois, Wisconsin, Iowa, Minnesota, North Dakota and South Dakota, a region as much more fertile, as much larger in extent, as much greater in possibilities than Normandy as is the mission and destiny of free America greater than that of any European country, this, the purest branch of the Teutonic race, will again make history, shape destiny, and help determine the weal and woe of millions yet to come. Among the marks and evidences that shall tell the spirit and temper of these Norse pioneers this monu-

ment will bear unimpeachable testimony as to their sympathies and as to the things they prized and placed foremost among their sacred possessions. A thousand years have intervened between their invasion and peaceful occupation of northern America . . . the desire for freedom in these qualities still lives [in] the Viking spirit of ancient days and of those qualities Bjørnson stands as the leader of his people.[44]

Local Norwegian-American leaders narrowed these ideas further. In 1910, in an article concerning the forthcoming Rollo celebration, Dr. Fjelde argued: "The Red River Valley ought to be the center in the Normandy of America. And Fargo must be regarded as the capital city in this region." The statue of Rollo placed in Fargo was a copy of the statue of the Rollo millennium dedicated in 1911 in Rouen, France, and for Norwegian Americans of the valley it offered a metaphor of their regional identity. The *Fargo Forum and Daily Republican* agreed, noting that it was fitting to have all these affairs in Fargo, for "this city and this state are the strongest Norwegian centers in the United States." The dedication ceremony coincided with the convention of the Norman-American Congress, which further cemented the concept of a New Normandy. During the 1912 ceremony, H. J. Hagen, chairman of the Rollo Committee, mentioned in his speech that "Rollo had planted the seeds of liberty, which had grown and flourished across the water until they reached these shores, the greatest liberty-loving nation on the face of the globe." In the language of metaphor, local Norwegian-American leaders claimed that the Red River Valley Norwegian settlements were the strongest and most Norwegian of all the immigrant settlements and had best preserved Norwegian culture in America, a clear challenge to the hegemony of the Twin Cities as the capital of Norwegian America.[45]

Such bold proclamations, however, did not always sit well with those excluded or victimized by the sometimes strong language of Norwegian racial superiority. In his speech at the 1912 Ibsen ceremony, Fjelde joked about how such a German-American city as Wahpeton had been made over suddenly to become Norwegian and celebrate May 17. *Fram* reported that the joke was in poor taste and chided him with a mocking "Bravo doctor!" During his speech at the 1912 Rollo ceremony, Olson alienated many of the Catholic and French guests for his ideas about Teutonic civilization overcoming the effete cultures of Greece and Rome. As a result, the French delegation refused to attend the banquet later that evening. In an editorial, the Norwegian-American paper *Normanden* observed that Olson's speech proved a major embarrassment. The affair prompted a formal apology from J. C. Charest, the secretary of the Rollo Statue Committee, noting that Olson's speech made them "feel deeply ashamed and insulted."[46]

Furthermore, as noted by Daniel J. Sherman, the act of erecting statues, or monuments in general, was inherently unstable. The monuments had a tendency to blend into the landscape, thereby embodying that instability in an ironic way, which was not the intent of the organizers.[47]

Despite Olson's faux pas, Norwegian-American leaders of the valley clung to the analogy of their region as a new Normandy. Their vision would have favored a more nuanced interpretation, such as the one offered by Mayor W. D. Sweet of Fargo, whose speech occurred after Olson's. He referred to Normans as a composite race, and when its descendants converged "with the course of those other vikings, they reached the spot which we now mark today as the new world of the Norman and Scandinavian races."[48] As a people loyal to both America and Norway, Norwegian Americans of the Red River Valley likewise were beginning to view themselves as a hybrid nation whose future and identity belonged to their new world.

In spite of its regional orientation, the identity constructed by Norwegian Americans of the Red River Valley largely supported the basic ideas of the Norwegian-American identity articulated by the community's more nation-oriented leaders. In addition, the valley identity shared with the more inclusive Norwegian-American identity an increasing realization that Norwegian Americans and homeland Norwegians shared in a common national, or more accurately, *transnational* identity.

Closer organizational ties between Norwegian America and Norway were evident with the forming of Nordmands-Forbundet (the Norsemen's Federation) in 1907. During the momentous year 1905, when Norway gained full separation from Sweden, a number of leading Norwegians, including Bjørnstjerne Bjørnson, had noticed the ardent support evidenced among their compatriots in America, including several who volunteered to fight for Norway if the union crisis led to war. Members of the Norwegian government and leading members of Norway's elite formed the Norsemen's Federation to promote closer cultural and business ties with emigrated Norwegians. Established in Norway rather than America, the federation's existence demonstrated the new recognition Norwegian Americans were now accorded in their old homeland. At this point, homeland Norwegians also sought to add their viewpoints to the emerging Norwegian-American identity. The federation published a monthly journal, also named *Nordmands-Forbundet,* and in its inaugural issue it urged greater ties across national boundaries: "Our national strength will grow and provide convincing proof both at home and abroad of our great national character. This goal can only be realized, however, if all Norwegians, in the homeland and the emigrated, learn to become more unified and take part in the mutual assistance and work that fuels these impulses and promotes an exchange of ideas."[49]

An example of the increased importance of the business and professional elite was the creation of the Norwegian-American Line in 1911, a steamship passenger line intended to profit from the increased travel between the two nations. Prominent Norwegian-American businessmen provided a majority of the funding, which amounted to $750,000. A Chicago Norwegian American, Birger Osland, who belonged to the city's Norwegian club, spearheaded the fund-raising effort. A Norwegian-American Line ship would transport members of the Sons of Norway to Norway for the 1914 centennial of Norway's constitution.[50]

The strong ties between Nordmands-Forbundet and the Norwegian government were in evidence at the 1915 Panama Exhibition in San Francisco. Nordmands-Forbundet's goal was to make Norway, especially its manufactured goods, better known in America. A related goal was to improve contacts with the influential Norwegian-American business community based on America's West Coast. A Norwegian-American businessman, A. C. Floan, who visited the exhibition, observed that Norway's building was replete with pictures of Norway's fishing industry and other industries, including its resources in hydroelectric power. On October 16, Norgesbygning (Norway's Building) hosted a celebration in honor of Consul F. Herman Gade and his wife. The evening celebration featured a plentiful dinner spread, including the famous fish pudding à la Norway. As the concluding speaker, Consul Gade thanked everyone and proposed a *skaal* (toast) to Norway, which was met with thunderous hurrahs. The evening finished with a stirring rendition of Norway's national anthem, which the correspondent remarked was "sung by hundreds of robust voices."[51]

In reaction to the elitism of these organizations, rural and many urban Norwegian immigrants turned to the *bygdelag* movement, which operated at the grass-roots level by stressing emotional ties to specific old home localities in Norway rather than to Norway as a nation. The leaders of the *bygdelag* tended to be prominent second-generation Norwegians who often had a nostalgic longing for the culture of a homeland they had not experienced. Its principal activities were the *stevnes* at which several hundred or even thousands of ordinary Norwegian Americans would gather to share in fellowship honoring their pioneer ancestors. With its emphasis on rural peasant traditions from Norway, the *bygdelag* movement represented an alternative vision to the more urban high-culture vision held by other Norwegian elite. As historian Odd Lovoll observes, the *bygdelag* movement was a distinctly Norwegian-American phenomenon, but it influenced movements in Norway such as the youth movement, the temperance movement, and the emergence of an interest in local history in Norway.[52]

The rivalry between the *bygdelags*, with their rural orientation, and the urban Norwegian-American elites, with their image of Norway and Norwegian Americans as modern and progressive, was an example of the tensions between common folk and elite groups found in most, if not all, immigrants. But in the case of Norwegian America, it was particularly interesting since it reflected the heated contemporary conflict over *who* and *what* was truly Norwegian in Norway itself. As historian Anne-Lise Seip has shown, there were strong tensions around the turn of the century between the two competing visions of Norway. Many, if not most, rural Norwegians clung to Norway's earlier nineteenth-century national identity, based on a romantic glorification of peasant culture and a heroic Viking past. But urban Norwegian elites wanted to adapt the romantic symbols to demonstrate how Norway had become a modern nation, both politically and economically.[53]

Because of the competition among these sets of elites, Norwegian-American festival days often had competing ceremonies, such as had occurred on May 17. To commemorate the centennial of Norway's constitution, Norway's government scheduled a large celebration to take place in Kristiania (Oslo) during the summer months of 1914. Efforts to celebrate the Eidsvold centennial among Norwegian Americans seemed a plausible counterpart, and the *bygdelag* took the initiative to organize the event beginning in 1910. Representing as it did a multifaceted and decidedly local rather than national self-image, such efforts among the leaders of the *bygdelag* might have seemed like a contradiction. However, the appeal of the local identities for many of the Norwegian immigrants had given the movement organizational muscle, and its members were active in charities that gave relief to the rural poor in Norway. The local lodges also were highly active in acquiring and cataloging genealogical and historical materials concerning their respective *bygds*.⁵⁴

The efforts of the *bygdelag* to promote a nationalist celebration may be understood as a phenomenon in which the foundations of nationalism are often rooted in local symbols. In his study on German nationalism, *The Nation as a Local Metaphor,* Alon Confino has demonstrated how German nationalism became acceptable to the mass of Germans through its association with local symbols.⁵⁵ In this context, the *bygdelag* worked to present Norwegian-American nationalism's strength as residing in the rugged descendants of those rural pioneers, an attempt to negate the interpretation offered by the urban elites. Yet, the urban professionals reacted with disdain, and one Chicago newspaper warned, "The peasants are coming! The peasants are coming!"⁵⁶

Fearing that a competing ceremony might take place, the *bygdelag* committee decided to cooperate with the other organizations, and a united celebration took place in the Twin Cities from May 16 to 18, 1914. The celebrations commenced on May 16 with two processions, one from St. Paul and one from Minneapolis, and they convened at the fairgrounds between the two cities. The celebration touched on popular aspects of the Norwegian-American identity; some participants wore traditional peasant costumes (featuring regional dress); one float featured Vikings in a Viking ship, another was a re-creation of the Eidsvold Assembly, and another represented women's suffrage; survivors of the Fifteenth Wisconsin Regiment marched in the procession; and there was a children's parade by Minneapolis schoolchildren.

At the Eidsvold Centennial Jubilee held at Frogner Park the same year in the Norwegian capital, Norway celebrated its national heritage, including an exhibition titled "The Emigrated Norway," which featured pictures and artifacts from Norwegian life in America. At a banquet held on May 15, the Norwegian government, represented by King Haakon VII and Carl Berner, the president of Nordmands-Forbundet and a former president of the Norwegian parliament, offered a toast to the Norwegian-American delegates. Olaf I. Rove, the Norwegian consul in Milwaukee and the Supreme President of the Sons of Norway, responded to the toast for "the Emigrated Norway." At the May 17 parade in Kristiania, representatives of the various Norwegian-American groups, including the Sons of Norway, marched beneath American flags.⁵⁷

Norway gave further recognition to the emigrated Norwegians on the July 4 "Americans' Day" held in Frogner Park. L. B. Hanna, the governor of North Dakota, "the most Norwegian of all states," presented a bust of Abraham Lincoln as a gift of the people of his state. The *bygdelag* had been particularly active in raising money for the bust. The prominent Norwegian-American societies were present at the ceremony, and it featured participation by the Luther College band and surviving veterans of the Fifteenth Wisconsin Regiment. The Sons of Norway presented a banner to the veterans. The Norwegian synod also participated in a ceremony at the American legation where Hans G. Stub, a leading figure in the church, presented a Norwegian-American memorial gift to Norway. Numerous individuals also participated—an estimated twenty thousand emigrated Norwegians visited the homeland that summer.[58]

Competing visions of this transatlantic celebration were still present, especially in the written literature associated with the event. The official program of the three-day American ceremony was largely the work of the *bygdelag* organizing committee, and most of its pages were devoted to a history of the *bygdelag* movement. The urban elite, meanwhile, produced a *Festskrift*, or literary celebration, edited by Johannes B. Wist in commemoration of the occasion, and it presented a Norwegian-American self-image that focused on the cultural and progressive achievements of the immigrants. Under the editorship of J. S. Johnson, a leading member of the Sons of Norway, the publication *Minnesota* offered another interpretation that represented a position between the other two. And in the official program of the celebration in Norway, a section was devoted to the emigrated Norway, reflecting the ideas of the emerging business and technical elite found among Norwegians on both sides of the Atlantic. Moreover, the League of Norsemen had been largely responsible for the inclusion of the emigrated Norway at the festivities held in Norway. Its secretary-general Carl J. Hambro had spent the previous year soliciting support among Norwegians in America.[59]

The Norwegian government was aware of the tensions present within Norwegian-American society. To celebrate the dedication of the Wergeland statue in 1908, it had sent Bishop Bang as its official representative, an attempt to appeal to the clergy and rural Norwegian immigrants. Bang's companion, Thoralv Klaveness, was secretary of the League of Norsemen, and he represented ties to the secular business and professional elite. A similar situation arose in 1913, when the Norwegian parliament decided to

Johannes B. Wist, an early intellectual leader of the Norwegian-American community. Courtesy of the National Library of Norway, Norwegian-American Collection.

have the nation's Lutheran clergy strongly represented at the Twin Cities Eidsvold centennial the next year.[60]

Despite these tensions, by the time of the Eidsvold Jubilee, the concept of Norway in America had become widely accepted, at least in the public's mind. Writing in the official Norwegian program of the jubilee, Wilhelm Morgenstierne, secretary of Nordmands-Forbundet, mentioned the sense of a shared identity between Norway and its emigrated people:

> It is that closer famliarity towards each other and thereby that greater understanding and sympathy that is a result of the cooperation over the summer between the emigrated and the homeland Norwegians. There is hardly a one of them, who has witnessed up close the so-called work of building bridges between the two peoples, who now and then has not regretfully seen how the lack of mutual familiarity between Norwegians at home and abroad has led to mistrust and misunderstanding. It now appears actually possible to believe that we have taken great strides forward to rectify that situation. On one side went the thousands, who after several years of absence have seen Norway again, a changed and wealthier visage in the land and the people. What they receive are impressions of a richer and more independent Norway than that which stories and memories from their childhood related to them. From traveling across the country, they have noticed the changes in the home parish, the development of cities, and from beginning to end the display of an image shown by the new Norway, working energetically for the many. Amazement and delight over what they have seen comes again and again in expressions of unity.[61]

The sentiments of Morgenstierne further revealed how visits by Norwegian Americans provided opportunities for Norway to promote its self-image as well. In promoting the Eidsvold Jubilee, Norway's image-makers catered to the nostalgia of the returning immigrant, but they shared with the Norwegian-American elite an understanding of the need to offer a progressive vision of their national identities.

By 1914, the concept of Norway in America had become well known among homeland Norwegians, and Norway's public education system helped to further disseminate this concept. The school primer used in most Norwegian schools, that of the aforementioned Nordahl Rolfsen, had a fifth volume added to the series in 1915. Titled *Norge i Amerika* (Norway in America) it included contributions by prominent Norwegian-Americans on the achievements of their group in America. The lengthy foreword by the author explained the importance of "Norway in America":

Norwegian-American visitors to Norway were not always greeted with warmth. This cartoon poked fun at the ostentatious display of wealth by an arrogant Norwegian-American couple visiting the 1914 Eidsvold Centennial. "By holding the finger in the nose momentarily, it allows you to show off your diamond rings to people." Courtesy of the National Library of Norway, Norwegian-American Collection.

This book about Norway is written by Norwegians in America and it seeks to provide a picture of Norwegian organizational life, Norwegian nature and folklife, Norwegian literature, and Norwegian history through the ages. But this latest addition to the series must be comprehensive if it is to be successfully combined with a number of living images from that part of Norway's history that can be characterized as Norway in America. I have believed that these living images could have meaning also for the old country, which through innumerable personal contacts is tied to the emigrated Norway, even if that knowledge is most often confined to those personal contacts. I have believed that a more common knowledge and a clearer understanding would be welcomed. Therefore, *Norway in America* will become available simultaneously in the new and the old land.[62]

Rolfsen's *Norge i Amerika* thus reflected the extent to which the Norwegian-American self-image had been developed by Norwegian-American leaders interacting with their homeland counterparts. It contained a section devoted to the pioneering efforts of the Norwegian immigrants, honoring their religious piety as well as their sacrifice to their adopted land during the American Civil War. It also demonstrated how Norwegians had a long association with America going back to the Viking age, which supported the modern Vikings concept in its descriptions of the latter-day accomplishments of Norwegian Americans in business, education, the professions, and industry. In effect, it showed how Norwegian Americans had become the best Americans owing to their innate values such as love of freedom and support for democratic institutions. Moreover, the success of Norwegians in America reinforced the greatness of the Norwegian national character.[63]

The desire among Norwegian-American leaders to have the importance of their group recognized by Norway's elite and general population had motivated the concept of Norway in America. Although it contributed to the Norwegian-American self-image and was, therefore, useful in an American context, the Norway in America concept primarily aimed to win recognition from Norwegians. The inclusion of the Norwegian-American experience in celebrations of Norway's major national holiday as well as in its popular history validated the Norwegian-American self-image. Furthermore, the success of Norwegian Americans had bolstered

Norway's own national image, and Norwegian image-makers used their contacts with their emigrated countrymen to proclaim the success of modern Norway as well.

Norwegians Are the Best Americans

Conditions in America between 1890 and 1914 created a favorable environment for Norwegian Americans. The last heavy wave of Norwegian immigration occurred during these years, and it provided a critical mass for the ethnic Norwegian population in America. Norwegian Americans had achieved success economically as well as socially, and their confidence was reflected by their greater numbers in American social and political life. An emerging Norwegian-American literature also gave hope to the group's leaders, who envisioned the possibility of a sustainable ethnic literature.[64] The Norwegian-American community likewise benefited from comparisons between the "older," mostly northern and western European immigrants and the "newer" immigrants from predominantly southern and eastern Europe. Yankee leaders viewed the Norwegians, as members of the former group, much more favorably than they did groups such as the Jews or Italians.[65]

Leading American scholars of the late nineteenth century trumpeted the virtuous Norwegians. Historian Benson John Lossing wrote, "It is back to the Norwegian Vikings we must look for the hardiest elements of progress in the United States." Another American scholar, B. F. De Costa, expressed similar ideas: "Let us remember that in vindicating the Norsemen we honor those who not only give us the first knowledge possessed of the American continent, but to whom we are indebted for much beside that we esteem valuable." He added, "We fable in a great measure when we speak of our Saxon inheritance. It is rather from the Northmen that we have derived our vital energy, our freedom of thought, and in measure that we do not yet suspect our strength."[66]

A larger American audience viewed Norwegians favorably owing to the positive portrayals of Norway found in nineteenth-century travel accounts authored by Americans. These accounts painted a positive portrait of a highly romanticized Norway, a land of majestic mountains, rugged beauty, and rustic peasants. Moreover, they depicted Norway as the land of Viking-age heroes, and Americans came to share this highly stylized vision of Norway, which made them predisposed to having favorable impressions of Norwegian immigrants and their descendants. The Franco-American Paul Du Chaillu authored his immensely popular *Land of the Midnight Sun* in 1881, which addressed his travels throughout Scandinavia, though Norway featured prominently. The activities of the Norwegian violinist Ole Bull, who eventually acquired American citizenship, also served to enhance the reputation of Norway.[67]

Armed with the approval of the dominant class in America, Norwegian-American leaders felt confident in proclaiming that Norwegians were the best immigrant group. Noting how the appearance of the "Viking" ship at the World's Columbian Exposition had gained the attention of prominent Americans, Lars A. Stenholt commented that the event in 1893 substantiated in a striking manner the Norwegians' claim to be the first Europeans in North America. He heaped special praise on Captain Magnus Andersen: "Norwegians in America shall remember your great deed, Magnus, for as long as our hearts are beating." He stated that "in America's history we shall thus receive our rightful place."[68]

In his 1894 history of the Fifteenth Wisconsin Regiment, Norwegian-American author Ole Buslett used the theme of Norwegian service to insist that his compatriots were the best immigrant group: "In relation to the size of the population, no other nation was as greatly and bravely represented in the war as the Norwegian one." At a banquet held in Chicago in 1905, for the purposes of toasting the visiting Norwegian student singing societies, Nicolay A. Grevstad, the editor of *Skandinaven,* boasted that "here in the land Norwegians are becoming Americans" and that they are "good and law-abiding citizens, who are one of the best immigrant groups in this nation."[69]

Norwegian visitors to America shared this evaluation. Writing in 1904, Hans Seland, who was active in the agrarian movement in Norway, commented, "Among the immigrants . . . they [the Norwegians] have easily earned themselves a reputation in the land . . . as the best Americans." Similarly, the liberal author Thoralv Klaveness had observed that Norwegian Americans represented the "best part of our nation" in America. In his presentation speech for the Wergeland statue, given at Minneapolis on May 17, 1908, Bishop Bang asserted that it represented "a heartfelt appreciation for the moral support and encouragement that our compatriots had offered to Norway during the tribulations of 1905."[70]

During these same years, the growing perception among Anglo-American leaders that the "newer" immigrants threatened their position led them to enlist allies among the more favored immigrants. To maintain its dominant hegemony, the ruling Anglo-Americans adopted a racial ideology that classified Europeans into three main groups. To the best group belonged the Nordic races, which included the Anglo-Saxons, Germans, Dutch, and Scandinavians. The middle group, the Alpine group, included the French, the Swiss, and most central Europeans. Lastly, there was the Mediterranean group, which included Italians, Greeks, and Jews. It should be noted that Anglo-Americans did not create these categories; they were well developed and widespread in Europe, not least in Scandinavia, by that time. But to Anglo-Americans and northern Europeans in America they seemed particularly relevant in their multiethnic society. Moreover, these categories did not always make for easy classification because they were based on both race and religion. Thus the Irish, for example, could be viewed as either Nordic (northern European) or Alpine since they were predominantly Catholic. Mostly Protestant groups from the British Isles also posed some problems. Presbyterian Scots, for instance, tended to be seen as Nordic, but they were sometimes depicted as Alpine because they were Celtic.[71]

Against this backdrop Norwegian-American identity-makers could proudly point out that they met all the criteria: Norwegians were Nordic, they were overwhelmingly Protestant, and their success in American life seemed to confirm their worthiness as being among the best Americans, or at least the best immigrant group. Anglo-American leaders could tolerate this assertion because it did not challenge the one idea that was fixed in stone: that Anglo-Americans were naturally the best Americans because they were the standard against which all other groups were compared. Some Norwegian-American leaders, however, did not accept this basic assumption. They interpreted the Anglo-American racial ideology as an *idealized standard* against which all Americans, including Anglo-Americans, should be measured. Against this idealized standard, argued some Norwegian-American leaders, the Norwegian American, rather than the Anglo-American, emerged as the best American.

Rasmus B. Anderson fired the first shot across the bow in the attack on Anglo-American superiority. In his 1875 speech on themes of Norwegian-American identity, he concluded by advancing the idea that Norwegians were the best Americans: "Let us move quickly into the future when it will be recognized that the Norseman is America's best citizen from whom deliverance will come when our land is threatened."[72]

Waldemar Ager, a prominent Norwegian-American novelist and essayist, refined and expanded the argument during the early years of the twentieth century. As the editor of *Kvartalskrift*, the journal of the Norwegian Society of America, Ager published several articles in which he presented the themes of Norwegian-American self-image, demonstrating how Norwegian Americans were the best Americans. His innovation derived from his ability to transform the traditional Anglo-American racial typology into an idealized one in which the Norwegian American bested the Anglo-American on the latter's own terms.

Among Ager's first attempts at this new approach was an October 1905 article appearing in *Kvartalskrift*, "Om at bevare vort modersmaal" (Preserving Our Mother Tongue). He advanced the idea that the preservation of Norwegian actually served the cause of American ideals:

> One might rightly expect much from the Norwegian youth here. The Viking blood, the rockbound steadfastness, the honesty, the desire for action, the frugality—all that which is received as a gift from the cradle should, when added to the real unvarnished American smartness and grit, create a class which would thrive like fish in water. They should, as it were, become the key spiritual and industrial troops in the vanguard in their adopted land.[73]

Ager claimed the Norwegians were racially superior even to the Anglo-Americans owing to those "Americanized" traits that first appeared in the Viking age. To suppress those traits via assimilation would be a great loss for America. In addition, he introduced a further refinement to the Norwegian-American identity, namely, that a hybrid race, the Norwegian American, would become the standard-bearer for the emerging society. Here Ager reflected a sense shared by other Norwegian-American leaders that they combined the best traits of Norway and America.[74]

Yet Ager cautioned his countrymen not to confuse Norwegian Americans with Americans, noting that assimilation would forfeit any racial advantages. Maintaining one's Norwegian language and culture was the only means that assured success in America. As proof, he wrote that native-born Norwegian Americans had the advantage of knowledge of the language and local customs yet "they become more or less 'Yankeefied,' [while] the 'greenhorns' who came over a few years ago have gone ahead of them."[75] Ager needed to emphasize the maintenance of Norwegian language and

Waldemar Ager, the foremost proponent of Norwegian-American superiority and severe critic of the melting-pot assimilation model of America. Courtesy of Nordmanns-Forbundet Archive.

culture because if race were all that mattered, then Norwegians, as inherently superior racially, would succeed regardless of which language they used. As a cultural preservationist, he viewed Norwegian racial traits as latent, capable of full development only in an environment exposed to Norwegian culture and language.

Assimilation of Norwegians, Ager stated in 1908, was not necessary. "It has been demonstrated here in America that immigrants have been fully as good citizens as the natives—and even better." He further challenged the quasi-mythical status that some Anglo-American leaders ascribed to their group: "Why, then, should we display our subservience in such an exaggerated, humble, and prostate worship of the Yankees? What their American forefathers have done for this country, ours have done as well."[76]

Lastly, Ager challenged the notion of the American melting pot, made popular in Israel Zangwill's 1908 theatrical production of the same name. Rather than accepting an idealized America in which all immigrants became homogenized citizens, he foresaw that it was a mixing pot that would only serve to destroy the best traits of Norwegians.

> We will not become "Americans" in any better sense than we are now. We will only lose our own racial characteristics without acquiring theirs. Everyone—including all races now in America—is, to a considerable extent, in the process of being absorbed in the melting pot. The Norwegian Americans can be said to have entered upon a fortunate path for their own good, as well as that of this country. These immigrants produce fewer criminals than the Americans. They are, on average, just as prosperous. As pioneers, they have shown themselves to be as competent as the other Americans, and they are just as loyal citizens. They have already supplied that nation with evidences of significant mental abilities. In short, they have measured up—and then some.[77]

Forcing Norwegian Americans to assimilate, Ager argued, would violate the tenets of Anglo-American racial theory. By using the racial arguments of the day as an idealized standard, he could substitute Norwegian Americans in place of Anglo-Americans at the top of the racial hierarchy. Given this exalted position, it was not logical to deny Norwegian Americans the right to retain their language and promote their culture, not only because of their tremendous contributions to the making of America but also because of the *tremendous potential* of Norwegian Americans. Even during the height of wartime nativism, Ager did not back down in his criticism of the melting pot. In a 1917 essay he maintained, "We cannot render *our* contributions on the basis of their Anglo heritage. If we are to contribute anything, it must be on the basis of our Norwegian heritage." He added that Norwegians were more spiritual and, hence, more Protestant than Yankee Americans. "Norwegians take the evangelical attitude more seriously than do Anglo-Americans. There is more inside and less outside." Norwegian Lutheran churches were also true folk churches, whose worshippers were primarily workers, he insisted, a trait sorely lacking in American Protestant churches. "The common people—those who are less well off—are snatched up by the Catholics, they have the greatest folk church."[78]

Like some Swedish-American leaders, Ager also expressed the idea that the old Anglo-American population was degenerating, losing its original vigor and growing soft in wealth and luxury, whereas the Norwegian, as well as other Scandinavian or even German immigrants, remained strong and venturesome and thus actively contributed to the making of America. He also used this argument to discredit those immigrants who entered the melting pot for they "no longer want to work with saw and hammer."[79]

Measured against an idealized standard, Ager could argue that Norwegian Americans were better than Anglo-Americans because they were more racially Nordic, more Protestant, and more supportive of "American" values than the dominant Yankee class. These ideas demonstrate how the purpose of constructing a Norwegian-American identity had shifted from the earlier concern with proving that the Norwegian had a long association with the New World to one that now proclaimed that Norwegians were the best Americans. In effect, the new myths, which might be termed *hegemonic myths,* had supplanted the earlier *origin myths.*

Observations by homeland Norwegians concerning American national characteristics likely influenced proclamations of Norwegian-American superiority in regard to Anglo-Americans during this period. During his 1908 tour of Norwegian America in conjunction with the dedication of the Wergeland statue, Bishop Bang of Norway appeared at a luncheon at the Chicago Club hosted by the city's Norwegian-American leaders. In his address, the bishop revealed that at an earlier meeting with Theodore Roosevelt the American president had told him, "Yes, the Norwegians are our best citizens. We can never have enough of them. We are all Norwegians over here."[80]

Other homeland Norwegians found the United States to have an exaggerated reputation. The Norwegian historian Halvdan Koht's 1910 account of the nefarious influence of the "money aristocracy" had alerted many Norwegian intellectuals to the possibility that American society was not as classless or egalitarian as it might pretend to be. In a 1913 travel account, the anti-emigration writer Knut Takla claimed that Norway was more egalitarian and democratic than the "corrupt America," and that corruption and crime had prevented the superior Norwegians from realizing their true potential. Such arguments served to lower the reputation of Anglo-Americans, seen as corrupted by greed and materialism, and concomitantly raised the prestige of Norwegian Americans and Norwegians, who were depicted as espousing noble values and being less tainted by worldly temptations.[81]

More common, though, were the comments that reflected on how well Norwegian Americans had preserved their traditions. As one of the featured speakers at the 1908 May 17 celebration in the Twin Cities, which focused on the dedication of the Henrik Wergeland statue, Thoralv Klaveness asked his largely Norwegian-American audience rhetorically: "Is it truly possible that I find myself 4,000 miles from Norway? Is it possible that a celebration such as this is found at this place in a city so far from Norway's kingdom?" Of course, the implication was that one might mistake Minneapolis–St. Paul for Norway because of the preserved traditions of Norwegian Americans.[82]

Within the Norwegian-American community, not everyone espoused the dominant ideology. From the 1890s and on, following serious labor disputes in both Norway and America, a growing Marxist socialist and labor movement came into being, especially among urban Norwegian workers. In Chicago in 1904, Norwegian American socialists organized the Skandinavisk Socialist Forening for Chicago med Omegn (Scandinavian Socialist Association of Chicago and Vicinity), which operated under the auspices of the Socialist Party of America. Its first chairman, Adolf Bay, was a bakery worker who shortly thereafter returned to Norway to become head of the Norwegian Bakery Workers Union. Other notables included Claus Nicoll, a former Social-Democratic councilman from Bergen, Norway, and Martin Tranmæl, who was active in the International Workers of the World and returned to Norway where he became a leader of the

Norwegian labor movement. There was a Norwegian-Danish chapter of the Socialist Party organized in Kenosha, Wisconsin, around this time.[83]

Norwegians in Chicago were active in the more radical Socialist Labor Party, which cooperated with Swedish, Danish, and German socialists of the city. Hallvard Hande reported in the Norwegian-American newspaper *Norden* (The North) that a great number of Norwegians had participated in the 1886 Haymarket Riot in Chicago. In Minneapolis, Emil Lauritz Mengshoel operated the newspaper *Gaa Paa* (Strike Forth), which appeared in 1903 and lasted until around 1920. A strong labor movement existed among Norwegians in New York, centered on the shipping industry. As late as 1941, 60 percent of all Norwegian laborers in the city belonged to labor unions, and many espoused socialist views.[84] Only a small fraction of predominantly rural Norwegian Americans were political and labor radicals.

The various publications arising out of the 1914 Eidsvold Jubilee also provided Norwegian-American leaders with opportunities to proclaim the superiority of their group. In the official program of the American celebration, A. A. Veblen, a second-generation academic and leader of the Valdres *bygdelag,* implied that the peasant-based lodges were the most Norwegian. "Norwegian members, who organize themselves, as a rule, display no greater Nationalism than in relation [with the *bygdelags*]." It was "their religious fervor" and "especially their conception of the language, which articulated the boundaries of that relationship." Participation in the *bygdelags,* stated Veblen, was the most effective way of ensuring that the American-born Norwegians would "grow in a national direction" as leaders in American politics and society.[85]

Leaders of the Norwegian-American academic and professional elite, meanwhile, pooled their efforts to produce the *Norsk-Amerikanernes festskrift* (the Norwegian-American Literary Celebration) in 1914. Under the direction of Johannes B. Wist, the publication sought to detail the immense cultural and social contributions of Norwegian Americans in a variety of fields. The *Norsk-Amerikanernes festskrift* mirrored the recent emphasis among Norwegian-American elites to stress modern contributions, especially in the arts and the professions. In the foreword to the volume, Wist wrote, "A celebration of this kind should not be of interest to only Norwegian Americans, but it sought to also be of some use for many in Norway who seek enlightenment concerning the entire operations of the Norwegian America."[86]

Stressing the modern contributions of Norwegian Americans was indicative of the increased value of the ties between the two countries being promoted by a business and professional elite. According to this image, Norwegian Americans were more than simple farmers; they were educated, literate, and prosperous; in a word, they were sophisticated. Norwegian Americans had not abandoned their heritage; they had promoted their Norwegian ancestry. In the chapter on Norwegian organizational life in America, Carl G. O. Hansen, editor of *Minneapolis Tidende*, notes that the various Norwegian organizations are based "entirely on Norwegian models," and they have been "designed to promote Norwegian nationalism." Denying the American nature of these organizations, he further explains that the associations "are imbued with a Norwegian national element, which in orders like the Sons of Norway and similar organizations, [make] Norwegians feel right at home."[87]

As for their contributions to American public life, Juul Dieserud mentions that the considerable participation in American politics by Norwegians "signifies the greatness of their values" and that President Roosevelt singled them out as the nation's "most valuable citizens." Their Norwegian heritage, he adds, marks their "steady path in their climb as the [nation's] greatest and best."[88]

Another centennial publication that echoed the praises of Norwegian-American contributions was the aforementioned *Minnesota*, published by the Minnesota–Norway 1914 Centennial Exposition Association. Its primary author, J. S. Johnson, was secretary of the association and a leader in the Sons of Norway. Like the *Norsk-Amerikanernes festskrift*, it chronicled the latter-day achievements of Norwegians in a number of fields, including education, business, literature, religious life, and of course, their sacrifice to the nation during the Civil War. "The sacrifice made by the Norwegians for their adopted land was neither easy nor without tremendous cost! They were good soldiers and warriors, who upheld the old Vikings' renown for strife and battlelust."[89]

Johnson also paid homage to the robust spirit of the pioneers: "It can therefore safely be stated that the Norwegian pioneers were better endowed in almost every aspect, both earthly and spiritually, than their contemporary neighbors of other nationalities." He noted Norwegian superiority in other fields as well, noting how they had not succumbed to political corruption: "There has never been any scandal because of embezzlement for 'graft,' or corruption by any Norwegian public official."[90]

Despite the popularity of Lincoln Steffen's 1904 book *Shame of the Cities,* which showed ethnic corruption among all groups, including Norwegians, the idea of inherent Norwegian honesty remained an essential component of the Norwegian-American identity.[91]

In claiming to be the best Americans, Norwegian Americans were not alone. As Orm Øverland has demonstrated in his study of American homemaking myths, nearly all immigrant groups insisted that their ethnic characteristics and actions earned for them the distinction of being the best Americans. Furthermore, he states, the Dutch, Swedish, Finnish, and German immigrant groups made especially strong claims as the best Americans, superior to even Anglo-Americans. Not surprisingly, the Swedish-American author Johan A. Enander, in making his claim that Swedes were the best Americans, utilized almost exactly the same arguments—cultural, racial, and religious—as Norwegian-American leaders used in claiming that their group was the best.[92]

However, with the exception of Swedish Americans, only the Norwegian Americans could challenge the Anglo-Americans on their own ground, claiming to be inherently the best Americans, surpassing in their essentially American qualities even the Anglo-Americans themselves. The large Catholic element among the German-American population meant that they could not challenge the Anglo-Americans on the basis of religious Protestantism. The Finnish Americans, although descended from a northern European country, could not claim to be racially Nordic according to the theories of the time. And while the Dutch immigrants could offer a substantial challenge, they do not as a group seem to have had much inclination to lay claim to being the best immigrant group.[93] In challenging the Anglo-American hierarchy, Norwegian Americans (and Swedish Americans) alone possessed the combination of aggressive ethnic leadership and group consensus necessary to wage such a campaign.

Negative Anglo-American reactions to the large influx of immigrants from southern and eastern Europe since the 1890s had benefited the position of the Norwegians in America. Unlike the "swarthy" newcomers, who were mostly Catholic or Jewish, the Anglo-Americans found the Scandinavians to be highly desirable. In his 1914 work, *The Scandinavian Element in the United States,* Kendric Charles Babcock viewed the Scandinavians as allies in the racial struggle that threatened the American way of life. He contrasted the immigrants from the North, who were "decently educated, able-bodied, law-abiding men and women," with the new immigrants, whom he characterized as "illiterates, paupers, or criminals." To him, Scandinavians represented a positive force for America: "They will be builders, not destroyers; their greatest service will be as a silent, steadying influence, re-enforcing those qualities which are sometimes called Puritan, sometimes American, but which in any case make for local and national peace, progress, and righteousness."[94]

As late as 1916, on the eve of America's entry into World War I, many prominent Anglo-Americans believed their fellow Nordic peoples could be useful allies. In his 1916 book, *The Passing of the Great Race*, Madison Grant warned that the strength of the white race had been weakened through war, excessively hot climates, and miscegenation with inferior breeds and that it was threatened with extinction. He contended that America needed to adopt measures to exclude inferior types from southern and eastern Europe while making conditions more favorable to those preferable types from northern Europe, especially the Scandinavian element.[95] The war, however, would create a climate in America that demanded absolute loyalty and complete assimilation to American ways, requiring immigrant groups to abandon their ethnic tongues and cultures.

For a period of nearly thirty years, a Norwegian-American golden age had existed that made it possible for Norwegian-American leaders to articulate their challenge to Anglo-American cultural hegemony. Waldemar Ager contended that the Anglo-American racial identity represented an idealized standard by which all Americans should be judged, and he found Norwegian Americans to be superior to Anglo-Americans because Norwegians in America were more Nordic, more Protestant, and more innately imbued with the proper racial traits, such as love of freedom and proclivity for democratic institutions.

Another development in the Norwegian-American self-image was the shift in emphasis from an identity based solely on a romanticized peasant-oriented past to one that featured elements of a romantic past and a progressive-oriented, modernist present, albeit one in which both images coexisted in an uneasy modus vivendi. Crafted by such leaders as Johannes B. Wist, J. S. Johnson, and Carl G. O. Hansen, this orientation pointed to the numerous contributions made by Norwegian Americans in the building of America. This shift in self-image became necessary because Norwegian-American leaders needed to demonstrate to their counterparts in Norway that they had advanced beyond their initial role as farmers and had spread their expertise to all phases of American life.

A hybrid identity, it attracted the immigrant community for whom old peasant Norway still held powerful appeal while concomitantly upholding Norway as a modern, progressive nation. The concepts of latter-day Vikings and Norway in America must be seen in this context as the results of negotiation over the respective national identities of Norwegian America and Norway. It was these concepts that permitted Norwegian-American image-makers to construct an identity that placed their group in the area of overlap between the two nationalisms. This constructed, latter-day self-image allowed Norwegian-American leaders to advance the idea that their immigrant compatriots were fulfilling their duties as good (Norwegian) Americans and as good Norwegians.

· CHAPTER 4 ·

Backlash

Xenophobia and the Pressure to Assimilate,
1917–1929

WARTIME ZEAL often makes people suspicious of those perceived as different, and this was most evident in America during the Great War. Though a nation of immigrants, patriotic fanaticism created an atmosphere of distrust toward "foreigners," and America in many ways fought a war on two fronts: one abroad and one domestic. As a result of the Anglo-American counteroffensive against immigrant groups, even the Norwegian-American community, despite being usually viewed as a highly desirable ethnic group, sensed the severe pressure to conform to American practices. At the 1918 convention of the Norwegian Lutheran Church in America, church leaders voted 533 to 61 to remove the word "Norwegian" from the synod's name. The proposed name change brought great indignation from the Norwegian-American community, many of whom saw the church as one of the primary institutions of Norwegian-American culture, and the proposal was dropped.[1]

Despite the popular resistance among Norwegian Americans in defense of Norwegian culture, the new political and cultural American landscape initiated by the pressures of the Great War had radically changed the environment in which the Norwegian-American identity was calculated. The intense pressure to assimilate and conform to American norms would make it nearly impossible to argue that Norwegian Americans were better than Anglo-Americans as they had prior to the war. America's political system aimed to curtail virtually all expressions deemed foreign by a twin-pronged strategy that attacked incessantly the use of languages other than English and designed legislation to severely limit further immigration from Europe, especially from southern and eastern Europe.

To cope with these new realities, Norwegian-American leaders had to adjust their tactics. The most notable change was the almost hyperbolic emphasis on the loyalty of Norwegian Americans to America and to American values. Although this was not a new tactic, it was featured front and center in the new Norwegian-American articulation of characteristics shared with Anglo-Americans. Norwegian-American leaders argued that owing to the close similarity in values between the two groups, the Norwegian community served as a conservative bulwark in defense of America against "radical" challengers. In return, Norwegian-American leaders hoped that American leaders would see fit to include the Norwegian-American story within the larger American narrative. This strategy—the creation of legacy myths—underscored the primary efforts of Norwegian-American image-makers in the postwar years.

The success of the 1925 Norse-American Centennial was perceived as a confirmation of these legacy myths. When President Calvin Coolidge spoke at the event touting Norwegians as among the best immigrants, it appeared that Anglo-America had endorsed the Norwegian-American legacy. Norwegian-American leaders had regained a position of prominence for Norwegians within the American racial hierarchy.

At the same time, the reduced flow of emigrants from Norway changed the context of relations between Norwegian America and the homeland. No longer threatened by the mass exodus, Norway could now view the emigrants in more positive terms. Homeland leaders used the reputation of Norwegians in America as evidence of the prestige of Norway's cultural traditions. In addition, the business and professional elite of the homeland used the emigrants' success to promote an image of Norway as a modern and progressive nation, which enhanced Norway's international reputation.

All came to a crashing halt, however, when America passed the National Origins Act in 1929, which curtailed the quotas for all immigrants except those of the British Isles. Moreover, it signaled the failure of the legacy myths approach, and it appeared that the Norwegian-American identity had been dealt a blow from which it might never recover. However, the Norwegian-American identity was rehabilitated, although the impetus came largely from Norway. During the 1920s, leaders in Norway realized the extent to which Norway's national identity and the Norwegian-American identity had become mutually intertwined. Although the legacy myths approach was abandoned, elite leaders in both Norway and Norwegian America endorsed most rigorously the greater Norway concept, the idea that Norwegian Americans were loyal citizens of a Norwegian nation that existed beyond the physical boundaries of the homeland. While this idea had been around since 1907, by the late 1920s the greater Norway had become the new standard-bearer in promoting a transnational Norwegian identity.

World War I and Its Aftermath

The advent of World War I changed the situation for all immigrant groups in America. Of course, no group suffered more than the German Americans, the main targets of the One Hundred Percent American campaign. Among Scandinavian Americans, the situation had mixed results. For Swedish Americans, whose homeland tended to have a more pro-German orientation than either Norway or Denmark, the situation in America made them a somewhat suspect group in Anglo-American eyes. Norwegian Americans fared better. Their press tended to be cautious with regard to the war, and Senator Knute Nelson enjoyed a solid reputation as a responsible American among Anglo-American patriots. Perhaps the single greatest perceived flaw was the overwhelming Lutheran religious affiliation of Norwegian Americans, which proved to be a slight embarrassment owing to the German origins of the creed.[2]

As America inched closer to becoming an active participant in the war, the level of mass hysteria over all things "foreign" likewise increased, and both federal and state governments reacted accordingly. The U.S. Congress, overriding President Wilson's veto, passed a literacy test for immigrants in 1917. More ominous from the standpoint of the immigrant groups, including Norwegian Americans, was the campaign to suppress the use of all languages other than English. In 1918, Governor Harding of Iowa outlawed oral communication in any language but English, and Nebraska soon afterward implemented a similar policy. Other states with large Scandinavian populations such as Minnesota, Wisconsin, and North Dakota resisted such extreme measures, but in almost all states private patriotic citizen groups used vocal intimidation and even violence to discourage "free speech." Censorship of the foreign-language press extended to Wilson's 1917 presidential order requiring all foreign-language publications to file an English translation with their local postmaster.

The Great War did not result in the complete assimilation of Norwegian Americans (and other immigrant groups), but it certainly hastened the process. A striking example was the use of Norwegian among Norwegian

Lutheran congregations. The percent of English-language services in the different Lutheran synods increased from none in 1900 to 22 percent in 1915. But at the height of war hysteria, in 1918, approximately nine thousand services in the Norwegian Lutheran churches changed from Norwegian to English, which represented a loss of nearly 11 percent of Norwegian-language services. By 1925 there was roughly an equal balance between the number of services in the two languages, and as the older immigrants died and fewer new immigrants were available to replace them, the use of English increased dramatically. By the 1930s all congregations had abandoned Norwegian for the religious instruction of young people, and by the end of World War II, less than 7 percent of all services in Lutheran churches were conducted in Norwegian.[3]

The end of World War I did not diminish the American effort to limit immigration. The 1917 literacy test had failed to significantly reduce immigration, so the U.S. Congress passed the 1921 quota law, which permitted the annual immigration of the equivalent of 3 percent of each nationality (excluding Orientals) already in the United States, based on the 1910 federal census. Although this census tended to favor immigrants from southern and eastern Europe, the law received generally muted comment from the Norwegian-American press. The old push factors, primarily economic ones, no longer served as inducements for immigration to America. Still, in a 1922 editorial, Johannes B. Wist noted that Scandinavian immigration for the previous year—roughly 16,700—accounted for 5.4 percent of the grand total of 309,556. At the same time, he pointed out that 53,000 Jews and 41,000 Italians were among the newcomers. Immigration from southern and eastern Europe, he implied, was apparently not being discouraged.[4]

In 1924 Congress passed the Immigration Restriction Act with the intended effect of curtailing the influx of these "undesirables." The act had a more pronounced pro–North European bias since it limited annual immigration to 2 percent of each nationality according to the 1890 federal census. Since the heaviest rates of emigration from southern and eastern Europe occurred in the years following 1890, the act's authors chose the 1890 census to ensure that a higher proportion of immigrants would continue to come from northern European countries. For the most part the Norwegian-American press did not complain, although some, like Waldemar Ager, a staunch prohibitionist, saw southern and eastern European immigrants as playing a sinister role in the then-illegal whiskey trade. As Arlow W. Andersen notes, the Norwegian-American press tended to view the 1924 act more favorably than negatively.[5]

Despite these measures, the Anglo-American elite were often pessimistic about the ultimate assimilation of ethnic Americans. They strongly believed that American identity equated with conformity to the culture and religion of the earliest American settlers, viewing ethnic church services, fairs, songs, food, and other activities as proof of disloyalty to core American values. Writing in 1925, Madison Grant, while commenting on the condition of the Pennsylvania Amish, wrote, "It will take centuries before the foreigners now become Americans." The principal author of the 1924 Immigration Restriction Act, Albert Johnson, stated, "The myth of the melting pot has been discredited." Writing in 1926, Henry Pratt Fairchild in his book *The Melting Pot Mistake* noted that the immigrants could not be Americanized because their "deepest feelings of love and affection" lay with their ancestral homelands.[6]

Historian Gary Gerstle refers to this period as one in which Anglo-Americans were fearful of the large-scale changes affecting America. He argues that Anglo-American efforts to pass Americanization, Prohibition, and antiradical initiatives had been blocked or limited (although Prohibition would soon be passed) and so embraced immigration restriction as an alternative way of excluding or subordinating radicals, Jews, Catholics, and other groups whom they feared.[7]

The American backlash against immigrants likewise highlighted the limits of America's culture of civic nationalism. As shown by Aviel Roshwald, even nations whose national identity was largely predicated on allegiance to shared civic values required a formulation of what he terms "figurative kinship" to bind their diverse elements together. In the case of America, Roshwald notes how Social Darwinist concepts of race claimed that nineteenth-century America had been forged "through the admixture of Anglo-Saxon with other Northern European races." Essential to this definition was the idea that the mingling of diverse races would take place through the joint shedding of blood. Yet at a time such as at the end of World War I, popular aversions against mingled blood would lead to attempts to limit the "pollution" to the blood of the nation, and 1918 became the watershed for this new paradigm.[8]

That same year the Norwegian novelist Ole E. Rølvaag opined in an article that the Great War had served to bolster the Anglo-American attack on ethnic cultures, including the Norwegian-American. "In these latter years, especially since our nation has become involved in the world war, everything that is not of Anglo-American origin has been rendered suspect to an ominous degree.... In some places ill will and suspicion turned into the most rancorous persecution.... All that was strange and dangerous; so it had to be extirpated. They were not particular about the means, and woe to anyone who tried to object."[9]

A contemporary critic of "Americanism," Horace Kallen, wrote in 1924 about how the Anglo-American elite followed the Great War with a battle of ideas designed to eradicate the enemy, meaning immigrant cultures. He observed "the growing uneasiness of the native-born in the presence of the immigrant from an unconscious strain to a conscious repulsion, the condescending certainty of native superiority into an alarmed proclamation of it, and the native assurance that it cannot be otherwise into a frenzied argument that it must be sheltered to survive."[10] Thus, Norwegian-American leaders realized that the days when they were considered a highly desirable immigrant group had passed, and now they were perceived as just another group of foreigners.

Homeland Norwegians likewise rushed to the defense of Norwegian Americans. In an article from early 1919, Thoralv Klaveness argued that Yankee Americans had benefited from all immigrants but especially from Norwegian Americans. He pointed out how Norwegians had first arrived in America nearly a century ago, willing to tame the American frontier filled with Indians, bison, and grasshoppers. States along the northern tier, from Illinois to Washington, had prospered in large part because of the economic value added by hardworking Norwegians. According to Klaveness, the economic value of Norwegians in America was worth ten times the national wealth of Norway. Moreover, Norwegians had been loyal to their new land so he was puzzled as to why America would now want to severely limit the numbers of immigrant Norwegians. After all, he reasoned, Norwegians made good citizens because Norway shared similar values. Klaveness even claimed, "Norway was and still is constitutionally a freer land than America."[11]

The years between 1918 and 1925, culminating in the Norwegian-American centennial, must therefore be viewed as part of the struggle by which Norwegian-American leaders reacted against Anglo-American conformity and attempted to once again lay claim to their group's rightful place within the American cultural sphere. It represented a resurgence of *norskhet* (Norwegianness), an effort to affirm the superiority of Norwegian culture. The circumstances of the era meant that Norwegian-American identity-makers would have to frame their arguments with even greater regard to questions of loyalty to America. Yet it also afforded them the opportunity to once again seek validation for the Norwegian-American identity both in America and in Norway. The increasing ties between the Norwegian-American elite and their counterparts in Norway would also mean that the evolving Norwegian-American identity would be influenced by Norway's evolving national identity.

Refining the Norwegian-American Identity

The emergence of Anglo-centric American nationalism in the years after the Great War required refinements to the Norwegian-American self-image. Although that identity still upheld notions of Norwegian-American superiority, it tended to place increasing emphasis on the characteristics it shared with Anglo-Americans. Realizing that English would undoubtedly gain in use among Norwegian Americans, some within the community hoped that Norwegian language and culture would become a popular area of study in American high schools and universities, especially those located in areas with a high concentration of ethnic Norwegians. For Professor Ole E. Rølvaag of St. Olaf College in Northfield, Minnesota, the emerging study of Norwegian language and culture during the 1920s seemed to confirm this idea.

In 1920, Rølvaag produced a three-volume *Norsk læsebok* (Norwegian reader) that he hoped would be adopted by schools at all levels. The second volume, designed for high schools and colleges, was written in Norwegian with a Norwegian–English lexicon at the end. It contained a number of articles, written by Rølvaag and others, that reinforced the main themes of the Norwegian-American identity.

The first section highlighted the early Norwegian contributions to the foundation of America. Especially prominent was the image of Leif Erikson, who is introduced in a lengthy poem by Sigurd Folkestad. The last stanza of the poem contends that as the first Europeans in America, the Norwegians had earned their place within the cultural landscape of America:

> So now we live with our claim to be first
> We people of Leif Erikson's own descent.
> He kindled for our nation that historical day,

Ole E. Rølvaag, author of Giants in the Earth. The success of the novel, which became a best seller in both Norway and America, pointed to the transnational identity of Norwegians during the 1920s and beyond. Courtesy of St. Olaf College Archives.

The spark that was the birth of our people's saga.
Indeed we approach a million strong,
With a vibrant cultural life that will forever remain,
And just as he was the first to find our land,
So we shall receive the inheritance that our spirit has conquered.[12]

Rølvaag then presented many of the familiar themes of the Norwegian-American identity. After establishing an early Norwegian presence in the New World during the Viking age, he proceeds with the immigration to America. Despite the great hardships facing the Norwegian settlers, they, like the Vikings of old, conquered the "wild and untamed prairie." The ordeal of taming this wild land proved that Norwegian Americans had retained that ruggedness, that physical prowess that set them apart as one of the manly races.[13]

The military service rendered by Norwegian Americans reflected another important theme, but it was updated to include the gallantry of Norwegian Americans during World War I. The author of this section, Carl G. O. Hansen, details the heroic exploits of decorated Norwegian Americans. He notes that of the seventy-eight Americans who received the Congressional Medal of Honor, four were Norwegian. Hansen observes how Norwegian Americans displayed great bravery on the battlefields of France and that the phrase "conspicuous gallantry" seemed to "cling to them like glue." Furthermore, he related that Norwegians had a long record of serving America. "That moving spirit, which today appears in every endeavor among those called Norwegians, especially in people of American origins, becomes most manifest during wartime service to the cause of the United States."[14]

The *Norsk læsebok* also touched on the solid religious character of Norwegian Americans. Peder Tangjerd makes a comparison between the biblical Abraham's search for Canaan and the journey by Norwegian immigrants across the Atlantic during the nineteenth century. The Norwegians were "a 'godly people' who took the Promised Land into their possession." Moreover, realized Tangjerd, the Norwegians had "inherited a wealth that was more valuable than gold. For the aforementioned inheritance, both the national and especially the spiritual, was of immeasurable value." And finally he claims, "The cornerstone for our church in America, both spiritually and financially, has come from Norway."[15]

In keeping with the progressive self-image of Norwegian Americans,

Rølvaag authored the final section, "Skogen som klædde fjeldet" (The Forest That Clothed the Mountain). The heading was taken from Bjørnson's novel *Arne* and was a symbol of humankind's age-long struggle to give meaning and beauty to life.[16] He observes how the nearly one million Norwegian Americans had "clothed the mountain that was America." The analogy suggests that America was great, like a gigantic yet bare mountain. But what really gave the mountain its character, its clothes, were the contributions of those who worked hard to transform the naked mountain into its lush present-day landscape. The alchemy that led to this wonderful transformation owed its success to the Norwegian-American race, which was loyal to its civic American duty, its Lutheran faith, and its Norwegian heritage, which was shared with the Anglo-Americans:

> And this family is likewise the people of Vesterheim [the Old Norse name for America], the Norwegian Americans. This is yours and my people in the narrowest sense, for we have a common origin. And the blood we share ties us together in a great family. And not just the blood, but also our histories and our cultures bind us together. We all have the shared ethnic culture and family culture, and that is different from all the other Americans. Everything great and noble that our people throughout the ages have built up can be traced to our heritage, and it is that heritage that we who are the inheritors must demand to be preserved. That heritage makes us brothers. And no other than precisely the heritage we have can be given to our glorious land. It must be further understood that we naturally are all Americans, politically and civically—wholly and entirely American. Our destiny is the nation's. We are therefore Americans. But our ancestry, our ethnicity, is Norwegian. Hence, by blood, by history, and by cultural bonds are you and I forever linked to the Norwegian family of peoples.[17]

One other aspect of Rølvaag's narrative bears mention. On several occasions, he uses the term "we Americans of Norwegian ancestry" rather than Norwegian Americans. Although a subtle change, it signaled erosion in the use of the prevailing term "Norwegian American." The most obvious cause was the rising proportion of the American-born generation in relation to the Norwegian-born. The group itself was being transformed as time passed. The change reflected a growing realization among ethnic leaders that their Norwegian compatriots were becoming Americans whose ethnicity was Norwegian.

Members of the Norwegian-American press likewise recognized the shift that was taking place. A 1921 volume, *Norwegian Immigrant Contributions to America's Making*, sought to present the progressive contributions of Norwegian Americans in the context of increasing assimilation. The editor of the volume, Harry Sundby-Hansen, and the other contributors tended to have a more liberal orientation than that of more conservative preservationists like Ager and Rølvaag. However, this did not mean that they were opposed to efforts to promote a highly positive Norwegian-American self-image. While they acknowledged that English would be the language of Norwegians in the future, they still believed it feasible to promote interest in the study of Norwegian culture and immigrant contributions. Such studies would attract not only Americans of Norwegian ancestry but other Americans as well.

In the introduction, Sundby-Hansen noted that Norwegian Americans were "a substantial part of the American people, which by loyalty and demonstrated achievements in material and cultural advancement, has earned the right to be Americans." He also hoped that Anglo-Americans would recognize the accomplishments of Norwegian Americans: "It is hoped, however, that this modest effort in the treatment of an important subject will serve to stimulate an interest in the study of the material and intellectual part Norwegian immigrants and their descendants have played in the upbuilding of America."[18] In effect, Sundby-Hansen was arguing for recognition of the legacy of Norwegian Americans in the story of America.

Like other progressive interpretations of the Norwegian-American identity, the volume explained in detail the immense contributions made by Norwegian Americans. A subtle shift can be detected, however, for it stresses how modern-day Norway had provided highly skilled immigrants who had greatly enriched America. This new emphasis on the progressive rather than the romanticized Norway coincided with the breakthrough period of Norway's industrialization, which occurred largely between the years 1900 to 1940. As Sundby-Hansen writes, "Norway has not only given America a greater number of her people than any other sovereign nation on earth, but she has also given this country proportionately a greater number of technically educated men than any other country."[19]

Another theme of *Norwegian Immigrant Contributions* was the idea that Norwegian Americans served as a bulwark in defending American values against the onslaught of dangerous newcomers from southern and eastern Europe. In the chapter dealing with Norwegian-American literature, Julius E. Olson argued, "Norwegian churches, schools, press, and other activities of allied character have not been antagonistic to republican institutions and a stable state of society in this country." Furthermore, Olson cites a recent study on the question that demonstrates that Norwegian-American institutions, "instead of being a menace to our state, form one of the main safe-guards of this country against the dangers accompanying the large influx of people of foreign nationality."[20] It is worth noting that Norwegian-American leaders could now view themselves as defenders of American values, especially against foreign peoples. They viewed themselves as Americans, even if many of their compatriots had only recently come ashore.

There was also recognition of the need to reorient the Norwegian-American identity in the homeland. Writing in late 1918, Sigurd Folkestad, the secretary of Nordmands-Forbundet, observed how Norwegian immigration had first experienced a colonization stage, in which Norwegian communities in America were communities of people who shared the cultural values of Norway. Later, the pattern shifted to the settlement stage, in which Norwegians and their descendants came to see themselves increasingly as Americans who were nonetheless proud of their Norwegian heritage. However, these settler Norwegians never intended to return to Norway, for America was their home. Ironically, noted Folkestad, their love of Norway was bound to the past, to an idealized and romanticized image of the homeland that no longer existed. Therefore, he argued, the key was to promote a realization that Norway was no longer a "poor and uncultured land, but that its schools and institutions can be said to be among the best in the world and that the Norwegian people are the world's model of democracy."[21]

The dilemma facing Norwegian-American leaders who did not seek to resist the unavoidable adoption of English by Norwegians was how to create a viable self-image that would not completely obliterate the Norwegian influence. In this regard they were not strict adherents of Ager's more conservative preservationist model. Simply stated, the conservatives feared that if the Norwegian language died off in America, the Norwegian-American culture would then by definition no longer exist. What Sundby-Hansen and his fellow contributors aimed for was a model that would foster promotion of an *American-Norwegian ideal*, in which Anglo-American leaders would recognize the unique *racial, civic,* and *religious* contributions made by Norwegians to America. In addition, enlightened Anglo-American leaders would make the Norwegian-American contribution a significant component of the dominant Anglo-American hegemonic model. Hence, the dominant ideology of America would soon become an Anglo-Norwegian racial identity.

One can discern this argument in the chapter on "Church and Education." Its author, Gisle Bothne, professor of Scandinavian studies at the University of Minnesota, called for the widespread study of Norwegian-American history and culture. He argues that the promotion of Norwegian-American studies would enrich and preserve the true American identity:

> The emigration from Norway to America had been very great, greater proportionately than from any other independent nation in Europe. To transplant this nation to American soil without losing the best traits of their character, to make it a fully harmonious part of our American people so as to enrich and strengthen it, has, as it should be, been the general aim and the only justification of the American institutions established by the Norwegian contingent of our people.... The higher institutions of learning established by Americans of Norwegian birth or ancestry owe it to the people whose money has built these schools and who have done their share in building America by conquering the wilderness, by clearing and cultivating the land, to give in the curricula a prominent place to the intelligent and intensive study of Norwegian literature and history. They owe it to themselves as American institutions to hit back and hit back hard, at the ignorance and arrogance which dare to call everything "foreign" that does not conform with the narrowest conception of Americanism. They owe it, in true understanding of the idea underlying the Norwegian-American institutions of learning, to our glorious America which they want to make more glorious and rich in good things by doing their share, by contributing what the Norwegian element had that is worth while to the sum total of America's spiritual, intellectual and moral values.[22]

This change in emphasis from a Norwegian-American identity to an American-Norwegian identity was not confined to only the Norwegians in America. As H. Arnold Barton mentions in his study on the evolving identity of Swedes in America, similar pressures to conform in the postwar years led to an emphasis on an American-Swedish identity rather than the older Swedish-American. Many of their ethnic institutions, such as the American Swedish Historical Museum or the American Swedish Institute, reflected this change in emphasis in the ordering of their names and the idea of promoting the study of Swedish culture and history in America.[23]

By 1922, the Norwegian-American identity attained its most comprehensive summation with a series of essays authored by Rølvaag. *Omkring fædrearven* (Concerning Our Heritage) articulated the major themes of the latter-day Norwegian-American identity. He acknowledged that the inevitable assimilation of the Norwegian people and their wholesale conversion to English could not be prevented. He further observed, "Literature written in English will blossom among us, and will be so beautiful and truthful that it will be a joy and a benefit to mankind. However, this will happen only if our national characteristics are not erased too soon."[24] Here Rølvaag argues for the preservation of Norwegian language and culture owing to the exceptional value that it contributes to America. Assimilation should be postponed as long as possible to ensure that Norwegian racial characteristics could be as fully absorbed as possible within the larger American culture.

Rølvaag identifies seven main characteristics of Norwegian Americans. The first is an *idealistic view of nature,* which fosters among them a feeling of place. As such, they love the places where they live. A second, closely related trait was the Norwegian *love of home.* In America, this trait meant that Norwegian Americans desired to own land and houses, which well equipped them for their role as pioneers on the frontier.[25]

He then proceeds to identify traits that had been suggested previously by other Norwegian-American leaders. Owing to their Viking heritage, Norwegians had an *innate sense of freedom* and an inherent distrust of aristocratic forms of power. Rølvaag maintained that Norwegian Americans served as guarantors and defenders of American liberty: "One of the strongest brakes to this trend [toward American decline] is a strong, enlightened population of farmers with the democratic-aristocratic view of ownership, family, and home that has characterized the best of the Norwegian farming population."[26]

Norwegian Americans had *respect for the law of the land.* Rølvaag noted that wherever "our Viking ancestors" settled they organized themselves in ways that promoted law and order. He further stated that America had a higher rate of criminal activity than any other civilized country and that the preservation of Norwegian culture might serve to counter this dangerous trend. "Those who do not care about preserving our national [American] heritage better take note of this and consider their choice of words more carefully when they speak out against the usefulness of the Norwegian heritage for America."[27]

Norwegian culture also displayed a *desire for knowledge and appreciation for art*. On higher education, he mentions, "Of all the ethnic groups in the United States, we do more for higher education in proportion to our numbers than any other group in the country." With pride, he pointed out the cultural achievements of Norway, and noted that America, despite a population of 100 million, had not produced a single great writer, while Norway, with its tiny population, had produced great writers such as Bjørnson, Ibsen, and Hamsun. "No other nation in proportion to its population has made such an impact on world culture in the area of the arts as the small country of Norway has done in the last hundred years."[28]

Norwegians were *strongly inclined toward religion,* according to Rølvaag, arguing that Norwegian children encounter God everywhere, in the home and in school as well as in church. Moreover, he contended, "Norwegians have a *distinctly personal* relationship to God," and it is this trait that characterizes Norwegian Christianity. This trait makes Norwegians well suited to being good Americans. "This is closely related to our national character, with its focus on individualism and personal freedom. Norwegian Lutheranism suits our national character and our national character suits it."[29]

The seventh and most essential trait of the Norwegian-American self-image, Rølvaag stipulates, a trait present from Viking times, was that Norwegian societies had always striven to provide the greatest possible *freedom for the individual*. He stresses that this idea was at the core of the American ideal and that the history of the Norwegian people revealed this shared principle. And like other Norwegian-American leaders, Rølvaag reiterates the Norwegian origins of American values: "It is even possible that this ideal and many of America's free institutions are actually inherited from ancient Norwegian traditions, that they have their origins in Norway."[30]

While Rølvaag could point to the impressive accomplishments of Norwegian Americans, he still had to confront their inevitable assimilation. His effort to promote the study of Norwegian language, history, and culture provided one means of offsetting this loss. However, the possibility remained that Norwegian-American culture would vanish and ethnic contributions would be forgotten as the dominant Anglo-American culture absorbed the English-speaking children of the immigrants. Waldemar Ager had argued that Norwegian culture was superior to Anglo-American culture because the Norwegians were superior in their civic virtues, religious Protestantism, and racial purity. However, he insisted that Norwegian racial contributions could only be realized through the maintenance of the Norwegian language. Trends in the America of the 1920s did not bode well for the long-term survival of the Norwegian language. Rølvaag needed to develop an argument that would maintain the concept of Norwegian racial supremacy—including the future study of Norwegian history and culture in American schools—while still allowing for the eventual use of English.

His solution was to transform the definition of Americanism beyond a set of civic, religious, and racial traits into a definition that equated the essential makeup of Americanism with Norwegian ethnicity. Put more simply, he argued that the Norwegian was an American prior to his emigration to America:

> We have often heard that the Norwegian immigrant, in comparison with other immigrant groups, makes a good American. Everyone seems astonished at how easily and quickly the process of transformation takes place. What people say and write in this regard is correct. However, it would be even more true if they changed the tense of the verb. The Norwegian immigrant doesn't become a good American. He is one already before he emigrates. He was one already in the saga age.... Through countless battles and endless sacrifice we have made progress. And our ancestors have always been among the leaders. The greatest possible freedom under the common law of the land is the social-political ideal they have striven for ever since the dawn of history broke over our people. This passion and drive and will is one of our main character traits. God grant that it will continue to be! Then we will be a blessing for our new country in the days to come. Those who promote our Norwegian heritage and give it to our country in the greatest measure will become the greatest Americans in the future. It will be to our everlasting honor if we can lead in the great march of progress and not hang back with the masses and the stragglers. Here we stand before a seeming paradox: The best Norwegian is the greatest American![31]

Rølvaag's latter-day Viking, placed in the context of the 1920s, had evolved into a latent American hero. Of course, Norwegians were not alone among immigrant groups in their claims as being Americans prior to their arrival, as shown by comparative studies on immigrant identities by Orm Øverland and George M. Stephenson.[32] As previously discussed in chapter 3, what makes the Norwegian case unique was the extent to which they made their clams before a wider American audience than other immigrant groups.

Ole E. Rølvaag deserves much of the credit for disseminating these ideas to the American public. The concept of the latter-day Viking was found in his most famous novel, *Giants in the Earth*. Originally published in Norwegian in 1924 as *I de dage* (In Those Days) and *Riket grundlægges* (Founding the Kingdom), the novel appeared in English in 1927, when it became a sensation in America. The novel traces the tribulations of a Norwegian family as it travels by wagon across the prairie of Minnesota toward their ultimate destination in Dakota Territory. Traveling through the prairie grass, the wagon caravan evokes an image of a line of ships: "A small caravan was pushing its way through the tall grass. The track that it left behind was like the wake of a boat—except that instead of widening out astern it closed in again." The imagery implies that the immigrants were like Vikings on the prairie.[33]

In their 1939 biography of Rølvaag, Theodore Jorgenson and Nora O. Solum describe this metaphor in a chapter that showcases his attempt to depict Norwegian immigrants as latter-day Vikings. The authors note that the main character, Per Hansa, represents this twentieth-century Norwegian archetype, "the Viking of the prairie," whose "Viking heart is in this book; there it will beat through the ages."[34]

Yet the greater lesson to be learned from Rølvaag's latter-day Vikings is the peril of abandoning one's cultural roots. Per Hansa is tempted by American wealth if he will only "sell out" his Norwegian heritage. In the end, a horrific snowstorm claims his life. The one who survives, his wife, Beret—although ostensibly the frail one—is loyal to her Norwegian heritage, and it is she who perseveres the longest. In *Peder Victorious* and *Their Fathers' God*, sequels to *Giants in the Earth*, the author admonishes Norwegians to preserve their heritage for as long as possible, for it provides the best chance of survival in America. Beret's concern for ethics and religion, the soul, proves stronger than Per Hansa's preoccupation with the materialism of the future.[35]

Other Norwegian-American image-makers linked the Viking spirit with a strong devotion to Christian ideals. A poem, "The Cross at the Prow," from the 1918 edition of *Jul i Vesterheimen* (Christmas in the Western World), showed how replacing the dragon's head on the prow of a Viking ship with a cross signified how the Norwegians' Viking-age vigor had been adapted to a more modern, Christianizing mission. The text was accompanied by an illustration based on the Viking window, located in the chapel at St. Olaf College. The window depicts a Viking ship sailing across the sea between Norway and America. The homeland is represented by a medieval stave church (a transitional design incorporating Christian and pagan elements), and America—toward which the ship is sailing—is represented by a modern Christian church. As noted by Kristin Ann Risley, the poem and the illustration, contained in an Augsburg Publishing House edition, affirmed that Norwegian Americans were steadfast Christians and latter-day Vikings.[36]

These adjustments to the metaphor of modern Vikings continued into the 1920s. In 1928, Rølvaag rehashed many of his ideas in "The Vikings of the Midwest," which appeared in *American Magazine* and aimed for a wider American audience. He argued for the dedicated study of the Norwegian heritage in America, urging that the group's deeds be recorded before the irreversible process of assimilation erased Norwegian culture entirely. Risley terms Rølvaag's article a plea for the creation of collective memory and a legacy for Norwegian Americans.[37]

In their reaction to the Anglo-American counteroffensive, Norwegian-American identity-makers sought to present their group as allies and defenders of conservative American values. They argued that a long, historical association between Norwegians and English-speaking peoples had produced a set of shared cultural values. Leaders from Rølvaag to Sundby-Hansen promoted the image of Norwegian-Americans as frontline soldiers in the defense of American values, particularly those whom they viewed as swarthy, non-Protestant, and politically radical newcomers. To a large degree, the Norwegian-American leaders were trying to make their group as Anglo-American as possible, thus representing a departure from the advocacy of cultural pluralism. To prevent their group from becoming faceless members of white America, however, the Norwegian-American leaders tried to advance the idea that Norwegian Americans had earned respect from Anglo-America and, therefore, ought to have their ethnic accomplishments become part of the American cultural landscape. This strategy can be seen as part of the process of building *legacy myths* for the Norwegian Americans.

The 1925 Norse-American Centennial

A century after the arrival of the first Norwegian immigrants aboard the *Restaurationen,* the 1925 Norse-American Centennial offered leaders of Norwegian America an opportunity to both challenge Anglo-American superiority and reaffirm the values shared between the two groups. In her study of the Norse-American Centennial, April Rose Schultz contends that the affair was "a dual celebration of Norwegian and American nationalisms" whose organizers "wanted to portray a particular image about the Norwegian Americans—that they had easily become American citizens because, as Norwegians and descendants of Norwegians, they innately possessed American ideals." Moreover, she notes, the organizers of the centennial "constructed an ethnic identity that placed their community at the center of forming a democratic, American society" and that the constructed narrative of their group's history "signified Norwegian-American ethnicity in the 1920s as 'safe' for American politics, business, and culture."[38]

The organizational genesis of the centennial drew on the model of the successful 1914 Eidsvold Constitution celebration in Norway. The *bygdelag* leaders had decided that they should continue to cooperate in organizing future festivals. The joint council of the *bygdelag* reformed in 1917 and passed a resolution in 1920 to organize an immigration centennial celebration with the purpose of launching a Norwegian-American counteroffensive.[39]

Schultz observes that despite the folk connotations of the *bygdelag,* by early 1924 a centennial committee, consisting largely of members of the professional and business classes, had taken on the task of organizing the event. The joint council elected to this committee an elite group, including Gisle Bothne from the University of Minnesota; state representative N. T. Moen as vice president; S. H. Holstad, owner of a coffee company, as managing director; and Knut Gjerset, the curator of the Norwegian pioneer museum in Decorah, Iowa, as chairman of the committee on exhibits. The committee also included Caroline Storlie, a member of several Scandianvian organizations, a member of the Minnesota Democratic Party, and an active member of the National Women's Party. Having constituted itself in July 1924 as the Norse-American Centennial, Inc., the committee worked diligently to promote what Schultz describes as a conservative orientation, one that would protect the Norwegian-American community from nativist attacks and also attract the younger generation of Norwegian Americans who were succumbing to the "individualist" pressures of the emerging consumer culture of 1920s America.[40]

The success of the constructed narrative of the centennial would ultimately depend on the ability of Norwegian-American leaders to get Anglo-American leaders to buy into the concept that Norwegians made good Americans. On February 24, 1925, Congressman Ole J. Kvale of Minnesota delivered a lengthy speech to the U.S. House of Representatives in which he offered a personal invitation to each House member to attend the Norse-American Centennial. Kvale recounted to his colleagues how the historical record of the Norwegian people revealed their long association with the New World, their racial pedigree, and the cultural values they shared with Anglo-America.

He further noted how Norwegian immigrants had become Frenchmen in France, Englishmen in England, and were now Americans in America. "Our people have not built, nor attempted to build, a little Kingdom of Norway on American soil. The immigrants from Norway and their descendants have become as thoroughly and genuinely American as have the immigrants from any other country of Europe, not excepting even England." Yet Kvale observed that Norwegians were not "unmindful of the deeds and the traditions of their forefathers, nor ashamed of... their love and reverence for 'the old country.' Quite the contrary; every Norseman worthy of the name is proud of all the heritage that from his ancestors and their loved little land is his."[41]

These comments reflect the concerns of Norwegian-American leaders in pitching their ethnic identity to Anglo-Americans. If they could secure the participation of important Anglo-American leaders in the Norse-American Centennial, they would gain validation of the Norwegian-American self-image. On the eve of the centennial, a headline in the *Decorah-Posten* announced, "Uncle Sam and Mother Norway Can Be Proud." Kvale played an important role in getting the U.S. Congress to partake in the celebration. An editorial written in *Nordisk Tidende* on June 11, 1925, acknowledged his role in getting Congress to create two commemorative stamps and a silver coin medallion in honor of the occasion. One stamp contained an image of the *Restaurationen,* the other of a Viking ship; the medallion featured a

Viking chieftain setting foot on American soil on one side and a Viking ship on the other side.⁴²

Through the celebration of both American and Norwegian nationalisms, the Norse-American Centennial solicited the involvement of Norwegian Americans, non-Norwegian Americans, and guests from Norway. From June 6 to 9, 1925, in the Twin Cities, the celebration brought together these groups in a symbolic affirmation of the Norwegian-American identity. This intersection created a context in which the centennial organizers could achieve validation of the Norwegian-American self-image by wrapping it in the safe and acceptable language of Americanism. At the opening ceremony, five hundred Norwegian-American schoolchildren draped in red, white, and blue capes stood arranged as the flag of Norway. They sang Norway's national anthem and then transformed themselves into the Star-Spangled Banner as they broke into America's national anthem. This living flag served to remind the audience of the ease with which Norwegian immigrants became solid American citizens.⁴³

This living Norwegian flag, composed of children wearing the colors of Norway's flag (red, white, and blue), would transform into an American flag, thus revealing how loyalty to Norway did not prevent loyalty to America. Photograph by the K. L. Fenney Company. Courtesy of the Minnesota Historical Society.

On June 8, the featured speaker, President Calvin Coolidge, confirmed the success of this formula in his speech. He distinguished between solid citizens such as the Norwegian Americans and the more "suspect" and "foreign" immigrants. He rejected the nation's current immigration restriction laws because it "puts up bars against some of the most superior races," which included Norwegians. He added:

> The institutions and the manners of democracy came naturally to them. Their glory is all about you, their living and their mighty dead. They have been great soldiers, statesmen, scientists, educators and men of business to the upbuilding of their adopted country. They have been rapidly amalgamated into the body of citizenship, contributing to it many of its best and most characteristic elements. To their adaptability the Nation owes much for its success in the enormous process of assimilation and spiritual unification that has made our Nation what it is and our people what they are.[44]

In the course of his speech Coolidge praised Norwegian contributions to American life and even acknowledged that Leif Erikson discovered America long before Columbus. A local journalist reported the reaction of the seventy-five thousand listeners: "The great roar that rose from Nordic throats to Thor and Odin above the lowering gray clouds told that the pride of the race had been touched." The Norwegian-language press reacted enthusiastically. Calling it the "Norwegian People's Greatest Day," the *Decorah-Posten* proclaimed, "The nation's President salutes and pays homage to the Norwegian and American flags as they wave side by side."[45]

The *Decorah-Posten* used the president's speech to denote the convergence of the twin nationalisms while still extolling the superiority of the Norwegian people:

> There blazed great pride in the eyes of every woman and man who possessed even a few drops of Norwegian blood in their veins. They went confidently and proudly; something they had every right to do. They looked upon the American flag with reverence in their gazes and gratitude in their hearts for the Norwegian colors, which have given them strength and the noble spirit to salute the Stars and Stripes. It also provided them with the conviction to believe that they are the best citizens in this land. There is also

something else that the Norwegian-American people have learned this day, something they perhaps have not noticed before. This realization has escaped in particular those born in this country: That we Norwegian people, wherever we eventually settle and live, become recognized as one of the greatest peoples in the world, yes even the greatest of all, not just as the people of God's Mammon, but in all things cultural as well.[46]

The Norse-American Centennial also relied on visual displays to convey this message. Two parades, one starting in Minneapolis and the other in St. Paul, marched toward each other, meeting at the Minnesota State Fairgrounds in the center. In this respect, it matched the pattern of the earlier 1914 Eidsvold Celebration. However, this time the celebration was a Norwegian-American occasion rather than a Norwegian national one. The parade route featured numerous Norwegian and American flags draped side by side by local businesses. Slogans in Norwegian, including *velkommen* (welcome) greeted those attending the celebration.

The two parades converged at the fairgrounds for the crowning event: *The Pageant of the Northmen*. It presented the story of the Norwegian immigrants by centering on the life of Colonel Hans Christian Heg, the Norwegian-American Civil War hero and martyr. In the 1830s, Heg as a young boy listened to family stories about Norway's glorious past. These stories illustrated the ties between the greatness of Norway's Viking age and the robust character found in the common folk who would immigrate to America. Vikings, trolls, and folk dancers appeared on the stage. The pageant highlighted Leif Erikson's discovery of the New World and the Viking king St. Olaf, who established Christianity in Norway.

As the pageant moved to the nineteenth century, it reminded the audience of the heroic exploits of Cleng Peerson, the early slooper immigrants, and more commonplace heroes such as ministers, soldiers, and pioneers. It contained a fictional but peaceful encounter between Norwegians and Native Americans, reflecting the notion that Norwegians were agents of civilization. Then the pageant finally focused on Heg's life, including his opposition to slavery. The pageant concluded with the story of Heg's Civil War service and death at Chickamauga. The poignant death scene showed President Lincoln and General Grant standing behind Heg's funeral bier.

The culminating scenes of the pageant featured a minister, a choir, and a confirmation class. As they retreated to the back of the stage, other groups

Colonel Hans Christian Heg, who died in 1862 serving for the Union in the Civil War, symbolized the sacrifices made by Norwegians to the building of America. In time, he became a transatlantic symbol of the greater Norway vision. Courtesy of the National Library of Norway, Norwegian-American Collection.

joined them in succession, including Norwegian-Americans in business, art and literature, industry and commerce, World War I soldiers, Red Cross nurses, and women war workers. They remained for the final scene in which a statue of Heg was unveiled. A speaker reminded the audience that Heg "proved himself all is highest in the citizen of a republic and who gave his life in battle for his adopted country." The pageant manuscript stated that ancient kings and Vikings appeared "as in a dream," joined by sturdy immigrants, slaves, soldiers, and spirits—all "who had an influence upon the colonel's life."[47]

According to Schultz, the 1925 Norse-American Centennial reflected the sentiments of the Progressive Era in that it emphasized the easy assimilation of the Norwegians. The organizers, she notes, hoped to preserve their positions within an ethnic community without posing a threat to American culture. In this context, the centennial was a conservative endeavor. However, she also observes how the narrative of the centennial contained an inherent challenge to Anglo-American superiority that delivered a Janus-faced message: it was both accommodationist and resistant.[48]

The most compelling example was Waldemar Ager's essay in the official program. Ager stressed that peculiarity and difference, rather than accommodation, should be the real message of the Norse-American Centennial. It is significant that Ager's was the only essay printed in Norwegian and that it was the prize-winning essay. His solution to the evils of assimilation was that Norwegian Americans should continue "to honor their fathers." He noted further that "our constitution and our institutions" could not be guaranteed without a knowledge of the group's past. "We who have learned to respect and honor our fathers will not surrender what our fathers, with blood, sweat, and brains have built. The father's flag becomes their flag and the father's beliefs theirs." Ole E. Rølvaag echoed Ager's sentiments in his speech at the centennial.[49]

Professor Olaf M. Norlie, whose essay won second prize, also challenged Anglo-American superiority. He accused Americans of British ancestry of ignorance, for they "do not seem to know, or want to know, that Norwegians are of their race, or that they have as good a right to be called Americans as anybody else, or that they are entitled to the same opportunities as their Anglo-Saxon brothers. The Centennial ought to secure from these good neighbors a more just recognition of what the Norwegian really is."[50]

In connection with the centennial, the Norwegian Lutheran Church commissioned Norlie to publish his *History of the Norwegian People in America* (1925) in which he recounted the standard themes of the Norwegian-American self-image. Norlie used the opportunity to state his case for Norwegian-American superiority:

> Ethnographically, the Norwegians are Teutons, the most typical of Teutons. Physically, they are tall and lank, healthy and hardy, a vigorous, handsome race. Intellectually, they are like other Teutons, highly endowed with a boundless capacity for civilization. Morally, they are a clean, chaste race with the highest standards and most tender conscience. Religiously, they are God-fearing—in olden days, according to their Norse mythology, they had the highest type of natural religion recorded; and in our day, according to the Lutheran faith, the purest type of Christianity ever formulated. Socially, they are a friendly, hospitable, thrifty, home-loving race, reverencing womanhood and respecting conjugal ties. Industrially, they love to work at any honest calling.... Politically, they are independent and democratic, anxious to make their own laws and willing to abide by them, loyal to their chosen rulers and magistrates, patriotically living for their country in times of peace and dying for it in times of war. Linguistically, they are Teutons of the purest type, and their written language as well as its dialects are clear, strong, beautiful, extremely simple, yet fully adequate to express the widest range of thought and feeling. Culturally, they have from the dawn of their history been far advanced in civilization and have contributed liberally to art, science and literature, affecting the spiritual uplift and the material progress of the world.[51]

The Norse-American Centennial, furthermore, sought to impress homeland Norwegians. An April 17, 1925, editorial from *Decorah-Posten*, "Norge og vi" (Norway and We), acknowledged the success of Norway in fashioning a new national consciousness. The editorial claimed that the greatness of the new Norway should be viewed as "two parts of the Norwegian heritage, on each side of the Atlantic."

Other Norwegian-American papers proclaimed the stunning success of the centennial. *Minneapolis Daglig Tidende* pointed to the tremendous participation from homeland Norwegians, including representatives of

Norway's parliament, its government, the university, churches, the press, literature, agriculture, industry, and other institutions. The paper commented on how these homeland Norwegians had expressed "feelings of gratitude and joy towards us." Observing that the four-day event had attracted over two hundred thousand visitors, *Nordisk Tidende* stated that the tens of thousands of homeland Norwegians in attendance were now connected to the experiences of Norwegian immigrants. In a similar vein, it quoted the speech of Carl J. Hambro, president of Norway's parliament, and the reaction of one member of the American press, who concluded that Hambro's speech was "paving the way for ever closer friendship between the people of Norway and those of Minneapolis and the Northwest."[52]

The Norwegian-American press also pointed out how well the centennial was received in Norway's papers. *Aftenposten* observed that President Coolidge's speech was a historic event and a source of great pride for Americans of Norwegian descent and for every Norwegian. It further noted that Coolidge's "unqualified recognition of Leif Eriksson as the discoverer of America would become noticed by the historians in all the lands." *Handels og Sjøfartstidende* (Business and Shipping Times) remarked that the president's speech would lead to "belief and confidence in the Norwegian people and the abilities of Norwegians in all lands."[53] Approval from Norway further heightened the sense among Norwegian Americans that they had remained enduringly loyal to the culture of the homeland.

Absalom Taranger, a Norwegian historian, attended the Norse-American Centennial and wrote a book, *Inntrykk fra Amerka* (Impressions from America), which he published in 1927. The author had been invited as a guest of the Nordhordalland *bygdelag*. Observing that Norwegians had been colonists in the New World since Viking times, Taranger viewed positively the contributions of his countrymen to America's development. Their "Norge I Amerika" (Norway in America), he observes, reflects that "from the first," the Norwegians in America have "maintained their affections to the motherland and to the heritage of their fathers."[54]

The author also attended a meeting of the Norwegian Lutheran Church Council, which took place in the Twin Cities from June 10 to 14, 1925. He cites how Bishop Johan Lunde from Norway, an attendee of the centennial, addressed the Church Council and observed, "These [Norwegian-American] Churches are full of people," unlike similar Lutheran churches in Norway. Another Norwegian speaker, Hans Seland, a representative of Norway's Agrarian party, compared favorably the church-going regularity of Norwegian Americans, which contrasted greatly with Norway's labor classes, whose "Labor Party took its orders from Moscow." Earlier Norwegian visitors to America, such as Thoralv Klaveness and Christian Gierløff, had made similar observations, perceiving in the stalwart Norwegian-American farmer what they saw as true, time-honored Norwegian qualities, as opposed to their countrymen at home, especially the urban working classes. These visitors in particular praised the immigrants' proud self-reliance and capacity for hard work.[55] Thus, the Norwegian-American self-image served as an idealized standard for Norwegian elites often frustrated by developments in the homeland.

Although the largest celebration of the century of Norwegian immigration took place in the Twin Cities, it was not the only major celebration that year. The Norwegian-American Centennial Festival was held in Chicago on June 28, 1925. During the afternoon portion of the celebration, a crowd of six thousand gathered at the Municipal Pier for a program of music and speeches. The featured speaker, Bishop Johan P. Lunde of Norway, affirmed the link between Norwegian America and the homeland. He mentioned how he had found the Norwegian Americans to be highly regarded citizens in the new land and that they "had not withered away while longing for the homeland, but instead had directed themselves to accomplishing great deeds."[56]

The second half of the Chicago centennial involved a banquet at the Chicago Auditorium—filled to the last place—in the evening. The featured speaker, Congressman Ole J. Kvale of Minnesota, took the opportunity to reiterate the familiar themes of the Norwegian-American identity, especially his tribute to the immigrant pioneers, among "the noblest and most valuable citizens." It was these nameless heroes, he noted, the men and women who did not hold any official positions in either church or state, who "had led inspired lives." Moreover, Kvale assumed the voice of Norwegian Americans, stating that "[we] loved the land in which we were born, and that we hope to maintain its best traditions."[57]

On the same day nearly ten thousand people rallied to the Norse-American Centennial of the Pacific Northwest in Seattle. Highlighting the celebration was the Leiv Eiriksson aar 1000 (Leif Erikson 1,000 Years) parade, which the local Leif Eiriksson Lodge of the Sons of Norway had organized. Involving one thousand participants, the parade marched twice around the field of the local stadium and focused on such familiar themes as the sloopers with Cleng Peerson in the lead, followed by stout Norwegian pioneers in their prairie schooners, and then Norwegians of various occupations such as fishermen, miners, and others. Naturally, the parade paid tribute to Colonel Heg and the Fifteenth Wisconsin Regiment, which was followed by floats commemorating Norwegian-American churches, schools, newspapers, hospitals, orphanages, and elder-care homes. There was also the customary array of music, art, and literature with Norwegian-Americans dressed in the traditional costumes of their ancestral regions in Norway.[58]

Both official Norway and America were represented at the Seattle celebration. Minister Wilhelm Morgenstierne read the official greeting from Norway's government while pianist Signe Lunde read a greeting from Norway's women, which invoked the image of Gudrid, the wife of one of the first Norwegian settlers in the New World. President Coolidge sent a telegram greeting the Norwegian Americans, who from the first had been "among the leaders in the march towards the west." It should be noted that Norway's consul in Seattle, Thomas H. Kolderup, read the president's telegram and had served as the president of the local organizing committee for the centennial. Following several more greetings, the Luther College Band and then the Kystens norske Sangerforbund (The Coast's Norwegian Singing Association) entertained the audience with music and song. Senator Peter Norbeck of South Dakota, whose ancestry was Norwegian, gave the keynote address in which he spoke about the life and work of Norwegian ancestors on both sides of the Atlantic, about the need for Norwegian Americans to honor the memory of their ancestral fathers, and the need for the modern-day children of the immigrants to strive to be their best as their pioneering ancestors had done. He concluded his speech with a stirring crescendo: "We love Norway, we cannot forget that our ancestors lie in its meager soil, but we acknowledge only one master: America!"[59]

The Norse-American Centennial of Illinois, held in Ottawa, Illinois, on September 6 and 7, 1925, offered Norwegian-American leaders an additional opportunity to promote their group's self-image. Around three thousand people attended the festival and *Minneapolis Daglig Tidende* observed that many were likely descendants of the original settlers to the Fox River community in northern Illinois. The Illinois centennial emphasized the fact that the Fox River settlement was the oldest surviving Norwegian colony. Unlike the more secular urban celebrations, the Ottawa one was more religious and featured several prominent Norwegian Lutheran pastors from small towns in Illinois, Wisconsin, and Minnesota as well as churches in Chicago and Minneapolis.[60]

As might be expected, the Ottawa celebration highlighted the achievements of the Norwegians as pioneers and contributors to civilization. Olaf M. Norlie, who figured prominently in the official program of the Illinois centennial, wrote, "The Norwegians in America, like their brothers in the Old Country, have enriched the world by their notable discoveries and inventions, their systems and applications." Similarly, Mrs. Manley L. Fosteen of Minneapolis, a daughter of one of the original Fox River settlers, paid tribute to the contributions of Norwegians in the Middle Ages in the fields of shipping, business, statecraft, literature, and the arts. She was impressed by their patriotism and related the fact that the original sloopers had departed from Norway on the Fourth of July, a sign that they intended to be "loyal American citizens." She further reflected on how Norwegians had sacrificed their lives in service to America from the Revolutionary War to present times. And finally, she concluded that no greater tribute to the saga of the Norwegians in the New World could be found than that given in the speech of President Coolidge at the Norse-American Centennial in the Twin Cities, which she had witnessed.[61]

In New York, the Norwegian-American Centennial, 1825–1925, was held from October 9 to 11, 1925. The official program featured on its cover a painting by Dwight Franklin, *The Vikings,* which showed a Viking dragon ship with a standing chieftain at the helm. In a short article contained in the official program, Rasmus B. Anderson urged Norwegians to promote "the great and good Norwegian character" and "to transfer this same spirit to the entire American people, bringing the distinctive, impressive Norwegian spirit into the consciousness of the American people."[62]

According to *Nordisk Tidende,* the New York centennial centered on three highly successful events. On Friday, October 9, the Academy of Music was the site for a performance involving the New York Philharmonic Orchestra under the direction of Ole Windingstad and accompanied by the opera singer Borgny Hammer. As expected, the performance consisted of several Norwegian compositions. The next day, Saturday, October 10, the centennial observers gathered at the New York Armory to watch Norwegian folk dancers, reenactments of historical situations, gymnastic exercises, and Norwegian songs offered by the various Norwegian-

American male choirs. Gracing the event were the Norwegian minister Helmer Bryn and the president of the upper chamber of Norway's parliament, Carl Wilhelm Wefring, who both delivered speeches. The centennial concluded on Sunday, October 11, with a patriotic celebration at the Armory of the Seventy-first Regiment, which was fitting since many Norwegian Americans had served in the regiment. The highlight of the armory ceremony was a speech delivered by the famous Norwegian explorer Roald Amundsen. That same day Bishop J. C. Petersen of Norway officiated a religious service at the Academy of Music before an assembly of three thousand. The finale of the centennial was a banquet held at the St. George's Hotel before a gathering of one thousand.[63]

The presence of these luminaries from Norway strengthened the idea that Norwegian Americans had remained loyal to Norway and were participating in a celebration of Norway's nationalism as well as that of Norwegian America. Bishop Petersen, for instance, stated that the achievements of Norwegian Americans, and their deep religious and moral values, had made Norway "greater and richer... at home and abroad." At the armory ceremony, General Consul Hans Fay introduced the Arctic explorer Amundsen, comparing his modern-day exploits to those of Leif Erikson. In his own remarks, Amundsen noted how Norwegians, despite coming from a small land, had succeeded beyond expectation in helping to build the world's greatest nation. He also expressed how many of his expeditions would not have been possible without "the moral and financial support of Norwegians on both sides of the Atlantic."[64]

At the same ceremony Minister Bryn offered ample evidence that Norway's monarch and government had given their endorsement to the Norwegian-American self-image. He spoke highly of the "good, favorable, and sound conditions [Norwegian Americans were] obtaining here, and it is natural that the Norwegian government looks with favor on immigration to this country as long as Norway cannot keep all her children at home." During his speech he read the official greetings from King Haakon VII who was proud of what "Norwegians have achieved in the new land." Next, Bryn referred to Prime Minister Johan Ludvig Mowinckel who had noted "the love for Norway that the emigrants have made on this day to such a robust degree and the appreciation for the great respect that the emigrants have been capable of obtaining for themselves in that foreign land. With their diligence, trustworthiness, and abilities they have cast their brilliance over Norway's name, and the Motherland is deeply grateful for it."[65]

These other celebrations offered additional opportunities for homeland Norwegians to comment on the position of their Norwegian-American cousins. Wilhelm Morgenstierne, Norway's chief consul to America, gave an address at the Norse-American Centennial of the Pacific Northwest held in Seattle. He invoked the image of Norwegians as pioneers of the frontier, noting how Norwegians had contributed greatly to this "incessant march to the West." Furthermore, he stressed how the accomplishments of Norwegian-Americans were a great source of pride for all Norwegians and that they had preserved the values of their heritage. The official handbook of the New York centennial, meanwhile, offered Norway's prime minister, Johan Ludwig Mowinckel, an additional opportunity to praise Norwegian-Americans: "The memory of the first Norwegian immigrants and what they and their descendants have achieved through their pioneering work, has brought Norwegians throughout the entire world to realize how strong are the bonds that bind them together." In the same work, the Norwegian author Johan Bojer commented that Norway owed much to Norwegian-Americans. "Our marshes, waterfalls, our tempo of work and our economy are derived from the Norwegian American—perhaps above all our parliament. Here is the place, here are the possibilities, here is our greatest loss."[66]

The Norse-American centennial celebrations coincided with a steep decline in the rate of emigration from Norway, which no longer posed the threat it once had to Norway. Thus, during the 1920s, homeland Norwegians could view the accomplishments of Norwegian immigrants as evidence of the superior virtues of Norwegian nationhood.

On the eve of the Norse-American Centennial held in Minneapolis–St. Paul, *Aftenposten* ran a long article titled "Norge i Amerika" (Norway in America), which gave an overview of Norwegian-American history from Leif Erikson to the centennial. The paper noted how the "over 2 million persons of unmixed Norwegian ancestry in the U.S.A. . . . have an [economic] value 4 times as great as Norway." *Aftenposten* noted further, "It makes us proud here in the homeland to know that so many of our countrymen have achieved high standing and a good home over there." The paper concluded, "These new citizens of the great land have not forgotten the little land of their birth."[67]

Nationen (The Nation) offered similar sentiments in the context of the centennial: "Through their labors and the accomplishments of their descendants, our people have earned themselves a great star among the various nations of their new fatherland." The paper also observed how "from the land's [Norway's] earliest history to the present day, the spirit... of the Norwegians has made the Norwegian people a healthy and vibrant nation that has spread its reputation worldwide. And that spirit has attained for them considerable influence in other lands, which instills respect and provides the reason for their feelings of great pride."[68]

As part of the Norse-American Centennial, a corresponding celebration at Stavangèr, Norway, the original departure site for the sloopers, took place to celebrate the emigrants' legacy. In its Norwegian context, the event was in honor of the founding of the city of Stavanger some nine centuries earlier, and it featured an appearance by King Haakon VII of Norway and an address by the American minister to Norway, Laurits S. Swenson. In his remarks, Swenson mentioned that "Norwegians belong to the land's [America's] best and most worthy citizens. Their greatest legacy is their work in building churches." Pastor Frederick Ring, a Norwegian-American Methodist, wrote an account of his attendance at the centennial celebration in Norway. In a conversation he had with King Haakon VII, Ring noted how proud the monarch was of the emigrated Norwegians. "I am proud of the emigrated Norway, for the way it has presented itself and worked itself up in the New World. It has in all honesty brought our beloved Norway great acclaim, which makes us all very delighted."[69]

Other influential Norwegians saw in Norwegian emigration to America the proof of Norway's real greatness. Carl J. Hambro, a member of Norway's parliament and a leader in Nordmands-Forbundet, opined that the Norwegian-American century was the greatest in Norway's history. "We celebrate the Centennial of the journey that opened the greatest Viking expedition our race knows, the first of the expeditions that let us claim a larger land than Northumberland and Normandy, than Iceland and the Norwegian islands and the Irish coasts under Norwegian ploughs." Wilhelm Morgenstierne, stationed with the Norwegian consulate in Washington, D.C., posited similar ideas: "Of primary significance is the consciousness concerning the place our compatriots have won for themselves in the New World and their contributions in the development of the world's greatest republic." Like Hambro, Morgenstierne used allusions to the modern Norwegian saga: "And I will just say that our people's journey to the west in these hundred years, everything that signifies the great Norwegian America of today; it cannot be denied that it is the most powerful factor in the saga of our people, which in reality it truly is."[70]

The success of the Norse-American Centennial served to proclaim the greatness of Norwegian America. Likewise, the success of the immigrants bolstered Norway's own national self-image; the modern immigrants represented Norway's greatest colonists. In addition, the centennial also brought forth the idea that the Norwegian American incorporated the best traits of Norway and America. Morgenstierne understood this concept, which he attempted to summarize in an article in *Normands-Forbundet*:

> The American of Norwegian ancestry, who is lucky enough to be aware of his father's heritage from the old country—love of nature and the fantastic, the mind's depth and dignity—that is the gift of the Norwegian peasant to the people, which is simultaneously characterized by the most valuable American traits: optimism, enthusiasm, a bright mind, helpfulness and the true democratic sociability, they appear to me as some of the most attractive human types one in general can ever meet.[71]

Morgenstierne's comments reflected the way many Norwegians in America came to view themselves during the 1920s. Historian John Jenswold observed how this change was a result of the tumultuous events of the decade. Norwegians in America had to be especially vigilant in proving their loyalty as Americans, yet they also needed an identity that would allow them to distinguish their unique character with regard to other immigrant groups, whom they often encountered as they moved into suburban communities. The Norwegian-American identity solved this dilemma and allowed its members to remain loyal to what it meant to be Norwegian.[72]

Although the organizers of the Norse-American Centennial sought to fit the Norwegian-American identity within the framework of accommodation with Anglo-American superiority and sought to be acceptable to Anglo-American sensibilities, their narrative concomitantly restated ideas of Norwegian-American superiority in the coded language of pageantry and the ideas surrounding the occasion. As such, the Norse-American Centennial did not represent "the final hurrah" of Norwegian America but rather a strong rebuke to Anglo-American superiority. And although the Norwegian-American image-makers realized that the Norwegian language would ultimately die off in America, they wished to use public festivals like the Norse-American Centennial, in combination with the ideology of the Norwegian-American self-image, to produce legacy myths that would ensure that achievements of their group received their proper recognition within the American, and the Norwegian, national pantheons.

Promoting the Norwegian-American Self-Image in Norway

Once large-scale emigration from Norway ceased, as it did by the time of World War I, the activities and achievements of "the emigrated Norway" came to be viewed in a different context in Norway. No longer did the immigrants remind homeland Norwegians of what was wrong with the Fatherland; rather, they became symbols for the greatness of Norway. In the decade of the 1920s the Norwegian media, especially the newspapers associated with the conservative and agrarian political parties, expanded their coverage and discussion of emigrated Norwegians. For the bourgeois parties occupying the political right and center in Norway, the Norwegian-American self-image could be analyzed in fairly straightforward nationalist terms. In other words, the center and right parties wanted to promote a Norwegian national identity that emphasized the cultural and material achievements, often in business, industry, and agriculture, of both Norway and Norwegian America.

For the parties on the left, especially Norway's Arbeider (Labor) party, issues of nationalism were deemed anachronistic within a Marxist perspective and considered far less important than issues of labor solidarity and economic justice. The Marxists in Norway, as well as elsewhere, developed a distinctly anti-American stance by the 1920s, coming to regard America as "Capitalism's Promised Land" and "Proletarian Hell." However, this was still very much a minority viewpoint in Norway at the time. Many individual working-class trade unionists in Norway and members of the Arbeiderpartiet, who had close ties with emigrated relatives and friends in America, likely had feelings that did not reflect the official party line.[73]

During the 1920s, much of the debate over Norwegian Americans centered on whether the emigrated really had anything in common with the land they left behind. The Norwegian poet Nils Collett Vogt, who had attended the 1925 centennial in the Twin Cites, gave a speech in Norway in December of that same year in which he stated that the two peoples had diverged too much to be considered part of the same nation. As H. Arnold Barton has shown in his *A Folk Divided*, a similar debate raged among Swedish Americans and homeland Swedes during the years following World War I. In response to Vogt, Arne Kildal, the general secretary for

Nordmands-Forbundet, authored an article titled "Norskheten i Amerika" (Norwegian Identity in America). According to Kildal, it was true that the use of Norwegian was rapidly declining in America among the immigrant communities, but it was countered by the avid participation of Norwegian Americans in their organizational life such as the Norwegian Lutheran Church and especially the *bygdelags,* which he claimed numbered around four hundred thousand members. In response to Kildal's criticism, Vogt defended his claims and stated, "Future developments would travel from Norway to America. From Norwegian culture to American."[74]

Despite the arguments of critics like Vogt, the idea that Norwegian Americans represented an extension of Norway remained popular in the homeland. Rølvaag's pioneer novels attained their first successes in Norway around 1924 and remained popular for many years thereafter. In his novel *The Immigrants,* the Norwegian author Johan Bojer painted a sympathetic portrait of emigrated Norwegians.[75]

In 1925, Carl J. Hambro released his work *Glimt fra Amerika* (Glimpses from America), which featured articles he had written about Norwegian America in the previous fifteen years. At the end of the book he comments, "Each generation of Norwegian Americans becomes attached to the land more deeply because for them it implies not just hope, but the memory of their father's land built with their yearning.... With the growth of Americanism comes a further understanding of the Norwegian, better comprehension of the double kingdom that means having ancestral lands on both sides of the ocean—freer possibilities for growth for those who have faith in Norwegianness."[76] Hambro's ideas reveal a growing realization that Norway's greatness as a nation extended beyond its geopolitical borders. Norway's "colonists" in America, those latter-day Vikings, had demonstrated conclusively the superiority of Norwegian national traits.

One of the most popular accounts of the Norwegian emigration to America appeared in 1925 with Christian Gierløff's *Folket som Utvandrer* (The People Who Emigrate). A journalist by trade, Gierløff had authored an early travel account of Norwegian America in 1904. *Folket som Utvandrer* used the constructed Norwegian-American history, including the Viking-age discovery of the New World, the colonial era, the age of immigration, and the accomplishments of present-day Norwegian Americans. Elaborating further, he argued that throughout its history Norway's "stoutest, smartest and most virile" members, its emigrants, had been its greatest export. If Norway had only retained its emigrants throughout the years, it "would today be the most democratic, the most moral, the most just and the most freedom and peace-seeking of all the great powers." Subsequently, the greatness of present-day America, he contended, was due to the Nordic race, of which the Norwegians were the purest. He quotes an American sociologist, Luther Stoddard, to emphasize his point: "Had it not been for the Nordic race, which is the supreme among all the races, America would not rank as highly as it does today."[77]

Such race-based arguments were prevalent in the 1920s, and Norwegian-American leaders such as Ager and Rølvaag had used similar language. In the interwar period nationalism in Norway had an especially aggressive character. The nation had flexed its muscles in the international realm by successfully reclaiming a number of Arctic islands, including Spitsbergen, which was renamed Svalbard, its Old Norse name. Norway also tried to obtain rights to the unpopulated eastern portion of Greenland, controlled by Denmark, through a series of legal challenges in the International Court of Arbitration in The Hague. Although the challenge ultimately proved unsuccessful in 1932, Norwegian leaders made great efforts to prove the greatness of the Norwegian race. The construction of Norway's national self-image emanated from a group of intellectuals in the academic and literary world. As Halvdan Koht observed, Norway's historians played a significant role in articulating that self-image.[78]

Nearly all Norwegian historians during this period ignored the emigration to America, and for them, the Norwegian-American experience did not figure into their national formula. However, a rival elite faction, consisting of businesspeople and professionals in Norway, sought to partake in formulating Norway's national identity. Many of these people had ties to Norway's shipping industry and Høyre, Norway's conservative party. This set of elites had also been instrumental in the creation of Nordmands-Forbundet in 1907. These business elites wanted to project an image of Norway as a great trading nation and a highly cosmopolitan society. They utilized their contacts with other businesspeople, particularly in Norwegian-American business and professional circles, to promote an alternative vision of Norway. Central to this image was the idea that the greatness of Norway extended far beyond its political boundaries. *Et større Norge,* a greater Norway, became the key concept to this alternate vision of Norwegian nationalism.[79]

Promoting the Norwegian-American identity in both Norway and America thus was a prime objective for Nordmands-Forbundet. One of its endeavors was the erection of a statue to Colonel Hans C. Heg at his birthplace of Lier, Norway, in January 1925. (Under the auspices of Det Norske Selskab [The Norwegian Society], a replica statue was dedicated on the state capitol grounds in Madison, Wisconsin, on October 17, 1926.) Nordmands-Forbundet was also active in coordinating activities around the 1925 Norse-American Centennial. It sponsored Norwegian Week, the Norwegian-American component of the Stavanger celebration in Norway. At the centennial held in the Twin Cities, Carl J. Hambro, chair of Nordmands-Forbundet and the president of Norway's parliament, read the official greeting of the Norwegian government.[80]

Norway's government and Nordmands-Forbundet combined their efforts in the summer of 1927 when they invited twelve American newspapermen, four of whom were Norwegian-Americans, to participate in a national tour of Norway. The state-sponsored tour aimed to develop a greater awareness about Norway among Americans, particularly in the hope that greater tourism would result. Norwegian officials expected that the affiliated newspapers of the respective correspondents would write glowing accounts about the Nordic land in their American newspapers, especially the English-language ones. Although the tour—despite the lavish accommodations and visits with high-level Norwegians—did not lead to the level of English-language coverage anticipated, it did receive highly positive coverage in the Norwegian-American press.

The historian Terje Leiren observes that the tour reached a core constituency, Norwegian Americans, and received selective coverage in the wider American press, thus making it a qualified success. Furthermore, the tour showed that Norwegian Americans had achieved a high level of acceptance by the Norwegian government, providing a boost to the self-image of Norwegian Americans. Writing about the tour a year later in *En sommer i Norge* (A Summer in Norway), Kristian Prestgard of *Decorah-Posten* compared it to a pilgrimage to the holy land.[81]

That same summer the *Leif Erikson*, a Viking-age replica ship, arrived at its final destination in Duluth, Minnesota. Captained by Gerhard Folgerø, the ship had sailed from Bergen, Norway, in 1926 to retrace the likely route of Leif Erikson in 997 CE. It had been part of Norway's contribution during the 1926 World's Fair in Philadelphia, a commemoration of the sesquicentennial of America. Once the ship arrived in Duluth, Captain Folgerø and his crew received a heartfelt reception. Numerous photographers and a robust crowd greeted the ship as the S.S. *Paducah* swung around and past the Viking ship, on whose decks stood "blue-clad Vikings in gleaming silver helmets." A band on the Paducah played rousing music to complete the scene. *Duluth Skandinav* reported that the scene was "a living reenactment of history, a realistic portrayal of the dream of a generation in heartfelt harmony with a thousand-year-old history."[82]

Providing organizational "muscle" for the event were Norwegian-American organizations such as the Normanna Mandskor (Northmen's Male Chorus), members of the Nordlandslaget and Trønderlaget, Det Norske Nationalforbunde (Norwegian National League), and the Nortun Lodge of the Sons of Norway. Professor Gisle Bothne of the University of Minnesota and Carl G. O. Hansen of *Minneapolis Tidende* were among the prominent Norwegian Americans representing Minneapolis, and A. E. Williamsen, president of the Norwegian National League, was among the several prominent Norwegian Americans from Chicago who were likewise in attendance. In the evening, a banquet honoring the latter-day Vikings was held in the Hotel Spalding, and the speeches embraced the Vikings' discovery of America and the pride of Norwegians in being a leading people in America. Captain Folgerø used his speech from that afternoon to deliver greetings from Norway, from the King of Norway, the Norwegian parliament, and the people across the Atlantic. He thanked the people, observing that he and his men had received "a reception that we never will forget." The *Leif Erikson* was placed in a park in Duluth, which in 1929 was named Leif Erikson Park.[83]

In an interview a few days later, Folgerø admitted that the journey was highly important for Norway's national self-image, noting that it "was worth millions for the land." He also pointed to what he termed the "class" struggle in America between the Latin "class" (he probably meant race) and the Nordic race. The impressive exploits of the *Leif Erikson* in 1927 and Magnus Andersen's *Viking* in 1893, he noted, had solidified the position of Norwegians in America.[84] The tangible voyage of the *Leif Erikson*, therefore, provided powerful reinforcement for the ideological constructs centered on the Viking explorer, whose legacy greatly enhanced the self-image of Norwegian Americans as well as the national identity of Norway.

Nordmands-Forbundet took the lead in establishing Leif Erikson Day in Norway, which was first observed on September 25, 1926. The Norwegian government proclaimed the festival, noting that it would be celebrated in Norway's schools. The Norwegian press tended to give the new celebration favorable reviews. On the eve of the day, one small newspaper reported,

"Tomorrow Norway shall also celebrate its first Leiv Eriksøn Day, the day of celebration we now share with our emigrated kinsmen; a Norway Day for them—an American Day for us." *Aftenposten* stated that the new observance "will inspire happiness and enthusiasm among our compatriots in America knowing that Norwegians in the homeland will unite with them in celebrating a festival they steadfastly have maintained."[85]

The next year Leif Erikson Day in Norway was moved to October 9 to coincide with the day it was usually celebrated in America. The Icelandic sagas indicated that Leif had reached Vinland sometime in autumn. Since the Norwegians on board the *Restaurationen* had landed at New York on October 9, 1825, it had become the custom to celebrate Leif Erikson on that date in America. The 1927 Leif Erikson Day celebration in Norway featured a radio broadcast from Oslo. In his speech on the subject, Arne Kildal noted that for more than two generations Norwegian Americans had struggled to have the Norwegian discovery of America recognized in the United States. The dedication of statues to Leif Erikson in Boston and Chicago, the naming of Leif Erikson Square in Brooklyn, and President Coolidge's speech in 1925 all pointed to the growing realization among Americans of the Norwegian legacy. He urged his Norwegian listeners to make Leif Erikson day in Norway an occasion on which to honor the Norwegian emigrants:

> Leiv Eiriksson Day should gain a foothold in Norway not just in the schools and the press, but in the churches, in the youth lodges, and in the homes. Then it would become a day of cooperation, the day that reminds us that there is a greater Norway in the world today that has nothing to do with our national boundaries. Let us hope that the youth will take the lead and work for such a celebration of Leiv Eiriksson Day here in this country. A better handshake across the sea and the sand we could not give our emigrated kinsmen.[86]

The next year Kildal gave a speech commemorating Leif Erikson Day in Norway. He repeated his demands to make the day a celebration of the Norwegian emigrants. "We have today about as many Norwegians outside as within Norway. In the United States and Canada men and women of Norwegian ancestry have shaped a new society, moving Norwegian traditions ever forward and creating new reverence for the Norwegian name."[87]

Leif Erikson Day continues to be celebrated in Norway. By promoting the most important Norwegian-American festival and making it into a dual celebration, the leaders of Nordmands-Forbundet were building bridges that sought to unite the two peoples on both sides of the Atlantic. It also signified validation of the Norwegian-American identity in Norway, which helped to offset the loss of prestige wrought by nativist sentiments in America.

Furthermore, in promoting the accomplishments of Norwegian Americans, the elites of organizations such as Nordmands-Forbundet created a Norwegian national identity that extended beyond the national territory of Norway. Norwegian America thus became an extension of Norway, evidence of the success of Norwegian national traits. In the highly competitive environment of America, the relative success of Norwegian Americans improved Norway's prestige in the eyes of the international community. The creation of Leif Erikson Day in Norway, at least at a popular level, thus served to tie Norway's national identity to that of the Norwegian-American identity.

The National Origins Act of 1927

In passing the 1924 Immigration Restriction Act, which limited annual immigration to 2 percent of the population of each nationality present according to the 1890 federal census, the U.S. Congress hoped to give future immigration an even more pronounced North European bias. However, when Congress passed further quotas under the Reed Amendment, the resulting National Origins Act of 1927 limited annual immigration to 150,000, based on the proportion of nationalities of the 1920 federal census. The Quota Board, which made the final determination, did not limit its statistical determination to nineteenth- and twentieth-century data but also sought to determine the ethnic composition of colonial America. Using a study produced by Marcus Lee Hansen and Howard Baker, the board concluded that persons of colonial stock composed 43.5 percent of the 1920 population, and later immigrants and their descendants accounted for 56.5 percent of the total. The effect was to favor immigrants from Britain, Northern Ireland, and certain southern and eastern European countries at the expense of immigrants from Ireland, Germany, and the Scandinavian countries. The amendment produced an indignant outcry among the Swedish-American press. One editorial questioned how the act's makers could possibly believe that true settlers and nation-builders like the Swedes, Norwegians, Danes, and Germans were less desirable than the Russians, Italians, and English.[88]

Much of the impetus for the stricter immigration limits came from what John Higham terms the racial and cultural defensiveness of the Deep South and the Far West. Southerners and Westerners tended to regard the unfamiliar peoples of southeastern Europe as less than completely white, not to mention their deep-seated resentment toward Asian immigrants. The war hysteria against German Americans served to light a fuse that did not go out during the 1920s. Although Norwegians, Swedes, Germans, Dutch, and other northern Europeans had been regarded as good Nordics and desirable as immigrants, they became caught up in the crossfire of racial and ethnic prejudice that prompted the ultimate passage of the National Origins Act.[89]

Indignation also marked the reactions of many Norwegian-American newspapers. Set to become law on July 1, 1929, the Quota Law (as it was popularly called) would reduce the annual number of Norwegian immigrants from 6,453 to 2,377 while increasing the numbers of immigrants from Great Britain and Northern Ireland from 34,007 to 65,721. *Skandinaven* observed that "[with] the quota for Northern Europe [that] is being proposed, the law will work actually against the intended objective, which was then adopted, namely, to allow a proportionately greater immigration of the Nordic races." *Minneapolis Tidende* remarked that for Scandinavians the law "would label [them] as undesirable immigrants." Another article from *Skandinaven* calculated that approximately 20,000 Norwegians a year desired to immigrate to the United States. "With a quota limit of 2,377, it will take around 15 to 20 years before the last of the now would-be immigrants comes over." *Norgesposten* made a similar claim, but listed the number of potential immigrants from the homeland at 45,000. Further dissent occurred when *Norgesposten* complained, "The defense of Norwegianness in this land stands and falls with immigration; by stopping it, which could be termed the question of our times, then all work on behalf of Norwegianness must cease."[90]

Individual Norwegian-Americans expressed their disapproval of the act as well. South Dakota senator Peter Norbeck expressed concerns that the law would actually threaten white America: "People of all races and all parts of the world come in under the British quota. . . . Negro[es] from Jamaica or other British islands in the West Indies, or from a British colony in Africa ... are British citizens and have the same right to immigrate to the United States as a white man born in England, Scotland, Wales, or Northern Ireland." The Norwegian-American author Franklin Petersen questioned the racial purity of Anglo-Americans. "Our [Norwegian] traditions go back over 1,000 years—how far back go the Americans'? We Norwegians are a pure and unblemished race. Can the Americans say the same?"[91]

This latest salvo offended many Norwegian Americans since it made them appear less desirable than those of "Anglo-Saxon" stock. The apparent victory of the 1925 Norse-American Centennial appeared to have been short-lived. The Anglo-American validation of the Norwegian-American self-image now seemed to have been reversed, and the reputation of Norwegian America had suffered a significant setback.

Reaction to the National Origins Act in Norway was highly negative. During a debate in the Norwegian parliament in the spring of 1929, President Carl J. Hambro offered a "very sharp critique" of the Quota Law. Acording to the editor of *Nordisk Tidende,* in Norway "Hambro's protest has raised an amazingly swift and sympathetic response especially from public reaction in the press and a broad spectrum of the people." The same article stated that Norway's cabinet was drafting a protest intended for the American president. *Morgenbladet* mentioned that twenty thousand Norwegians were on a waiting list to emigrate to America and that they "anxiously awaited the fate of the American immigration law," while *Aftenposten* cited the number as forty thousand. In noting that attempts to increase Norwegian quotas had failed, *Aftenposten* remarked that "the so-called hundred-percent Americans spearheaded an energetic agitation in [congressional] corridors against revision of the proposal. The agitation is supported primarily outside the Senate by the American Legion and the Ku Klux Klan."[92]

Such a negative reaction to the new immigration restrictions reveal how badly the Norwegian-American image had been tarnished. In the hierarchy of nations, Norway's position had declined, and Norwegian-American leaders realized that their group's self-image had suffered a similar decline. The negative reaction in Norway, even though it likely prevented thousands of Norwegians from leaving the homeland, also reveals how closely Norway's national prestige had become tied to that of the Norwegian-American identity. In this sense, it revealed how successful had been the effort to have homeland Norwegians validate the Norwegian-American self-image. It further revealed the mutual interdependence that the two national identities shared. For leaders of Norway's business and professional elite, it necessitated a coordinated effort with Norwegian-American leaders to rehabilitate the Norwegian-American self-image, thereby strengthening Norway's national identity. Beginning in the late 1920s, the two sets of that elite would engage in vigorously promoting the concept of a greater Norway.

· CHAPTER 5 ·

A Shared Homeland

Celebrating Norwegian Identity across the Atlantic, 1929–1945

ON THE TWENTY-FIFTH ANNIVERSARY of Nordmanns-Forbundet in 1932, H. Aschehoug and Company published a commemoration of the federation titled *Et større Norge* (A Greater Norway). Edited by Wilhelm Morgenstierne, who became Norway's *sendemann* (envoy) to America in 1929, the book celebrated the achievement of a greater Norway. Morgenstierne expressed how Norwegian emigration had made this possible: "The application of a greater Norway has in recent years been employed in several different aspects. Most strikingly it has been used in connection with the Norway that knows no borders but which extends everywhere Norwegians have celebrated the homeland and Norwegian contributions have been recognized."[1]

Morgenstierne's insight succinctly highlighted the main ideas of the greater Norway concept. In creating "the Norway that knows no borders," the leaders of this effort sought to expand the nation of Norway beyond its physical borders. This transcendent Norway, the greater Norway, would be defined by both the homeland (the traditional nationalist understanding of the nation) and by communities of ethnic Norwegians living outside Norway's territorial borders. It would create a Norway that was transnational, a nation that existed across political borders.

The second half of Morgenstierne's statement reveals how membership in the greater Norway would be determined. The greater Norway "extends everywhere Norwegians have celebrated the homeland and Norwegian contributions have been recognized." Certainly one could belong to the Norwegian nation by living within the physical boundaries of the homeland, but the greater Norway asserted that ethnic Norwegians living outside those boundaries could still belong to the nation by demonstrating their loyalty to the homeland. Regardless of where they resided, the body of loyal Norwegians, including the descendants of immigrants, constituted the greater Norway, which existed in a transnational, extraterritorial space.

Since the largest number of emigrant Norwegians resided in the United States, the leaders of the greater Norway concept focused their efforts on building close connections between Norwegian Americans and the homeland. Through a series of transnational celebrations between the late 1920s and 1939, the evolution of the greater Norway unfolded. Promoters of this ideology structured the celebrations to bring together Norwegians on both sides of the Atlantic, which allowed the participants to share in honoring the legacy of Norway. The commemoration of *norskhet* involved a number of different occasions, and these celebrations honored homeland heroes and Norwegian-American heroes, future Norwegian sailors, Norwegian immigrants to America, and Norway's royal family. The celebrations usually had matching ceremonies in both Norway and America, further signifying the transatlantic character of the emerging identity. Participation in these celebrations, moreover, extended beyond those physically present at the ceremonies to include those listening on the radio, thereby creating an "imagined Norway" that existed in the transnational space.

The greater Norway, though, represented more than an abstract imagining. The ordeal of World War II and the foreign occupation of Norway proved to be the ultimate test for the greater Norway concept. Loyalty to Norway became more than symbolic; it required real sacrifice. As a government in exile, Norway's leaders, including the royal family, upheld and put into practice the greater Norway, asking Norwegians living outside Norway to contribute financially and also through military service to the restoration of a free Norway. The actions of Norwegian Americans in this regard, including the creation of the Viking Battalion, a unit composed entirely of those of Norwegian ancestry, proved to the homeland that their emigrated cousins were indeed loyal to Norway.

Promoting "A Greater Norway," 1929–1939

By the mid-1920s, the basic outlines of the Norwegian-American identity had been established. The challenge to image-makers in America and Norway involved restoring the self-image of Norwegian America following the sense of loss associated with the implementation of the National Origins Act in 1929. Leaders among Norwegian Americans and homeland Norwegians attempted to show how vibrant Norwegian-American culture remained despite the diminished use of the Norwegian language. Whereas up to the 1920s it had been the Norwegian Americans who had sought anxiously—and often under discouraging circumstances—to maintain close ties, it was now Norway that showed a particular eagerness to preserve the bonds that attached Norwegian Americans to their old homeland. In constructing their legacy myths, these leaders promoted the concept of *et større Norge*, which advanced the idea that Norwegian Americans had remained faithful to their Norwegian heritage and thus constituted the "other half of the Norwegian nation."

The idea of a greater Norway became especially popular in Norway starting around the mid-1920s. In a self-promoting article from 1926, Arne Kildal claimed that "the way to a greater Norway goes through Nordmands-Forbundet." The concept was relevant, he argued, because 1.7 to 2 million "of our people reside today in the United States of America," and "the bonds between Norwegians in America and Norway are becoming even stronger so that they seem like flesh of the same flesh and blood of the same blood."[2]

A greater Norway existed as an idealized place. In a May 17 speech given in New York in 1932, Morgenstierne asked his Norwegian-American audience, "Who does not remember May in Norway? Where in the world is there such springtime, such powerful extremes in nature?" He described a vibrant Norway where "the new breaks forth, wild and effervescent waterfalls, the thousand brooks and rivers on their course to the sea. One sees the sprouting growth on hills and mountainsides, the birch stands lively and green right against the snow line. And this is precisely the spirit of Eidsvold." By invoking Norwegian landscapes in reference to the place where Norway's constitution had been promulgated, Morgenstierne invoked a Norway that could be imagined both spiritually and physically.[3]

The Norwegian-American press enthusiastically received *Et større Norge* because the book underscored a sense of shared community between the immigrants and the homeland. *Minneapolis Tidende*, for instance, stated that the book revealed "a people on the path to convergence." This idea had tremendous appeal despite the fact that for many of the immigrants the Norway they had known no longer existed.[4] Similar praise greeted the work in the Norwegian papers. A reviewer for *Aftenposten* exclaimed, "There is the greater Norway ... and the goal that we should be working for, single-mindedly and enthusiastically, is to build and strengthen this greater Norway." *Nationen* mentioned, "Our

Despite the pressures of assimilation and the decline of the use of the Norwegian language, ethnic Norwegians still honored Norway as demonstrated by this photograph of a Syttende mai celebration in Chicago in 1935.

land is greater than the maps and the historians teach."[5] Such comments reveal the realization that a greater Norway benefited Norway's self-image and that the relationship between emigrated Norwegians and homeland Norwegians had to be nurtured.

Norway's active role in promoting the successes of its emigrated population was unusual. To be sure, virtually all immigrant groups in America looked to the homeland for vindication of their efforts at preserving their ethnic traditions. What is unique about the case of Norway is how the emigrants were welcomed into the national community. One finds a similar phenomenon among the Poles in America, who tended to see themselves as members of a greater Poland, namely, Polonia. However, as William J. Galush observes, Poland did not typically pay attention to the emigrated kinfolk save in times of crisis. It was largely the emigrated Poles, the Polonians, who were invested in the transatlantic relationship through their desire for an independent Poland. The homeland did not reciprocate.[6]

The elite leaders of Nordmanns-Forbundet understood that Norway's national identity was tied to the Norwegian-American self-image. In 1936 general secretary Arne Kildal stressed the importance of this relationship:

> [We] Norwegians in the "Old Country" should seek in earnest to construct a more intimate solidarity with our relatives over in America, a solidarity that is—and will be—based on the greatest cultural and economic significance for both parties. By most accounts one can find around 2 million persons of Norwegian ancestry in the States. Naturally, the greatest percentage of these Norwegian descendents has become strongly Americanized, yet this notwithstanding they are all tied to Norway. If one could maintain the ancestral ties that now exist between Norway and America, and further deepen the connection with the newer generations, it would be undoubtedly of the greatest significance for both parties. But we cannot continue to rely on the Norwegian Americans to uphold this connection; the impulses must come from "the Old Country."[7]

In the same article, Kildal observed how Norway thus had the responsibility to help restore the Norwegian-American legacy. "It is naturally of the greatest urgency that we stimulate a sense of shared sentiment, and we must therefore hope to emphasize how quickly our undertaking can be realized."[8] During the 1930s, therefore, the safeguarding and the restoration of the Norwegian-American self-image was very much a shared endeavor between Norwegian Americans and homeland Norwegians. In effect, the elite of the two nations worked to promote a transatlantic national identity that served both Norwegian-American and homeland Norwegian interests.

Leaders from Norway were anxious to promote this message in America as well. In a radio address delivered as part of the Festival of Nations series on November 17, 1932, Morgenstierne's speech, "Norway and America," demonstrated the long association and close affinity that the two nations had for each other:

> A peculiar understanding and friendship has grown up between these two nations—the United States, the oldest of the modern republics, and Norway, one of the oldest of Europe's kingdoms. It is a relationship that goes back about a thousand years, and which has found nourishment and inspiration in the democratic ideals and institutions and practices which both nations have in Common [sic]. It is, maybe, no chance happening that in Norway, Abraham Lincoln is perhaps better known and more beloved than any other

man outside our own country, and Ibsen's greatest poem, "Upon the Death of Abraham Lincoln," is one of our literary treasures. There is something fine and inspiring in the fact that no question of geographical or statistical bigness plays any part in this fundamental understanding and friendship between a people of 120 millions and one of 2¾ millions. This is indeed a triumph for culture and civilization and true human and spiritual values. Here are the two great nations, in the true sense of that word, who join hands across the sea, realizing that not only do they have the same colors in their flags, but also the same ideals in their hearts.[9]

Such arguments increased Norway's national prestige by tying its self-image to that of the powerful American nation. Moreover, this shared identity of a greater Norway usually generated a conservative interpretation of Norwegian Americans, namely, that they had preserved their homeland traditions. Recognition of the Norwegian-American success story was not a universal given, however. In 1939, Einar Lund, editor for *Decorah-Posten,* complained that Wilhelm Keilau's recent history of the Norwegian people, *Vaar egen tid* (Our Own Times), had devoted only four pages out of more than five hundred to the Norwegian emigration. He argued that Norway needed to do more from its side in recording the achievements of Norwegian Americans.[10]

Despite the misgivings of Lund and others, the promotion of a greater Norway proved highly successful in both Norway and America. It is true that Norway's academic community seldom paid homage to the immigrants, but at most levels of Norwegian society, especially at the popular level, the Norwegian-American self-image had become an addendum to Norway's national identity. Norway's business and professional elite utilized the success of Norwegian Americans to increase Norway's national prestige. Most important, it allowed them to tie Norway's self-image to the greatness of America by showing how historic Norwegian national traits could explain the success of Norwegian Americans.

Shared Celebrations and Commemorations

Despite the hardship of Depression-era America, the 1930s actually witnessed an ethnic resurgence. Economic privation meant that to survive many Americans sought help in their ethnic communities. Ethnic organizations allowed individuals to pool their resources and to utilize networks of mutual assistance during hard times. Many of these ethnic organizations also served as outlets for socialization and entertainment, since a lack of funds precluded many Americans from engaging in more expensive forms of entertainment. The Norwegian community of the Twin Cities, for example, established the celebration of Norway Day in 1929 and continued to observe it during the 1930s and World War II years. Ethnic artists flourished in many of America's big cities during the Depresssion, and as scholars Mary Anne Thatcher, Lizabeth Cohen, Sture Lindmark, Jon Gjerde, and David Mauk have shown, ethnic groups were highly adaptive in meeting the challenges posed during the 1930s.[11]

Public celebrations and commemorations provided the "testing grounds" against which the mettle of the greater Norway concept could be measured. Moreover, such celebrations required dual observances on both sides of the Atlantic. From the late 1920s until the onset of World War II, a number of successful shared celebrations were observed, reinforcing the idea of a greater Norway.

The initial test of the greater Norway concept, the dry run, so to speak, was the centennial of Henrik Ibsen's birth in 1928. Norway commemorated its renowned author with a five-day celebration from March 16 to 20—the final day being Ibsen's birthday—in Oslo. In the streets of the capital, Ibsen statues and paintings were ubiquitous, while merchants displayed their tributes to the author, including one confectioner who sold "Ibsen chocolates."[12]

At a luncheon on March 17 at the house of Laurits S. Swenson, the American ambassador to Norway, leading elites from both sides of the Atlantic met to honor Ibsen. Robert Underwood Johnson, the poet, represented the American delegation along with Ole E. Rølvaag. Representing Norway were two cabinet ministers, Carl J. Hambro, president of Norway's parliament, and the historians Halfdan Koht and Francis Bull. Koht delivered a lecture on "En folkefiende (An Enemy of the People), while Bull's lecture dealt with "Gjengangere" (Ghosts). Johnson concluded the program with a speech on the author, including a toast to Norway's well-being and to the memory of Ibsen. The day ended with a performance of *Ghosts* at the National Theater at which King Haakon and Crown Prince Olav were in attendance.[13]

On Sunday, March 18, the celebration continued with a concert in honor of Ibsen by the Oslo Philharmonic Orchestra. The next day's main activity was a procession of the guests, who walked along Karl Johans Avenue to the royal castle where they were greeted by King Haakon. Robert Underwood Johnson was the first in line, and he used the opportunity to express America's greetings to the monarch. The day concluded with a lecture by Bull on Ibsen's *Vildanden* (The Wild Duck) at the National Theater.[14]

The culmination of the celebration took place on March 20, Ibsen's birthday. In the morning, a ceremony was held at Our Savior's Cemetery in Oslo, where Ibsen's legacy was honored with the laying of numerous wreaths, several speeches, and the firing of cannons. Mr. Johnson read a poem in honor of the man who "had made Norway's name known among the nations." The evening ceremonies took place within the auditorium of the University of Oslo, as the king and crown prince received diplomats and guests from the numerous foreign countries in attendance. The various speakers offering praise of the author reflected on Ibsen's universal fame. For instance, Professor Vasenius of Finland, Sir Edmund Gosse of England, and Professor Woerner of Germany all gave speeches, a testimony to Ibsen's cosmopolitan appeal. In his speech, Carl J. Hambro concluded that "we cannot make Ibsen greater than he is" but hoped that the canonization of him would "inspire Norwegians to remember for a moment the day's activities and to cast their eyes toward heaven in thanks." Later, Johnson reprised his verse to Ibsen, of which the final four lines were: "Dividing wrong from right and strong from weak / Kindred to Sophocles he well may be / When to the Three Fates of the Ancient Greek / He adds a fourth, in man's heredity."[15]

Across the Atlantic, Norwegian America participated in the commemoration of Ibsen as well. On March 20 at the Lyceum in Minneapolis, the Ibsen celebration took place during a three-hour-long evening celebration. According to *Minneapolis Daglig Tidende,* the Norwegian National League decorated the Lyceum splendidly. The backdrop featured large American and Norwegian flags on both sides of additional flags bearing the titles of Ibsen's works, and behind the stage hung a large portrait of Ibsen. Important Norwegian-American organizations were present, including the Norwegian Singing Association, the St. Olaf College Band, the Dovre Male Choir, and the Norwegian Glee Club. Fred Krohn, president of the Norwegian National League, read a telegram greeting from the Oslo Ibsen Committee. Important Norwegians and Norwegian Americans were in attendance, thus ensuring that the event paid homage to both nationalisms.[16]

As with many of these transnational ceremonies, the Minneapolis Ibsen celebration offered speeches in both English and Norwegian. Martin B. Ruud, professor of philosophy at the University of Minnesota, supplied the English-language speech. In his remarks, he acknowledged that Ibsen's greatest initial popularity occurred in Germany and England because of his often biting criticism of Norwegian society. But toward the end of his life, Norwegians finally realized that his advanced ideas on such issues as women's rights and the aspirations of younger generations had earned him a place alongside Sophocles and Shakespeare. Meanwhile, the Norwegian speech given by Carl G. O. Hansen, editor of *Minneapolis Tidende,* paid tribute to Ibsen's values. Hansen declared that Ibsen stood for truth and freedom and that he was a radical individualist whose gift to the Norwegian people was his unflinching support for freedom, even though his life was filled with controversy and ruin. Most of all he was an artist with an artist's view of life, which meant that he saw life for both its beauty and its darker side.[17]

Seattle's Norwegian community likewise honored Ibsen, albeit a day earlier, on March 19, at Meany Hall on the campus of the University of Washington. Once again, numerous Norwegian-American organizations participated, such as the Norwegian Singing Association, and the hall was decked out with numerous American and Norwegian flags. The Oslo Ibsen Committee sent a telegram, which was read aloud. Prominent Norwegians and Norwegian Americans attended the event, including the Norwegian consul for Seattle. The keynote speaker, E. J. Vickner of the University of Washington, emphasized Ibsen's support for progressive ideas in his time such as the eight-hour workday and greater civil rights. He compared Ibsen with Bjørnstjerne Bjørnson, concluding that while Bjørnson was the champion of freedom and justice in Norway, Ibsen directed his energies toward more universal causes, supporting the rights of all people. He noted that Ibsen's life and work were deeply appreciated.[18]

Many Norwegian Americans realized that Ibsen's more universal appeal meant that he was the most significant Norwegian author and playwright for most Americans. There was a certain irony arising from the fact that Ibsen's value to Norwegian America was more suitable to the Norwegian America of the 1920s then it had been during the author's heyday during the 1870s and 1880s. Like Norway, Norwegian America during those decades found his works of social realism far less desirable than his earlier peasant-based works such as *Peer Gynt.* Despite this situation,

Norwegian-American leaders could envision how the various celebrations would lead to a greater appreciation for the man. A *Nordisk Tidende* editorial voiced this anticipation: "*Nordisk Tidende* expresses the hope that the festivals of the various kinds that have been arranged in coordination with the centennial day of the great author's birthday might lead to a fine and deserving future course, which to its greatest extent, will inspire greater respect than already exists for the Norwegian culture in America."[19]

As the template for the greater Norway ideal, the Ibsen celebration displayed the characteristics that would be common to these transnational ceremonies. They had representation, often in an official capacity, from both Norway and Norwegian America. Moreover, the speeches involved participation from the representatives of the two nations. They also employed symbols from the two nations, usually a display of American and Norwegian flags, but there were often other physical symbols present such as Vikings, peasant costumes, or religious items and more ethereal symbols such as references to Norway's parliament, king, constitution, or May 17. And most important, these commemorations allowed both Norway and Norwegian America to point to the success of Norwegians in the homeland and abroad as proof of the fortitude of their respective national identities.

From July 28 to August 3, 1930, Norway celebrated the nine-hundredth anniversary of the death of King Olav Haraldsson, better known as St. Olav. Considered Norway's greatest Christian king, his death at the Battle of Stiklestad in 1030 had earned him an almost mythic reputation. According to the Norwegian scholar Svein Ivar Angell, this celebration of his death in Norway was both a religious and a national event in that it marked the founding of the Norwegian state and its acceptance of Christianity. The celebration, moreover, was important for Norway owing to societal divisions that had occurred after World War I between the nation's socialist left and the bourgeois parties.[20]

Angell further observes that the St. Olav celebration was an attempt "to define the content of the national process of consolidation which it itself sought to enforce" and that it took the form that tried to "define the process of how the collective memory of national foundation should be constructed." The leaders of the event, he contends, were using that constructed memory to advance the progress of the country and to strengthen the will of the people toward a unified nation.[21]

The St. Olav celebration was literally a shared celebration between

Norway and Norwegian America. The July 30 program from the Nidaros Cathedral in Trondheim featured a simultaneous radio broadcast in Norway and in America. Successive greater Norway celebrations would usually employ similar large-scale radio broadcasts, and it was this feature that allowed these commemorations to be truly shared, or transnational, something not experienced in the previous ones. The program featured a greeting by Carl J. Hambro, in his role as president of Norway's parliament, followed by a speech from the king and a speech in honor of Norwegian Americans by the Norwegian author Johan Bojer. The program concluded with a performance by the St. Olaf College Choir, which sang "America" and the Norwegian national anthem. As noted in *Nordisk Tidende*, "This broadcast represents a new phase in the bridge-building process between the emigrated and those in the homeland."[22]

This newest phase of "bridge-building" represented the process of putting a greater Norway into action. The Norwegian-American delegation to the festivities, led by Bishop J. S. Aasgaard, president of the Norwegian Lutheran Church in America, presented a silver cross and altar, representing Christ's crucifixion, to Nidaros Cathedral on behalf of Norwegian Americans. Furthering the sense of shared national identity was Det Utflyttede Norges Mottagelsepaviljong (The Emigrated Norway's Pavilion), which was located adjacent to the cathedral. By sharing in Norway's national celebration, Norwegian Americans could reinforce their claim to two of Norway's strongest national symbols, its Christian heritage and the glory of its Viking-age past.

Bishop Aasgaard resolutely affirmed those symbols in his speech dedicating the cross. "One can be permitted to muse about the place where men and women of Norwegian ancestry live today. It is something to marvel about the king of such a church in Leif Eriksson's Vinland with 3,000 churches and 1,200 ministers—a church whose source is in Olaf's church."[23]

As might be expected, Norwegian America honored St. Olaf with its own activities. In Minneapolis, a large gathering of Norwegians assembled in the Norwegian Memorial Church. The festivities featured members of the local Norske Nationalforbund (Norwegian National League), the city's three Norwegian male choruses, and numerous dignitaries. Vice consul Harry Eberhardt delivered a greeting from Norway in which he observed that nothing makes the heart beat more warmly for Norway than the "thousands of us from all the world's lands who have flocked home to partake in this celebration." He further described the celebration in Minneapolis as a chance for Norwegian men and women to celebrate together with the thousands in Stiklestad and Nidaros, in honor of "our God for what has blessed us for 900 years in our Fatherland."[24]

The keynote speaker at the Minneapolis celebration was R. Malmin, professor at Augsburg Seminary. In his concluding remarks, Malmin elucidated the connection between Norwegian America and the legacy of St. Olaf:

> Finally, we Norwegian churchgoers in America share in St. Olaf's legacy: A people with Christian evangelism as life's greatest goal. A people whose life receives its consecration from the Church with the Word and the Sacraments. A people who have upheld their great duty to the state and the Church—a people who learned to organize themselves under the Church's arch and to work for the country's welfare and progress, especially in a new, adopted homeland. And a people who shall cooperate in the completion of the solemn mission. That is our legacy. God gave us his spirit so that we must fulfill that promise. God gave us that spiritual strength, which gives our life its purpose, a God-ordained life to Christian glory! Amen.[25]

The Norwegian community in the New York area likewise celebrated St. Olaf; they congregated at Lake Telemark, New Jersey. The celebration centered on a picnic luncheon and was graced by the appearance of the Nordmændenes Sangforening (Norwegian Singing Association) under the direction of Ole Windingstad. The keynote speakers were seaman's minister Hoiland of the Norwegian Seaman's Church and general consul Wilhelm Morgenstierne, who delivered their speeches within the *hytte*, or Norwegian-style cabin. *Nordisk Tidende* reported that Hoiland intoned the psalms and his sermon in clear and ringing Landsmaal. Morgenstierne used his speech to laud the achievements of Norway's latter-day heroes, linking the achievements of St. Olaf with Fridtjof Nansen, the famed Arctic explorer. He observed that the day should remind Norwegians of all that they had achieved, but especially to direct their thoughts toward the land that "God himself gave to us, with its beautiful nature, its fields and fjords, and the smiling mountainsides and meadows." Morgenstierne concluded that Norway's rugged beauty, which had imbued its people with a strong character, was a lesson of the St. Olaf legacy.[26]

Commenting on the ultimate meaning of the St. Olaf's celebration, *Washington Posten* in Seattle titled its editorial "Norge, vaar mor" (Norway, Our Mother). The paper argued that emigrated Norwegians were part of a constant theme in Norway's history. Norway, the paper contended, had always been a nation whose people were attracted to trade and adventure, and its sailors had traveled to all parts of the globe. And just as Norwegians from across the world had traveled to bring gifts and thanks to St. Olaf nine hundred years ago, so today must Norwegians take a lesson from St. Olaf's time and realize that they all were working for the Norwegian people's good fortune and prosperity in modern times.[27]

Two years later, the greater Norway participated in another national celebration. To honor the father of Norwegian nationalism, Bjørnstjerne Bjørnson, Norway held a nationwide celebration on December 8, 1932, on the one hundredth anniversary of his birth. The main celebration was held in Oslo from December 4 to 8, and it featured nightly torchlight parades. On the final day, a large crowd gathered at Bjørnson's grave where "a long procession laid down wreaths." The festivities concluded with a memorial at the University of Oslo's main auditorium. There, many speakers honored the legacy of the poet. Nicolay A. Grevstad, who represented the Norwegian-American press, spoke on behalf of emigrated Norway. "We of the Norwegian race, who have established homes in Vinland, are here to honor Bjørnstjerne Bjørnson, Norway's greatest national writer, because he is also ours."[28]

Norwegian America likewise celebrated Bjørnson's legacy in the New World. One of the largest took place in New York, where eighteen hundred people turned out to participate. The highlight of the New York celebration was the program held at the Academy of Music in Brooklyn, including a stirring rendition of Norway's national anthem by De Forenede Norske Sanger (The United Norwegian Singers). Following the performance, the singers sent a telegram to Karoline Bjørnson, the poet's widow, at her home in Aulestad, Norway. Included in the message was a claim that "never has 'Ja vi elsker' [Norway's anthem] sounded more beautiful, nor a more enthusiastic gathering, than this evening." Norway's minister to the United States, H. H. Bachke, offered his tribute to Bjørnson and the Norwegian Americans for "celebrating the memory of our great countryman, whose name this evening we honor. We would have perceived the fullest appreciation of how loved and cherished is Bjørnson's name, whose place has been anchored in the hearts of the Norwegian people."[29]

On that same day, December 8, Minneapolis was host to a large Bjørnson celebration at which the local chapter of the Norwegian National League was again present. Although the day was celebrated in several locations, the primary celebration was at Cyrus Northrup Memorial Auditorium on the University of Minnesota campus. Martin Ruud, professor of English at the university, served as master of ceremonies. The ceremony featured several musical numbers in honor of Bjørnson performed by the university's symphony, the Nordraak Twin Cities Male Singers' Association, and a solo sung by Mrs. Carlo Fücher. Lotus D. Coffman, president of the university, delivered a speech in English praising Bjørnson, while vice consul Harry Eberhardt once again read the official greeting from Norway, as he had at the St. Olaf Celebration in 1930.[30]

The highlight of the Minneapolis celebration undoubtedly was the speech delivered by Minnesota governor Floyd Bjørnsterne Olson, whose middle name clearly was homage to the Norwegian author. Olson compared Bjørnson with the American poet Walt Whitman because both "had grown close with the common people." He elaborated further by noting that Bjørnson was "a great statesman with his finger on the pulse of the people," and that his was the "modern democratic project to ... protect the people's freedom and rights." Later, Gisle Bothne of the University of Minnesota delivered the major speech in Norwegian. Bothne referred to Bjørnson as Norway's "uncrowned king for fifty years" since his poetry, dramas, speeches, and political activities all had been in service to the liberation of the common man.[31]

Of course these Norwegian-American celebrations glossed over the fact that during Bjørnson's only visit to America in 1880–81 he had been at the center of a stormy controversy owing to his antibiblical and freethinking views. *Nordisk Tidende* acknowledged this fact in an April 1932 editorial, when it urged its readers to consider Bjørnson in the light of his times and to judge him without bitterness. Norwegians the world over, it noted, had drawn closer to him over time. Concerning the author's spirituality, *Minneapolis Tidende* quoted Bishop Eivind Berggrav of Norway who opined that Bjørnson was inwardly religious and that much of his criticism was directed toward what he perceived as the corrupt, outer trappings of Christianity. The passage of more than fifty years and the processes of memory accumulation had turned Bjørnson into a hero for both homeland Norwegians and Norwegian Americans. As Bothne stressed in his speech, Bjørnson loved Norway, had an unfailing belief in the Norwegian people's will and right to live an independent life, and had dedicated his life to Norway's independence.³² The latter sentiment typified the Bjørnson remembered in the Norwegian-American identity.

Additional Bjørnson celebrations were held in other Norwegian-American communities, and they likewise featured prominent Norwegian-American leaders and representatives from Norway. In particular, a number of Midwestern cities, including Madison and Milwaukee, Wisconsin; St. Olaf College at Northfield, Minnesota; and Decorah and Forest City, Iowa, conducted celebrations in honor of the father of Norwegian nationalism.³³

Thus, in a little over four years, Norwegian Americans had shared in three of Norway's greatest national celebrations. Moreover, their inclusion as partners in these ceremonies reinforced their place as part of the Norwegian people. This confirmation from the homeland helped to restore much of the lost luster of the Norwegian-American self-image.

These binational celebrations of a greater Norway were also put into practice within larger, international contexts such as the 1933 Chicago World's Fair, whose slogan was "A Century of Progress." As might be expected, Nordmanns-Forbundet served as coordinator between the representatives of Norway and Norwegian America. Norway's main exhibit at the fair was the training ship *Sørlandet* (South Land), a sailing ship of the type still used for training potential Norwegian seamen. In a voyage designed to remind fairgoers of the 1893 Chicago World's Fair, when the replica of a Viking ship sailed from Norway to Chicago, *Sørlandet* followed a similar path. A speech delivered by the Norwegian-American Arthur Andersen, founder of the famed accounting firm, invoked the memory of the 1893 voyage of the ship *Viking*, which reinforced the idea of a greater Norway, especially the concept of latter-day Vikings.³⁴

During the week honoring the Scandinavian countries, the commemoration of *Sørlandet* was the central theme in the Norway Day celebration of June 20, 1933. A large contingent assembled on the south end of Northerly Island to greet the ship, featuring four hundred Norwegian-American singers from Chicago; Minneapolis; Sioux Falls, South Dakota; Madison, Wisconsin; Seattle; and other cities. Leading dignitaries, including John W. Sinding, president of the Norwegian-American World's Exposition Committee, Norway's envoy H. H. Bachke and cabinet minister Nils Trædel, and Captain Magnus Andersen, joined members of the press for a luncheon onboard *Sørlandet*.³⁵

In the evening a festive banquet held at the Stevens Hotel on Michigan

Avenue honored the captain and crew of the Norwegian training ship. Members of prominent Norwegian-American organizations, such as the Chicago Norske Klub (Chicago Norwegian Club), the Normennenes Klubhus (Norwegians' Club House), and the Chicago Sangerforbundet (Chicago Singers' Association) were present at the banquet. Bands from Luther College and Concordia College played "Nordic" music, including several rousing marches. The Queen of the Exposition, Lillian Anderson of Racine, Wisconsin, herself of Swedish-Finnish ancestry, extolled the exploits of *Sørlandet*'s crew, noting, "They will become the symbol for the first groups of Scandinavians and their Nordic racial characteristics."[36]

Two publications in Norway from this time fostered a sense of shared nationalism between Norwegian America and Norway. Magnus Andersen's *70 Års tilbakkeblikk* (Seventy Years of Looking Back) reflected on the fortieth anniversary of the voyage of the *Viking* and served to again remind homeland Norwegians that the Viking spirit could still be found among Norwegians on both sides of the Atlantic. Aksel Akselson's *Våre yngste vikinger* (Our Youngest Vikings) was an account of the exploits of *Sørlandet* and its crew. Its central point was that the "youngest Vikings" were a symbol of Norway's power as a nation, a young, vibrant nation that still possessed the vitality of its Viking-age forbears. To enforce this point, Akselson quotes the American president of the exhibition, Rufus Dawes: "Norway could not send us any better exhibition than these young men, who follow in Leif Erikson's footsteps, and who are a symbol of Norway's power on the oceans."[37]

At the local level, the greater Norway concept also had utility. On June 22–24, 1934, Norwegian America celebrated the Centennial Celebration of the First Permanent Norwegian Settlement in the United States in the Fox River Valley, La Salle County, Illinois. A commemoration of the longest-surviving Norwegian-American colony, the celebration centered on the dedication of a stone monument to Cleng Peerson, the man who located the land for the original settlers.

The celebration involved the collaboration of the Illinois State Historical Society, the Norwegian-American Historical Association, and the Department of History at the University of Illinois. Representing Norway at the ceremony was Chicago consul Olaf Bernts, while Birger Osland was present among the many Chicago-area and northern Illinois Norwegian-American leaders. According to *Nordisk Tidende*, the three-day celebration was marked by parades, concerts, religious services, lunches, Norwegian films, lectures, and speeches. At the dedication, a small *bautastein*, or stone monolith, with a bronze plate commemorating the first settlers from 1834, was unveiled amid the backdrop of Norwegian and American flags.[38]

Minister Morgenstierne and Arne Kildal, representing Nordmanns-Forbundet, attended the festivities, and both gave speeches. The minister was the event's featured speaker, and to him the Fox River settlement symbolized the virtues of the early pioneers and the concept of a greater Norway: "There is in reality a greater Norway, greater than any map or any census in any fashion can show." He claimed that the eight hundred thousand Norwegian immigrants to America and their descendants now numbered "perhaps as many as three million."[39]

Likewise, Kildal stressed the importance of the migration: "There is no event in the new Norway's history that has played a greater role than the emigration; economically and socially it has impacted the development of our nation and for a long time into the future will it determine our course." Elaborating further, he mentioned how the democratic lifestyle of America had its origins in Norway's democratic past, echoing Rasmus Bjørn Anderson in the 1870s and 1880s and others thereafter.[40] Local celebration was likewise adapted as a metaphor for the greater Norway concept.

To completely rehabilitate the Norwegian-American self-image following the Great War, both the American and the Norwegian governments had to validate it. Two events—the American government's official proclamation of Leif Erikson Day on October 9, 1935, and the 1939 visit to America by Crown Prince Olav and Crown Princess Märtha—achieved this result. Thus, on the eve of World War II, the Norwegian-American self-image had been restored to its 1914 status.

Norwegian-American leaders pushed for the American government to proclaim a national Leif Erikson day. The Leif Erikson Memorial Association of America was created in 1929 with the intended purpose of securing a national day for the Viking explorer. In conjunction with a number of other Norwegian-American organizations, such as the Sons of Norway and the Norwegian National League, plus the efforts of elected Norwegian-American representatives, the association achieved its goal. In 1935, Congress passed a resolution authorizing a national Leif Erikson Day, and on June 25, 1935, President Franklin D. Roosevelt by presidential proclamation designated October 9, 1935, for it. In addition, Norway's Per Krogh, the son of the painter Christian Krogh, produced a copy of his father's 1893 painting of Leif Erikson discovering the New World, which was emplaced in Statuary Hall in the Capitol Building on March 24, 1936.[41]

America's official recognition of Leif Erikson revitalized the Norwegian-American self-image. In a letter to *Decorah-Posten,* Theodore Jorgenson, professor at St. Olaf College, admitted that "Leif Erikson and the work of other [Norwegians] as explorers, which is to a large degree symbolic, has been transformed into a symbol of a retro-looking modern type." Jorgenson's somewhat awkward description meant that Erikson had become a contemporary symbol of Norwegian America. He further commented, "We come to the conclusion that Leif Erikson symbolizes the expansion of the Norwegian race." *Decorah-Posten* offered similar analysis when it noted in September of that year: "But it is not only in America that Leif's Day, the 9th of October, has become a universal, national day of celebration and memory. The same has occurred in Norway—and it has been so these past years."[42]

Of equal importance to Norwegian-American leaders was the idea that Leif Erikson's legacy had achieved something akin to equal footing with that of Christopher Columbus. In October 1934, a *Nordisk Tidende* editorial wryly noted that at a park dedicated to Leif Erikson in New York, the New York mayor had arrived only a half hour after dedicating a city park to Columbus, and it noted that Leif Erickson's park still lacked a monument of the Norse explorer. After the dedication of the Leif Erikson painting in the U.S. Capitol, the paper commented in 1936 that "recognition of Leiv Eriksson as America's first explorer . . . has at last been nearly fulfilled." It did admit that most American textbooks referred to Columbus as the "discoverer of America," but the paper preferred to call him "the re-discoverer of America."[43]

Vigilance, however, had to be maintained, warned *Nordisk Tidende,* owing to concerted opposition to recognition of the Leif Erikson legacy. It noted how two Italian-American congressmen were critical of the placement of the Leif Erikson picture in the Capitol rotunda and that the New York City press tended to be negative toward the explorer, which implied that they were catering to the biases of New York's Italian-American community. To bolster its case, *Nordisk Tidende* reprinted an editorial from the *Washington Evening Star,* which argued that further scientific research in the years to follow would only add greater credence to the notion that Leif Erikson, not Christopher Columbus, was the real discoverer of America. Furthermore, the *Washington Evening Star* praised Norwegian Americans who had helped to build the American nation, sustaining it through their dedication to its traditions of liberty, progress, and peace. It added, "Norway, too, is motivated by similar ideals. All that is wanted is the fruition of their mutual hopes for all mankind."[44]

Notwithstanding its rivalry with the city's Italian-American community, New York's Norwegian community used the positive publicity resulting from the Leif Erikson proclamation to bolster the self-image of Norwegian America. On October 9, 1935, *Nordisk Tidende* published a special English insert, the "Leiv Eiriksson Review," which devoted nineteen pages to the legacy of Leif Erikson. It reported that the Norwegian people in America should be proud of "the contributions it has made in the up-building of this nation. It has pioneered in new states, in the wilderness of the virgin territories, and by dint of brain and brawn, efficiency and thrift, honesty and upright dealing, added an empire to the American Union."[45] By printing a special English edition, the paper used the occasion of Leif Erikson Day to promote the Norwegian-American self-image to a larger American audience.

Leif Erikson Day elicited a positive response from Norway, for the recognition of Norwegian Americans strengthened Norway's national image. King Haakon VII sent a telegram to President Roosevelt: "On the occasion of the first official celebration of Leiv Eiriksson day, I wish to transmit to all Americans the warm greetings of all Norwegians." Norway's prime minister Johan Nygaardsvold gave a speech from Norway that was simultaneously broadcast in America. In the speech he sent his greetings to note that the Norwegian-American contribution "has led America forward to what it is today: one of the world's greatest nations."[46]

Norway's press recognized the significance of Leif Erikson Day for Norway. In 1934 *Aftenposten* observed that the forthcoming observance of Leif Erikson Day in America represented a great victory for Norwegian America, and it urged that one day soon Norway should celebrate October 9 as "Emigrated Norwegians' Day." Trondheim's *Dagsposten* reasoned that Leif Erikson should be remembered because "today one finds almost as many Norwegians living abroad as here at home." It also stated that because of "the great work ethic and energy that most Norwegians have demonstrated these days, they are well-liked in America and they have in most instances done quite well for themselves." *Tidens Tegn,* meanwhile, commented on how Leif Erikson Day "to a greater extent than ever before has attained a beautiful and emotional expression on both sides of the Atlantic."[47]

Numerous platitudes similarly resonated at the dedication of the Leif Erikson painting, which a large Norwegian delegation attended. Alf Bjercke, representing the Norske Venner av Amerika (Norwegian Friends of America) and, along with Wilhelm Morgenstierne, the Norwegian government, delivered the painting to the Norwegian-American delegation. The Norwegian Friends of America had solicited individual Norwegians to raise the necessary funds to produce the Erikson painting. In his remarks, Bjercke stated that the painting was a gift in friendship to the American people and a tribute to the contributions of Norwegians to America, in cultural as well as in commercial and industrial ways. Continuing, he noted:

> In addition to this recognition of Norwegian-born men and women's good work as American citizens, the American people in general are more and more realizing that Norwegians' feelings for this continent are so to speak rooted in tradition. I refer here to all the memorials and other marks of appreciation that are dedicated to the name of Leiv Eriksson, America's discoverer. All Norwegian-bred American citizens and all Norwegians in the mother country received with great pleasure the information that Congress last year instituted the 9th of October as Leiv Eriksson's day. And we entertain hope that the day will continue to be devoted to his memory.[48]

The success of Leif Erikson Day even attracted the attention of Norway's academic community. The Norwegian historian A. W. Brøgger authored a four-page essay that appeared in *Tidens Tegn* on October 12, 1935. Brøgger stated the case for the strong connection between Norway and America:

> As the discovery was tied to Norwegian seamanship, so the rediscovered history and Leif Erikson Day once again are tied to the Norwegian race. They are likewise tied to the knowledge that the other Norwegian colonization in America, which began eight hundred years after the first, has been of great importance in the formation of the modern U.S.A. And this same U.S.A. owes much more to the Norwegian and Anglo-Saxon races; it has more in common with them than it does with the Latin discoverers of the fifteenth and sixteenth centuries."[49]

Official American government recognition of Norwegian America, therefore, impacted the Norwegian-American self-image profoundly. It reinforced powerful Anglo-American validation of the importance of the Norwegian-American community. The official Leif Erikson Day signaled to Norway's image-makers that their Norwegian compatriots in America had established a worthy legacy in America. And it was that legacy that also served to advance Norway's national identity. The benefits of the relationship also meant that the fortunes of Norwegian America would remain highly important in cultivating Norway's image abroad.

When Norway's Crown Prince Olav and Crown Princess Märtha visited America in 1939, it marked the high point in Norway's validation of the Norwegian-American self-image. Norway's government had planned the royal visit as early as November 1937, and it was likely aware of the successful visit to America in 1938 by Sweden's Crown Prince Gustav Adolf to commemorate the tercentenary celebration of the Swedes in America. The government had charged Nordmanns-Forbundet with the responsibility of organizing the tour. The visit would also coincide with the 1939 New York World's Fair, offering further opportunities to promote Norway's national image.

In a letter dated April 14, 1939, Norway's consul general in New York, Rolf A. Christensen, wrote to Carl Søyland, editor of *Nordisk Tidende*, explaining the reasons for the royal visit. It would allow Norway to pay its greatest compliment to the Norwegian Americans, showing to the world the high esteem that Norway had for the emigrants and their sense of devotion to Norway's royal house. The visit would hopefully bring Norway's name to the foreground of world attention.[50] The visit by Norway's crown prince and princess was part of the Norwegian government's attempt to promote a modern national image for Norway, which would capitalize on the success of Norwegian-American identity.

The royal couple arrived at New York on April 27, 1939, and they met with President Roosevelt the next day. For over two months, the couple visited Norwegian America. Highlights of their tour included their participation at the opening of Norway's pavilion at the World's Fair, including the dedication of a stone monument to Leif Erikson in Leif Eiriksson Square. They also had stops in Chicago; Northfield, Minnesota; Minneapolis–St. Paul; and several stops along the Pacific Coast.

Each stop on the tour permitted Norwegian Americans to participate in a mutual celebration of Norwegian and Norwegian-American nationalisms, and the turnout was impressive. On May 1, when the royal couple attended the opening ceremonies of Norway's pavilion at the World Fair, attendance was estimated at fifty thousand, including ten thousand children waving Norwegian flags. The day also included visits to various Norwegian-American institutions in the city. The theme of the World's Fair was "Building the World of Tomorrow," and Crown Prince Olav delivered a speech to dedicate the opening of the Norwegian pavilion, noting, "We Norwegians are taking the most keen interest in the American efforts for the building of a better world of tomorrow."[51]

At a later welcoming ceremony held at the Metropolitan Museum, the crown prince gave a stirring homage to his emigrated kinsmen, reflecting on their contributions to their new homeland:

> May I say to the Americans of Norwegian birth or parentage that this you could do and can do without the slightest risk of being misunderstood. Your loyalty to your new country in war and peace has indeed stood its test. The spirit of Colonel Heg and Knute Nelson has been and is today your spirit. You are in the fortunate situation that your Norwegian heritage, your *fedrearv*, blends harmoniously with your American foundations and environment. You are in a position to draw on the cultural and national treasures of two great peoples—You find in this your new country that same love of liberty, those same free, democratic institutions, the same freedom of religion, of speech and of action within the law, the same human brotherliness, the same love of justice and peace, which has been carried down to you from your fathers. And so by keeping alive your Norwegian heritage you can become only better Americans and in addition you will increasingly become the most important and vital link between our two peoples who have so much in common and nothing to separate them but the ocean![52]

Even small venues had impressive turnouts. Decorah, Iowa, had a population of five thousand, yet when it received the royal couple on May 6 and 7, it had a turnout of twenty thousand. At the main ceremony held at Luther College, Crown Prince Olav thanked several Norwegian-American institutions, including the college and *Decorah-Posten*, "for the contributions they had made to the preservation of Norwegianness." Reciprocating the compliment, congressman H. O. Talle spoke of the energy and youthful spirit linking America and Norway and praised the crown prince for coming to this young land as "the highest representative of Norway's youthfulness."[53]

On the couple's next stop, at St. Olaf College in Northfield, Minnesota,

As the royal ambassadors of the greater Norway, Crown Prince Olav and Princess Märtha were often photographed in formal dress during their tour of Norwegian America in 1939. This photograph was taken in Fargo, North Dakota. Courtesy of the Institute for Regional Studies, North Dakota State University, Fargo.

five thousand people greeted them at the train station, and there were six thousand at the ceremony at the college. The college welcomed the couple with an impressive ceremony, including the awarding of an honorary doctorate to the crown prince. Sigvald Holden, one of the college's students, greeted the royal couple with a speech in Norwegian, which greatly impressed the guests from the homeland. The crown prince thanked and greeted St. Olaf College for the achievements it had made in American cultural life. One of the most expressive moments occurred at a luncheon the next day when a greeting by Professor Theodore Jorgenson, who was ill and unable to attend, was read by Dean J. Jørgen Thompson. According to the Norwegian press attaché Hans Olav, it was a poetic work of great beauty that attested to the importance of Crown Prince Olav's name in Norwegian history.[54]

In addition to their swing through the upper Midwest, the royal couple visited several important cities along America's West Coast, greeted by large crowds of Americans of Norwegian ancestry. An article by Hans Olav, which appeared in *Washington Posten,* referred to the journey of the royal couple as "a triumphal procession from coast to coast." The paper noted that the couple's early celebration of May 17 (on May 14) in Los Angeles attracted twenty thousand people. In his speech, delivered in Norwegian, Crown Prince Olav paid special attention to the work of the Peer Gynt Lodge of the Sons of Norway, especially their efforts to protect Norwegian language and cultural values, which bound together Norwegian people on both sides of the ocean.[55]

The royal couple celebrated Norway's Constitution Day in San Francisco on May 17. In conjunction with the New York World's Fair, the city was to host the Golden Gate Exhibition later that summer. The centerpiece was a banquet held that evening in the California Hall of the Golden Gate Exhibition. The crown prince's speech on the occasion was broadcast in both Norway and America. He assured his Norwegian-American audience that people back in the homeland "are proud of what our compatriots in America have achieved." He remarked that May 17 brought ties of fellowship between America and Norway and that "it represents even more the strong and living bond between them. . . . Freedom and peace are our common slogans."[56]

It should be noted that the Golden Gate Exhibition offered another opportunity for Norwegian Americans and Norway to celebrate their shared heritage. Although it did not have the presence of the royal couple to bring the same luster as to the New York World's Fair or to the crown prince's lecture tour, nonetheless, it did provide additional exposure for that shared heritage, especially on Norway's Day, which was held on August 27 of that year. Traditional Norwegian culture could be found at the authentic Norwegian-style ski cabin where visitors were greeted by Norwegians in their traditional *bunader.* At the evening celebration, visitors were entertained by Norwegian singing associations and traditional dances.[57]

Governor John Moses of North Dakota, whose ancestry was, of course, Norwegian, hailed the "spirit of Norway" in his talk on Norway's Day. The governor related common themes, such as the idea that men and women of Norwegian descent had been a major factor in the development of many areas of the United States. Furthermore, the governor noted, Norwegian Americans had come to love America. He praised them for the rugged individualism inherited from their Viking forebears, their adherence to democracy, and their ability to adjust to new surroundings. Yet, he pointed out that Norway was a modern, industrial nation that had made great strides in social legislation, including health care, education, and the care of its elderly. Most important, Norway was a steadfastly neutral country whose aspirations spoke of the desire for peace, unlike the acts of its aggressive neighbor Germany.[58]

Seattle, home to the largest concentration of Norwegian-Americans on the West Coast, received a visit from Crown Prince Olav and Princess Märtha on May 25 and 26. A contingent led by Mayor Arthur B. Langlie and his wife greeted them in the plaza outside city hall. The Norwegians among the audience revealed themselves by throwing their hats into the air when the band broke into "Ja, vi elsker dette landet." The next day, May 26, featured a lunch at the Chamber of Commerce, at which the members of the Norwegian Chamber of Commerce figured prominently. Colonel Howard Hansen gave a speech in which he initiated the crown prince as a member of the organization. The highlight of the visit took place that evening at the Civic Auditorium where over six thousand attended. Numerous Norwegian-American organizations were represented, and August Werner and his orchestra played selections from the Sigurd Jorsalfar Suite as the royal couple made their entrance.[59]

Dignitaries, including vice consul Christian Stang-Andersen and consul Einar Beyer, expressed what *Washington Posten* termed "strong words wishing the honored guests and everyone else welcome." Governor Clarence D. Martin likewise spoke, and singers from the Olav Trygvason Choir entertained the audience. Major Langlie concluded the evening with a rousing speech, referred to by *Washington Posten* as the best mayoral speech the royal couple had heard on their entire trip.[60]

After leaving the Pacific Northwest, the royal tour ventured into the strongly Norwegian-American areas of the northern plains. Stopping at numerous small towns and cities, the tour involved countless luncheons and endless handshaking. During their stop at the small town of Mayville, North Dakota, a heavily Norwegian area, three thousand people turned out to see the Norwegian couple. Presiding over the ceremony, Mayor Selmer Groth told them that the assembly was "almost ninety-nine percent Norwegian." The tour provided ample opportunities for the crown prince to symbolically reaffirm the authentic Norwegian character of the immigrants' heroes. For example, the crown prince visited the grave of Carl Ben Eielson in Hatton, North Dakota, and at Alexandria, Minnesota, he visited the grave of Senator Knute Nelson, laying flowered wreaths on both gravestones.[61]

Two of the most impressive receptions for the crown prince and his wife occurred in the twin towns of Fargo, North Dakota, and Moorhead, Minnesota, on June 8 and June 9. On Thursday, June 8, Concordia College in Moorhead held its graduation ceremony at which it bestowed an honorary doctor of laws degree on the crown prince. As the featured speaker at the ceremony, the crown prince addressed the seventy-nine graduates, praising Norwegian Americans and their institutions for preserving the common heritage shared with Norway. He also urged the young people present to "hold the window open toward the land from which their fathers had come," and to seek "stronger ties between the two freedom-loving peoples."[62]

On the following day, Friday, June 9, the royal couple rode in an open car at the head of a parade that followed a two-and-a-half-mile route through Moorhead and Fargo. At the corner of Broadway and Northern Pacific avenues, the parade traveled past a tribute in the form of a large flag-adorned Viking ship. At this point, the crown prince stepped out to greet the members of the passing parade. The group then assembled in Island Park, where the crown prince spoke in Norwegian to the throng of fifty thousand, including forty-two *bygdelags* that had assembled in Fargo–Moorhead. The remainder of the official "people's fest" took place at the North Dakota Agricultural College, which featured several Norwegian music corps and singing choruses. Among the speech givers was John Moses, North Dakota's governor, a man of Norwegian ancestry.[63]

A large, three-day ceremony greeted the crown prince and crown princess in Minneapolis–St. Paul from June 11 to 13. On the first day they partook in a Norwegian-style church service, conducted entirely in Norwegian, at the Hippodrome in St. Paul. The planners had decided to hold the service in Norwegian because they felt it might be the last time such a massed Norwegian service could be conducted in America.[64] The official banquet was held on the evening of June 12, 1939, and featured the elite of the Twin Cities, including Governor Harold Stassen and J. A. Aasgaard, president of the Norwegian Lutheran Church in America; as well as prominent homeland Norwegians, such as Aage Brun, attaché for the Norwegian Legation in Washington, D.C.; Guy Stanton Ford, president of the University of Minnesota; Wilhelm Morgenstierne, Norway's minister to America; and consul F. H. Hobe. The inaugural speaker, Aasgard, commented, "We Norwegians are proud to have participated in the building of this land. We are, first and foremost, citizens of America, which we combine with the finest and purest of our cultural traditions." In a similar vein, Mrs. Manley L. Fosteen, a former Republican Party committeewoman from Minnesota, observed, "We are proud of our legacy, proud of the little land Norway, which has contributed so much to civilization and whose immigrants have worked with such productive inspiration."[65]

At last, the couple was introduced by Governor Stassen. In his speech, the crown prince noted that Norwegian Americans had strong ties to both Norway and America:

> St. Paul and Minneapolis are a Norwegian tribute to the making of America. And while the Norwegian ethnic group has preserved its heritage, it has never taken a backseat to anyone in its loyalty to the United States. The Norwegian Americans are today the most important link between two peoples who stand very close to each other because both believe in the democratic form of government and in freedom through responsibility.[66]

Three days later, on June 15, the royal couple paid a visit to the twin cities of Duluth, Minnesota, and Superior, Wisconsin. There the couple participated in the dedication of the Bert J. Enger Memorial Observation Tower, located in Enger Park in Duluth. Of Norwegian ancestry, Enger had been a successful businessman and philanthropist, having dedicated land for Enger Park a few years earlier. The dedication of Enger Tower provided a chance to comment on the generosity and commitment to public service found in all Norwegian Americans, a trait traceable to Norway. At the ceremony, Mayor E. R. Berghult stated that the park "will become a lasting memorial to a progressive American citizen of Norwegian ancestry." Crown Prince Olav likewise utilized his speech to laud the attributes of Enger and, by extension, Norwegian Americans. Noting that Enger had a typical Norwegian name, the crown prince emphasized that he "had been born and had grown up in Norway, where he learned the core principles of his life."[67]

By paying homage to American and Norwegian-American nationalism, the crown prince participated as the symbolic link in the commemoration of the two nationalisms. On June 22, the crown prince traveled to Springfield, Illinois, to visit President Lincoln's home. The visit represented a pilgrimage to one of America's most revered places.[68] In New York, on July 6, 1939, they were present at the dedication of the monument to Leif Erikson, which was attended by ten thousand people. Attached to the ten-foot-high stone monument was a bronze plate that read, in runic-style letters, "Leiv Eiriksson discovered America Year 1000." In an act of interethnic solidarity, New York City mayor Fiorello LaGuardia remarked that he was receiving the monument in the name of the city not only as mayor but also "as a son of Columbus who greets the son of a Viking." The crown prince's speech restated the idea of shared Norwegian and American values:

> Leif Eiriksson finally is becoming known as the first discoverer of the American continent, and he would be glad to see that the monument was raised where so many Norwegians have journeyed. It shall always be a reminder of the close friendship and the common ideas—freedom, brotherhood, and democracy—that bind the two democracies together.[69]

Drawing on ideas first articulated by Norwegian-American image-makers, the crown prince used the royal tour to drive home the idea that Norway and America had a long association and shared core values. In most of his speeches given on the tour he repeated those ideas that culminated in the speech he gave at the dedication of the Leif Erikson monument.[70]

Norwegian Americans could achieve their place within the Norwegian nation because of their strong ethnic ties. As Anthony D. Smith has shown, nationalism ultimately derives from a core ethnic group, and though the nation initially was identified with the territorial homeland, it was possible for those living outside the homeland to still belong to the nation owing to those ethnic ties. For Norwegian Americans, their strong Norwegian cultural practices and ethnic character qualified them to be members of the Norwegian nation, a point repeatedly confirmed by the transnational celebrations.[71]

Although homeland reaction to the royal visit was mostly positive, some negative coverage did arise. After visiting the Norwegian pavilion at the World's Fair, one correspondent wrote that "Norwegians are being snubbed" and that Norwegians in New York are "seen with Swedish eyes," which implied that fairgoers often mistook Norwegians for Swedes.[72]

Other Norwegian papers, however, viewed the royal visit positively. On May 2, 1939, *Aftenposten* displayed a photograph of Crown Prince Olav and President Roosevelt sharing a hearty laugh. Over this picture ran the caption: "Godt å være norsk i Amerika nå" (Good to be Norwegian in America now).[73]

On the whole, coverage of the latter type predominated, especially when the Norwegian press evaluated the tour as it neared its completion. For instance, *Nationen* reported that the visit was "a Norwegian-American commemoration." The comments of the crown prince reflected the realization in Norway that the Norwegian-American reputation bolstered Norway's national self-image. The paper stated that the exposure of the fair, coupled with the high profile created by the visit of the royal couple, would ensure that Norway received substantial publicity from the two events.[74]

According to *Aftenposten*, Crown Prince Olav had made a triumphant tour among Norwegian Americans, who by "being good Norwegians and good Americans at the same time ... are contributing to binding Norway and America closer together." In another article, *Aftenposten* congratulated the crown prince "for bringing his message to the American people." It reported that the crown prince had made a "forceful" case that the American and Norwegian peoples were becoming more closely united by their shared ideals.[75] The success of the royal couple's tour thus served to validate the importance of Norwegian-Americans to Norway's national self-image. And by becoming successful Americans, the emigrated Norwegians had helped to define Norway's national image through a set of values it shared with America.

Not surprisingly, the Norwegian-American response to the tour was likewise positive. Commenting in *Decorah-Posten* as well as *Dagbladet*, editor Kristian Prestgard exclaimed, "Not since the first emigration from Norway began more than a hundred years ago have there been such feelings of joy and unity across Norwegian America, as with Crown Prince Olav and Crown Princess Märtha's present goodwill tour." After attending the festivities in Minneapolis–St. Paul, the Norwegian-American Bishop J. A. Aasgaard hoped that the couple would take "a greeting home to Norway with the warm thanks and affection that still throbs in the hearts of Norwegians for the land of their fathers." On the day of their return voyage to Norway, *Nordisk Tidende* proclaimed the tour a success and described how Crown Prince Olav and Princess Märtha "were bidding farewell to the U.S.A. with tears in their eyes."[76]

Skandinaven observed how the efforts of Nordmanns-Forbundet to promote the tour had allowed homeland Norway to "discover" Norwegian America:

> In recent years, one has Nordmanns-Forbundet to thank for the increasing friendship between the people of Norway and her emigrated friends here in the United States. In addition, they have learned to see that our Norwegian America is a society that in many respects can be spoken of favorably with the motherland and in some areas is now more advanced. All branches of the Norwegian tree stand in debt to Nordmanns-Forbundet for its priceless work in bringing closer family connections among Norwegians, both at home and abroad, and for the acknowledgment that the homeland has shown for our loyalty to the inheritance from our fathers' land.[77]

As representatives of the state of Norway, Crown Prince Olav and Crown Princess Märtha succeeded in establishing greater recognition of the ties between Norway and Norwegian America. Their efforts added tremendous value to the Norwegian-American self-image, and the prestige of the visit added the luster of official recognition, which validated that self-image. Norwegian-American leaders at last had realized the dream of having the emigrated Norway viewed as a vital component of Norway's national identity. The visit by Crown Prince Olav and Crown Princess Märtha had proven the existence of a greater Norway. Germany's invasion of Norway in World War II, moreover, would prove just how valuable it was for Norway to have strong ties with ethnic Norwegians outside its homeland borders.

World War II

On the eve of World War II, the Norwegian-American community had reached what might be termed the mature phase of its development. It had been more than a generation since the last large wave of immigration, and Norwegian language use had declined. Third- and fourth-generation Norwegian Americans were now English speakers; they might still know Norwegian, but they were no longer tied to Norwegian-language activities.[78]

Yet Norwegian Americans remained active in certain types of ethnic organizations through what H. Arnold Barton has termed "elective ethnicity." For instance, the Sons of Norway had a membership increase of three thousand in 1939. Many Norwegian-American communities continued to celebrate May 17 and Leif Erikson Day. Prominent Norwegian-Americans continued to meet at their Norwegian clubs in the large cities. And as Jane Marie Pederson's study has revealed, some rural Norwegian-American communities maintained their ethnic identities well into the 1940s. Peter A. Munch's 1952 study of Norwegian communities in Wisconsin revealed how tenaciously the Norwegian cultural identity remained.[79]

The German invasion of Norway on April 9, 1940, and the subsequent five-year occupation offered a severe test of the greater Norway concept. Hitler chose to invade Norway to prevent a British naval blockade as in the First World War, as well as for ideological reasons. According to the ideology of National Socialism, the Nordic racial purity of Norwegians should have made them the natural allies of Germany. However, the resolute resistance of Norway's King Haakon VII, the Norwegian government, and the Norwegian people belied that assumption. Both the king and the government fled into exile in Britain, and in their place the Germans installed Major Vidkun Quisling, the leader of Norway's anemic fascist movement Nasjonal Samling (National Gathering), as the figurehead of the new regime.

Norway's greatest asset was its merchant marine, and the government in exile attempted to maintain it by establishing its base of operations in New York. Although America was still officially neutral, many prominent Norwegians, including Crown Princess Märtha and her children, took up residence in America. In fact, during the visit of Crown Prince Olav and his wife to the United States in 1939, President Roosevelt had offered them sanctuary in the event that such a calamity might befall Norway. In addition, many large Norwegian corporations had offices in New York, and so America was a logical place from which to base the fleet. The strong relationship between Norway and its emigrated cousins offered additional inducement, including an affluent constituency that could lobby for Norway's interests.[80]

In the early days of the war, however, it proved difficult to promote the idea that Norway was a victim of the Nazi war machine. A major reason was an article published in *Life* on May 6, 1940, by the American journalist Leland Stowe. According to Stowe, the Germans had bluffed their way into Oslo, taking control of the Norwegian capital with a modest force of only fifteen hundred men. The reason, Stowe concluded, was large-scale Norwegian indifference: not a single Norwegian had resisted, and the government had fled north to Hamar almost immediately. But even more damaging was his charge that Norwegian traitors had allowed disguised German ships (loaded with armed soldiers) to slip into Norway's major ports undetected, thus becoming the spearhead of the invasion.[81]

It became imperative, therefore, for the Norwegian government in exile to wage a major campaign to sway American public opinion and prove that Stowe's assertions were not valid. Norwegian Americans would play a crucial role in that effort since they enjoyed a reputation for being solid, patriotic citizens, especially among Anglo-American opinion makers.[82]

Despite the goodwill that existed between Norway and Norwegian America, tension sometimes marked the early years of the partnership. The Norwegian Americans of New York expected that the newcomers would take advantage of existing Norwegian-American institutions, especially their maritime institutions. Many homeland Norwegians, however, wanted little to do with the immigrant community. The Norwegian government in exile created the Norwegian Shipping and Trade Mission, better known as Nortraships, to handle all activities, including the foundation of a new infrastructure largely from scratch.[83]

The response from the Norwegian-American community sometimes reflected a sense of betrayal. In September 1941, an article about the Seaman's Hotel by Pastor C. O. Pedersen of the Norwegian Seaman's Mission expressed this indignation. His article was titled "Brobygning—et varsku!" (Bridge Building—a Warning), and he commented on the strained relationship between "snobbish" Norwegians and "hayseed" Norwegian Americans.[84]

Sometimes outright animosity broke out between the two halves of the Norwegian nation, as it did on November 22, 1941. In an article for *Collier's Magazine*, Norway's Major Ole Reistad used the opportunity to criticize Norwegian Americans. As commander of Camp Little Norway in Canada, where the Norwegian Royal Air Force trained its pilots, the major's denouncement struck a raw nerve. "From the Norwegian Americans come sayings that they must help us. We hope for their support but there is not much that they have done. They call themselves 'Sons of Norway' and prattle about 'the Viking heritage.' But you cannot count yourself a son when you experience seeing Norway in a struggle to the death and being beaten to a pulp, and you nonetheless do nothing about it."[85]

Despite the tensions between the two halves of the Norwegian nation, however, the high stakes involved demanded that the concept of a greater Norway must ultimately prevail. Even Major Reistad, despite his early remarks, became popular at Norwegian-American organizations after he realized the importance of the immigrant community to Norway's war effort. Goodwill between Norway and the Norwegian-American community was essential to Norway's strategy for winning the war. At a speech delivered in London in November 1941, Minister Wilhelm Morgenstierne stressed that Norway had an exceptionally strong position in the United States owing to both sympathy for Norway and the steadfast support of Norwegian Americans.[86] The concept proved useful on Norway's side because the government understood that defeating Hitler would involve securing the cooperation of the United States. It therefore utilized the strong ties it had cultivated with both the Norwegian-American community and the American government to secure financial and ideological support for Norway. In this context, the activities of Nordmanns-Forbundet also proved important.

On the American side, Norwegian-American leaders led the effort to secure financial support for Norway, and they promoted the idea that Norwegians and Norwegian Americans were brothers, that is, "modern Vikings" engaged in a struggle to rescue the homeland. The administration of President Franklin D. Roosevelt offered material support as well as strong ideological support for the idea that Norway represented the truest ideals of democracy and freedom.

Norwegian leaders took advantage of every opportunity to relate these ideas to the American public. Because Crown Princess Märtha and her children resided at Pook's Hill, a short distance from the American capitol, Crown Prince Olav traveled frequently to America. On the anniversary of the German invasion of Norway, he was in Boston, where he gave a radio speech about the Norwegian people at home. During the course of his speech he invoked the concept of a greater Norway to argue that Norway's strength was far from diminished:

> The greatest of everything that is still to be reckoned is that the overwhelming and most valuable part of our people, who naturally reside outside the land, today stand completely together in their duty to free our land. Let us remember that we have strong and good friends in the world who are fighting for the same cause as us [sic], and who will do everything possible so that we shall win our

freedom. I have spent some time myself in the United States and here have on many occasions noticed the sympathy and good will with which the American people follow our cause and realize the effective help that is to be contributed for the ideas, which are also America's own.[87]

Once America and Norway became wartime allies in December 1941, Norway could resort to more direct appeals for aid. Less than a month after the attack on Pearl Harbor, the director of Norway's Public Health department, Karl Evang, spoke in Washington, D.C., to thank Norwegian Americans and other friends of Norway for their material assistance prior to America's involvement in the war. Now that America and Norway were "brothers in arms," he expressed the hope that greater opportunities for assistance would be possible in the war to preserve democracy. Speaking in London in June 1942, Crown Prince Olav observed the deep sympathy for Norway's cause in America among "endless men and women—especially those of Norwegian birth or descent."[88]

Recognizing how successful the visit of the royal couple had been in 1939, the government in exile arranged another visit, which primarily featured Olav's lecture tour of America between April 11 and May 1, 1942, but also included a handful of public appearances beforehand along the eastern seaboard. Unlike the 1939 visit, marked by the pomp and circumstance of parades and celebrations, this time the visit was a low-key, Spartan affair whose mission was "business." During his visit to the Twin Cities, the crown prince admitted that the purpose of the speaking tour was to raise money among Norwegian Americans.[89] During the visit, he expressed at every opportunity the idea that Norwegians, like Americans, were strongly individualistic:

> There is disagreement and serious discussion among us Norwegians in foreign lands; that is a natural consequence of our individualism, of our ancient right to each individual to express his beliefs. But we all know that the Norwegian people have never stood more united than today in their basic beliefs. We will all free Norway, and it means not least that there can be rule based on differences of opinion concerning the course of action and its forces when the issue appears so clear. Everything that mattered to us before becomes so very small compared to that which unites us now.[90]

Another official Norwegian strategy involved sharing public rituals between Norway and Norwegian America. It thus became common for a representative of the government to be present at major Norwegian-American organizational events.[91] One of the most salient examples occurred on May 17, 1942, when Norway's prime minister Johan Nygaardsvold gave a speech at the Constitution Day celebration in Minneapolis. He observed how the Old Norse sagas revealed an "attempt to obtain this people's [the Norwegians'] ancient right to freedom." He further proclaimed that when faced by "tyranny and dictatorial oppression, the people journeyed—in spite of their love of their homes and the land—out from Norway so they might build homes in other lands. But they never forgot Norway. In deed and in words they expressed their love for Norway." Here, the prime minister was alluding to the exodus to Iceland and Normandy in Harald Fairhair's time, comparing the present struggle with an earlier attempt to resist tyranny.[92]

Yet this symbolic, Viking-inspired struggle was very much one fought on behalf of the modern and progressive Norway. At a speech given a few days later in Seattle, Nygaardsvold strongly refuted the Nazi claim that the German invasion had been necessary because Norway had been on the brink of chaos and revolution. Instead, he insisted that Norway had been peaceful, prosperous, and neutral prior to the conflict. Most important, the prime minister observed, Nazi plundering and brutality had united the Norwegian people in their opposition, making them determined to win the struggle for Norway's freedom. And it was a fight for a modern Norway, whose symbols were the Storting, its constitution, and its constitutional monarch, Haakon VII.[93]

On July 4, 1942, Tryggve Lie, Norway's minister of foreign affairs, provided confirmation of the importance of the greater Norway concept, especially the link between Norwegians and Americans:

> The 4th of July is marked by an endless stream of good wishes to the United States from all the freedom-loving peoples in the entire world. The Norwegian people are bound to the great republic on the other side of the Atlantic Ocean through many strong bonds. Hundreds of thousands of men and women of Norwegian ancestry have found a home in the New World, and they have been active in building up the powerful American democracy. Both the nation's president and the American people during the entire war have provided help to Norway and supported our war against the Nazi oppressors.[94]

Although Norway was a small, occupied nation, its public relations campaign made sure that its contributions in waging the war were well known. On behalf of the government in exile, foreign minister Lie made it clear that Norway would have no territorial demands after the war.[95] The anthology *Tusen norske skip* (A Thousand Norwegian Ships), published in November 1943, offered the thesis that through its merchant fleet, which carried war materials for the allies, Norway had been a significant combatant. Another common wartime idea was that the Germans considered Norway's merchant marine to be worth a million-man army to England. Moreover, the top-scoring squadron in the Royal Air Force during 1943 was Norsk Jægerskvadron (the Norwegian Hunter Squadron), which shot down over 160 German planes. In connection with the 130th anniversary of Norway's constitution in 1944, the Norwegian government sponsored an exhibition titled "Norway, a Fighting Ally," which featured a book in English by the same name as well as a traveling exhibit.[96] These efforts all promoted the idea that Norway was a significant contributor to the war effort, an attempt to boost Norway's prestige in the world.

From the Norwegian-American side came ample financial contributions to the war effort. Just ten days after the German invasion, Norwegian-American leaders formed Norwegian Relief, Inc., which was later renamed American Relief for Norway at the request of the American government. Organized in virtually all major Norwegian-American communities, its structure reflected the need to balance representation among the major cultural centers. As a consequence, despite the fact that it had been incorporated in Illinois, its executive committee included representatives from the major Norwegian-American urban centers. Throughout most of the war, J. A. Aasgaard of Minneapolis served as president of the board, and he was joined by other Norwegian Americans from cities including New York, Seattle, Boston, Los Angeles, and San Francisco.

In 1947, A. N. Rygg of New York published a book outlining the activities of American Relief for Norway. The project raised 1.8 million dollars, which were used to send humanitarian aid to Norway and also provided funding for Camp Little Norway, a training center for Norwegian pilots in Canada. In recognition of these efforts, the book contained a dedication from King Haakon VII: "The memorial about American Relief for Norway's work will always be a strong bond of friendship between the Norwegian people and the population in the Unites States of America."[97]

Norwegian Americans continued to celebrate Norwegian holidays, such as May 17, but with the purpose of raising money for Norway's relief. During the war, on the anniversary of the German invasion, April 9, Norwegian Americans would gather in support of the homeland to "remember that black day which has brought all Norwegians together." In Minneapolis–St. Paul, Norwegian Americans used the day to hold their annual Norway Liberation Rally; in Seattle, the Norwegian-American community began celebrating a new Norway Day on August 21. The old Norway Day had been celebrated in the autumn, but Norwegian-American leaders believed they could raise more money for the war effort by moving the celebration to the more temperate summer season.[98]

Another strategy involved Norwegian-American efforts to counter the Nazi appropriation of Viking-age symbolism. Under the Quisling regime, official propaganda portrayed National Socialism as the inheritor of Norway's Viking spirit. Most homeland Norwegians objected strongly to the Nazi appropriation, labeling it the stealing of Norway's national symbols for evil purposes. Among Norwegian-Americans, whose national identity equated with the concept of latter-day Vikings, every effort was made to counter the negative National Socialist–appropriated images of the Viking era. Thus, after a March 1941 joint British–Norwegian commando raid on the Lofoten Islands in northern Norway, *Nordisk Tidende* stated, "Modern Vikings make beach raid in Lofoten, freeing 300 Norwegians."[99]

The paper also ran cartoons that countered the association between Vikings and National Socialists. One from February 1942 showed a Viking holding his nose in disgust as Hitler pins a medal on Quisling. That same year, a more positive cartoon showed a Viking with one arm on a fighter pilot and the other on a sailor. The caption read, "To Norway's Fighting Forces." In Seattle, *Washington Posten* ran a similar cartoon two days before Syttende mai, 1942, in which a Norwegian fighter pilot and a Norwegian soldier are shown marching across the North Atlantic, while behind them lurks a Viking warrior with spear and shield. Over this cartoon is the caption, "The Norse Spirit of Old on the March to Victory." Norway's government offered considerable support in this campaign as well. Crown Prince Olav gave a radio address in early 1942, "The Spirit of the Vikings," in which he claimed the true Viking spirit resided in the love of all Norwegians for individualism and liberty.[100]

As might be expected, Norwegian America often invoked the tested and true symbol of Leif Erikson in word and celebration to promote a positive image of the Viking legacy during the war. In 1943 New York governor

To counter the attempted Nazi appropriation of Norway's Viking past, cartoons such as this one were often printed in Norwegian-language papers. This cartoon appeared in Nordisk Tidende in 1942 and depicts the disgust of the true Viking as Hitler pins a medal on the traitor Vidkun Quisling.

Norwegian-language newspapers ran cartoons linking the World War II effort to restore Norway's independence with imagery of the Viking. This cartoon was published in Nordisk Tidende *in 1942.*

The struggle to regain Norwegian independence in World War II was linked with the Viking spirit of the past. This illustration appeared in the Norwegian-language paper Washington Posten *in 1942.*

Thomas E. Dewey proclaimed October 9 as Leif Erikson Day, urging New Yorkers to "honor the memory of Leif Erikson and in so doing pay a tribute to the gallant race from which he came—a people now suffering under the Nazi yoke but uncrushed and unafraid after two years of cruelty and enslavement."[101]

In the same issue in which it printed Governor Dewey's proclamation, *Nordisk Tidende* printed an editorial titled "Nytt lys over Leiv Eiriksson" (New Light over Leif Erikson). The editorial told how modern technology, especially the airplane, had effectively made our "one world" a smaller place, while also increasing geographic knowledge of the planet. Against that backdrop, it argued that Leif Erikson's voyage of discovery, most notably his discovery of Vinland, or the New World, must be viewed as a tremendous accomplishment. And it concluded by quoting Einar Haugen:

"The Norse Vikings were the first American pioneers, and as such they deserve an honorable place in the pageant of American history."[102]

Perhaps the most striking Norwegian-American example of the latter-day Viking concept was the creation by the U.S. Army of the Ninety-ninth (Separate) Battalion on May 9, 1942. Also known as the Viking Battalion (their unit patch featured a Viking ship), the Ninety-ninth recruited men of Norwegian ancestry. The battalion was intended to spearhead the liberation of Norway, but the German surrender in May 1945 precluded it. Until then, the battalion saw action on the Western Front, from Normandy to the Rhine. The unit newspaper, the *Viking*, summed up the feelings among many of the Norwegian Americans who formed the unit:

> For centuries the Vikings sailed along Europe's coasts, as they terrorized the inhabitants, and in the 20th century the spirit from the old Vikings will live again anew and they will again sail down European coasts ... not to terrorize but to liberate. Norwegians both in the U.S. and Norway, as well as Americans, will be proud of the final character of the New Vikings, which the Norwegian Battalion will become.[103]

The Ninety-ninth Battalion did serve in Norway after the war, where they were in charge of German prisoners. They were present when King Haakon VII returned to Norway for the first time on June 7, 1945, and they participated in the American Forces Day parade held in Oslo on July 4, 1945. According to one Norwegian account, "the Americans' parade took Oslo by storm," while another stated that "the 99th Battalion received an extra-hearty welcome from the crowd." Members of the Viking Battalion developed close ties with the Norwegians on many levels. In fact, seventy men from the battalion married Norwegian women. "Strong ties are being knitted between Norwegians and Americans," commented Colonel Walker, the commander of the unit.[104]

From an official standpoint, Norway was well aware of the Norwegian-American military contribution. While in London during the summer of 1944, Wilhelm Morgenstierne, Norway's ambassador to America, commented on the significance of the wartime experience. "This is the greatest [thing] that has happened in our people's long history. There is a new national heritage, which is bequeathed to us all, and which will live among Norwegians and Americans of Norwegian ancestry for time immemorial."[105]

Morgenstierne realized that through their contributions to Norway's liberation, whether as combatants or through their generous monetary donations, Norwegian Americans had helped to shape a Norwegian national identity that extended beyond Norway's borders.

Individual Norwegians also contributed significantly during the war. As a Norwegian exile in America, author Sigrid Undset lectured extensively to instill among Norwegians and Americans the sense that "we stand on common ground." In 1942 she published the book *Return to the Future,* which was her account of the Nazi invasion of Norway and her subsequent escape into exile. On October 9, 1943, she was the keynote speaker at New York's Leif Erikson Day celebration where she urged Norwegian Americans and Norwegians living in America "to help a Norway that is being bled white." She added that by contributing to relief for Norway they were securing justice and assistance "for the people from whom you are descended."[106]

Another veteran of the American speaking circuit was Halvdan Koht, historian and Norway's former minister of defense. In 1941 Koht authored *Norway: Neutral and Invaded,* in which he argued that Norway was fighting for true democracy, a society where all class privileges are abolished, an argument that surely resonated with the architects of America's New Deal. Koht and his son-in-law Sigmund Skard coauthored the highly popular work *The Voice of Norway* in 1944. In the preface Koht observed that for years Norway "has shared the struggle of the United Nations against the enemies of our civilization." He also disavowed Germany's appropriation of Viking-age symbolism. Instead, the Viking age was based on the ideals of freedom and individualism. "Only Germany escaped the activities of the Vikings, perhaps to her own lasting disadvantage."[107]

A long-standing goal of Norwegian-American leaders had been the inclusion of their story in Norway's academic scholarship. Through the efforts of Nordmanns-Forbundet, which since 1933 had lobbied for a history of Norwegian Americans written by a member of Norway's academic community, the dream bore fruit in 1941 with the first volume of Ingrid Semmingsen's *Veien mot Vest* (The Way to the West). The second volume, which treated emigration up to 1914, was published after the war in 1950. Halvdan Koht offered additional confirmation of this history in his positive 1942 review of the second volume *(The American Transition)* of Theodore C. Blegen's *Norwegian Migration to America,* which had been published in 1940.[108] Such academic endorsement was further proof of Norwegian America's increased stature among homeland Norwegians.

Of course, the Norwegian press came under Nazi censorship during the war, and Nordmanns-Forbundet was no exception. On September 11, 1941, the organization's editor and office staff were replaced with "approved" personnel.[109] To counter this move, the leaders of Nordmanns-Forbundet moved their activities to America. The editorial board was located at Princeton, New Jersey, and the journal *Nordmanns-Forbundet* was published in Grand Forks, North Dakota, where North Dakota's lieutenant governor Henry Holt operated a printing firm. Holt, of course, was of Norwegian ancestry. Thus from December 1941 through May 1945, there were two competing versions of *Nordmanns-Forbundet*.

The occupying Nazi forces had attempted to enlist Nordsmanns-Forbundet in its effort to contact Norwegians abroad, especially seamen. Odd S. Lovoll observes that the organization's long-earned respect would have offered cover to the Norwegian Nazis in their dream to attain a kind of Norwegian–German supernationalism. This effort, however, including the use of the motto *Enige og tro* (United and Faithful), was firmly rejected. During the summer months of 1941, Nasjonal Samling arranged an exhibition titled "Normannafolket" (The Norman people) in Oslo, and its attempt to gain the blessing of Nordmanns-Forbundet failed on July 15, 1941, when the organization's board unanimously voted not to take part nor to let the Nordmanns-Forbundet name be used. Lovoll notes that these two actions led to Nasjonal Samling taking over the organization.[110]

In the first edition published in the United States, Carl J. Hambro identified how the Germans and their helpers in Norway "have since the occupation dreamt of shaping a kind of Norwegian-German greatnationalism," especially by promising to restore to Norway its medieval possessions such as the Orkneys, the Shetlands, the Isle of Man, and northern Scotland. Elaborating further, he described the Nazi takeover of Nordmanns-Forbundet as an attempt "to smuggle the Nazi virus among Norwegians in all the lands."[111]

Thus, the situation during the war marked the "Janus-faced years" for *Nordmanns-Forbundet*. As might be expected, the two journals differed radically in their approach. The American version made the prosecution of the war its primary focus, as pictures of airplanes, ships, and fighting men replaced its formerly tranquil landscape covers, and every issue addressed some aspect of Norway's liberation fighting forces or the tributes to Norwegian resistance at home. The Nazi version, meanwhile, virtually ignored the war, and even minister-president Quisling was scarce in its issues. Naturally, the American version took every opportunity to poke ridicule at the hated puppet dictator. As for symbolism, since the Nazis were attempting to appropriate Norway's Viking-age and romantic peasant past, the American version strongly emphasized modern-day symbols of Norway: its constitution, the Storting, May 17, and King Haakon VII. And while the Nazi version attempted to place the journal in the service of a greater Germanic supernationalism, in which Norway's future would be tied to the fortunes of Hitler's Germany, in contrast the American version of *Nordmanns-Forbundet* promoted the greater Norway concept, which called for close ties between a democratic and free Norway and its emigrated population living in other areas of the world.[112]

As might be expected, Nordmanns-Forbundet paid tribute to the services rendered by Norwegian America during the war. Arne Kildal, a frequent speaker at Norwegian-American gatherings, published a tribute to Norwegian Americans, *De gjorde Norge større* (They Made Norway Greater), in 1945. Kildal recounted the long history of emigrated Norwegians in the New World, ending his book by saying, "And then much will be heard about [them] in addition to their many great and good deeds, which have contributed to 'making Norway greater' out in the world."[113] It was a fitting tribute to the Norwegian-American role in restoring the independence of Norway, thereby proving their steadfast loyalty to the ideals of the homeland.

The heroic stand of Norway secured American appreciation of Norway's image and, by extension, the Norwegian-American self-image. The crowning achievement for Norway's cause in America occurred on September 16, 1942, when the American government donated a submarine chaser to Norway. In honor of the seventieth birthday that year of Norway's King Haakon, the ship bore his name. During the ceremony at the Washington Navy Yard, President Roosevelt made his famous "Look to Norway" speech:

> If there is anyone who still wonders why this war is being fought, let him look to Norway. If there is anyone who has any delusions that this war could have been averted, let him look to Norway. And if there is anyone who doubts the democratic *will* to win, again I say, let him look to Norway.
>
> He will find in Norway, at once conquered and unconquered, the answer to his questioning.[114]

In the remainder of the speech, Roosevelt outlined the immense contributions that Norway had made, despite its small size, to the Allied war effort. In her responding remarks, Crown Princess Märtha mentioned that the American people had heard Roosevelt's words and that his speech "about the Norwegian people and its contributions to our common cause" will "find its way into every Norwegian home, every Norwegian ship on the seven seas, yes, to every place where Norwegian men and women labor and struggle to win the free and fortunate Norway that we all long for."[115]

The Norwegian-American reaction to Roosevelt's speech reflected the sense that America had at last fully recognized the unique Norwegian heritage. An editorial in *Nordisk Tidende*, "Se på Norge" (Look to Norway), observed, "There is a desire for justice in our Norwegian people that has shaped the home front [in Norway]; it blazes like a lighthouse in a dark world. It is this lighthouse that Roosevelt points to.... We Norwegian Americans do not take Roosevelt's words as national flattery. We know they were not meant like that. It was a logical and sober appraisal of the people and the result of such analysis must today be: Look to Norway."[116]

According to *Washington Posten*, "On this simple occasion the American authorities had captured the true sentiments that America's president and people ascribe to Norway's contribution in the war against the Axis powers."[117] With Norway as the world's shining beacon of freedom, the Norwegian-American community could take great pride in its heritage, and the Norwegian-American legacy received a tremendous boost.

Roosevelt offered further reinforcement on the occasion of the May 17 celebration in 1944. The year marked the one hundred thirtieth anniversary of Norway's constitution. He wrote, "With the help of God, the brave men and women of Norway will celebrate the one hundred and thirty-first anniversary of the Norwegian Constitution in a country once again free and democratic." Roosevelt's words proved prophetic, for Norway was liberated on May 7, 1945, though the president did not live to see the event.[118]

This commemoration of a Norwegian national symbol by the American president served as an endorsement of the Norwegian-American identity. E. B. Hauke, president of the Sons of Norway, wrote of the occasion that it demonstrated the unity between Norwegians and Norwegian Americans: "Since April 9, 1940, this unity has grown stronger every day." He noted that the Eidsvold Constitution was connected with "the Norwegians' discovery of America and the contributions they have made in the progress of this land.... It is now a ... symbol of the freedom and the peace that shall come to Norway in the not-too-distant future."[119] During the war, Norwegian Americans held somber celebrations of May 17, which the American government had proclaimed as "America Day." As a result May 17 became a shared symbol of both Norway and America, which further legitimized the prestige of the Norwegian community in America.

A prime example of a shared transnational heritage occurred at New York City's May 17 parade in 1944. The large procession, which totaled more than one thousand, included numerous children dressed in traditional Norwegian costumes and waving Norwegian flags, whose route naturally passed by Leiv Erikson square. According to *Nordisk Tidende*, the most impressive contingents in the parade were the Norwegian marines, the Norwegian merchant marines, and the tightly ordered march of officers, including captains, mates, and machinists. The keynote speaker, Sverre Norborg, solemnly offered hope: "When we see the grayness that every day hangs over Norway, it is nonetheless clear that we think ahead to the new society that will grow out of four years of night.... We certainly know that this will be continued in our common social, national, and moral values."[120]

The latter-day symbolic synthesis of Norway's national identity came together in the May 1944 issue of the American version of *Nordmanns-Forbundet*, commemorating the one hundred and thirtieth anniversary of Norway's constitution. The cover featured a flight of birds flying a V formation toward Norway, which symbolized the triple V slogan of the home front, *vi vil vine* (we will win), and King Haakon VII. Dedicated to Norway's constitution day, the issue affirmed May 17 as a powerful symbol of Norway. In his tribute to "our constitutional day," Carl J. Hambro explained that the Storting was the "living expression of our constitution, as its active symbol," and that May 17 represented the public spirit that made the nation great. In the same issue, Prime Minister Nygaardsvold reflected that May 17 showed respect for the constitution that had "shaped our independence and freedom"; Minister W. Neuman of the diplomatic corps simply stated, "Norway is freedom." King Haakon VII contended that May 17 represented Norway's cause to liberate itself from Germany's attempt to impose a slave state.[121]

The widespread popularity of Norway's cause in America, which was highly publicized in both print and film, had now made it possible for the Norwegian-American self-image to attain a greater degree of public exposure than it had ever achieved before. An example of the solidarity between America and Norway was the October 28, 1944, *New York Times* article "Our Norwegian Ally," which commended Norway's stout resistance to Nazi tyranny. In literature, John Steinbeck's 1942 novel *The Moon Is Down* struck a responsive chord among Americans. Based in a fictitious American town that represented Norway, it depicted the town's resistance to a group of outside invaders, which represented the Germans. In the 1943 film *Edge of Darkness*, which starred Errol Flynn, the inhabitants of the small Norwegian fishing village of Trollness display their resistance to Nazi rule, ultimately taking up arms and dying en masse as a symbol of widespread Norwegian resistance to tyranny. In the October 23, 1943, issue of the *Saturday Evening Post*, Joseph Auslander published "An Open Letter to the Unconquerable Norwegians" in which he wrote, "They will return, O Norway, mother of heroes.... They will burn the filth of the Nazi Neros.... As you linger there in your doorway. Ah, dear mother of my little daughter! Norway!"[122] As a result of the mass exposure given to Norway's plight, the American public came to view Norway as an important partner in the larger struggle to preserve freedom.

A September 1944 editorial in *Nordisk Tidende* commented that the war had led to a greater exchange of ideas between Norway and America. Specifically, homeland Norwegians who had resided in America had gained a greater understanding of America and the new ideas it represented and, by implication, of Norwegian America as well—a positive by-product of the shared sacrifice.[123]

That sense of a shared mission was manifest in President Roosevelt's 1944 Leif Erikson Day proclamation. It also showed how nicely the Norwegian-American identity dovetailed with the ideology of wartime America:

> We hail the Norwegians as our fellow fighters in the sacred cause of democracy, battling fearlessly against the enemies of mankind on their home soil, in the air, and on the seven seas. And we greet our own fellow citizens of Leif Erikson's blood, fighting in the battle lines and on the home front, ferrying the victorious armies and the arms of the United Nations across the ocean that once their fathers furrowed in their frail boats in man's undying quest for liberty.[124]

In this short passage, President Roosevelt tied together the two halves of the Norwegian people through their service to the American-led war effort. A greater Norway did exist on both sides of the Atlantic Ocean, and its members were the descendants of the intrepid, liberty-loving Vikings, the latter-day Vikings of the modern world.

In the aftermath of Norway's liberation on May 7, 1945, Norway's Constitution Day celebration took on special significance. On May 17, 1945, jubilant celebrations were held on both sides of the Atlantic. In Norway, however, because King Haakon and the government had not yet returned, the occasion was somewhat muted. In America, a number of Norwegian communities held joyous May 17 celebrations that often featured prominent homeland Norwegians. For instance, Ambassador Morgenstierne gave the keynote address at San Francisco's May 17 celebration, while the May 17 celebration in the Twin Cities featured a speech by Consul Reidar Solum.[125]

Norwegian Americans likewise flocked to Chicago where a large and boisterous May 17 celebration was observed. The various Norwegian-American organizations took to the streets of the Windy City with the type of joyous exultation not seen in over five years as the various Norwegian singing choruses joined with the city's Nordmændenes Sangforening, Den norske Klubben, a children's parade, and other manifestations of Norwegian spirit, all under the watchful eyes of Leif Erikson's statue. The keynote speaker, Bjørn Stallare, who had served in the Norwegian underground, observed, "The Seventeenth of May has something of the original flavor to it for the emigrants," a ringing endorsement for the idea that emigrated Norwegians were now part of the Norwegian nation.[126]

At Seattle's May 17 celebration, Consul Christen A. Stang expressed Norway's thanks for the efforts of Norwegian Americans. Under the direction of August Werner, the orchestra pulled out all the stops, playing at full strength, with hundreds of violins and trumpets. The celebration featured the auction of Prime Minister Nygaardsvold's old hat, which raised $36,000 in war bonds. The sentiments of Seattle's Norwegian Americans were perhaps expressed best by the local Sons of Norway lodge, which placed a greeting in *Washington Posten* that read: "To our courageous people and to everyone who has stood behind our Motherland Norway during the war and the heavy years of oppression since 9 April, 1940, we send in deep gratitude our best wishes for a *syttende mai* filled with jubilation as has never before been seen."[127]

Although Norwegians in the New York City area celebrated May 17 with several smaller local ceremonies, the city's big festival came on May 30 for the Norsk Fylkings (Norwegian Counties) Free Norway Festival in Carnegie Hall. The event was broadcast in New York and England, with three thousand people crowding into the famous hall. The evening ceremony featured the New York Philharmonic Orchestra and a 140-person choir composed of Norwegians from every part of Norway. Performing on a stage decked with two Norwegian flags on either side of an American one, the orchestra and choir performed several Norwegian songs, including Johan Svendsens's "Kroningsmarj" (Crowning March), which he had composed and which had been played at the coronation of King Haakon VII at Trondheim in 1906. Rees Edgar Tullos, president of the United Lutheran Council, exclaimed that all Americans of Norwegian ancestry could be proud of their compatriots in Norway who had fought against oppression. He added that Lutherans from around the world sent him greetings expressing admiration for "the Norwegian people and what they had done in winning the war for Christian ideals and universal justice."[128]

Above all, the war had involved tremendous sacrifice. Sigrid Undset's comments pinpointed what the war had meant to Norway in human terms:

> And let us not forget—in the march of the dead from these war years our Norwegian dead were an extremely small portion. They seemed to number quite a few for such a small people as ours, but that was before we had made ourselves realize that these precious human beings were better than most people in the world. But we shall commemorate the dead from all the other lands, large and small, who have fought with us, many of whom were not perceived of until the war against them brought its worldwide vision of the glorification of violence and the thirst for power, with words and murder as its instruments. Our fallen men and boys and women and children died for Norway, and Norway is free today. They gave their lives for our peace, but these dead shall be remembered by us forever because that peace came at a steep price; it came to cost a people their freedom and lives under laws that are supposed to be expressions of our thoughts about human dignity, justice, tradition and honor. For Norway could have had peace every day during the war years if the people had been willing to yield to the superior force of the conquerors and been content with slavery in their own land.[129]

Norway's great ceremony of liberation occurred on June 7, 1945, the fortieth anniversary of the dissolution of the union with Sweden. The capital Oslo was host to what was described as "the greatest mass meeting in the city's history." The celebration featured King Haakon, Crown Prince Olav, Crown Princess Märtha and their children, and members of the government including Prime Minister Nygaardsvold and Carl J. Hambro. The centerpiece of the day was an automobile parade in which the king and other dignitaries were driven along Karl Johan's Avenue to the Royal Palace, where the royal family once again assumed residence. *Nordisk Tidende* again reminded its readers to "Look to Norway" on "the day when Norway once again flew its true Norwegian flags, King Haakon had returned to Norway, [and] the church bells in every city and rural area from Lindesnes to Nordkapp rang the joyful message." *Aftenposten* described it as "the greatest and most beautiful day in free Norway's history."[130]

In the wake of the Norwegian-American contributions made to Norway's wartime cause, homeland Norway likewise shared in the exaltation of their emigrated cousins. A major revelation concerned how much money and aid American Relief for Norway had raised. Because America was at war with Germany, almost everything, mainly clothing and other humanitarian aid, had to be shipped to neutral Sweden first and then sent to Norway. As a consequence, most homeland Norwegians were unaware that many of their relief packages actually had come from Norwegian America.

In writing on the relief activity in July 1945, *Nationen* observed, "Americans of Norwegian descent have not forgotten the Old Country." The article concluded by noting, "It was a revelation for many of the Norwegians who worked in the U.S.A. during the war to see the love for Norway that ruled the many Norwegian Americans and friends of Norway in the United States." In a related article, *Dagbladet* praised the Norwegian Americans for establishing "an entire network of humanitarian assistance."[131]

Official Norway was very much aware of the contributions made by Norwegian Americans to a greater Norway. Speaking at a July 16, 1945, press conference in Oslo, Crown Prince Olav urged Norwegians to shape a society based on justice, freedom, and tolerance. At the end of his remarks, he offered "a special thank you to the states of 'the middle West' in the U.S.A., where Norwegian-descended people have distinguished themselves in the service of the Allied cause. He gave thanks for the reception the Norwegian armed forces members received there and for all the help America had rendered during the war."[132]

For homeland Norwegians, World War II had proven just how true the concept of a greater Norway really was. The contributions of Norwegian Americans had been a major factor in the liberation of Norway. Some, like Torstein Høverstad, a Norwegian scholar, even argued that the key to Norway's future lay in nurturing "a greater Norway." Postwar Norway's recovery would require greater cooperation among all Norwegians. "Few things are more obvious than that lighthouse which guides all Norwegians in our time, which is to devote ourselves to building a greater Norway.... In this endeavor Norway can attain great power through a much stronger unification of all the Norwegian people." Moreover, Norwegian America was most important: "The Norwegian communities in America are today as never before the first line of defense for Norwegian cultural values, for both Norway and the world."[133]

Such expressions concerning the importance of a greater Norway served to validate the Norwegian-American self-image, surely to a greater extent than could ever have been imagined. The dramatic circumstances that projected Norway onto the world's stage had offered the ultimate test of the bonds between Norway and Norwegians in America. For roughly eighty years, Norwegian-American leaders had argued that the immigrants were worthy of their Norwegian heritage and that they deserved to be considered as equals by their homeland. After all, they were the Vikings of the latter-day era, blazing new trails of adventure across the vast ocean prairies of the New World. Through their service to Norway during World War II, the Norwegian Americans had at last gained that measure of respect from their ancestral homeland. But perhaps more important, they had finally achieved full recognition of their cultural legacy from America, the land to which they belonged. For over eighty years, the Norwegian-American identity had been based on a love of two countries. By 1945, both Norway and America had reciprocated that love.

· CONCLUSION ·

Building a Greater Norway

Prior to our time there was a great divide between the nations, between *Vesterheimen* and the motherland. Over time they have drawn more and more together. In so many ways the unity has become stronger between the emigrated people and those in the homeland.... The old gray-haired Norwegian, who has for the most part been virtually forgotten in the homeland, came here with a delightful memory of his childhood, his valley, the mountains and the fjords, where he played as a small boy.[1]

Thus wrote the Norwegian-American Engel Meslo to a Norwegian newspaper in 1933 as he urged closer ties between the youth of Norway and those of Norwegian ancestry in *Vesterheim*. By stressing these themes—memories of a romanticized Norway, the emigrated kinsman who is nearly forgotten by his homeland, and the present-day realization that there are two halves to the Norwegian nation—Meslo was summarizing the basic evolution of the Norwegian-American identity.

Despite his concern that the accomplishments of Norwegian Americans might be forgotten, Meslo demonstrated how he (and other Norwegian Americans) had internalized the basic components of the Norwegian-American identity. He reminded his readers that it is not at all difficult "to find Norwegian churches" in the Norwegian-American landscape. One found churches in "the large and small towns, on the far-flung prairies and in the forested valleys." He referred to Norwegian films that showed the "natural pictures" of Norway's "coasts, the exceptionally breathtaking mountains, fjords and scattered towns."[2]

The French sociologist Maurice Halbwachs argued that memory is a conscious, collective, and purposeful process. Indeed, memory is not a passive process but one, he stressed, that takes place in a complex network of power relations, customs, discourses, and symbols. According to Halbwachs, a group sustains itself by manipulating images of the past for present purposes, and individuals experience their own personal memories through the context of that group. As such, he maintains that memory must be viewed as "commemoration," or an active process dependent on collective agency and rational choice.[3]

The greater Norway was imagined through idealized landscapes, both Norwegian-American and Norwegian. What it meant to be Norwegian thus was defined as membership in an imagined community that transcended the physical—and ultimately language—boundaries of *mor Norge* (mother Norway). Instead, true *norskhet* (Norwegianness) was the active process of continually *commemorating* and *reinventing* Norway through collective means, even as English supplanted Norwegian among the immigrant population. For the individual, participation in the collective process of defining *norskhet* gave context to one's personal identity.

For the soldiers of the Viking Battalion, their triumphal return to Norway, the ancestral homeland, meant that the collective and personal experiences of the greater Norway had converged. Through the personal stories of these prodigal Vikings, one can discern the poignancy with which the two Norways (homeland and immigrant) were reunited. For example, Arnold Everson, a second-generation Norwegian American, related that he knew that his grandmother on his father's side had come from Nord-Aurdal in Norway. Traveling by train and then bus to Leira, he located a cousin named Einar Fossbraaten. After spending a night in town, a young girl on a bicycle came to take him to the Fossbraaten summer farm, a trip that meant that Everson and the young girl had to alternate taking turns riding and walking up the steep hill. Once he arrived at the summer farm, Everson was greeted by relatives who served cheese and butter cream. There he came to learn that he had also encountered relatives from his grandmother's family on his mother's side. In all, Everson had an impromptu family reunion with forty-eight relatives.[4]

Another soldier, Fritz Carlsen, was Norwegian by birth, and on his return to Norway he wanted to look up his parents in Torshov, a suburb of Oslo. He and his fellow soldiers sailed to Norway aboard a steamer, and on the morning of their arrival in Norway the ship sailed up the Oslo fjord. He remembered how "the tears were streaming" for the Norwegian-born in anticipation of reunion with their families. After some humorous mix-ups involving the Oslo trolley system, Fritz arrived at his parents' home, but they were not there. He then rang the neighbor's doorbell, who told him they were at his mother's sister's home. The neighbor assumed that

Fritz was his brother, who had recently returned home after serving with the Norwegian Navy in England. Unknown to Fritz, his parents thought him dead. When his mother saw him, she asked, "Is it really you? I thought you were dead."[5]

After a couple days Carlsen had to rejoin the battalion at Smestad outside Oslo. There his old sweetheart came to see him. They found a park bench and talked about old times and decided to get married in August. The young couple went to the old family church, the Sagene Church, but the local pastor would not marry them because he considered Fritz to still be an enemy. But because his mother had been baptized, confirmed, and married at Sagene Church, Fritz remained adamant, and Pastor Olner from Torshov Church came and performed the ceremony at Sagene Church on August 4, 1945. The church was packed, and two sergeants from the battalion served as Carlsen's best men. For the reception afterward, the couple had to scramble to find enough food to feed the guests in war-torn Norway. A farmer in Asker had promised the bride two big hams, but they did not materialize, and a similar promise for a whole lamb likewise ended without success. In the end, Carlsen managed to get food and other convivial items from the captain at the Smestad base, who told him, "Just take what you need, Fritz, as long as there is enough for the boys."[6]

In these two anecdotes one sees the poignant side of the greater Norway. Through the liberation of Norway the various branches of the Norwegian family tree became reunited, providing tangible evidence that the imagined community was real. Throughout most of the time frame of this study, this transnational space was and remained a metaphorical space, one envisioned and idealized on behalf of an ideological construct aimed to promote what might be termed the higher calling of Norwegian nationalism. But it must be acknowledged that the struggle for life during World War II created a unique set of circumstances, and while this study has argued that the greater Norway was ultimately realized through the shedding of blood, it must be recognized that it was also realized through ties of friendship, family, and love.

Although the creators of the greater Norway imagined Norway as existing in a transnational space, the nation had often been conceived as an idealized landscape, both within Norway and outside her. Another transnational impulse for Norway's identity came from those living outside Norway who were not of Norwegian ancestry. H. Arnold Barton's study of nineteenth-century foreign travelers to Norway demonstrates that they interpreted it in three aspects: majestic Norway, Norway the land of heroes, and picturesque Norway. In other words, they held a highly romantic view of Norway as the rugged land of resolute and proud peasants. In addition, Barton observes that the austere and awe-inspiring Norwegian landscape invoked a reverence for Norway as the home of the heroes of the Viking Age. Travelers from Britain, Germany, and America were especially fond of perceiving Norway in these terms, and American writers such as Charles Loring Brace and Bayard Taylor published some of the most favorable accounts of Norway. A somewhat paradoxical development, however, was what Barton terms the image of progressive Norway, a view that was especially popular in neighboring Sweden during the nineteenth century. The Scotsman Samuel Laing went so far as to claim that Norway was the embodiment of liberty and equality, even surpassing the United States, while American travel writers Brace and Taylor favorably compared Norway's liberal constitution with their own.[7] Norway's identity was to a certain degree fashioned beyond the nation's borders, and the contributions of emigrated Norwegians toward this end were likewise important.

Foreign observers articulated these mixed impressions of Norway owing to the conflicting trends present within Norway itself. Bodil Stenseth has described how three parties contested for control of Norway's national identity around 1900. The ultranationalist Ungdomssrørsla, or rural youth movement, emphasized that the peasantry and their traditions, including Landsmaal, were the only true representation of authentic Norwegian culture. The Lysaker Circle, which included Fridtjof Nansen, Erik Werenskiold, and Gerhard Munthe, aimed for an identity that balanced images of traditional Norway with the modern world. The third party was the Kristiania intelligentsia led by the painter Christian Krogh and his friends who embraced a cosmopolitan worldview that held little room for old traditions.[8] This conflict in Norway between traditional and modern impulses mirrored the struggle among Norwegian Americans to reconcile a romantic self-image with a progressive, or modern, self-image.

In comparing the two halves of the Norwegian nation, however, one must note that there was not complete symmetry. Orm Øverland has identified a functional difference between the ethnic character of immigrant groups and the ethnic character of national groups. An ethnic minority will try to emphasize its resistance to the dominant culture. In comparison, he argues that ethnic groups in America created homemaking myths that promoted the superiority of the group in order to claim their allegiance to American nationalism.[9] Such an assessment is correct with regard to the creation of homemaking myths in an American context. However, as this study has shown, Norwegian Americans created myths that were designed for a Norwegian context as well as an American context. They attempted to create an identity that satisfied the requirements of both American and Norwegian nationalisms. Among immigration specialists, more attention needs to be paid to how the immigrants impacted the development of the homeland's identity. Thomas N. Brown's study of Irish-American nationalism and Timothy J. Kloberdanz's study of German-Russian immigrants, and their impact on the identity of Germans from the Volga region of Russia, offer two such examples.[10]

For scholars who study European emigration, there has been increased awareness in recent years concerning the link between emigration and nation building. In "Emigration and Nation Building during the Mass Migrations from Europe," Donna R. Gabaccia, Dirk Hoerder, and Adam Walaszek show that during the nineteenth and early twentieth centuries mass emigration from Germany, Italy, and Poland became tied to nationalist aspirations. More specifically, they argue that the positively perceived "traveling cultures" of emigrants were tied to dreams of national expansion and that the "colonization" efforts of the emigrants represented opportunities for expansion of the homeland's national identity and culture. Historian Emilio Franzina's study suggests that emigrants were nation builders, and the work of other scholars supports his idea. Caroline Douki maintains that Italian emigrants helped the modern Italian managerial state come into being, and François Weil shows how the concern over French emigrants led to an increased specialization of the French bureaucratic state, creating legal, administrative, and statistical tools to keep track of and to protect the emigrants.[11]

One might question why the concept of a greater Norway became popular during the 1930s and the 1940s, especially given the significantly decreased use of Norwegian among the immigrants and their descendants in America. Its appeal among homeland Norwegians can be attributed to the success of the emigrated Norwegians, which showcased the greatness of a small nation like Norway in a larger international context. In addition, by the 1930s, emigration from Norway was no longer a threat as only about one hundred Norwegians per year on average left for America.[12]

For the increasingly Americanized Norwegians, however, one might expect that they would not be so enthralled with their ties to the distant homeland. Much of the explanation is due to the nature of ethnicity. As Marcus Lee Hansen argued in 1937, the third-generation immigrant chooses to remember what his parents wanted to forget, the traditions of the old country. Secure in his American identity, Hansen opined, the third-generation immigrant would embrace the culture of his grandparents as a way of expressing his membership in a shared community.[13]

There has been a tendency among scholars of Norwegian America to end their studies at 1925, or in some cases 1930, a reflection of the belief that the 1925 Norse-American Centennial was truly the last hurrah of the immigrant community. April Rose Schultz is especially critical of the historians of Norwegian America, accusing them of embracing fully the assimilation of the Norwegians in America, although such a viewpoint is too harsh. Odd S. Lovoll, for instance, acknowledges that while Theodore C. Blegen's historical narrative was assimilative in nature, his bottom-up, egalitarian, and pluralist history foreshadowed the social history of the 1960s. With the foundation of the Norwegian-American Historical Association in 1925—the professionalization of historians of Norwegian America—the focus turned to the establishment of legacy myths rather than the earlier hegemonic or creation myths. A similar process occurred at Vesterheim, the Norwegian-American museum in Decorah, Iowa, that same year when historian Knut Gjerset became its director. Professional scholars would be entrusted with the mission of preserving and promoting the Norwegian-American self-image, albeit in the language of scientific scholarship.[14]

Newer approaches to ethnicity and identity formation, moreover, raise questions about the ability to date the end of a group's identity. Studies by Mary Waters and Richard Alba contend that ethnicity can tend to fluctuate according to contemporary social conditions. Waters points out that for white immigrants, who are not subjected to the limits of racial prejudice, ethnicity becomes a symbolic option that allows them to gain membership within a community without having to make sacrifices to that ethnic culture, such as coping with language barriers or limited employment opportunities. Alba, meanwhile, maintains that ethnic identity can increase when new arrivals threaten the status quo. He further asserts that ethnic identity can establish boundaries that empower one's group. Both Waters and Alba tend to see present-day ethnicity as largely symbolic, or perceived, and not necessarily authentic.[15]

Scholars who have studied Norwegian-American identity, however, have often emphasized that ethnicity is indeed authentic. Øverland, for instance, argues that while Norwegian-American culture might have been marginal, the basic ideas of the Norwegian-American self-image were important to the immigrants. Øyvind T. Gulliksen goes further and argues that practitioners of Norwegian-American culture, such as its writers, did not consider themselves marginal but rather in a special position to draw on two rich cultures. Odd S. Lovoll contends that present-day Norwegian Americans engage in a constant "re-creation and inventiveness" to promote the historical symbolism of their group's identity. He adds that "ethnicity is not invented fiction, but instead rests upon social and cultural realities," and that Norwegian-American ethnicity is just as authentic as the ethnicity of homeland Norwegians.[16]

Current theories of national identity likewise raise questions about what has been traditionally seen as the authentic incubator of national identity, namely, the nation-state. According to Aviel Roshwald, one must be deeply skeptical about the "widely prevalent claim that the nation is a culturally and socially homogenous collectivity and the kaleidoscopic reality of human loyalties and affections." He notes, "There is no one set of objective socio-cultural criteria that defines national identity." In effect, Roshwald's study of nationalism suggests that membership in a national community is by necessity flexibly defined in order to accommodate globalizing forces of the modern era. Nationalism only succeeds when it is linked to, co-opts, or otherwise embraces other "loyalties and affiliations, ranging from the religious to the familial."[17]

A related problem concerns the authenticity of the modern nation-state. Chris A. Bayly, a leading transnational historian, has observed that nations were not the originary elements of such products as national identity; instead, nations were the products of transnational elements. Matthew Connelly proceeds further by arguing that nation-states are continually reconstituted through conflict with transnational forces or impulses, and he contends that these transnational forces result from a dialogue between the material and the ideological.[18] One should not therefore expect that the nation-state of Norway and its national identity were simply the product of forces contained within the boundaries of modern Norway. Rather, as this study has shown, the Norwegian national identity was reconstituted through interaction with transnational forces, which in this case have focused on the activities of the emigrated Norwegian population to the

United States. The greater Norway was a transnational identity that resulted from the impact of transnational forces.

Yet despite these considerations, the question remains as to whether Norwegian Americans through their participation in the greater Norway were true members of Norway's national community. At the core of this problem is how to define the nation. Anthony D. Smith's theories on the close relationship between nations and ethnic communities provide a working model. Smith defines the nation as "a named human community residing in a perceived homeland, and having common myths and a shared history, a distinct public culture, and common laws and customs for all members." He defines an ethnie or ethnic community as "a named human community connected to a homeland, possessing common myths of ancestry, shared memories, one or more elements of a shared culture, and a measure of solidarity, at least among elites."[19]

Smith acknowledges that these are really pure or ideal types of "nation" and "ethnie," derived from a stylization of the respective beliefs and sentiments of elite members of ethnie and of nations. As such, his scheme tends to highlight differences rather than common denominators. He further notes that ethnic communities and nations belong to the same category of phenomena since they share the attributes of collective names, common myths, and shared memories. Conversely, he observes how nations are differentiated from ethnic communities by their members sharing common laws and a distinct public culture. Moreover, he stresses that in the ideal, nations occupy the homeland and ethnic communities may be linked only symbolically to the homeland. Finally, Smith points out that ethnic communities need not have a public culture, only some common cultural element—be it language, religion, customs, or shared institutions—while in contrast a nation has a distinct public culture as one of its key attributes.[20]

At first glance this divide would seem to negate the concept of the greater Norway since Norwegian Americans—the ethnic community—did not share in all the attributes of the nation of Norway. But as this study has argued, homeland Norwegian leaders attempted to integrate Norwegian-American cultural achievements and history into both the public culture of Norway and its standardized national history. And although it may appear that Norway and Norwegian America did not share common laws and cultures, Norway's leaders constantly attempted to show that Norway and the United States (the home of Norwegian Americans) shared many laws and legal practices such as commitment to democracy, love of freedom, and constitutional government. The Norwegian homeland was not occupied by Norwegian Americans; the creators of the greater Norway overcame this limitation by reimagining the homeland as a transnational social space in which membership was bound to bonds of loyalty to Norway and its customs, which existed beyond the physical space of Norway. The greater Norway involved the "ethno-symbolic reconstruction"[21] of the national identity of Norway, but it was a plausible reconstruction because Norwegian Americans shared many, if not most, of the cultural elements and traditions of the homeland. In effect, the creators of the greater Norway aimed to overcome the traditional differences between nation and ethnic community by envisioning Norway in a transnational context, thereby making emigrated Norwegians and their descendants into bona fide members of the Norwegian nation.

Smith further elaborates how national identity is a discursive ideology that need not be confined exclusively to those citizens living within the territorial boundaries of the nation. Stressing that nationalism is an ideology of the nation, not the state, he contends that national identity can be primarily defined as a cultural doctrine. For example, Smith defines national identity as "the continuous reproduction and reinterpretation of the pattern of values, symbols, memories, myths, and traditions that compose the distinctive heritage of nations, and the identifications of individuals with that pattern and its cultural elements." Reinforcing the cultural doctrine, he adds, relies on the introduction of new concepts, languages, and symbols to attain and maintain "the *autonomy, unity,* and *identity* of the nation." Smith notes how unity signifies social cohesion, and by creating national symbols and ceremonies every member of the community participates in the nation as it "assures the continuity of an abstract community of history and destiny."[22] Homeland leaders in Norway grasped this concept and therefore sought to create a sense of national belonging among emigrated Norwegians by involving them in transnational celebrations of the ceremonies, myths, and symbols of Norway and its national identity.

After 1925 Norway took the lead in promoting the greater Norway concept, which validated membership among Norwegian Americans within the nation. Thus from the late 1920s until the conclusion of World War II in 1945, the relationship between Norway (homeland) and Norwegians who emigrated to America (migrant community) closely resembled a diaspora. In her study of the Irish-American diaspora, Astrid Wonneberger identifies the four major elements of a diaspora: (1) a diaspora consists of at least two communities of one ethnic group who live outside their homeland; (2) a diaspora consists of a relatively large number of people who maintain a common cultural identity that they use to distinguish themselves from other groups as well as their home society; (3) the country of origin takes a central place in the process of maintaining a collective memory and solidarity; and (4) diasporic communities maintain permanent contact with each other and keep up different kinds of relationships to the home country if possible.[23]

It is element three that is especially striking. Norway's promotion of the greater Norway involved a reconfiguration of identities so as to allow Norwegian Americans to see themselves as legitimate members of the collective identity (national identity in this case) even though they were outside Norway's borders. It is not uncommon for countries of emigration, such as Norway, to invoke national solidarity across borders.[24] Although it is problematic to view the entire history of the Norwegian migration to America as a diaspora, especially since the idea of coerced migration is not the issue, the relationship between Norway and emigrated Norwegians from the late 1920s until the conclusion of World War II nonetheless strongly suggests that a diaspora dynamic was in play.

Viewing nations in an extraterritorial context is also found among the newer transnational approaches to the role of the nation-state, which are useful in understanding the relationship between Norway and its emigrants, although some of these approaches would seem to counter the possibility of a transnational nationalism. Glick Schiller et al.'s formulation of transnational theory argued that the forces of globalization of the modern era mean that theory must be recast from analysis based on the nation-state to analysis based on a global or world-systems perspective. This "nations unbound" perspective, however, has received much criticism for its all-or-nothing approach that tends to severely downplay the role of the nation-state in any transnational analysis.[25] The nation-state, and by extension nationalism, remains viable to the creation of identities even across national borders. A point of contestation is how national identity can be both territorial and transnational.

A number of transnational scholars now view nationalism and national identity as an extraterritorial phenomenon. Despite having reservations about nationalism, Nyla Ali Khan concedes, "The dissemination of transnational practices entails the transterritorialization of various socioeconomic, political, and cultural practices and identities that frequently bolster the formation and reconstitution of the nation-state." In her study of kin-state nationalism in Hungary, Myra A. Waterbury states that nation-states often reach out to ethnic kin across their borders not out of an altruistic sense of community but to mobilize feelings of ethnic solidarity for some other purpose that suits the homeland politically. Similarly, one could argue that the business and political elites in Norway who promoted a greater Norway did so for reasons of economic or political advantage. In studying Polish transnationalism, Kathy Burrell observes how past and present are tied together in the homeland. She notes that for Polish migrants the homeland means the past, but it is often imagined as a site of future return. She reflects that transnationalism brings the past and the homeland together into the present, a process very similar to the one described in this study.[26]

The flexibility of nationalism to remake itself also suggests that it needs to be understood more broadly than it has been traditionally, even in lieu of postmodern theories. Although a harsh critic of the nation, Peter Hitchcock acknowledges:

> But however pinned to modernity the Nation has been, it can also attach itself to postmodern narrativity in alarmingly fluid fashion. Indeed, the ideological purview of Nation is imbued with its own sense of border crossing that makes the ascription of intrinsic radicality to this move extremely difficult to gainsay. A successful ideology does not remain so by monologism. . . . It continually renegotiates the form of its hegemony in terms of current contingencies (which is also a lesson from Antonio Gramsci). Ironically, the political attraction of the contingent, provisional, and unfinished has been very alluring to the idea of Nation all along. The need to rearticulate Nation is a raison d'être of national governments. Thus just as one must specify the condition of hybridity in counter-hegemonic discourse, so must one pay careful attention to the tactical virtuosity of the Nation as idea.[27]

The greater Norway concept, therefore, can be understood as a national identity that was both territorial and extraterritorial, or centered and de-centered.

The most important consideration, though, is that the ordeal of World War II tested the validity of the greater Norway concept. The loss of

Norway, the homeland, to Nazi invasion meant that real sacrifice in terms of blood was required. Furthermore, the loss of the homeland from 1940 to 1945 created a short-term diaspora, and both homeland Norwegians, whether living under foreign occupation or in exile, and emigrated Norwegians and their descendants yearned for the return of an independent Norway. During the war years the greater Norway concept operated very much like a transnational diaspora identity.

Thus, it is best to view the greater Norway as a result of processes occurring on both sides of the Atlantic. The Norwegian-American identity had its origins during the decade of the American Civil War as the immigrants attempted to show how they were the best immigrant group. The sacrifice of Norwegians to their adopted land legitimized their standing, and early immigrant leaders, most notably Rasmus Bjørn Anderson, constructed an ideology based on origin myths, which were designed to show that Norwegians had a long association with the New World. Norwegians, they argued, were desirable both racially and because their traditions and values mirrored those cherished by Anglo-Americans.

Between 1890 and 1917, the Norwegian-American identity was based on hegemony myths designed to demonstrate that Norwegians were superior to all Americans, including Anglo-Americans. The leading proponent of this view, Waldemar Ager, took advantage of the Social Darwinist ideas then popular in the United States and Europe to argue that Norwegians were the most Nordic, most freedom-loving, and most Protestant of all Americans. It was during this same period that increasing contacts between emigrated Norwegians and homeland Norwegians meant that the Norwegian-American self-image became known in the old country. The willingness of many Norwegian Americans to fight on behalf of Norway during the 1905 union crisis with Sweden earned the immigrants a healthy reputation among leaders in Norway. From 1907—the year Nordmands-Forbundet was organized—the success of Norwegian Americans would serve to advance Norway's own national identity. A tangible measure of that success was the exhibit dedicated to the emigrated Norway at the 1914 Constitutional Centennial in Norway.

Taking its form during these years, the Norwegian-American identity represented a consensus between two rival camps. The rural and church-oriented Norwegian America preferred the romantic vision of the stalwart Norwegian peasant, a vision that had developed in Norway during the strong nationalist phase of the mid-nineteenth century. The secular, urban-oriented Norwegian-American elite offered a vision of Norwegians as modern, progressive citizens who could succeed in business and the professions. The dominant Norwegian-American identity included both visions: the Norwegian-American was a virile, hard-working, enterprising citizen owing to those traits that had their origins in the Viking age of his ancestors.

During the years of the Anglo-American counteroffensive, Norwegian-American and homeland Norwegian leaders engaged in strategies to bolster the Norwegian-American self-image in America. Realizing that assimilation meant that a viable Norwegian-language-based culture could not be maintained, they constructed legacy myths to argue that the Norwegian culture should be recognized and celebrated by the dominant Anglo-American element. The highlight occurred in 1925 at the Norse-American Centennial, which featured participation by Norwegians on both sides of the Atlantic. The ringing endorsement of the Norwegian-American identity by President Calvin Coolidge represented the apogee of that effort. However, the severe limitations imposed on further Norwegian immigration to America by the National Origins Act appeared to signal the defeat of the Norwegian-American ideal.

From 1929 to 1940, Norway took the initiative by promoting an image of Norwegian-American success. Leaders of Norway's business elite believed it would benefit Norway's identity in the world community, especially in the United States. A series of shared celebrations involving Norway and Norwegian America reinforced the idea that there was a greater Norway. President Roosevelt's proclamation of Leif Erikson Day in 1935 and the 1939 visit to America by Crown Prince Olav and Crown Princess Märtha showcased the success of this strategy. The tribulations of World War II, when Norway was invaded, and the substantial support offered by Norwegian Americans to the homeland proved that the greater Norway concept was valid, and it secured a long-standing goal of Norwegian-Americans to have the homeland recognize their steadfast defense of their Norwegian heritage.

In endorsing the concept of a greater Norway, Norwegian Americans of the Depression era and World War II were not simply engaging in largely symbolic ethnicity, but instead were involved in a constructive process of identity building that transcended the limitations of language and the boundaries of place. In effect, they were constructing a transnational identity. Although Norwegian was no longer the primary language of Norwegian Americans, they conceived of themselves as belonging to Norway's greater national community. They had internalized their ethnic identity, basing it less on language and culture and more on abstract concepts such as loyalty and friendship to the homeland. Furthermore, the legitimacy of the greater Norway concept, both in America and the homeland, meant that Norwegian Americans belonged to the Norwegian nation in a concrete sense and not just in a symbolic sense. The very real contributions made by Norwegian Americans to Norway during World War II were proof of that sense of shared national identity. The greater Norway had not only been imagined; it had been built on both sides of the Atlantic.

Acknowledgments

I WISH TO THANK NUMEROUS PEOPLE for making this work possible. I am especially indebted to my dissertation adviser, H. Arnold Barton, whose patience, constructive criticism, and friendship greatly improved the quality of my work. I also thank James Smith Allen of Southern Illinois University for his tutelage and insights, both of which enhanced my scholarship, as well as his friendship and encouragement. I am likewise indebted to other history professors at Southern Illinois University Carbondale for their valuable observations: Kay Carr, Charles Fanning, Jonathan Wiesen, Ed O'Day, Margie Morgan (now at Central Washington University), and Joseph Sramek. Special thanks must be given to Odd S. Lovoll of St. Olaf College for his suggestions and support. I single out Mike Batinski of Southern Illinois University, who retired after forty years of service; he recruited me to SIUC and has treated me wonderfully, both as former graduate director and most recently as my chair.

I have benefited immensely from the supportive environment at Indiana University East, where I am assistant professor of European and world history. My fellow historian, colleague, and former dean, Joanne Passet, has been most encouraging and always willing to offer constructive feedback. Paul Kriese, my colleague in political science, has been both friend and mentor and ever willing to share his insights. I give specific thanks to Mary Fell of the English department for her sage advice and tremendous friendship; I also thank English professors Alisa Clapp-Itnyre and T. J. Rivard for their camaraderie and willingness to motivate me. Justin Carroll also deserves mention for his wit and sense of humor. I appreciate the great friendship and moral support of Duane Lundy and Julien Simon.

My book has been a collaborative effort, and I pay special thanks in this regard to the University of Minnesota Press. I am grateful to my editor, Pieter Martin, for his judgment, constructive suggestions, and unwavering devotion in guiding the book's development. Kristian Tvedten, editorial assistant, has likewise been instrumental and offered sapient insights that benefited the book. I thank the editorial board at the Press as well as the outside readers; they contributed highly useful recommendations that significantly improved my effort.

At both Indiana University East and Southern Illinois University I have had the privilege to serve outstanding students. At SIU, I especially want to thank Kevin Chrisman (now at the University of Nebraska), Christina and Roy Bearden-White, Deb Wilson, Paula Bilyeu, Christi McCallum, and Kevin Pryor, plus many others too numerous to mention. At Indiana University East, I thank my fellow Whisters (world history students) for their love of history, which has greatly inspired me: Toby Bonwell, Andrew Britt, Jason Clark, Clayton Haisley, Mara Pennycuff, and Kraig Rose. Rick Madden and David Barger were two of my advisees who share a love of American history. I am also thankful to two other IU East students, Vicki Colley and Beth Crose. I warmly thank you all and others I have not mentioned.

In the course of conducting research in Norway, I met several people who assisted me. Cheryl Storø of the Norway–America Association was most helpful in setting up contacts. I am thankful for Dina Tolfsby of the Norwegian-American Collection for her kindly assistance as well as Knut Djupedal of the Norwegian Emigrant Museum. Several scholars in Norway provided essential criticisms: Øystein Sørensen, David C. Mauk, the late Dorothy Burton Skårdal, and Ingeborg Kongslien.

Two former advisers, Kenneth Smemo of Minnesota State University, Moorhead and Playford Thorson of the University of North Dakota, provided guidance during my formative years. I thank Playford's wife, Harriet, for her kindness and the great meals she cooked for me over the years.

Without the cheerful assistance of the office staff at SIUC this work would not have been possible. I offer my heartfelt thanks to the history department secretaries, Barb Mueller and Chasity Shea, and the staff at the Morris Library. I am indebted to the hardworking staff at IU East, including secretaries Michelle King and Reva J. Woodall and the ever-friendly custodial staff, Bo, Connie, Cindy, Bill, Tom, David, Tony, and the others; from day one you have all been very welcoming to me. I also thank the IU East Library staff, including Frances Yates, Mandi Moning, Sue McFadden, Matt Dilworth, and Heidi Huff.

On a personal level, I am thankful to numerous friends who have been very supportive during the years.

I dedicate this book to my late mother, Arla Olson. Throughout the various and difficult moments in my life, she never stopped believing in me, and she continued to support me with her love and understanding. Special mention goes to my father, Earl Olson, for his kindness and encouragement and to the aforementioned H. Arnold Barton. Although I could expound at length on his numerous qualities, the best thing I can say about him is that he is a true gentleman and a scholar. I am also grateful to Arnold's wife, Aina, who has been my "northern mom" during these recent years. Thank you all.

Notes

Introduction

1. The various spellings of the Viking-era explorer's name depended on the language being used. The usual Norwegian spelling was "Leif Erikson" (or "Eriksson"), the Icelandic spelling was "Leifur Eiríksson," and the Swedish spelling rendered his surname as "Eriksson." The matter was further complicated by the 1932 language reforms in Norway, which made "Leiv Eriksson" or "Eiriksson" the standard. English writers normally wrote his name as "Leif Erikson," which is the form used in this study.

2. *The Vinland Sagas: The Norse Discovery of America; Grænlendinga Saga and Eirik's Saga*, trans. and with introduction by Magnus Magnusson and Hermann Pálsson (Harmondsworth, England: Penguin Books, 1965), 54–58.

3. Gerd Nyquist, *The 99th Battalion*, translated by Inger-Johanne Gerwig, Henrik M. Hansen, and Mr. and Mrs. Oddvar Nass (Oslo: H. Aschehoug [W. Nygaard], 1981), 15–17, 177, 196–99.

4. Bernhard Giesen, "National Identity as Trauma: The German Case," in *Myth and Memory in the Construction of Community: Historical Patterns in Europe and Beyond*, ed. Bo Stråth (Brussels: P.I.E.-Peter Lang, 2000), 235–36.

5. Odd Sverre Lovoll, *Celebrating a Century: Nordmanns-Forbundet and Norwegians in the World Community 1907–2007* (Oslo: Nordmanns-Forbundet, 2009), 13–15; Olav Tysdal, "The Dissolution of the Union between Norway and Sweden and the Scandinavian Americans," *Scandinavian Studies*, Summer 2007, 174–75; *Minneapolis Daglig Tidende*, June 8 and 9, 1905.

6. Wolfgang Kaschuba, "The Emergence and Transformation of Foundation Myths," in *Myth and Memory*, ed. Stråth, 217–26; Arve Thorsen, "Foundation Myths at Work: National Day Celebrations in France, Germany, and Norway in a Comparative Perspective," in *Myth and Memory*, ed. Stråth, 331–50. Kaschuba's article describes the theoretical considerations of foundation myths, while Thorsen provides a comparative analysis of successful and unsuccessful foundation myths. Kaschuba defines foundation myths as "tightly woven fabrics of data and ideologies, of semantics and aesthetics, of values and practices. They represent extremely highly condensed cultural codifications that tell us 'quote me, use me, believe me, but don't ask me!' because myths discard their concrete temporal and spatial

references and try to assume *universal* meaning" (218). Thorsen, meanwhile, sees Norway's nationalism as that of the small nation-state, "a national ideology that has been formed by a period of opposition to a stronger power, and that has stylised the justness of its cause and the will to embrace its youth and innocence as its national identity" (349).

7. Lovoll, *Celebrating a Century*, 8–11.

8. Orm Øverland, *Immigrant Minds, American Identities: Making the United States Home, 1870–1930* (Urbana: University of Illinois Press, 2000), 54–119.

9. Orm Øverland, *The Western Home: A Literary History of Norwegian America* (Northfield, Minn.: Norwegian-American Historical Association, 1996), 5.

10. Elliot R. Barkan, "Introduction: Immigration, Incorporation, Assimilation, and the Limits of Transnationalism," in *Immigration, Incorporation, and Transnationalism*, ed. Elliot R. Barkan (New Brunswick, N.J.: Transaction Publishers, 2007), 6–9; Peter Kivisto, "Theorizing Transnational Immigration: A Critical Review of Current Efforts," *Ethnic and Racial Studies* 24, no. 4 (2001): 549–577, 551–52.

11. Thomas Faist, *The Volume and Dynamics of International Migration and Transnational Social Spaces* (Oxford: Clarendon Press, 2000), 45–46, 200, 207–8, 210–11. A similar concept is "social fields." See Nina Glick Schiller, Linda Basch, and Christina Szanton Blanc, eds., *Towards a Transnational Perspective on Migration: Race, Class, Ethnicity, and Nationalism Reconsidered* (New York: New York Academy of Sciences, 1992); and Alejandro Portes, Luis E. Guarnizo, and Patricia Landholt, "The Study of Transnationalism: Pitfalls and Promise of an Emergent Research Field," *Ethnic and Racial Studies* 22, no. 2 (1999): 217–37.

12. John W. Meyer, John Boli, George M. Thomas, and Francisco O. Ramirez, "World Society and the Nation-State," *American Journal of Sociology* 102, no. 1 (1997): 144–45.

13. Thomas Faist, "Diaspora and Transnationalism: What Kind of Dance Partners?," in *Diaspora and Transnationalism: Concepts, Theories, and Methods*, ed. Rainer Bauböck and Thomas Faist (Amsterdam: Amsterdam University Press, 2010), 13–14; Schiller, Basch, and Szanton Blanc, eds., *Towards a Transnational Perspective on Migration*, 13–19; Kivisto, "Theorizing Transnational Immigration," 554–55; Luis Eduardo Guarnizo and Michael Peter Smith, "The Location of Transnationalism," in *Transnationalism from Below*, ed. Michael Peter Smith and Luis Eduardo Guarnizo (New Brunswick, N.J.: Transaction Publishers, 1998), 8–10, 18. Nancy Foner, "Then *and* Now or Then *to* Now: Immigration to New York in Contemporary and Historical Perspective," in *Immigration, Incorporation, and Transnationalism*, ed. Barkan, 28.

14. See Kivisto, "Theorizing Transnational Immigration," 554–55, 561–62; Ewa Morawska, "The Sociology and History of Immigration: Reflections of a Practitioner," in *European University Institute Workshop on Reflections on Migration*

Research, May 20–21 (Florence, Italy: European University Institute, 1999); and Ronald Takaki, *A Different Mirror: A History of Multicultural America* (Boston: Little, Brown, 1993). See also Herbert J. Gans, "Symbolic Ethnicity: The Future of Ethnic Groups and Cultures in America," *Ethnic and Racial Studies* 2, no. 1 (1979): 1–20; and Nancy Foner, "Then *and* Now or Then *to* Now," in *Immigration, Incorporation, and Transnationalism*, ed. Barkan, 28–29. Another good summary of this problem in transnationalism is offered by Steven Vertovec, "Introduction: Transnationalism, Migrant Transnationalism, and Transformation," in *Transnationalism*, ed. Steven Vertovec (London: Routledge, 2009), 13–18.

15. Richard Handler, "Is 'Identity' a Useful Cross-Cultural Concept?," in *Commemoration: The Politics of National Identity*, ed. John R. Gillis (Oxford: Oxford University Press, 1994), 122–31. For a full explanation of how the nation is bounded by territory and ethnicity, see Anthony D. Smith, *National Identity* (Reno: University of Nevada Press, 1991), 8–15.

16. Benedict Anderson, *Imagined Communities: Reflections on the Origin and Spread of Nationalism*, new ed. (London: Verso, 2006), 5–7.

17. Felicia Medved, "The Concept of Homeland," in *Migrants and the Homeland: Images, Symbols, and Realities*, ed. Harald Runblom, Uppsala Multiethnic Papers 44 (Uppsala, Sweden: Centre for Multiethnic Research, 2000), 81–96.

18. John Hutchinson, "Cultural Nationalism and Moral Regeneration," in *Nationalism*, ed. John Hutchinson and Anthony D. Smith (Oxford: Oxford University Press, 1994), 122–31; John Hutchinson, *The Dynamics of Cultural Nationalism: The Gaelic Revival and the Creation of the Irish Nation State* (London: Allen and Unwin, 1987), 8–23; John Hutchinson, *Modern Nationalism* (London: Fontana, 1994), 1–38; Øystein Sørensen, "Elitenes nasjonbyggingsprojekter 1770–1945," in *Jakten på det norske: Perspektiver på utviklingen av en norsk nasjonal identitet på 1800-tallet*, ed. Øystein Sørensen (Oslo: Gyldendal, 2001), 17–21, 26–35; Anne-Lise Seip, "Det norske 'vi'-kulturnasjonalisme i Norge," in *Jakten på det norske*, ed. Sørensen, 95–111.

19. Eric Hobsbawm and Terrance Ranger, eds., *The Invention of Tradition* (Cambridge: Cambridge University Press, 1995); Eric Hobsbawm, "The Nation as Invented Tradition," in *Nationalism*, ed. Hutchinson and Smith, 76–79.

20. Hutchinson and Smith, eds., *Nationalism*, 11.

21. Rogers Brubaker, *Nationalism Reframed: Nationhood and the National Question in the New Europe* (Cambridge: Cambridge University Press, 1996), 21; Hutchinson and Smith, eds., *Nationalism*, 27.

22. Anthony Smith, "Ethno-Symbolism and the Study of Nationalism," in *Nations and Nationalism: A Reader*, ed. Philip Spencer and Howard Wollman (New Brunswick, N.J.: Rutgers University Press, 2005), 23–32; Anthony D. Smith, *The Cultural Foundations of Nations: Hierarchy, Covenant, and Republic* (Malden, Mass.: Blackwell Publishing, 2008), 1–12, 28–47; Daniele Conversi, "Mapping the

Field: Theories of Nationalism and the Ethnosymbolist Approach," in *Nationalism and Ethnosymbolism: History, Culture, and Ethnicity in the Formation of Nations*, ed. Athena S. Leoussi and Steven Grosby (Edinburgh: Edinburgh University Press, 2007), 15–30; Anthony D. Smith, "Epilogue: The Power of Ethnic Traditions in the Modern World," in *Nationalism and Ethnosymbolism*, ed. Leoussi and Grosby, 325–36; Hutchinson and Smith, eds., *Nationalism*, 32.

23. Faist, "What Kind of Dance Partners?," 9.

24. Ibid., 9–13; William Safran, "Deconstructing and Comparing Diasporas," in *Diaspora, Identity, and Religion: New Directions in Theory and Research*, ed. Waltraud Kokot, Khachig Tölölyan, and Carolin Alfonso (London: Routledge, 2004), 12–13; Robert C. Smith, "Transnational Localities: Community Technology and the Politics of Membership within the Context of Mexico and U.S. Migration," in *Transnationalism from Below*, ed. Smith and Guarnizo, 229; James Clifford, "Diasporas," *Cultural Anthropology* 9, no. 3 (1994): 302–38; William Safran, "Diasporas," *Diaspora* 1, no. 1 (1991): 83–99. See also Arjun Appadurai, *Modernity at Large: Cultural Dimensions of Globalization* (Minneapolis: University of Minnesota Press, 1996).

25. Faist, "What Kind of Dance Partners?," 21.

26. See Roben Cohen, *Global Diasporas: An Introduction* (London: UCL Press, 1997); and Gabriel Sheffer, *Diaspora Politics: At Home Abroad* (Cambridge: Cambridge University Press, 2003).

27. Michael Bruneau, "Diasporas, Transnational Spaces, and Communities," in *Diaspora and Transnationalism*, ed. Bauböck and Faist, 36–37.

28. Agnieszka Weinar, "Instrumentalizing Diasporas for Development: International and European Policy Discourses," in *Diaspora and Transnationalism*, ed. Bauböck and Faist, 81–82; Susane Schwalgin, "Why Locality Matters: Diaspora Consciousness and Sedentariness in the Armenian Diaspora in Greece," in *Diaspora, Identity, Religion*, ed. Kokot, Tölölyan, and Alfonso, 73–76; Faist, "What Kind of Dance Partners?," 13; Bruneau, "Diasporas, Transnational Spaces, and Communities," 40; Sharron P. Schwartz, "Bridging 'The Great Divide': The Evolution and Impact of Cornish Translocalism in Britain and the USA," in *Immigration, Incorporation, and Transnationalism*, ed. Barkan, 155–56.

29. Kachig Tölölyan, "Rethinking Diaspora(s): Stateless Power in the Transnational Moment," *Diaspora* 5, no. 1 (1996): 28; Vertovec, *Transnationalism*, 130–32.

1. Creating Home

1. *Robert Steensma Interview: Wallace Stegner Documentary*, interviewed by John Howe, http://www.kued.org/productions/wallacestegner/transcripts/robertSteensma.pdf (accessed May 31, 2011).

2. Wallace Stegner as quoted in Orm Øverland, *The Western Home: A Literary*

History of Norwegian America (Northfield, Minn.: Norwegian-American Historical Association, 1996), 6.

3. Linda Basch, Nina Glick Schiller, and Christina Szanton Blanc, *Nations Unbound: Transnational Projects, Postcolonial Predicaments, and Deterritorialized Nation-States* (Basel, Switzerland: Gordon and Breach, 1994), 7.

4. Arjun Appadurai, *Modernity at Large: Cultural Dimensions of Globalization* (Minneapolis: University of Minnesota Press, 1996), 32–34, 48–65.

5. Odd S. Lovoll, *The Promise of America: A History of the Norwegian-American People* (Minneapolis: University of Minnesota Press in cooperation with the Norwegian-American Historical Association, 1984), 12, 23, 26, 28; Tore Pryser, *Norsk historie 1800–1870: Frå standssamfunn mot klassesamfunn* (Oslo: Det Norske Samlaget, 1990), 304; Carlton C. Qualey, *Norwegian Settlement in the United States* (Northfield, Minn.: Norwegian-American Historical Association, 1938), 4.

6. Pryser, *Norsk historie 1800–1870*, 31.

7. Theodore C. Blegen, *Norwegian Migration to America: 1825–1860* (Northfield, Minn.: Norwegian-American Historical Association, 1931), 2; Peter A. Munch, *A Study of Cultural Change: Rural-Urban Conflicts in Norway* (Oslo: H. Aschehoug, 1956), 32–33.

8. Blegen, *Norwegian Migration to America*, 6–7; Oscar J. Falnes, *National Romanticism in Norway* (New York: Columbia University Press, 1933; repr., New York: AMS Press, 1968), 55–61, 77–87. For a good description of how national romanticism influenced Sweden's national identity, see Michelle Facos, *Nationalism and the Nordic Imagination: Swedish Art of the 1890s* (Berkeley: University of California Press, 1998).

9. Øyvind Østerud, *Agrarian Structure and Peasant Politics in Scandinavia: A Comparative Study of Rural Response to Economic Change* (Oslo: Universitetsforlaget, 1978), 124, 157–58, 160–61, 164–68, 175–76, 180, 233–35, 239; Øyvind Østerud, "Nytt perspektiv på det store hamskiftet," *Historisk Tidsskrift* 54 (1975): 120–27; Jon Gjerde, *From Peasants to Farmers: The Migration from Balestrand, Norway, to the Upper Middle West* (Cambridge: Cambridge University Press, 1985), 56–84; Blegen, *Norwegian Migration to America*, 7–8; Gabriel Øidne, "Lit tom motsetninga mellom Austlandet og Vestlandet," *Syn og Segn* 3 (1957): 99–100, 104–9. All translations are the author's unless otherwise stated.

10. Lovoll, *The Promise of America*, 9–10.

11. Thomas K. Derry, *A Short History of Norway* (London: George Allen and Unwin, 1957), 124; Munch, *A Study of Cultural Change*, 41–43; Ingrid Semmingsen, *Norway to America: A History of the Migration*, trans. Einar Haugen (Minneapolis: University of Minnesota Press, 1978), 35–36; Thomas K. Derry, *A History of Modern Norway, 1814–1972* (Oxford: Clarendon Press, 1973), 39.

12. Munch, *A Study of Cultural Change*, 44–46; Falnes, *National Romanticism*, 45–87.

13. Pryser, *Norges historie*, 329; Terje I. Leiren, *Marcus Thrane: A Norwegian Radical in America*, Biographical Series 2 (Northfield, Minn.: Norwegian-American Historical Association, 1987), 11–12; Birger Steiro, *Marcus Thranes politiske agitasjon 1849–1855* (Melhus, Norway: Snøfugl forlag, 1974), 97–98, 106–7.

14. Blegen, *Norwegian Migration to America*, 165–70; Gjerde, *From Peasants to Farmers*, 56–57.

15. Gjerde, *From Peasants to Farmers*, 112–14.

16. Ibid., 57, 83–84; Blegen, *Norwegian Migration to America*, 169–75. On the issue of disgrace among Swedish farmers, see H. Arnold Barton, *A Folk Divided: Homeland Swedes and Swedish Americans, 1840–1940* (Carbondale: Southern Illinois University Press, 1994), 150–51.

17. Gjerde, *From Peasants to Farmers*, 114–15; Semmingsen, *Norway to America*, 41–47.

18. Lovoll, *The Promise of America*, 92.

19. See David C. Mauk, *The Colony That Rose from the Sea: Norwegian Maritime Migration and Community in Brooklyn, 1850–1910* (Northfield, Minn.: Norwegian-American Historical Association, 1997).

20. See especially Mark Wyman, *Round-Trip to America: The Immigrants Return to Europe, 1880–1930* (Ithaca, N.Y.: Cornell University Press, 1993), 11–12; Semmingsen, *Norway to America*, 119–120; Mauk, *Colony That Rose from the Sea*, 213–21; David C. Mauk, "Going on Land: Maritime Influences on the Development of the Norwegian Colony in Brooklyn to 1940," in *Essays on Norwegian-American Literature and History*, vol. 2, ed. Øyvind T. Gulliksen, Ingeborg R. Kongslien, and Dina Tolfsby (Oslo: De norsk-amerikanske historielaget, avd. Norge, 1990), 145–71.

21. Lovoll, *The Promise of America*, 29.

22. Gjerde, *From Peasants to Farmers*, 116–67.

23. Lovoll, *The Promise of America*, 10–11; Blegen, *Norwegian Migration to America*, 56–61; Knud Langeland, *Nordmændene i Amerika: Nogle optegnelser om de norskes udvandring til Amerika* (Chicago: John Anderson, 1889), 18–19.

24. Gert Hovland, letter to Norway (1835), as quoted in Blegen, *Norwegian Migration to America*, 66–68.

25. "Bishop Neumann's Word of Admonition to the Peasants," trans. and ed. Gunnar J. Malmin, *Norwegian-American Studies and Records* 1 (1926): 95–109.

26. D. G. Ristad, "A Doctrinaire Idealist: Hans Barlien," *Norwegian-American Historical Association Studies and Records* 3 (1928): 13–22.

27. *Ole Rynning's True Account of America*, trans. and ed. Theodore C. Blegen, Travel and Description 1 (Minneapolis: University of Minnesota Press for the Norwegian-American Historical Association, 1926), 77, 87–88.

28. See Johan Reinert Reierson, *Pathfinder for Norwegian Emigrants*, trans. Frank G. Nelson, ed. Kenneth O. Bjork, Travel and Description 9 (Northfield, Minn.: Norwegian-American Historical Association, 1981).

29. Blegen, *Norwegian Migration to America*, 158–95; Reierson, *Pathfinder for Norwegian Emigrants*, 160–78.

30. See especially Lovoll, *The Promise of America*, 36–37; Jon Gjerde, *The Minds of the West: Ethnocultural Evolution in the Rural Middle West, 1830–1917* (Chapel Hill: University of North Carolina Press, 1997), 74–76; Ingrid Semmingsen, *Veien mot vest*, vol. 2, *Utvandringen fra Norge, 1865–1915* (Oslo: H. Aschehoug, 1950), 288–90; Ingrid Semmingsen, *Drøm og Dåd: Utvandringen til Amerika* (Oslo: H. Achehoug, 1975), 138–40. For a good case study on how a community from Rättvik, Sweden, attempted to transplant its culture and way of life onto American soil (in Isanti County, Minnesota), see Robert C. Ostergren, *A Community Transplanted: The Trans-Atlantic Experience of a Swedish Immigrant Settlement in the Upper Middle West, 1835–1915* (Madison: University of Wisconsin Press, 1988).

31. Qualey, *Norwegian Settlement in the United States*, 14–15.

32. Lovoll, *The Promise of America*, 81–83.

33. Ibid., 82–90, 153–56; Gjerde, *From Peasants to Farmers*, 166–67.

34. Theodore C. Blegen, *Norwegian Migration to America: The American Transition* (Northfield, Minn.: Norwegian-American Historical Association, 1940), 459. Hereafter referred to as *The American Transition*.

35. Semmingsen, *Norway to America*, 121–22.

36. For a good description of a similar process in Sweden, see Barton, *A Folk Divided*, 37–38.

37. Lovoll, *The Promise of America*, 153.

38. Arne Hassing, "Norway's Organized Response to Emigration," *Norwegian-American Studies* 25 (1972): 59–68. For a Swedish-American analogy, see Barton, *A Folk Divided*, 27–31.

39. Blegen, *The American Transition*, 460; Østerud, *Agrarian Structure*, 233–35.

40. Blegen, *The American Transition*, 460; Johan Melbye, "Utvandringen," *Mot emigration,* January 1909, 1–18; Knut Takla, "Forholdene i de Forenede Stater," *Ny jord*, March 1917, 58–83.

41. Cited in Blegen, *The American Transition*, 461.

42. See Thorstein Veblen, *Theory of the Leisure Class* (New York: Macmillan, 1899).

2. Belonging to the Nation

1. Nils Hanson Hilton, Christiania, Norway, letter to Anne Karine Foss, Nannestad, Akershus, Norway, April 20, 1866, in *Fra Amerika til Norge*, vol. 2, *Norske utvandrerbrev 1858–1868,* ed. Orm Øverland and Steinar Kjærheim (Oslo: Solum Forlag, 1992), 348.

2. Øystein Sørensen, "The Development of a Norwegian National Identity during the Nineteenth Century," in *Nordic Paths to National Identity in the Nineteenth Century*, ed. Sørensen, KULTs skriftserie 22 (Oslo: Research Council of

Norway, 1994), 17–18, 23–27; Øystein Sørensen, interview with the author, February 18, 2004. Sørensen acknowledges that much of the ideology of national identity is constructed or invented, yet he cautions that this process cannot be used for indiscriminate fabrication. He contends that identity-makers can only utilize the actual raw material—either high or low culture—to create their national myths. With regard to Norway, he argues that it had a rich trove of raw historical material available with which its leaders could construct a meaningful national identity.

3. *America in the Forties: The Letters of Ole Munch Ræder,* trans. and ed. Gunnar J. Malmin, Travel and Description Series 3 (Minneapolis: University of Minnesota Press for the Norwegian-American Historical Association, 1931), 18–21, 148–49; *Emigranten,* March 14, 1859, as cited in Theodore C. Blegen, *Norwegian Migration to America, 1825–1860,* 373, other material is from 336–37; Theodore C. Blegen, *Norwegian Migration to America: The American Transition,* 100–165; Betty A. Bergland, "Norwegian Immigrants and 'Indianerne' in the Landtaking, 1838–1862," *Norwegian-American Studies* 35 (2000): 330–36; A. N. Rygg, *Norwegians in New York, 1825–1925* (Brooklyn, N.Y.: Norwegian News, 1940), 25–28; Knut Gjerset, *Norwegian Sailors on the Great Lakes: A Study in the History of American Inland Transportation* (Northfield, Minn.: Norwegian-American Historical Association, 1928), 26.

4. See, for example, Richard White, *The Middle Ground: Indians, Empire, and Republics in the Great Lakes Region, 1650–1815* (Cambridge: Cambridge University Press, 1991), ix–x, 527. White shows how the re-creation of the American Indian went through successive stages as the Alien, the Exotic, and finally the Other. Once white Europeans had achieved economic and military leverage against the Native Americans, they depicted them as objects of study in a world of white learning. White's work, therefore, has application to identity studies. The objectification of an enemy, such as the Confederate American, often served as a springboard to a group's identity. This was the case for many immigrant groups that fought predominantly on the Union side during the American Civil War.

5. Hans Torgerson Dahl, Dunn Company, Wisconsin, letter to Tor Torgersen Øyen, Skåbu, Norway, July 10, 1860, in *Fra Amerika til Norge,* vol. 2, *Norske utvandrerbrev 1858–1868,* 134.

6. John A. Johnson, *Det Skandinaviske Regiments historie (15de Wisconsin Regiment)* (LaCrosse, Wisc.: Fædrelandet og Emigrantens Trykkeri, 1869), 14–15.

7. *A Chronicler of Immigrant Life: Svein Nilsson's Articles in "Billed-Magazin," 1868–1870,* trans. and introduction by C. A. Clausen, Authors Series 6 (Northfield, Minn.: Norwegian-American Historical Association, 1982), 46, 100–106. Hereafter referred to as Nilsson, *A Chronicler of Immigrant Life.*

8. Herman Amberg Preus, *Vivacious Daughter: Seven Lectures on the Religious Situation among Norwegians in America,* ed., trans., and with introduction by Todd W. Nichol, Travel and Description Series 11 (Northfield, Minn.: Norwegian-American Historical Association, 1990), 36–40.

9. Peter Henrichson, "Om det norske Nybyggerliv i Amerika," *Norden: Et Maanedsskrift* (Christiania) 5 (1868): 347–66.
10. David Monrad Schøyen, *Amerikas Forenede Staters Historie*, 3 vols. (Chicago: Skandinavens Bogtrykkeri, 1874–1876) 1:3–4, 3:108–9; Odd S. Lovoll, *A Century of Urban Life: The Norwegians in Chicago before 1930* (Northfield, Minn.: Norwegian-American Historical Association, 1988), 132.
11. Fredrik M. Wallem, *De Norske I Amerika: En række reisebrev fra "Bergenspostens" korrespondent* (Særtrykk av Bergensposten, 1871; Bergen, Norway: Bergensposten, 1875), 92–96, 134–36.
12. Jørgen Gjerdrum, "Fra Amerika II," *Dagbladet,* December 3, 1874, and "Fra Amerika VI," *Dagbladet,* January 9, 1875; Carlton C. Qualey, "Jørgen Gjerdrum's Letters from America, 1874–1875," *Norwegian-American Studies and Records* 11 (1940): 86–91; David C. Mauk, *The Colony That Rose from the Sea: Norwegian Maritime Migration and Community in Brooklyn, 1850–1910* (Northfield, Minn.: Norwegian-American Historical Association, 1997), 62, 66.
13. David Mauk, "Syttende mai Vignettes from Minneapolis–St. Paul: The Changing Meaning of Norway's Constitution Day in the Capital of Norwegian America, 1869–1914," *American Studies in Scandinavia* 34, no. 2 (Autumn 2002): 32–35. For a full explanation of the changing relationship of consent and descent in immigrant life, see Werner Sollors, *Beyond Ethnicity: Consent and Descent in American Culture* (New York: Oxford University Press, 1986).
14. Øverland, *Immigrant Minds,* 9–11, 142, 161.
15. H. Arnold Barton, *A Folk Divided: Homeland Swedes and Swedish Americans, 1840–1940* (Carbondale: Southern Illinois University Press, 1994), 120–25, 222–26; H. Arnold Barton, "Three Insiders' Views of Swedish America," *Swedish-American Historical Quarterly,* October 1994, 179–81.
16. Thus, by the 1880s, the term "Norwegian-American" started to supplant "Norwegian" in America or the unhyphenated "Norwegian American" in everyday use.
17. Øverland, *Immigrant Minds,* 143.
18. Sørensen, "The Development of a Norwegian National Identity," 21–25; Dahl, *Norsk historieforskning,* 39–41, 43–85.
19. Sørensen, "The Development of a Norwegian National Identity," 21–25; H. Arnold Barton, *Sweden and Visions of Norway: Politics and Culture, 1814–1905* (Carbondale and Edwardsville: Southern Illinois University Press, 2003), 91–99; Sørensen, "Elitenes nasjonsbyggingsprosjekter," 26–30; Ørnulf Hodne, "Sagn og eventyr som nasjonalkultur," in *Jakten på det norske,* ed. Sørensen, 128–32.
20. Dag Thorkildsen, "En nasjonal og moderne utdanning," in *Jakten på det norske,* ed. Sørensen, 267–75; Sørensen, "The Development of a Norwegian National Identity," 25.
21. Sørensen, "The Development of a Norwegian National Identity," 28; Gudleiv Bø, "'Land og lynne'—norske diktere om nasjonal identitet," in *Jakten på det norske,*

ed. Sørensen, 120–24; Øystein Sørensen, *Bjørnstjerne Bjørnson og nasjonalismen* (Oslo: J. W. Cappelens Forlag, 1997), 36–38, 76–125; Øystein Sørensen, *Kampen om Norges sjel, Norsk idéhistorie* (Oslo: Aschehoug, 2001), 3:184–89.

22. Jørund Mannsåker, *Emigrasjon og dikting: Utvandringa til Nord-Amerika i norsk skjønnlitteratur* (Oslo: Det Norske Samlaget, 1971), 35–36.

23. Ibid., 35–36.

24. Ibid., 300; Sørensen, "The Development of a Norwegian National Identity," 30–32.

25. Mannsåker, *Emigrasjon og dikting*, 300–304; Knut Gjerset, *History of the Norwegian People*, 2 vols. (New York: Macmillan, 1915), 2:500.

26. Mannsåker, *Emigrasjon og dikting*, 311–31.

27. Orm Øverland, *The Western Home: A Literary History of Norwegian America*, Authors Series 8 (Northfield, Minn.: Norwegian-American Historical Association, 1996), 144–45; Joel G. Winkjer, "About the Author Hans Anderson Foss," in Hans A. Foss, *The Cotter's Son: A Story from Sigdal*, trans. Joel G. Winkjer (1884; Bismarck, N.D.: Smoky Water Press, 1998), 290–91.

28. Liv Kristin Asheim, "*Husmannsgutten*—Uncle Tom's Cabin for Norwegian Cotters," in Foss, *The Cotter's Son: A Story from Sigdal*, 298–301; Svein Ore Sandvik, "H. A. Foss: Norwegian-American Author and Editor" (thesis, University of Oslo, 1977), 16–25.

29. Asheim, "*Husmannsgutten*—Uncle Tom's Cabin for Norwegian Cotters," 302–3.

30. Ibid., 303–6.

31. Rygg, *Norwegians in New York*, 62.

32. Clarence A. Glasrud, *Hjalmar Hjorth Boyesen*, Authors Series 1 (Northfield, Minn.: Norwegian-American Historical Association, 1963), 54–76; Clarence A. Glasrud, "Boyesen and the Norwegian Immigration," *Norwegian-American Studies and Records* 14 (1956): 17–44.

33. Hjalmar Hjorth Boyesen, *The Modern Vikings: Stories of Life and Sport in the Norseland* (New York: Charles Scribner's Sons, 1887); Boyesen, "The Cooper and the Wolves," in *Modern Vikings*, 91–101. Glasrud notes that *The Modern Vikings* was Boyesen's best seller. See Glasrud, *Hjalmar Hjorth Boyesen*, 107.

34. H. Arnold Barton, "Historians of the Scandinavians in North America," in *Scandinavians in America: Literary Life*, ed. J. R. Christianson (Decorah, Iowa: Symra Literary Society, 1985), 43–47.

35. Victor R. Greene, *American Immigrant Leaders 1800–1910: Marginality and Identity* (Baltimore, Md.: Johns Hopkins University Press, 1987), 12–16, 140–42.

36. Dag Blanck, *The Creation of an Ethnic Identity: Being Swedish American in the Augustana Synod, 1860–1917* (Carbondale: Southern Illinois University Press, 2006), 162–87.

37. Barton, *A Folk Divided*, 64, 66–68.

38. Øverland, *Immigrant Minds*, 17–21; Wilbur Zelinsky, *Nation into State: The Shifting Foundations of American Nationalism* (Chapel Hill: University of North Carolina Press, 1988), 223; Jon Gjerde, *The Minds of the West: Ethnocultural Evolution in the Rural Middle West, 1830–1917* (Chapel Hill: University of North Carolina Press, 1997), 4–11; Lawrence Fuchs, *The American Kaleidoscope: Race, Ethnicity, and the Civic Culture* (Hanover: Wesleyan University Press, 1990), 5.

39. Lloyd Hustvedt, *Rasmus Bjørn Anderson* (1966; repr. New York: Arno Press, 1979), 314; Einar Haugen, *Voyages to Vinland: The First American Saga* (New York: A. Knopf, 1942), 104–19.

40. Nilsson, *A Chronicler of Immigrant Life*, 42–43.

41. Ernst Sars, *Udsigt over den norske Historie*, 4 vols. (Kristiania: Cammermeyer, 1873–1891), 2:16, 2:400, 4:35–352; see also Arne Garborg, *Den ny-norske Sprog-og Nationalitetsbevægelse* (Kristiania: Cammermeyer, 1877).

42. Sørensen, "The Development of a Norwegian National Identity," 26–27; Ottar Dahl, *Norsk historieforskning i det 19. og 20. århundre* (Oslo: Universitetsforlaget, 1990), 47–51, 64–66; Oscar J. Falnes, *National Romanticism in Norway* (1933; repr., New York: AMS Press, 1968), 123–24; Øystein Sørensen, "Elitenes nasjonsbyggningsprojekter 1770–1945," in *Jakten på det norske*, ed. Sørensen, 28–30; Anne-Lise Seip, "Det norske 'vi'—kulturnasjonalisme i Norge," in *Jakten på det norske*, ed. Sørensen, 103–6.

43. Rasmus Bjørn Anderson, *America Not Discovered by Columbus: A Historical Sketch of the Discovery of America by the Norsemen in the Tenth Century*, 4th ed. (Chicago: S. C. Griggs, 1891), 36–37.

44. Rasmus Bjørn Anderson, *Tale ved femti-aarsfesten for den norske udvandring til Amerika* (Chicago: n.p., 1875), 3–5, 8.

45. Ibid., 9, 12; Øverland, *Immigrant Minds, American Identities*, 158; Dahl, *Norsk historieforskning*, 24–25, 54–55, 67–74, 210–18.

46. Anderson, *Tale*, 12; Øverland, *Immigrant Minds*, 158–61.

47. Anderson, *Tale*, 10.

48. Øverland, *Immigrant Minds*, 161.

49. Rasmus B. Anderson, *Amerikas første Opdagelse* (Copenhagen: Gyldendalske Boghandels Forlag, 1886), 7–8, 26–27, 36–37.

50. *Dagbladet*, July 18 and 19, 1892.

51. *Aftenposten*, September 23, 1886; *Morgenbladet*, November 13, 1886; *Dagbladet*, undated but likely from 1886, as quoted in Hustvedt, *Rasmus Bjørn Anderson*, 315–16.

52. Øverland, *Immigrant Minds*, 54–86.

53. Ibid., 120–43; on Anderson's 1875 speech, one should refer again to Anderson, *Tale*, 11–12.

54. Nilsson, *A Chronicler of Immigrant Life*, 42–43; Anderson, *America Not Discovered by Columbus*, 71–83, 85–89; Martin Ulvestad, *Nordmændene i Amerika*,

deres historie og record: Bidrag til og bindeled mellem Norges historie og Nord-Amerikas—De Forenede Stater i Særdeleshed, 2 vols. (Minneapolis: History Book Company's Forlag, 1907–1913), 1:5; Hjalmar Rued Holand, *De norske Settlementers Historie: En Oversigt over den norske Indvandring til og Bebyggelse af Amerikas Nordvesten fra Amerikas Opdagelse til Indianerkrigen i Nordvesten,* 4th rev. ed. (Chicago: John Anderson Publishing 1912), 8–9.

55. Waldemar Ager, "Preserving Our Mother Tongue," trans. Sigvald Stoylen, in *Cultural Pluralism versus Assimilation: The Views of Waldemar Ager,* ed. Odd S. Lovoll (Northfield, Minn.: Norwegian-American Historical Association, 1977), 55; O. E. Rølvaag, *Concerning Our Heritage,* trans. Solveig Zempel (Northfield, Minn.: Norwegian-American Historical Association, 1998), 107–13.

56. Anderson, *America Not Discovered by Columbus,* 71–83; Hustvedt, *Rasmus Bjørn Anderson,* 311–12.

57. Ulvestad, *Norsk-Amerikaneren Vikingesaga samt Pioneerhistorie, Statistik og biografiske Oplysninger om Nordmænd i Amerika* (Seattle: by the author, 1928), 195.

58. Anderson, *America Not Discovered by Columbus,* 75–77; Ulvestad, *Nordmændene,* 1:6; Holand, *De norske Settlementers Historie,* 11–12.

59. Anderson, *America Not Discovered by Columbus,* 84; Ulvestad, *Nordmændene,* 1:6; Barton, *A Folk Divided,* 65, plate 8; Holand, *De norske Settlementers Historie,* 11–14.

60. Holand, *De norske Settlementers Historie,* 14–21; Lovoll, *The Promise of America: A History of the Norwegian People* (Minneapolis: University of Minnesota Press in cooperation with the Norwegian-American Historical Association, 1984), 181; H. Arnold Barton, "Symposium on 'Nordic Immigrants: Builders of Nations' at California Lutheran University, Thousand Oaks, California, February 22–24, 2002," *Swedish-American Historical Quarterly* 3 (July 2002): 222.

61. Gjerset, *History of the Norwegian People,* 2:6–7, 2:608, 2:610.

62. Øverland, *Immigrant Minds,* 141–42, 150, 160–61.

63. Blanck, *Becoming Swedish American: The Construction of an Ethnic Identity in the Augustana Synod, 1860–1917: Acta Universitatis Upsaliensis,* Studia historica Upsaliensa 182 (Uppsala: Uppsala University Press, 1997), 186–87. Although in his *Creating an Ethnic Identity* Blanck does not use these terms, he describes a similar pattern that he places in the context of Øverland's foundation myths (162–72).

64. Knud Langeland, *Nordmændene i Amerika: Nogle Optegnelser om de Norskes Udvandring til Amerika* (Chicago: John Anderson, 1889), 9; John O. Evjen, *Scandinavian Immigrants in New York, 1630–1674* (Minneapolis: K. C. Holter Publishing, 1916), 14.

65. Holand, *De norske Settlementers Historie,* 23–25; Holand, *Den sidste folkevandring: Sagastubber fra nybyggerlivet i Amerika* (Oslo: H. Aschehoug, 1930), 20–21; Evjen, *Scandinavian Immigrants in New York, 1630–1674,* 60.

66. George T. Flom, *A History of Norwegian Immigration to the United States*

from the Earliest Beginning Down to the Year 1848 (Iowa City: privately printed, 1909), 36–40; Evjen, *Scandinavian Immigrants in New York, 1630–1674*, 19–147.

67. Flom, *A History of Norwegian Immigration to the United States*, 41–42.

68. Albert Welles, *The Pedigree and History of the Washington Family Derived from Odin, the Founder of Scandinavia B.C. 70, Involving a Period of Eighteen Centuries and Including Fifty-Five Generations Down to General George Washington, First President of the United States* (1879). I obtained this information from Øverland's *Immigrant Minds*, 59.

69. Ulvestad, *Nordmændene*, 1:25, and *Vikingesaga*, 201; Øverland, *Immigrant Minds*, 59.

70. Ole E. Rølvaag, *Their Fathers' God*, trans. Trygve M. Ager (New York: Harper, 1931), 209–10.

71. Greene, *American Immigrant Leaders 1800–1910*, 142; Blanck, *Creation of an Ethnic Identity*, 176–81; Blanck, *Becoming Swedish American*, 194.

72. Anderson, *The First Chapter of Norwegian Immigration (1821–1840): Its Causes and Results* (Madison, Wisc.: by the author, 1895), 54–63, 70–90; Ulvestad, *Nordmændene*, 1:13–14; Olaf M. Norlie, *History of the Norwegian People in America* (Minneapolis: Augsburg Publishing House, 1925), 119–20, 193–95, 487–88; Martin W. Odland, *The Life of Knute Nelson* (Minneapolis: Lund Press, 1926), 228–35, 319–27.

73. Johnson, *Det Skandinaviske Regiments historie*, 109.

74. Ole Amundsen Buslett, *Det Femtende Regiment Wisconsin Frivillige* (Decorah, Iowa: Forfatterens Forlag, 1894), 99–104, 300.

75. Waldemar Ager, *Colonel Heg and His Boys: A Norwegian Regiment in the American Civil War*, trans. Della Kittleson Catuna and Clarence A. Clausen (Northfield, Minn.: Norwegian-American Historical Association, 2000), xxi, 3.

76. Ibid., 201–2.

77. Øverland, *Immigrant Minds*, 150.

78. Odd S. Lovoll, *Norwegians on the Prairie: Ethnicity and the Development of the Country Town* (St. Paul: Minnesota Historical Society in cooperation with the Norwegian-American Historical Association, 2006), xiv, 4, 35–36, 47–48, 51–53, 56–58, 78–81, 96–101.

79. Nilsson, *A Chronicler of Immigrant Life*, 79–80.

80. Holand, *Den sidste folkevandring*, 11–12.

81. For an example of this type of argument, see Nilsson, *A Chronicler of Immigrant Life*, 80.

82. Holand, *Den sidste folkevandring*, 14.

83. Langeland, *Nordmændene i Amerika*, 114–15.

84. John Higham, *Strangers in the Land: Patterns of American Nativism, 1860–1925* (Westport, Conn.: Greenwood Press, 1981), 87–96, 102–4, 159–75.

85. Langeland, *Nordmændene i Amerika*, 50–51; Ulvestad, *Nordmændene*, 1:3;

Kendric Charles Babcock, *The Scandinavian Element in the United States* (Urbana: University of Illinois Press, 1914), 180, 182.

86. Norlie, *History of the Norwegian People in America*, 509; see also April Rose Schultz, *Ethnicity on Parade: Inventing the Norwegian American through Celebration* (Amherst: University of Massachusetts Press, 1994), 1–7.

87. J. R. Christianson, "Myth, History, and the Norwegian-American Historical Association," in *Nordics in America: The Future of Their Past*, ed. Odd S. Lovoll (Northfield, Minn.: Norwegian-American Historical Association, 1993), 64.

88. Lovoll, *A Century of Urban Life*, 89–90.

89. Odd S. Lovoll, "The Changing Role of May 17 as a Norwegian-American 'Key' Symbol," in *Nasjonaldagsfeiring i fleirkulturelle demokrati*, ed. Brit Marie Hovland and Olaf Aagedal, Nord 4 (Copenhagen: Nordisk Ministerråd, 2001), 4:67–68.

90. Lovoll, *A Century of Urban Life*, 102, 131; *Chicago Times*, July 19, 1872; *Skandinaven*, July 17, 19, and 24, 1872.

91. Hildegunn Bjørgen and Brit Marie Hovland, "I takt med nasjonen—Den nasjonale 17. mai-paraden gjennom historia," in *Nasjonaldagsfeiring*, ed. Hovland and Aagedal, 39. Bjørgen and Hovland note the changing context of May 17 celebrations in Norway. For example, between 1844 and 1881 it was celebrated largely in commemoration of the dynastic union between Sweden and Norway. However, the rise of the Liberal party, and its demands for a separate consular service for Norway—and ultimately an entirely independent Norwegian state—meant that May 17 came to be celebrated as a nationalist expression of Norwegian independence. See esp. 31–36.

92. Lovoll, *A Century of Urban Life*, 89. For a discussion of how Norwegian immigrants combined homeland traditions with American ones, see Lovoll, *The Promise of America*, 208–13, and Øverland, *Immigrant Minds*, 166–73.

93. Mauk, "Syttende mai Vignettes," 38–40; Carl G. O. Hansen, *My Minneapolis: A Chronicle of What Has Been Learned and Observed about the Norwegians in Minneapolis through One Hundred Years* (Minneapolis: privately printed, 1956), 62–63, 68, 142–44, 226–28.

94. Lovoll, "The Changing Role of May 17," 68–69; Mauk, "Syttende mai Vignettes," 34–39; Mauk, *The Colony That Rose from the Sea*, 67; Rygg, *Norwegians in New York*, 77–79; Kenneth O. Bjork, *West of the Great Divide: Norwegian Migration to the Pacific Coast, 1847–1893* (Northfield, Minn.: Norwegian-American Historical Association, 1958), 189–90, 616–19.

95. Lovoll, *A Century of Urban Life*, 135; Mauk, "Syttende mai Vignettes," 34–35; Hustvedt, *Rasmus Bjørn Anderson*, 82–83, 130–37; *Land of the Free: Bjørnstjerne Bjørnson's America Letters*, ed. Eva Lund Haugen and Einar Haugen, Authors Series 5 (Northfield, Minn.: Norwegian-American Historical Association, 1978), 8–13. Hereafter referred to as Bjørnstjerne, *Land of the Free*.

96. Bjørnstjerne, *Land of the Free*, 35–39.
97. *Dagbladet*, November 16, 1880; Bjørnstjerne, *Land of the Free*, 63, 66.
98. Bjørnstjerne, *Land of the Free*, 141–43.
99. Nina Draxten, *Kristofer Janson in America* (Boston: Twayne Publishers, 1976), 5–6, 9–41; Nina Draxten, "Kristofer Janson's Lecture Tour, 1879–1880," *Norwegian-American Studies* 22 (1965): 18–74.
100. *Skandinaven*, June 25, 1880, November 16, 1880, January 25, 1881; Bjørnstjerne, *Land of the Free*, 147–50.
101. Bjørnstjerne, *Land of the Free*, 151–55.
102. Ibid., 157–66, 254.
103. *Budstikken* (Minneapolis), as quoted in *Skandinaven*, January 25, 1881.
104. *Norden* (Chicago), February 9, 1881, as cited in Bjørnstjerne, *Land of the Free*, 174.
105. Bjørnstjerne, *Land of the Free*, 175–77.
106. Hustvedt, *Rasmus Bjørn Anderson*, 170–71.
107. *Dagbladet*, April 6, 1881, as cited in Bjørnstjerne, *Land of the Free*, 227; material is from pages 218–27.
108. Samuel F. Bætzmann, *Det udflyttede Norge: Udgivet af Folkeskriftselskabet* (Kristiania: I hovedkommission hos Olaf Huseby og Olaf Olsen, Nikolai Olsens Bogtrykkeri, 1884), 3–4, 188.
109. Knut Hamsun, *The Cultural Life of Modern America*, ed. and trans. Barbara Gordon Morgridge (1889; Cambridge, Mass.: Harvard University Press, 1969), 18, 22–23.
110. See Jon Gjerde, *The Minds of the West*, 1–22,

3. Modern Vikings

1. Magnus Andersen, *Vikingefærden: En illustreret beskrivelse af "Vikings" reise i 1893* (Kristiania: Eget forlag, 1895), 4–7; Odd S. Lovoll, *A Century of Urban Life: The Norwegians in Chicago before 1930* (Northfield, Minn.: Norwegian-American Historical Association, 1988), 184–88; Mauk, *The Colony That Rose from the Sea*, 90–91.
2. *Chicago Herald*, May 27, 1893; *Daily Inter Ocean* (Chicago), July 13 and 22, 1893; Andersen, *Vikingefærden*, 429–30.
3. *Skandinaven*, July 18, 1893; *Chicago Record*, July 13, 1893, as quoted in *Skandinaven*, July 16, 1893; *Minneapolis Journal*, July 13, 1893, as quoted in *Skandinaven*, July 16, 1893.
4. *Skandinaven*, July 18, 1893 (quote is from this source); *Norden*, July 22, 1893.
5. On the importance of the urban Norwegian-American leadership in spreading the cult of Leif Erikson, see Odd S. Lovoll, "Leiv Eriksson som symbol i det norske Amerika," in *Leiv Eriksson, Helge Ingstad og Vinland. Kjelder og tradisjonar:*

Innlegg ved et seminar i regi av det Kongelige Norske Videnskabers Selskab 13–14 october 2000, ed. Jan Ragnar Hagland and Steinar Supphellen (Trondheim, Norway: Tapir Akademisk Forlag, 2001), 124–27; Lars A. Stenholt, *Moderne Vikinger: Historisk skildring av Kapt. Magnus Andersens fredelige Vikingefærd* (Minneapolis: Waldemar Kriedt Publishing, 1894), 10, 77, 81, 86.

6. Lars A. Stenholt, *Nordmændenes opdagelse af Amerika: Historiske skildringer* (Minneapolis: Waldemar Kriedt Publishing, 1893), 3.

7. Thoralv Klaveness, *Blandt udvandrede Nordmænd: Vore landsmænds liv og vilkaar i den nye verden* (Kristiania: Alb. Cammermeyers Forlag, 1904), 83–84; Waldemar Ager, "Preserving Our Mother Tongue," trans. Sigvald Stoylen, in *Cultural Pluralism versus Assimilation: The Views of Waldemar Ager*, ed. Odd S. Lovoll, Topical Studies 2 (Northfield, Minn.: Norwegian-American Historical Association, 1977), 55; the volume will be cited hereafter as *Cultural Pluralism;* H. Arnold Barton, "Partners and Rivals: Norwegian and Swedish Emigration and Immigrants," *Swedish-American Historical Quarterly* 54 (April 2003): 100–105.

8. Knute Nelson, "Det nittende aarhundredes Vikingtog," in *Minnesota: En kortfattet historie av Nordmændenes bebyggelse av staten, deres Gjøremaal, foreninger og Livsvilkaar*, ed. J. S. Johnson (Minneapolis: Minnesota–Norway 1914 Centennial Exposition Association, 1914), 150–52; hereafter referred to as *Minnesota: En kortfattet historie*.

9. Ibid., 153–55.

10. Knute Nelson, "To Norway," *Samtiden* 25 (1914): 287–88.

11. Knute Nelson, "Norske vikinger i det 19de aarhundrede," *Samtiden* 26 (1915): 70–71.

12. Alexander Bugge, "Vikingetidens kultur og livanskuelse," *Samtiden* 12 (1901): 149, 163. For a full treatment of these themes, see Alexander Bugge, *Vikingerne: Billeder fra vore Forfædres liv* (Copenhagen: Gyldendalske Boghandel Nordisk Forlag, 1906), 112–35.

13. Nordahl Rolfsen, foreword to *Norge i Amerika*, ed. Nordahl Rolfsen, Boken om Norge 5 (Kristiania: Jacob Dybwad, 1915); Helge Danielsen and Ruth Hemstad, "Nasjonal oppdragelse," in *Jakten på det norske: En utstilling om nasjonal identitet* (pamphlet) (Oslo: Norsk Folkemuseum, 1997), 44.

14. Lars A. Stenholt, *Norge i Amerika: Skildringer av Nordmændenes liv i Amerika* (Kristiania: Sophus Kriedts, 1897), 7–11, 70–130; quote is on page 123.

15. A. Sollid, *En Amerikatur: Reiseerindringer* (Skien, Norway: Forfatterens, 1896), 59, 65–67, 152–56.

16. Hans Seland, *Um Amerika: Og frendefolket i Vesterheim* (Kristiania: Olaf Norlis, 1904), 10–14.

17. Christian Gierløff, *Til Amerika med emigranterne: Dagbogsblade sommeren 1903* (Kristiania: L. E. Tvedtes, 1904), 145–46.

18. Klaveness, *Blandt udvandrede Nordmænd*, 83–84, 108–9.

19. Bo Stråth, *Union og demokrati: Dei sameinte rika Noreg-Sverige 1814–1905* (Oslo: Pax, 2005), 441–42.

20. Ulf Jonas Björk, "Norwegian Idiocy and Swedish Indolence: Swedish Americans and the Dissolution of the Swedish–Norwegian Union," *Swedish-American Historical Quarterly,* July 2007, 165–72.

21. Olav Tysdal, "The Dissolution of the Union between Norway and Sweden and the Scandinavian Americans," *Scandinavian Studies,* Summer 2007, 174–75; John R. Jenswold, "The Rise and Fall of Pan-Scandinavianism in Urban America," in *Scandinavians and Other Immigrants in Urban America: The Proceedings of a Research Conference, October 26–27, 1984,* ed. Odd S. Lovoll (Northfield, Minn.: St. Olaf College Press, 1985), 166; *Minneapolis Daglig Tidende,* June 8 and 9, 1905.

22. *Minneapolis Daglig Tidende,* June 11, 1905.

23. *Minneapolis Daglig Tidende,* November 26, 1905, and June 24, 1906.

24. Matthew Frye Jacobson, *Special Sorrows: The Diasporic Imagination of Irish, Polish, and Jewish Immigrants in the United States* (Cambridge, Mass.: Harvard University Press, 1995), 13–53, 141–216.

25. D. G. Ristad, "Det ny Normandi i Minnesotas Park Region," *Jul i Vesterheim* (1932), no page number, quoted in Kristin Ann Risley, "Vikings of the Midwest: Place, Culture, and Ethnicity in Norwegian-American Literature, 1870–1940," (Ph.D diss., Ohio State University, 2003), 125–27.

26. Simon Johnson, *I et nyt rige* (Minneapolis: K. C. Holter Publishing, 1914), 3–4, 6–7; Simon Johnson, *From Fjord to Prairie, or In the New Kingdom,* trans. C. O. Solberg (Minneapolis: Augsburg Publishing House, 1916), 6–7, 9–10.

27. Birger Osland, *A Long Pull from Stavanger: The Reminiscences of a Norwegian Immigrant* (Northfield, Minn.: Norwegian-American Historical Association, 1945), 34–43; Birger Osland, "Norwegian Clubs in Chicago," *Norwegian-American Studies and Records* 12 (1941): 113–16; Carl G. O. Hansen, *My Minneapolis: A Chronicle of What Has Been Learned and Observed about the Norwegians in Minneapolis through One Hundred Years* (Minneapolis: privately printed, 1956), 252–53.

28. For example, see "Ibsen-festen i Wahpeton, N.D.," *Kvartalskrift,* October 1911, 13–27.

29. Odd S. Lovoll, "The Changing Role of May 17 as a Norwegian-American 'Key' Symbol," in *Nasjonaldagsfeiring i fleirkulturelle demokrati,* ed. Brit Marie Hovland and Olaf Aagedal, Nord 4 (Copenhagen: Nordisk Ministerråd, 2001), 65; *Decorah-Posten* (Iowa), May 23, 1905; David C. Mauk, "Syttende Mai Vignettes from Minneapolis–St. Paul: The Changing Meaning of Norway's Constitution Day in the Capital of Norwegian America, 1869–1914," *American Studies in Scandinavia* 34, no. 2 (Autumn 2002): 43–45; *Minneapolis Daglig Tidende,* May 18, 1905.

30. Odd S. Lovoll, *Norwegians on the Prairie: Ethnicity and the Development of the Country Town* (St. Paul: Minnesota Historical Society Press in cooperation with the Norwegian-American Historical Association, 2006), 77–81, 94–125, 182–94,

224–26, 231–57; H. Arnold Barton, review of Lovoll, *Norwegians on the Prairie*, in *Scandinavian Studies*, Spring 2007, 99.

31. David Glassberg, "History and the Public Legacies of the Progressive Era," *Journal of American History* 73 (March 1987): 958–961.

32. *Normanden*, May 25, 1904; *Fargo Forum and Daily Republican*, May 18, 1904. However, *Fram*, as cited in *Normanden*, June 1, 1904, claimed that the Bjørnson monument was the brainchild of Thoralv Klaveness, an author from Norway with connections to the Liberal party who had authored a travel account in 1904. Playford V. Thorson, "Scandinavians," in *Plains Folk: North Dakota's Ethnic History* (Fargo: North Dakota Institute for Regional Studies, 1988), 210; and see also http://www.Fargo-history.com/ndac-bjornson.htm, and Kenneth Smemo, "Dr. Herman Fjelde: Monument Builder," *Red River Valley Historian*, Winter 1977–78, 3–5. "Afsløringen i Fargo," *Kvartalskrift*, October 1908, 2–4, 6–7; *Fargo Forum and Daily Republican*, June 17, 1908, and May 28, 1910; "Haugesfesten," *Eidsvold*, July 1912, 17.

33. "Afsløringen i Fargo," 2–4, 6; *Fargo Forum and Daily Republican*, June 17, 1908, May 28, 1910, and July 13, 1912; conversation with Dr. Kenneth Smemo, professor of history, Minnesota State University, Moorhead, July 31, 2006; "Et Monument for Wergeland," *Kvartalskrift*, (April 1907): 28; David Mauk, "*Norskdommens Høydepunkt*: 1880–1914, the Golden Age of Norwegian Immigrant Community in Minneapolis–St. Paul," in *Norwegian-American Essays 2004*, ed. Ørm Øverland and Harry T. Cleven (Oslo: NAHA-Norge, 2005), 185, 187–95.

34. "Afsløringen i Fargo," 4, 6, 8; *Fargo Forum and Daily Republican*, June 17, 1908, July 11, 1912.

35. *Normanden*, May 25, 1904, May 29, 1912, June 19, 1912, June 9, 1916; *Fargo Forum and Daily Republican*, May 18, 1904, June 17, 1908, June 10, 1912, July 13, 1912; "Afsløringen i Fargo," 8–9; *Fram*, May 23, 1912, June 15, 1916; "Ivar Aasen festen" *Nordmands-Forbundet* (August 1913): 436.

36. *Normanden*, May 25, 1904, and June 19, 1912; *Fargo Forum and Daily Republican*, June 10, 1912, and July 13, 1912; Marina Warner, *Maidens and Monuments: The Allegory of the Female Form* (London: Weidenfeld and Nicolson, 1985), xix–xxi, 12, 18; Joseph Campbell, *The Power of Myth with Bill Moyers*, ed. Betty Sue Flowers (New York: Anchor Books, 1991), 209–10.

37. John Bodnar, "Public Memory in an American City: Commemoration in Cleveland," in *Commemorations: The Politics of National Identity*, ed. John R. Gillis (Princeton, N.J.: Princeton University Press, 1994), 76; "Afsløringen af Wergelands-Monument," *Kvartalskrift*, July 1908, 11; *Fargo Forum and Daily Republican*, July 12 and 13, 1912, May 18, 1904, and June 7, 1913; *Normanden*, June 19, 1912; *Fram*, June 13, 1912; "Haugesfesten," *Eidsvold*, July 1912, 13–14; "Ivar Aasen Festival," 436.

38. *Normanden*, May 25, 1904; *Fargo Forum and Daily Republican*, May 18, 1904, and June 17, 1908.

39. "Afsløringen i Fargo," 13–14, 21; Julius E. Olson, *The Teutonic Spirit: An Address Delivered on the Occasion of the Unveiling of a Statue to Rollo of Normandy, at Fargo, North Dakota, July 12th 1912* (Minneapolis: K. C. Holter Publishing, 1912), 8, 17.

40. *Fram*, June 13, 1912; "Haugefesten," 13–14.

41. *Fargo Forum and Daily Republican*, June 7, 1913; "Ivar Aasen festen," 435–36.

42. *Fargo Forum and Daily Republican*, June 11, 1912.

43. *Normanden*, June 9, 1916.

44. *Fargo Forum and Daily Republican*, May 18, 1904.

45. *Fargo Forum and Daily Republican*, June 1, 1910, July 11, 1912, and July 13, 1912.

46. Olson, *The Teutonic Spirit*, 4–16; *Fram*, May 23, 1912; *Normanden*, July 24, 1912; Thorson, "Scandinavians," 210.

47. Daniel J. Sherman, "Art, Commerce, and the Production of Memory in France after World War I," in *Commemorations*, 206.

48. *Fargo Forum and Daily Republican*, July 13, 1912.

49. See *De tok et Norge med seg: Nordmanns-Forbundet saga gjennom 50 år*, ed. Johan Hambro (Oslo: Dreyers Forlag, 1957), 13–20; F. G. Gade and Moltke Moe, "Et Forbund av alle Nordmænd," *Nordmands-Forbundet*, October 1907, 5; Mauk, "Syttende Mai Vignettes," 47.

50. Osland, *A Long Pull from Stavanger*, 70–75; Carl G. O. Hansen, *History of the Sons of Norway: An American Fraternal Organization of Men and Women of Norwegian Birth or Extraction* (Minneapolis: Sons of Norway Supreme Lodge, 1945), 118–19.

51. R. S. N. Sartz, "Norge ved San Francisco-utstillingen," *Nordmands-Forbundet*, 1915, 758–60.

52. Odd Sverre Lovoll, *A Folk Epic: The Bygdelag in America* (Twayne Publishers, 1975), 24–35; Mona Klippenberg, "Den frilynte ungdomsrørsla i framvektsårene," in *Jakten på det norske: Perspektiver på utviklingen av en norsk nasjonal identitet på 1800-tallet*, ed. Øystein Sørensen (Oslo: Gyldenal Norsk Forlag, 2001), 357–70; Ottar Dahl, *Norsk historieforskning i det 19. og 20. århundre*, 4th ed. (Oslo: Universitetsforlaget, 1990), 243–46.

53. Anne-Lise Seip, "Det norsk 'vi'—kulturnasjonalisme i Norge," in *Jakten på det norske*, 95–111.

54. Lovoll, *A Folk Epic*, 99–110.

55. See Alon Confino, *The Nation as a Local Metaphor: Württemberg, Imperial Germany, and National Memory, 1871–1918* (Chapel Hill: University of North Carolina Press, 1997).

56. Lovoll, "The Changing Role of May 17," 72.

57. Hansen, *History of Sons of Norway*, 119.

58. Ibid., 120; Lovoll, *A Folk Epic*, 96–97.

59. See *Syttende mai festskrift: Hundreaars festen*, ed. N. N. Rønning (St. Paul–Minneapolis: K. C. Holter Publishing, 1914); *Norsk-Amerikanernes festskrift 1914*,

ed. Johannes B. Wist (Decorah, Iowa: Symra, 1914); the aforementioned *Minnesota: En kortfattet historie;* Lovoll, *A Folk Epic,* 97.

60. "Angående kirkens deltagelse i utstillingen 1914," in *Forhandlinger i Stortinget,* Syvende Del, 1914, nr. 204 (Kristiania: Lundhske bogtrykkeri ved C. L. Roshaum, 1914), 1625–32.

61. "Det utflyttede Norge," in *Norges Jubilæumsutstilling 1914 officiel beretning,* ed. N. A. Brinchman, 2 vols. (Kristiania: Grøndahl and Son, 1914), 2:514.

62. Rolfsen, foreword to *Norge i Amerika.*

63. Ibid., foreword; see also 237–378, 417–578.

64. Orm Øverland, *The Western Home: A Literary History of Norwegian America,* Authors Series 8 (Northfield, Minn.: Norwegian-American Historical Association, 1996), 109–10, 195–208.

65. Carl H. Chrislock, "Introduction: The Historical Context," in *Cultural Pluralism,* 16.

66. Benson John Lossing and B. F. De Costa, quoted in Rasmus B. Anderson, *The First Chapter of Norwegian Immigration, (1821–1840): Its Causes and Results,* 2nd ed. (Madison, Wisc.: Rasmus B. Anderson, 1896), 32–33.

67. H. Arnold Barton, "The Discovery of Norway Abroad, 1760–1905," *Scandinavian Studies,* Spring 2007, 28–32; Paul Du Chaillu, *The Land of the Midnight Sun: Summer and Winter Journeys through Sweden, Norway, Lapland, and Northern Finland,* 2 vols. (London: John Murray, 1881); Einar Haugen and Camilla Cai, *Ole Bull: Norway's Romantic Musician and Cosmopolitan Patriot* (Madison: University of Wisconsin Press, 1993).

68. Stenholt, *Moderne Vikinger,* 88–100; quote is on page 92.

69. Ole Amundson Buslett, *Det Femtende Regiment Wisconsin frivillige* (Decorah, Iowa: Forfatterens Forlag, 1894), 7–8; *Den norske Studentersangforenings koncerttourné gjennem det norske Amerika i mai og juni 1905* (Kristiania: Cammermeyers boghandel, 1906), 69.

70. Seland, *Um Amerika,* 12–13; Klaveness, *Blandt udvandrede Nordmænd,* 112; *Minneapolis Daglig Tidende,* May 18, 1908.

71. See esp. Carlos C. Closson, "The Hierarchy of European Races," *American Journal of Sociology,* 1897, 314–27. This interpretation remained popular well into the 1920s and 1930s. See, for example, Frank H. Hankins, *The Racial Basis of Civilization* (New York: A. A. Knopf, 1926).

72. Rasmus Bjørn Anderson, *Tale ved femti-aarsfesten for den norske udvandring til Amerika* (Chicago: n.p., 1875), 25; Orm Øverland, *Immigrant Minds, American Identities: Making the United States Home, 1870–1930* (Urbana: University of Illinois Press, 2000), 160.

73. Ager, "Preserving Our Mother Tongue," 55.

74. Øverland, *The Western Home,* 190–95.

75. Ager, "Preserving Our Mother Tongue," 57.

76. Waldemar Ager, "The Language Is Most Important," in *Cultural Pluralism,* 72.

77. Ibid., 74.
78. Waldemar Ager, "The Great Leveling," in *Cultural Pluralism,* 111–13.
79. Waldemar Ager, "The Melting Pot," in *Cultural Pluralism,* 80–84. Swedish-American leaders posited this same idea. See H. Arnold Barton, *A Folk Divided: Homeland Swedes and Swedish Americans, 1840–1940* (Carbondale: Southern Illinois University Press, 1994), 124–25, 223–26.
80. *Skandinaven,* May 12, 1908.
81. Halvdan Koht, *Pengemagt og arbeid i Amerika* (Kristiania: H. Aschehoug, 1910), 1–6, 58–104, 134–52; Knut Takla, *Det norske folk i de Forenede Stater: Deres daglige liv og økonomiske stilling. Historiske over Amerika—landets fremtidsmuligheter for an indvandrer* (Kristiania: J. Stenersen, 1913), 296–301.
82. *Minneapolis Daglig Tidende,* May 18, 1908.
83. Henry Bengston, *On the Left in America: Memoirs of the Scandinavian-American Labor Movement,* trans. Kermit B. Westerberg, ed. and with an introduction by Michael Brook (Carbondale: Southern Illinois University Press, 1999), 42, 44.
84. Lovoll, *A Century of Urban Life,* 169–72; Leola Nelson Bergman, *Americans from Norway* (Philadelphia: Lippincott, 1950), 175.
85. *Syttende mai festskrift,* 73–74, 78.
86. Johannes B. Wist, foreword to *Norsk-Amerikanernes festskrift 1914,* 5.
87. Carl Hansen, "Det norske publingsliv i Amerika," in *Norsk-Amerikanernes festskrift 1914,* 266–67.
88. Juul Dieserud, "Nordmænd i det offentlige og politiske liv," in *Norsk-Amerikanernes festskrift 1914,* 328–29.
89. Dr. J. S. Johnson, *Minnesota: En kortfattet historie,* 100–104.
90. Ibid., 91–92.
91. See Lincoln Steffens, *The Shame of the Cities* (New York: McClure Phillips, 1904).
92. Øverland, *Immigrant Minds,* 146, 124–39; Barton, *A Folk Divided,* 66–67.
93. Øverland, *Immigrant Minds,* 78–79.
94. Kendric Charles Babcock, *The Scandinavian Element in the United States* (Urbana: University of Illinois Press, 1914), 181–82.
95. Madison Grant, *The Passing of the Great Race, or The Racial Basis of European History* (New York: Charles Scribner's Sons, 1918), 10–12, 18, 69, 90, 124, 168–69, 177, 193, 206–11, 228, 236.

4. Backlash

1. Lovoll, *A Century of Urban Life,* 276.
2. Carl H. Chrislock, "Introduction: The Historical Context," in *Cultural Pluralism,* ed. Lovoll, 30.
3. Lovoll, *The Promise of America,* 208–9.
4. Johannes B. Wist, as quoted in Arlow W. Andersen, *Rough Road to Glory:*

The Norwegian-American Press Speaks Out on Public Affairs, 1875–1925 (Philadelphia: Balch Institute Press, 1990), 197–98.

5. Andersen, *Rough Road to Glory*, 200–202.

6. Madison Grant, Albert Johnson, and Henry Pratt Fairchild, as quoted in Fuchs, *The American Kaleidoscope*, 61.

7. Gary Gerstle, *American Crucible: Race and Nation in the Twentieth Century* (Princeton, N.J.: Princeton University Press, 2001), 93–115.

8. Aviel Roshwald, *The Endurance of Nationalism: Ancient Roots and Modern Dilemma* (Cambridge: Cambridge University Press, 2006), 266–71.

9. O. E. Rølvaag, "Om navneforandringen og litt til," *Lutheraneren*, December 11, 1918, 1497; April R. Schultz, *Ethnicity on Parade: Inventing the Norwegian-American through Celebration* (Amherst: University of Massachusetts Press, 1994), 35.

10. Horace Kallen, *Culture and Democracy in the United States* (New York: Boni and Liveright, 1924), 12.

11. Thoralv Klaveness, "Spørsmaal, som bør besvares," *Nordmands-Forbundet*, 1919, 63–73, 68.

12. Sigurd Folkestad, "Leif Erikson," in *Norsk læsebok*, ed. O. E. Rølvaag and P. J. Eikeland, 3 vols. (Minneapolis: Augsburg Publishing House, 1920), 2:12. Hereafter cited as *Norsk læsebok*.

13. O. E. Rølvaag, "Landet vore fædre fandt," in *Norsk læsebok*, 2:12–16; O. E. Rølvaag, "Og saa reiste de," in *Norsk læsebok*, 2:16–27.

14. Carl G. O. Hansen, "Norske i verdenskrigen," in *Norsk læsebok*, 2:224–37.

15. Peder Tangjerd, "De norske lutheranere i Amerika," in *Norsk læsebok*, 2:294–95.

16. Theodore Jorgenson and Nora O. Solum, *Ole Edvard Rølvaag: A Biography* (New York: Harper and Brothers, 1939), 250.

17. O. E. Rølvaag, "Skogen som klædde fjeldet," in *Norsk læsebok*, 2:331.

18. Harry Sundby-Hansen, introduction to *Norwegian Immigrant Contributions to America's Making*, ed. Sundby-Hansen (New York: International Press, 1921). Hereafter referred to as *Norwegian Immigrant Contributions*.

19. Harry Sundby-Hansen, "Contributions to Industry," in *Norwegian Immigrant Contributions*, 57–58.

20. Julius E. Olson, "Literature and the Press," in *Norwegian Immigrant Contributions*, 128.

21. Sigurd Folkestad, "Det utflyttede Norge i Amerika," *Nordmands-Forbundet*, 1918, 474–85, 483.

22. Gisle Bothne, "Church and Education," in *Norwegian Immigrant Contributions*, 96–97.

23. H. Arnold Barton, *A Folk Divided: Homeland Swedes and Swedish Americans, 1840–1940* (Carbondale: Southern Illinois University Press, 1994), 293–94, 312–13.

24. Rølvaag, *Concerning Our Heritage*, 131.

25. Ibid., 55–62.
26. Ibid., 63–66.
27. Ibid., 70–71.
28. Ibid., 78–88, esp. 82.
29. Ibid., 114–26, esp. 123.
30. Ibid., 105–13, esp. 110.
31. Ibid., 110, 113.
32. Øverland, *Immigrant Minds, American Identities,* 120–43; George M. Stephenson, "The Attitude of Swedish Americans toward the World War," *Proceedings of the Mississippi Valley Historical Association* 10 (1918–1919): 79–94, esp. 93.
33. O. E. Rølvaag, *Giants in the Earth: A Saga of the Prairie,* trans. Lincoln Colcord and the author (New York: Harper and Row, 1927), 3.
34. Jorgenson and Solum, *Ole Edvard Rølvaag,* 345–46, 350.
35. See O. E. Rølvaag, *Peder Victorius, a Novel,* trans. Nora O. Solum and the author (New York: Harper and Brothers, 1929); and O. E. Rølvaag, *Their Fathers' God, a Novel,* trans. Trygve M. Ager (New York: Harper and Brothers, 1931).
36. "The Cross at the Prow," in *Jul i Vesterheim* (Minneapolis: Augsburg Publishing House, 1918), n.p., as quoted in Kristin Ann Risley, "Vikings of the Midwest: Place, Culture, and Ethnicity in Norwegian-American Literature, 1870–1940" (Ph.D diss., Ohio State University, 2003), 120.
37. O. E. Rølvaag, "The Vikings of the Middle West," *American Magazine,* October 1929, 44–46, as quoted in Risley, "Vikings of the Midwest," 1–3.
38. Schultz, *Ethnicity on Parade,* 51–52.
39. Ibid., 52; Lovoll, *A Folk Epic,* 150–51.
40. Schultz, *Ethnicity on Parade,* 56–57.
41. See U.S. Congress, *Speech of Honorable O. J. Kvale of Minnesota in the House of Representatives, Tuesday, February 24, 1925* (Washington, D.C.: GPO, 1925).
42. *Decorah-Posten,* June 5, 1925; *Nordisk Tidende* (New York), June 11, 1925; "The Norse-American Centennial Medal and Stamps," in *Norse-American Centennial, 1825–1925: Souvenir Edition* (Minneapolis: Augsburg Publishing House, 1925), 74. Hereafter referred to as *Norse-American Souvenir.*
43. Schultz, *Ethnicity on Parade,* 51.
44. Carl O. Pederson, "The Norse-American Centennial" (1925), 84, Box 303, Carl O. Pederson Papers, Norwegian-American Historical Society, Northfield, Minnesota, as quoted in Schultz, *Ethnicity on Parade,* 60; Hansen, *My Minneapolis,* 275–76.
45. Lovoll, *The Promise of America,* 195; *Decorah-Posten,* June 12, 1925.
46. *Decorah-Posten,* June 12, 1925.
47. Schultz, *Ethnicity on Parade,* 1–8; *Minneapolis Daglig Tidende,* June 11, 1925; *Decorah-Posten,* June 12, 15, and 18, 1925; *Nordisk Tidende,* June 11 and 18, 1925.
48. Schultz, *Ethnicity on Parade,* 91–122.

49. Ole E. Rølvaag's speech at the Norse-American Centennial largely restated the ideas he developed in *Concerning Our Heritage*; Rølvaag's speech as quoted in Schultz, *Ethnicity on Parade*, 97–102; Waldemar Agers, "Omkring hundreaarsfesten," in *Norse-American Souvenir*, 13.

50. Olaf M. Norlie, "Why We Celebrate," in *Norse-American Souvenir*, 54–55.

51. Norlie, *History of the Norwegian People in America*, 33.

52. *Minneapolis Daglig Tidende*, June 14, 1925; Hans Olav, "Hundreaars-Jubilæet," *Nordisk Tidende*, June 18, 1925.

53. As quoted in *Minneapolis Daglig Tidende*, June 14, 1925.

54. Absalon Taranger, *Inntrykk fra Amerika* (Oslo: Lutherstiftelsens Bokhandel, 1927), n.p.

55. Ibid., 15–18, 54, 58; Thoralv Klaveness, *Blandt udvandrede Nordmænd: Vore Landsmænds liv og vilkaar in den nye verden* (Kristiania: Alb. Cammermeyers Forlag, 1904), 33–34, 83–84; Christian Gierløff, *Til Amerika med Emigranterne: Dagbogsblade sommeren 1903* (Kristiania: L. E. Tvedtes forlag, 1904), 145–46, 162–72, 182–83.

56. *Skandinaven*, June 30, 1925.

57. Ibid.

58. *Washington Posten*, as quoted in *Minneapolis Daglig Tidende*, July 7, 1925; *Nordisk Tidende*, June 25 and August 27, 1925; Hans Olav, "Hundreaarsfesten i Seattle," *Nordisk Tidende*, July 16, 1925.

59. *Decorah-Posten*, July 10, 1925; *Washington Posten*, as quoted in *Minneapolis Daglig Tidende*, July 7, 1925; Olav, "Hundreaarsfesten i Seattle."

60. *Minneapolis Daglig Tidende*, September 13, 1925.

61. O. M. Norlie, "The Culture of the Norwegian People in America," in *The Norse-American Centennial of Illinois, 1825–1925* (Minneapolis: Augsburg Publishing House, 1925), 14–17; *Minneapolis Daglig Tidende*, September 13, 1925.

62. *Norwegian-American Centennial, 1825–1925: Commemorating the One Hundredth Anniversary of Norwegian Immigration to the United States, New York, and New Jersey, October 9, 10, 11, 1925* (New York: Norwegian-American Centennial Committee of New York and New Jersey, 1925), cover. Hereafter referred to as *Norwegian-American Centennial, New York*.

63. *Nordisk Tidende*, September 17 and October 15, 1925. See also *Skandinaven*, October 18, 1925.

64. *Nordisk Tidende*, October 15, 1925.

65. Ibid.

66. "Noen tanker ved 100-års jubileet" (1925), in Wilhelm Morgenstierne, *Et større Norge: Fra Nordmanns-Forbundet arbeidsmark; Artikler og taler* (Oslo: H. Aschehoug, 1932), 95–97; Morgenstierne gave a speech titled "En strålende norsk fest ved Stillehavet" (A Shining Norwegian Celebration on the Pacific Ocean) at the Norse-American Centennial of the Pacific, July 3–7, 1925, Seattle. For addi-

tional information on Morgenstierne's speech, see *Decorah-Posten,* July 10, 1925. Johan Ludwig Mowinckel, in *Norwegian-American Centennial, New York,* 9; Johan Bojer, in *Norwegian-American Centennial, New York,* 15.

67. *Aftenposten,* June 6, 1925.

68. *Nationen,* June 8, 1925.

69. Ibid.; Pastor Frederick Ring, *Hundreaarsfesten i Norge 4 juli 1925: En bok for mænd, kvinder og barn paa begge sider ov havet* (Oslo: Norsk Forlagsselskabs Trykkeri, 1925), 3-4.

70. C. J. Hambro, "1925," *Nordmands-Forbundet,* 1925, 1; Wilhelm Morgenstierne, "Nogen tanker ved 100-aars jubilæet," *Nordmands-Forbundet,* 1925, 244, 246.

71. Morgenstierne, "Nogen tanker ved 100-aars jubilæet," 248.

72. John Jenswold, "Becoming American, Becoming Suburban: Norwegians in the 1920s," *Norwegian-American Studies* 33 (1992): 3-26; Øyvind T. Gulliksen, *Twofold Identities: Norwegian-American Contributions to Midwestern Literature* (New York: Peter Lang, 2004), 1-19, 65-96, 185-218.

73. Sigmund Skard, *The United States in Norwegian History,* Contributions in American Studies 26 (Westport, Conn.: Greenwood Press, 1976), 161-66. For an analysis of a similar phenomenon involving Sweden, see H. Arnold Barton, "The New Deal and the People's Home: American and Swedish Perspectives from the 1930s," in *Migration och mångfald: Essäer om kultur kontakt och minoritetsfrågor tillämnade Harald Runblom,* ed. Dag Blanck et al. (Uppsala, Sweden: Centrum för multietnisk forskning, 1999), 201-17.

74. *Dagbladet,* December 7, 1925; Arne Kildal, "Norskheten i Amerika," *Nationen,* December 21, 1925; Nils Collet Vogt, "Norskheten i Amerika," *Nationen,* December 22, 1925; Barton, *A Folk Divided,* 245-64.

75. See Johan Bojer, *The Emigrants,* trans. A. G. Jayne (New York: Century, 1923).

76. Carl J. Hambro, *Glimt fra Amerika* (Oslo: H. Aschehoug, 1925), 159.

77. Christian Gierløff, *Folket som utvandrer* (Oslo: H. Aschehoug, 1925), 101, 233. See also his *Til Amerika med emigranterne* (1904).

78. Ida Blom, *Kampen om Eirik Raudes land: Pressgruppepolitikk i Grønlandsspørsmålet, 1921-1931* (Oslo: Gyldendal, 1973), 148-65; Svein Ivar Angell, *Frå splid til nasjonal integrasjon: Norsk nasjonalisme i mellomkrigstida,* KULTs skriftserie 29/Nasjonal Identitet 4 (Oslo: Noregs forskningsråd og forfatteren, 1994), 84-92. On the significant role played by Norway's historians in crafting a national identity, see Halvdan Koht, *Nasjonalkjensla i Noreg: Tale på femtiårs-møte i den Norske historiske forening 27de mai* (Kristiania: n.p., 1920).

79. See esp. Morgenstierne, *Et større Norge;* F. G. Gade, "Nordmands-Forbundet i 20 aar," *Nordmands-Forbundet,* 1927, 187-96.

80. Hansen, *My Minneapolis,* 158-69, 252. On the dedication of a statue to Colonel Hans Christian Heg in Norway, see *De tok et Norge med seg: Nordmanns-Forbundet saga gjennom 50 år,* ed. Johan Hambro (Oslo: Dreyers Forlag, 1957), 56,

63–64; Gade, "Nordmands-Forbundet i 20 aar," 196; Hambro, *Glimt fra Amerika,* 149.

81. Terje I. Leiren, "Pilgrimage and Propaganda: The American Newspapermen's Tour of Norway in 1927," *Norwegian-American Studies* 35 (2000): 199–213; Kristian Prestgard, *En sommer i Norge* (Minneapolis: Augsburg Publishing House, 1928), 66–199.

82. *Duluth Skandinav,* June 24, 1927; Odd S. Lovoll, "Leiv Eriksson som symbol i det norske Amerika," in *Leiv Eriksson, Helge Ingstad, og Vinland: Kjelder og tradisjonar; Innlegg ved eit seminar i regi av det Kongelige Norske Videnskabers Selskab 13–14 oktober 2000,* ed. Jan Ragnar Hagland and Steinar Supphellen (Trondheim, Norway: Tapir Akademisk Forlag, 2001), 128–29.

83. *Duluth Skandinav,* June 24 and July 1, 1927; Lovoll, "Leif Eriksson som symbol," 129.

84. *Duluth Skandinav,* July 1, 1927.

85. *Morgenavis* (Norway), September 25, 1926; *Aftenposten,* September 22, 1926.

86. Arne Kildal, "Leiv Eiriksson-dagen," *Nordmands-Forbundet,* 1927, 379–81.

87. "Leiv Eirikssøn-dagen som utflyttede Norges dag," *Nordmands-Forbundet,* 1928, 390.

88. John Higham, *Send These to Me: Jews and Other Immigrants in Urban America* (New York: Athenum, 1975), 56–57; Thomas J. Archdeacon, *Becoming American: An Ethnic History* (New York: Free Press, 1983), 174–76; Sture Lindmark, *Swedish America, 1914–1932: Studies with Emphasis on Illinois and Minnesota* (Stockholm: Läromedelsförlagen, 1971), 155–57.

89. Highan, *Send These to Me,* 48–55.

90. *Skandinaven,* March 16, 1928, and July 5, 1929; *Minneapolis Tidende,* February 7, 1929; *Norgesposten* (New York), February 19 and July 9, 1929.

91. "Norge og Kvotaloven," *Skandinaven Almanak og Kalendar,* 1930, 59.

92. *Nordisk Tidende,* May 2, 1929; *Morgenbladet,* January 2, 1929; *Aftenposten,* December 30, 1929, and March 4, 1929.

5. A Shared Homeland

1. Morgenstierne, *Et større Norge,* 6–7.

2. Arne Kildal, "Veien mot et større Norge gaar gjennom Nordmandsforbundet," *Dagen* (Bergen), January 21, 1926.

3. *Norgesposten,* June 9, 1932.

4. *Nordisk Tidende,* October 22, 1932. Morgenstierne's essay was titled "Et større Norge." *Minneapolis Tidende,* January 12, 1933.

5. *Aftenposten,* August 25, 1932; *Nationen,* August 26, 1932.

6. William J. Galush, *For More Than Bread: Community and Identity in American Polonia, 1880–1940* (Boulder, Colo.: East European Monographs, 2006), 131–32.

7. Arne Kildal, "Samholdet med 'det store Norge' i Amerika," *Nationen*, February 10, 1936.
8. Ibid.
9. *Norgesposten*, November 22, 1932.
10. Einar Lund, "Utvandrere og Norge," *Aftenposten*, May 3, 1939.
11. Hansen, *My Minneapolis*, 284, 286; Mary Anne Thatcher, *Immigrants and the 1930s: Ethnicity and Alienage in Depression and On-coming of War* (New York: Garland, 1990); Lizabeth Cohen, *Making a New Deal: Industrial Workers in Chicago, 1919–1939* (Cambridge: Cambridge University Press, 1990); Sture Lindmark, *Swedish America, 1914–1932*; Jon Gjerde, "'And you know, not all Norwegians are blond...': The Process of Ethnicization in the Norwegian Settlement Communities in the American Middle West," in *Norwegian-American Essays 1996*, ed. Øyvind Gulliksen, David C. Mauk, and Dina Tolfsby (Oslo: NAHA-Norge and the Norwegian Emigrant Museum, 1996), 81–90; David C. Mauk, "Ørkenen Sur and Other Cultural Adaptations to Economic Adversity among Brooklyn Norwegians during the 1930s," in *Norwegian-American Essays 1996*, 113–25; David Mauk, "Going on Land: Maritime Influences on the Development of the Norwegian Colony in Brooklyn to 1940," in *Essays on Norwegian-American Literature and History* (Oslo: NAHA-Norge and Det norsk-amerikanske historielaget, avd. Norge, 1990), 2:145–71; Gjerde and Mauk are careful to note that the Norwegian communities were not static, however, and that what it meant to be Norwegian was a process of adaptation to conflict and crisis within the communities.
12. *Nordisk Tidende*, March 22, 1928.
13. Ibid.
14. Ibid.
15. Ibid.
16. *Mineapolis Daglig Tidende*, March 21, 1928.
17. Ibid.
18. *Washington Posten*, March 23, 1928.
19. *Nordisk Tidende*, March 15, 1928.
20. Svein Ivar Angell, *Frå splid til nasjonal integrasjon: Norsk nasjonalisme i mellomkrigstida*, KULTs skriftserie 22 / Nasjonal Identitet 4 (Oslo: Noregs forskingsråd og forfatteren, 1994), 93–104.
21. Ibid., 98–101; *Aftenposten*, July 30, 1930.
22. *Skandinaven*, July 29, 1930; *Nationen*, July 28, 1930; *Nordisk Tidende*, July 24 and August 7, 1930.
23. *Minneapolis Daglig Tidende*, July 30, 1930.
24. Ibid.
25. Ibid.
26. *Nordisk Tidende*, July 31, 1930.
27. *Washington Posten*, August 1, 1930.

28. "Bjørnson-jubileet," *Nordmanns-Forbundet*, January 1933, 4–7.
29. *Norgesposten*, December 13, 1932.
30. *Minneapolis Tidende*, December 8 and 15, 1932.
31. *Minneapolis Tidende*, December 15, 1932.
32. *Nordisk Tidende*, April 7, 1932.
33. "Nordmenn jorden rundt: Bjørnson-jubileet," *Nordmanns-Forbundet*, February 1933, 54–55; *Minneapolis Tidende*, December 15, 1932.
34. Osland, *A Long Pull from Stavanger*, 1945, 215.
35. *Nordisk Tidende*, June 20, 1933.
36. Ibid.
37. Magnus Andersen, *70 års tilbakkeblikk på mitt virke på sjø og i land* (Oslo: Magnus Andersens Forlag, 1932), 9–173; Aksel Akselson, *Våre yngste vikinger: Skoleskibet "Sørlandet"'s tokt til Chicago i tekst og billeder* (Oslo: Johan Grundt Tanum, 1933), 6, 52–53.
38. *Nordisk Tidende*, June 27, 1934.
39. Arne Kildal, "Hundreårsfesten i Norway, Ill.," *Nordmanns-Forbundet*, 248–51; *Skandinaven*, June 29, 1934; *Nordisk Tidende*, June 27, 1934. The Illinois-Norwegian Centennial featured a three-day celebration held at Norway and Ottawa, Illinois, on June 22–24, 1934. See *Centennial Celebration of the First Permanent Norwegian Settlement in the United States in the Fox River Valley, LaSalle County, Illinois in 1834* (Urbana: Illinois State Historical Society, Norwegian-American Historical Association, and Department of History, University of Illinois, 1934). Not surprisingly, the cover featured a Viking ship.
40. Ibid.
41. Harry Sundby-Hansen, "The Saga of Leiv and His Voyages," in "Leiv Eriksson Review"; *Nordisk Tidende*, October 9, 1935, 1; Hansen, *My Minneapolis*, 289–90; *Skandinaven*, March 27, 1936.
42. Theodore Jorgenson, "Leif Erikson som Symbol," *Decorah-Posten*, September 13, 1935.
43. *Nordisk Tidende*, October 18, 1934, and March 26, 1936.
44. *Evening Star* (Washington, D. C.), as quoted in *Nordisk Tidende*, April 9, 1936.
45. Harry Sundby-Hansen, "Norwegians Add Empire to U.S.," in "Leiv Eiriksson Review," *Nordisk Tidende*, October 9, 1935, 10.
46. *Aftenposten*, October 9, 1935; *Dagbladet*, October 9, 1935; *Tidens Tegn*, October 10, 1935; *Stavanger Aftenblad*, October 10, 1935.
47. *Aftenposten*, October 9, 1934; *Dagsposten* (Trondheim), October 8, 1935; *Tidens Tegn*, October 10, 1935.
48. *Nordisk Tidende*, March 26, 1936.
49. A. W. Brøgger, "Da ga han landet navn—og kalte det Vinland," *Tidens Tegn*, October 12, 1935.

50. Rolf A. Christensen, consul general, letter to Arne Kildal, November 18, 1937, "Verdensutstillingen Norsk-Amerikansk deltakelse," Konsulatberetninger New York, Box 88, Riksarkivet, Oslo, Norway. Rolf A. Christensen, consul general, letter to Carl Søyland, April 14, 1939, "Kronprinsparets besøk 1938–1939," Konsulatberetninger New York, Box 30, Riksarkivet, Oslo, Norway.

51. *Aftenposten*, May 3, 1939; *Nordisk Tidende*, May 4, 1939.

52. *Nordisk Tidende*, May 4, 1939.

53. "Festferden gjennem Amerika," *Nordmanns-Forbundet*, 1939, 171–72; Hans Olav, "Smaa rørende menneskelige Trekk og store Festligheter blander sig in Kronprinsfølgets Reise," *Nordisk Tidende*, May 18, 1939.

54. Olav, "Smaa rørende menneskelige Trekk."

55. Hans Olav, "Kronprinsparets reise er blitt et triumftog fra kyst til kyst," *Washington Posten*, May 19, 1939; Lars Fedt, "Kronprinsparet feiret '17 mai' i Los Angeles med 20,000 mennesker," *Washington Posten*, May 19, 1939.

56. *Aftenposten*, May 19, 1939; *Dagbladet*, May 19, 1939; *Nationen*, May 19, 1939; Hans Olav, "Fest og fryd i San Francisco ved kronprinsparets besøk," *Washington Posten*, May 26, 1939.

57. "I San Francisco," *Nordmanns-Forbundet*, August 1939, 263; *Washington Posten*, September 1, 1939.

58. *Washington Posten*, September 7, 1939.

59. *Washington Posten*, June 2, 1939.

60. Ibid.

61. *Decorah-Posten*, June 13, 1939.

62. Ibid.

63. Ibid.

64. Hansen, *My Minneapolis*, 335–45; "Østover og hjem til Norge," *Nordmanns-Forbundet*, 1939, 239–43.

65. *Decorah-Posten*, June 16, 1939.

66. *Nationen*, June 14, 1939.

67. *Decorah-Posten*, June 17, 1939.

68. *Aftenposten*, July 5, 1939.

69. *Aftenposten*, July 7, 1939; *Nationen*, July 7, 1939; *Nordisk Tidende*, July 13, 1939.

70. *Aftenposten*, May 4, 1939. The crown prince voiced similar remarks in speeches made at the Twin Cities on June 13, 1939, and at Duluth, Minnesota, on June 17, 1939; see *Nationen*, June 14 and 20, 1939.

71. Anthony D. Smith, *The Ethnic Origins of Nations* (Malden, Mass.: Blackwell Publishing, 1986, 1988), 129–52.

72. *Dagbladet*, May 10 and 18, 1939.

73. *Aftenposten*, May 2, 1939.

74. *Nationen*, June 14 and July 6, 1939.

75. *Aftenposten*, July 3 and 7, 1939.

76. *Decorah-Posten*, May 7, 1939; *Dagbladet*, May 8, 1939; Bishop J. A. Aasgard, "En gledes og festdag," *Nationen*, June 17, 1939; *Nordisk Tidende*, July 13, 1939.
77. *Skandinaven*, as cited in "Det norske Amerika opdaget," *Nordmanns-Forbundet*, December 1939, 415–16.
78. Lovoll, *A Folk Epic*, 174–75.
79. Barton, *A Folk Divided*, 306–13, 332; Carl G. O. Hansen, *History of the Sons of Norway: An American Fraternal Organization of Men and Women of Norwegian Birth or Extraction* (Minneapolis: Sons of Norway Supreme Lodge, 1945), 328; Lovoll, "The Changing Role of May 17," 74–75; Jane Marie Pederson, *Between Memory and Reality: Family and Community in Rural Wisconsin, 1870–1970* (Madison: University of Wisconsin Press, 1992), 226–32; Peter A. Munch, "Segregation and Assimilation of Norwegian Settlements of Wisconsin," *Norwegian-American Studies and Records* 17 (1952): 102–40.
80. Annemor Møst, "The Norwegian Monarchy—100 Years," *Norseman* 1 (2004): 86.
81. Leland Stowe, "How a Few Thousand Nazis Seized Norway," *Life*, May 6, 1940, 90–103.
82. Karsten Roedder, *Av en utvandreavis' saga: Nordisk tidende i New York gjennom 75 år*, 2 vols. (New York: Nordmanns-Forbundet New York Avdeling, 1966, 1968) 2:30–31.
83. Ibid., 2:31, 2:57–58, 2:96–98.
84. Ibid., 2:96–97.
85. From *Collier's Magazine*, as quoted in ibid., 2: 66.
86. *Washington Posten*, November 21, 1941.
87. *Nordisk Tidende*, April 10, 1941.
88. *Washington Posten*, January 2 and June 19, 1942.
89. Hans Olav, "Kronprins Olavs foredragstur gav rike resultater for Norge," *Nordmanns-Forbundet* (Grand Forks, N.D.), June 1942, 138–40; *Minneapolis Star Journal*, April 29, 1942.
90. *Nordisk Tidende*, March 12, 1942.
91. Hansen, *My Minneapolis*, 351–53.
92. *Norsk Tidend* (London), May 17, 1942.
93. *Washington Posten*, May 29, 1942.
94. *Norsk Tidend*, July 4, 1942.
95. *Washington Posten*, November 28, 1941; Dr. Edvard Hambro, "Inteview med utenriksministeren," *Nordmanns-Forbundet* (Grand Forks, N.D.), April 1943, 83–85.
96. Lise Lindbæk, ed., *Tusen norske skip: En antologi over norsk sjøfolks innsats i den annen verdenskrig* (New York: Arnesen Press, 1943), 9–218; *Nordisk Tidende*, May 21, 1942; Kristen Johansen, "Norsk Jagereskadron [sic] toppscorer i 1943," *Nordmanns-Forbundet* (Grand Forks, N.D.), June 1944, 137–39; "Norway, a Fighting Ally," *Nordmanns-Forbundet* (Grand Forks, N.D.), June–July 1944, 159; "Nor-

way, a Fighting Ally—utstillingen til Chicago," *Nordmanns-Forbundet* (Grand Forks, N.D.), December 1944, 310–11.

97. A. N. Rygg, *American Relief for Norway: En oversikt over Amerikas hjelpearbeid for Norge under og etter den annen verdenskrig* (Chicago: Arnesen Press, 1947), 1–141; Orlando Ingvoldstad, "Norwegian Relief, Inc.," *Nordmanns-Forbundet* (Grand Forks, N.D.), October 1942, 255–57.

98. *Washington Posten*, April 2 and July 16, 1943; Hansen, *My Minneapolis*, 348–49.

99. *Nordisk Tidende*, March 13, 1941.

100. *Nordisk Tidende*, February 26, 1942; *Washington Posten*, May 15, 1942; "Tale ved den britiske P. E. N.-klubbs innvielsesfest for det norske P. E. N.-sentrum i London 31.mars 1941," in Wilhelm Keilau, *Norsk røst i London: Innlegg og stemminger på utefronten* (Oslo: H. Aschehoug, 1945), 7–11; N. R. Østgaard, adjutant to Crown Prince Olav, letter to consul general Rolf A. Christensen, February 2, 1942, in which he notes that the crown prince will give a radio address titled "The Spirit of the Vikings" on February 10, 1942, "Kronprinsparets besøk," Konsulatberetninger New York, Box 31, Riksarkivet, Oslo, Norway. In fact, the Norwegian government sponsored monthly radio broadcasts in the United States, titled "The Spirit of the Vikings," from 1941 to 1946.

101. *Nordisk Tidende*, October 7, 1943.

102. Ibid.

103. *The Viking*, quoted in Gerd Nyquist, *Bataljon 99* (Oslo: H. Aschehoug, 1981), 47.

104. Ibid., 180–82; *Aftenposten*, July 4, 1945; *Dagbladet*, July 4, 1945; *Nationen*, October 15, 1945.

105. *Norsk Tidend*, September 6, 1944.

106. Sigrid Undset, "Vi star på felles grunn," *Nordmanns-Forbundet* (Grand Forks, N.D.), March 1942, 57–59; Sigrid Undset, *Return to the Future*, trans. Henriette C. K. Næseth (New York: A. A. Knopf, 1942); "Leiv Eirikssonsfest i sjømannskirken i Brooklyn," *Nordmanns-Forbundet* (Grand Forks, N.D.), November 1943, 280.

107. See Halvdan Koht, *Norway, Neutral and Invaded* (New York: Macmillan, 1941); Halvdan Koht and Sigmund Skard, *The Voice of Norway* (Morningside Heights, N.Y.: Columbia University Press, 1944), viii, 3.

108. Sigrid Undset, "Veien mot vest," *Nordmanns-Forbundet* (Grand Forks, N.D.), June 1943, 146–48; Halvdan Koht, "Nordmennene i Amerika," *Nordmanns-Forbundet* (Grand Forks, N.D.), December 1941, 90–93.

109. F. Støren, "Nordmanns-Forbundet," *Nordmanns-Forbundet*, October 1941, 217.

110. Odd Sverre Lovoll, *Celebrating a Century: Nordmanns-Forbundet and Norwegians in the World Community 1907–2007* (Oslo: Nordmanns-Forbundet, 2009), 88–89.

111. Carl J. Hambro, "Nordmanns-Forbundet," *Nordmanns-Forbundet* (Grand Forks, N.D.), December 1941, 193–94.

112. I cover these developments more fully in my paper, "The Janus-Faced Years: *Nordmanns-Forbundet* during World War II," which I presented at the 2007 Society for the Advancement of Scandinavian Study annual conference, held in Davenport, Iowa.

113. Arne Kildal, *De gjorde Norge større: En bok for ungdom* (Oslo: Johan Griegs Forlag, 1945), 221.

114. *The Public Papers and Addresses of Franklin D. Roosevelt*, compiled with special material and explanatory notes by Samuel I. Rosenman, vol. 11, *1942: Humanity on the Defensive* (New York: Harper and Row Publishers, 1950), 377–78.

115. Ibid., 377–78; *Nordisk Tidende*, September 24, 1942; Ingeborg Barth, "Jageren [sic] 'King Haakon VII' skjenket Norge," *Nordmanns-Forbundet* (Grand Forks, N.D.), October 1942, 259.

116. *Nordisk Tidende*, September 24, 1942.

117. *Washington Posten*, September 25, 1942.

118. Franklin D. Roosevelt, letter dated March 30, 1944, *Nordmanns-Forbundet* (Grand Forks, N.D.), May 1944, 29.

119. E. B. Hauke, "Et håndtrykk," *Nordmanns-Forbundet* (Grand Forks, N.D.), May 1944, 79.

120. *Nordisk Tidende*, May 18 and 25, 1944.

121. C. J. Hambro, "Vår grunnlovsdag," *Nordmanns-Forbundet* (Grand Forks, N.D.), May 1944, 34–36; Johan Nygaardsvol, *Nordmanns-Fobundet* (Grand Forks, N.D.), May 1944, 39; W. Neuman, "Norge er frihet," *Nordmanns-Forbundet* (Grand Forks, N.D.), May 1944, 52–53; King Haakon VII, *Nordmanns-Forbundet* (Grand Forks, N.D.), May 1944, 25.

122. *New York Times*, October 28, 1944; John Steinbeck, *The Moon Is Down* (New York: Viking Press, 1942), 185–86; Bosley Crowther, review of *Edge of Darkness*, *New York Times Review*, April 10, 1943, http://movies.nytimes.com/movie/review?res; Joseph Auslander, "An Open Letter to the Unconquerable Norwegians," *Saturday Evening Post*, October 23, 1943, as printed in *Washington Posten*, October 22, 1943.

123. "Større utveksling mellem Norge og Amerika," *Nordisk Tidende*, September 21, 1944.

124. "Franklin D. Roosevelt hylder Leif Eriksons minne," *Nordmanns-Forbundet* (Grand Forks, N.D.), November 1944, 275.

125. "Nordmenn jorden rundt: Amerika—U.S.A.," *Nordmanns-Forbundet* (Grand Forks, N.D.), June–July 1945, 155–60.

126. *Nordisk Tidende*, May 17, 1945; *Washington Posten*, May 18, 1945.

127. *Washington Posten*, May 18 and 25, 1945. The greeting is from May 18.

128. *Nordisk Tidende*, May 24 and June 7, 1945.

129. *Nordisk Tidende,* June 7, 1945.
130. "Regjeringen vender hjem," *Nordmanns-Forbundet* (Grand Forks, N.D.), June–July 1945, 165; Magne Skodvin, ed., *Norge i krig: Fremmedåk og frihetskamp 1940–1945,* vol. 8, Knut Einar Eriksen and Terje Halvorsen, *Frigjøring* (Oslo: Aschehoug, 1987), 193; *Nordisk Tidende,* June 7, 1945; *Aftenposten,* June 8, 1945.
131. *Nationen,* July 19, 1945; *Dagbladet,* December 21, 1945.
132. *Nationen,* July 16, 1945.
133. Torstein Høverstad, "Eit større Noreg," *Arbeiderbladet* (Oslo), July 6, 1946.

Conclusion

1. Engel Meslo, "Betre samband millom ungdomen i Noreg og ungdomen av norsk ætt i Vesterheimen," *Den 17de mai* (Norway), February 10, 1933.
2. Ibid.
3. Maurice Halbwachs, *On Collective Memory,* ed., trans., and introduction by Lewis A. Coser, Heritage of Sociology Series (Chicago: University of Chicago Press, 1992), 38–40, 48–51, 148–60, 167–89.
4. Gerd Nyquist, *The 99th Battalion,* trans. Inger-johanne Gerwig, Henrik M. Hansen, and Mr. and Mrs. Oddvar Nass (Oslo: H. Aschehoug (W. Nygaard), 1981), 186–87.
5. Ibid., 187–88.
6. Ibid., 188.
7. H. Arnold Barton, "The Discovery of Norway Abroad, 1760–1905," *Scandinavian Studies,* Spring 2007, 28–31.
8. Ibid., 33–34. See Bodil Stenseth, *En norsk elite: Nasjonsbyggene på Lysaker 1880–1940* (Oslo: Aschehoug, 1993).
9. Orm Øverland, "Old and New Homelands, Old and New Mythologies: The Creation of Ethnic Memory in the United States," in *Migrants and the Homeland,* 43–44.
10. Thomas N. Brown, *Irish-American Nationalism, 1870–1890* (Philadelphia: J. B. Lippincott, 1966), 153–56, 166–74; Timothy J. Kloberdanz, "Die Auswanderung nach Amerika und ihre Auswirkung auf Identität und Weltanschaung der Wolgadeutschen in Rußland," in *Zwischen Reform und Revolution: Die Deutschen an der Wolga 1860–1917,* ed. Dittmar Dahlmann and Ralph Tuchtenhagen (Essen, Germany: Klartext Verlag, 1994), 172–89. Brown argues that wealthy Irish Americans, many of them native born, embraced the nationalist movement to improve their standing in the eyes of native-stock Americans. They believed they could not achieve respect in the New World until the stigma of Ireland's enslavement had been erased in the old. They emphasized the need for the nationalist movement to be based on peaceful, legal means. Their contributions, both money and ideas, influenced significantly the character of Charles Parnell and the Irish

independence movement during this period. Kloberdanz argues that the experiences of emigrated Volga Germans from Russia, particularly those who settled the American Middle West, greatly influenced the identity of their homeland in three areas. First, the economic and lifestyle changes achieved in America created a sense of "relative deprivation" among homeland Volga Germans. Second, the exposure to American society created challenges to the strong patriarchal system in the homeland. And third, it strengthened the overall image of the Volga Germans within Russian society, creating a large group identity that replaced the older one based on loyalty to local or religious identities.

11. Donna R. Gabaccia, Dirk Hoerder, and Adam Walaszek, "Emigration and Nation Building during the Mass Migrations from Europe," in *Citizenship and Those Who Leave: The Politics of Emigration and Expatriation*, ed. Nancy L. Green and François Weil (Urbana: University of Illinois Press, 2007), 63–90; Emilio Franzina, *Gli italiani al nuovo mondo* (Milan: Arnoldo Mondadori Editore, 1995), as cited in *Citizenship and Those Who Leave*, 63, 82; Caroline Douki, "The Liberal Italian State and Mass Emigration, 1860–1914," in *Citizenship and Those Who Leave*, 91–113; François Weil, "The French State and Transoceanic Emigration," in *Citizenship and Those Who Leave*, 114–31.

12. *Norges Offisielle Statistikk*, 12:245, table 33, as quoted in Hans Fredrik Dahl, *Norge mellom krigene: Det norske samfunnet i krise og konflikt 1918–1940* (Oslo: Pax Forlag, 1971), 86.

13. Marcus Lee Hansen, *The Problem of the Third Generation Immigrant*; a reprint of the 1937 address with introductions by Peter Kivisto and Oscar Handlin (Rock Island, Ill.: Swenson Swedish Immigration Research Center and Augustana College Library, 1987).

14. Blegen and Lovoll end their synthetic studies at 1925, while Øverland ends his work at 1930. See Blegen, *The American Transition*; Lovoll, *The Promise of America*; Øverland, *Immigrant Minds, American Identities*. For a criticism of the assimilationist narrative adopted by historians of the Norwegian Americans, see Schultz, *Ethnicity on Parade*, 14–17. A response is offered by Odd S. Lovoll, "The Creation of Historical Memory in a Multicultural Society," in *Norwegian-American Essays 2001*, ed. Harry T. Cleven, Knut Djupedal, Ingeborg Kongslien, and Dina Tolfsby (Oslo: NAHA-Norge, 2001), 32–33.

15. Mary C. Waters, *Ethnic Options: Choosing Identities in America* (Berkeley: University of California Press, 1990), 17, 36–37, 76, 87, 134, 148–53; Richard D. Alba, *Ethnic Identity: The Transformation of White America* (New Haven, Conn.: Yale University Press, 1990), 25–30, 240–245, 294–296, 300–301, 306–8.

16. Øverland, *The Western Home*, 8–13; Øyvind T. Gulliksen, *Twofold Identities: Norwegian-American Contributions to Midwestern Literature* (New York: Peter Lang, 2004), 12–13; Odd S. Lovoll, *The Promise Fulfilled: A Portrait of Norwegian Americans Today* (Minneapolis: University of Minnesota Press in cooperation with the Norwegian-American Historical Association, 1998), 256–262.

17. Aviel Roshwald, *The Endurance of Nationalism: Ancient Roots and Modern Dilemmas* (Cambridge: Cambridge University Press, 200), 4–6, 297–301.

18. "AHR Conversation: On Transnational History," *American Historical Review*, December 2006, 1440–64; for comments by Bayly and Connelly, see esp. 1447–49, 1452.

19. Anthony D. Smith, *Nationalism: Theory, Ideology, History*, 2nd ed. (Cambridge, England: Polity Press, 2010), 13.

20. Ibid., 14.

21. Ibid., 20–23.

22. A. D. Smith, *National Identity*, 72–78; A. D. Smith, *Nationalism: Theory, Ideology, History*, 12–14, 17–18, 28–39. His definition of national identity is quoted on p. 18.

23. Astrid Wonneberger, "The Invention of History in the Irish-American Diaspora: Myths of the Great Famine," in *Diaspora, Identity, and Religion*, ed. Kokot, Tölöyan, and Alfonso, 118.

24. Steven Vertovec, *Transnationalism* (London: Routledge, 2009), 96–97; Basch, Schiller, and Szanton Blanc, *Nations Unbound*, 1–4, 7–9; Yossi Shain, *Marketing the American Creed Abroad: Diasporas in the U.S. and Their Homelands* (Cambridge: Cambridge University Press, 1999), 5–7; David Fitzgerald, *Negotiating Extra-Territorial Citizenship: Mexican Migration and the Transnational Politics of Community* (La Jolla, Calif.: Center for Comparative Immigration Studies, 2000), 10, 106. See also Stuart Hall, "Cultural Identity and Diaspora" in *Identity: Community, Culture, Difference*, ed. J. Rutherford (London: Lawrence and Wishart, 1990).

25. Peter Kivisto, "Theorizing Transnational Migration: A Critical Review of Current Efforts," *Ethnic and Racial Studies* 24, no. 4 (2001): 553–54; Paul Kennedy and Victor Roudometof, "Transnationalism in a Global Age," in *Communities across Borders*, ed. Paul Kennedy and Victor Roudometof (London: Routledge, 2002), 2–5; Robert C. Smith, "Transnational Localities: Community, Technology, and the Politics of Membership within the Context of Mexico and U.S. Migration," in *Transnationalism from Below*, ed. Michael Peter Smith and Luis Eduardo Guarnizo (New Brunswick, N.J.: Transaction Publishers, 1998), 201–3.

26. Nyla Ali Khan, *The Fiction of Nationality in an Era of Transnationalism* (New York: Routledge, 2005), 2; Myra A. Waterbury, *Between State and Nation: Diaspora Politics and Kin-State Nationalism in Hungary* (New York: Palgrave Macmillan, 2010), 16; Kathy Burrell, "Time Matters: Temporal Contexts of Polish Transnationalism," in *Transnational Ties: Cities, Migrations, and Identities*, ed. Michael Peter Smith and John Eade (New Brunswick, N.J.: Transaction Publishers, 2008), 15–16, 25–26.

27. Peter Hitchcock, *Imaginary States: Studies in Cultural Transnationalism* (Urbana: University of Illinois Press, 2003), 11.

Index

Aaker, H. H., 85
Aasen, Bernt, 80
Aasen, Ivar, 35, 84; development of Landsmaal, 35; statue dedicated, 84, 88
Aasgaard, J. A. (president of Concordia College), 88, 194
Aasgaard, J. S. (president of the Norwegian Lutheran Church in America), 169, 184, 187
Abercrombie, North Dakota, 84
Abraham, 123
Academy of Music (New York), 144–45, 171
Africa, xiv, 157
Aftenposten (Norwegian newspaper), 48, 141, 146, 154, 157, 161, 177, 187, 208; article about New York World's Fair (1939), 187
Ager, Waldemar, xix, 49, 55, 72, 76, 104–7, 118, 125, 130, 139, 151, 222; essay for Norse-American Centennial, 139; history of Colonel Heg, 55; Norwegian culture superior to American culture, 130, 222; Norwegian was already an American before immigration, 130; praises Colonel Heg as exemplar of Norwegian-American virtues, 55; prohibitionist, 118–19
Agrarian Party (Norway), 142
Akselson, Aksel, 174; *Våre yngste vikinger* (Our Youngest Vikings), 174

Alaska Territory, 77
Alexandria, Minnesota, 50, 184
Allies, xii, 208
Alpine race, the, 103
America (the United States), viii–xii, xv–xvi, xviii, xx, 1–2, 6–7, 9, 11–15, 19, 22, 25–26, 30, 32, 34–37, 45, 54, 72, 75–77, 80, 87–88, 90–93, 101, 103–4, 106, 108, 111–12, 115, 117–19, 121, 123–27, 129, 131–32, 137, 142–43, 146, 148, 151, 154–57, 159, 163–64, 168, 176–80, 182, 185–89, 191–92, 201, 203–5, 208, 214, 218, 223; attraction to Norwegians, 22, 36; birthday, 45; classless society, 36; economic opportunity, 14; egalitarian society, 15; freedom, 36; greatest republic in the world, 87, 91, 147, 177; love of liberty, 91; modern society, 36; pioneer era, 17; religious toleration, 4, 15; threatened by immigrants, 111–12; uncivilized land, 34
"America Day" (May 17, 1944), 204
American civil liberties, 15
American Civil War, x–xi, xix, 12, 17–18, 25–27, 29, 33, 78, 137–38; Confederate rebel as the Other, 27; Confederate states, 27; the Union, 27, 137–38
American College for Genealogical Registry and Heraldry, 53
American colonial period, 53
American colonies, 78

American churches, 62
American cultural curriculum, xx, 132
American customs and practices, xviii, 11, 21, 115
American Dream, 36
American elite, 86
American experience, 1
American farmers, 17, 30
American farmland, 7
American flag(s), 59, 79, 86, 88, 90, 95, 136–37, 166–67, 175, 207; Stars and Stripes, 136
American government, 194
American heroes, 44
American history, 199
American idealism, 37, 104
American influences, 37
Americanization, 119, 120, 127, 150
American landscape, 80
American Legion, the, 157
American Magazine, 132
American nation, 26, 29, 76, 90, 124, 136, 177
American national identity, 40, 43, 119, 149, 163, 192, 216; democratic ideals shared with Norway, 163; individualism shared with Norway, 192
American nationalism, 31, 66, 119, 121, 133, 135–36, 215; limits of civic nationalism, 119
American nativism, 117–19, 132, 156
American newspapers (press), 70, 141, 152
American-Norwegian ideal, 126; American-Norwegian identity, 127
American political system and politics, xi, 109–10; Norwegian-American involvement, 109–10
American prairie (and prairies), 7–8, 28
American promise of riches, 21
American Protestant churches, 107

American Relief for Norway, 194, 208
Americans, 31, 37, 43, 45, 90, 101–4, 119, 124, 134–35, 144, 157, 192, 205
"Americans' Day," 96
American social freedoms, 15, 36, 45
"Americans of Norwegian ancestry," 124
American soldiers, vii
American-Swedish Historical Museum, 128
American-Swedish identity, 128
American-Swedish Institute, 128
American Transition, The (Blegen, 1942) (history of Norwegian immigration), 200
American way of life, 111
American West, 19
Amundsen, Roald, 74, 145
Andersen, Arthur, 23, 173
Andersen, Magnus (captain), 69–71, 102, 153, 173–74; *70 Års tilbakkeblikk* (Seventy Years of Looking Back), 174
Anderson, John (publisher of *Skandinaven*), 29
Anderson, Lillian (queen of the 1933 Chicago World's Fair), 174
Anderson, Rasmus Bjørn, x, xix, 27, 32, 38, 44–50, 53, 62, 65, 72, 103, 144, 175, 222; *America Not Discovered by Columbus* (1874), 45; *Amerikas første Opdagelse* (America's First Discovery, 1886), 47; articulation of Norwegian identity, x, xix, 38, 44–50, 53, 103; battle with Gustav Storm, 47; Chicago speech (July 5, 1875), x, 38, 45, 48, 103; gift of liberty, 45, 175; glorification of the Viking age, 44–47; Norwegians are best Americans, 103; Vikings reimport liberty to America, 46

INDEX

Anglo-American counteroffensive, 115, 117–19, 132, 222
Anglo-American culture, xi, 120, 130
Anglo-American leaders, 31, 40, 102–3, 111–12, 119, 126, 134, 190
Anglo-Americans, x, xix–xx, 25, 29, 56, 62, 103, 106–8, 111–12, 117, 121, 132, 157, 222; racial purity questioned, 157; racial theory, 106, 111–12, 116; trailblazers, 56
Anglo-Norwegian racial identity, 127
Anglo-Saxons, 103, 119, 157
Anglo-Saxon world, 75. *See also* English-speaking world
Arne (Bjørnson), 124
Arne Garborg Club, 82
Asbjørnson, Peter Christen, 33; *Norske Folkeventyr* (Norwegian Folktales), 33
Asbjørnson, Sigvald, 84
Asia, xiv
Asian immigrants, 156
assimilation, 76, 106, 112, 119, 129
Atlantic Ocean, vii–ix, xii, 19, 40, 75, 132, 145, 153–55, 160, 165–66, 174, 180, 182, 193, 206, 222, 224
Augsburg Seminary, 52, 64
Augustana Lutheran Synod, 42
Aulestad, Norway, 171

Babcock, Kendric Charles, 57, 111
Bachke, H. H. (Norway's minister to the United States), 171, 173
Baker, Howard, 155
Balestrand, Norway, 6–7, 19
Bang, Anton C. (bishop of Norway), 82, 96, 102, 107
Barlien, Hans, 14
Battle of Chickamauga, 54
Battle of Yorktown, 52
Bay, Adolf, 108
Beamish, North Ludlow: *Discovery of*

America in the Tenth Century, The (1841), 43
Bendiren, Ole, 71
Bergen, New Jersey, 52
Bergen, Norway, 14, 29, 52, 108, 152
Bergen op Zoom, Netherlands, 52
Berggrav, Eivind (bishop of Norway), 172
Berghult, E. R. (mayor of Duluth, Minnesota), 185
Bernadotte, Jean-Baptiste (marshal of France), 3. *See also* Karl XIV Johan
Berner, Carl, ix, 95
Bernts, Olaf (Chicago consul for Norway), 174
Bert J. Enger Memorial Observation Tower (Duluth, Minnesota), 185
Beyer, Einar (consul of Norway), 183
Bible, the, 74
Billed-Magazin (Picture Magazine), 28
Bishop Hill, Illinois, 7
Bjercke, Alf, 178
Bjørnson, Bjørnstjerne, xv, 3, 33–34, 36–37, 60–65, 82, 84–88, 90–92, 124, 129, 167, 171–73; anti-emigration bias, 34–35; centennial of his birth, 171–73; champion of freedom and justice, 167, 172; compared to Walt Whitman, 172; criticisms of America, 35; *Det nye system* (The New System), 35; "Father of Norwegian Nationalism," 33, 64, 171; hero for both homeland Norwegians and Norwegian Americans, 172; identified with the common people, 172; influenced by Norwegian historical school, 33; monument erected in Fargo, North Dakota, 1904, 82, 85–87, 90; Norwegian nationalist, 33, 91; personification of Norwegian character, 88, 129; secular attack on

Christianity, 62–65; social realism, 33, 37; speaking tour of America, 62–65, 172; spirituality, 172; statues erected, 82, 84; support for democracy, 172; Viking Spirit and success in modern society, 38
Bjørnson, Karoline (widow of Bjørnson), 171
Blegen, Theodore, 200
Bøckman, M. O. (bishop from Trondheim, Norway), 88
Bojer, Johan (Norwegian author), 146, 150, 169
Bønder (Norwegian farmers), 3, 4, 7
Bondestand (Norwegian freeholder class), 3
Bosque County, Texas, 17
Boston, Massachusetts, 54, 62, 191, 194
Bothne, Gilse (professor of Scandinavian studies at University of Minnesota), 127, 133, 153, 172
Boyesen, Hjalmar Hjorth, 36–38, 40; *Gunnar*, 37, 39; *Modern Vikings*, 39; *A Norseman's Pilgrimage*, 37; professor of German literature, 37; romantic orientation, 38; social realism, 38; Viking spirit and success in modern Society, 38–40
Brace, Charles Loring, 214
Britain, 155–56, 189, 214
British, the, 2, 51; cultural and political traditions, 51
British blockade, 189
British citizens, 157
British Isles, 116
British soldiers, vii, xii
Brøgger, A. W. (Norwegian historian), 178
Brooklyn, New York, 9, 171
Brownsboro, Texas, 15

Brun, Aage (attaché for the Norwegian Legation), 184
Bryan, William Jennings, 79
Bryn, Helmer H. (Norway's minister in Washington, D.C.), 82, 145
Budstikken (Norwegian-American newspaper), 64
Bugge, Alexander, 74
Bull, Francis, 165–66
Bull, Ole, xv, 7, 60, 62, 83, 102; acquires American citizenship, 102; statue dedicated at Minneapolis (1897), 83
Bull, Sarah Chapman, 62
bunad (pl., *bunader*; traditional Norwegian costume), 86, 88, 143, 182, 204
Burke, John (governor of North Dakota), 86
Buslett, Ole Amundsen, 54, 102; history of the Scandinavian Regiment, 54–55, 102
bygd (local region of Norway), 18–19, 83, 95
bygdelag movement, 81, 93–96, 133, 150, 184

California, 17, 54, 77; gold rush, 17, 54
California Hall, 182
Cambridge, Massachusetts, 62
Camp Little Norway (Canada), 190, 194
Canaan, 123
Canada, xiv, 154, 190, 194; prairie provinces, 19
capitalism, 1, 9, 19
Capitol Building, 176
Carlsen, Fritz, 212–13
Carnegie Hall, 207
Catholics, 49, 103, 107, 111
Celtic, 103
censorship of foreign-language press, 117
Centennial Celebration of the First

Permanent Norwegian Settlement in the United States in the Fox River Valley, La Salle County, Illinois, 174
chain migration, 2, 17
Chambers of Commerce, 82, 183
Charest, J. C. (secretary of the Rollo Statue Committee), 92
Chicago, 17–18, 20, 54, 59, 63–64, 69–70, 76, 79, 83, 93–94, 102, 107–9, 142, 144, 153, 162, 173–74, 179, 206
Chicago Auditorium, 142
Chicago Club, 107
Chicago Herald, 69
Chicago Norwegian Club, 82, 174
Chicago Record, 70
Chicago Sangerforbundet (Chicago Singers Association), 174
Chicago's Great Fire, 62
Chicago Times, 59
Chicago World's Fair, 173
Christendom, 88
Christensen, Rolf A. (Norway's consul general in New York), 179
Christiansand, Norway, 85
Christiansandposten (Christiansand Post, Norwegian newspaper), 15
Christianson, Lars, 85
Christmas, 39
"Church and Education," 127
Civic Auditorium (Seattle), 183
Clayton County, Iowa, 18
Coffman, Lotus D. (president of the University of Minnesota), 172
collective identity, xiv, xviii, 212
collective memory, xiv, 26, 86, 132, 168, 211–12; constructed memory, 86; public memory, 86
Collier's Magazine, 190
Columbia University, 37
Columbus, Christopher, xi, 43, 45, 49, 69, 176, 186. *See also* World's Columbian Exposition
Columbian Exposition in Chicago. *See* World's Columbian Exposition
Concordia College (Moorhead, Minnesota), 84, 88, 174, 184
Congress, U.S., xi, 19, 117–18, 134, 155, 175; authorizes national Leif Erikson Day, 175; literacy test (1917), 118; quota law (1921), 118
Congressional Medal of Honor (United States), 123
Coolidge, Calvin (president of the United States), xi, 116, 136, 141, 143–44, 154, 223
Coon Prairie, Wisconsin, 64
cooperative societies, 5
Copenhagen, Denmark, 47–48
cotters *(husmenn),* 3, 7, 19, 30
"Cross at the Prow, The," 132
Crusoe, Robinson, 72–73
Cuba, 80
Cyrus Northrup Memorial Auditorium, 172

Dagbladet (Norwegian newspaper), 30, 62, 65, 187, 208
Dagsposten (newspaper, Trondheim, Norway), 177
Dahl, J. C., 33
Dakotas, the, 17–18, 77
Dakota Territory, 131
Danes, 44, 156
Danish-Americans, 61
Dawes, Rufus, 174
Declaration of Independence, 46
Decorah, Iowa, 20, 81, 133, 173, 180, 216
Decorah-Posten (Norwegian-American newspaper), 134, 136, 140, 152, 164, 176, 180, 187
De Costa, B. F., 101

de dage, I (In Those Days). See *Giants in the Earth*
Deep South, 156
Defoe, Daniel, 72–73
De Forenede Norske Sanger (United Norwegian Singers), 171
De gjorde Norge større (They Made Norway Greater) (Kildal), 202
Delaware River, 51
Democratic Party, 27
Denmark, 3, 47, 51–52, 60, 70, 117, 151; alliance with France, 3; Danish influences, 32–33, 44; Danish rule, xviii, 3
Den norske Klubben (Norwegian Club of Chicago), 206
Den signede dag (Their Father's God), 53, 131. See also *Their Father's God*
Det Norske Nationalforbunde. See Norwegian National League
Det Norske Selskab. See Norwegian Society
Det Skandinaviske Regiments historie (The Scandinavian Regiment's History), 54
Det udflytte Norge (The Emigrated Norway), 66
Det Utflyttede Norges Mottagelsepaviljong (The Emigrated Norway's Pavilion), 169
Dewey, Thomas E. (governor of New York), 195, 198
Diaspora theories, xvii–xviii, 80, 219–20
Dieserud, Juul, 110
Dighton Writing Rock, 43, 49–50
Dinhart, Rabbi, 97
Douglas County, Minnesota, 18
Dovre Male Choir, 166
dragon imagery, 69–70
drot (monarch), 61

Du Chaillu, Paul, 102
Duluth, Minnesota, 152–53, 185
Duluth Skandinav (Norwegian-American newspaper), 153
Dutch, the, 103
Dutch immigrants, 111

Eberhardt, Harry (vice consul for Norway), 169, 172
Eddas, the, 44
Edge of Darkness (film), 205
Eidsvold, Norway, 161, 203
Eidsvold Centennial (1914), xi, xvi, 72, 94–95, 97–99, 109, 133, 222
Eielsen, Elling (Lutheran pastor), 54
Eielson, Carl Ben, 184
"elective ethnicity," 188–89
elite image-makers, xiv
"Emigrated Norway, The" (exhibition), 95
emigration, xiv, 4, 7; opponents, 14; strategies, 2
emigration and nation building, 214
Enander, Johan A., 42, 50, 111; best Americans, 111; constructed Swedish-American history, 42, 50; Swedes as colonizers of America, 42; Swedish Vikings were discoverers of America, 42
Enemy of the People, An (Ibsen), 165
Enger, Bert, 185
Enger Park (Duluth, Minnesota), 185
England, xix, 26, 44, 46–48, 53, 90, 134, 15, 166–67, 194, 207, 212–13; Norman invasion (1066), 48; Norwegian colonization, 44, 46, 90
English, the, 134, 156
English language, xviii, 39, 76, 115, 117–18, 121, 125, 128, 131, 167, 172, 177
English nation, 50
English royalty, 79

English-speaking world, xix, 44, 75, 132; Norwegians introduced democracy and freedom, 44, 75
Enige og tro (United and Faithful), original slogan of Nordmands-Forbundet, 201
Erikson, Leif (Leif the Lucky), vii–viii, xi–xii, xv–xvi, xix, 28, 43–44, 46–50, 54, 62, 69–71, 74, 121, 136–37, 141, 145, 152–54, 169, 174–79, 186, 189, 195, 198, 200, 204–6, 223; celebration, xv, 175–79; Crown Prince Olav of Norway, 186; dedication of monument in Leif Eiriksson Square, 179, 186; equal status with Columbus, 176; first European to discover America, 28, 43, 46–47, 121, 136, 137, 176, 186; Leif Erikson Day, xvi, 54, 153–55, 175–79, 189, 200, 205, 223; modern symbol of Norwegian America, 176, 178; Norwegian and American hero, 44, 141, 153–54, 204–5; portrait (1883), 69, 175–76; replica of portrait, 175–76, 178; statues erected to him, 54, 62, 154; voyage (997 AD) retraced, 152; used to promote a positive Viking legacy during World War II, 195–96, 204–6
Erik the Red, vii, 70
Errol Flynn (star of *Edge of Darkness*), 205
ethnicity, 216; authentic nature, 217; symbolic ethnicity, 216; theories, 214–17
ethnoscapes, 2
Europe, 2, 47, 101, 103, 111–12, 118, 126–27, 134, 156, 199
European homeland, 31
European nations, 27, 62, 65, 90, 111, 155
Europeans, 26, 43, 57, 103; eastern and southern Europeans, 57, 155
Evang, Karl (director of Norway's Public Health department), 192
Everson, Arnold, 212
Evjen, John O., 52

Fairchild, Henry Pratt, 119
Fargo, North Dakota, 20, 81, 83–86, 91, 184; capital of New Normandy, 91
Fargo Commercial Club, 85
Fargo Forum and Daily Republican, 85, 91
farms, 17; comparison of American and Norwegian farms, 17
Far West, 156
Fay, Hans (general consul of Norway), 145
federal census, U.S., 10, 21, 155
Fersen, Count Axel von, 52
Festival of Nations, 163
Festskrift, 96
Fifteenth Wisconsin Regiment, 54, 95–96, 102, 143. *See also* Scandinavian Regiment
"figurative kinship," 119
Fillmore County, Minnesota, 18
Finland, 3
Finnish immigrants, 111
Finnmarken (province of Norway), 14
First Evangelical Lutheran Church (Chicago), 60
Fjelde, Herman O., 84–85, 91
Fjelde, Jacob, 84
Fjelde, Paul, 84
Floan, A. C., 93
Flom, George T., 52–53, 72
Folgerø, Gerhard (captain of *Leif Erikson*), 152–53
Folkestad, Sigurd, 121, 126
Folket som Utvandrer (The People Who Emigrate) (Gierløff), 150
folk high schools, 33

Ford, Guy Stanton (president of the University of Minnesota), 184
foreign views of Norway, 213–14
Forest City, Iowa, 173
Foss, Hans A., 36–37; class differences in Norway, 36, 40; *Husmandsgutten: En Fortælling fra Sigdal* (The Cotter's Son: A Story from Sigdal), 36–37, 40
Fossbraaten, Einar, 212
Fosteen, Manley, L., Mrs., 144, 185
Founding the Kingdom (Rølvaag), 131
Fourth of July, 96, 144, 193
Fox River settlement, Illinois, 12, 14, 143–44, 174–75
Fra det moderne Amerikas aandsliv (The Cultural Life of Modern America) (Hamsun), 66
Fram (Norwegian-American newspaper), 85, 91
France, 3, 83; French tricolor (flag), 86, 123
Franklin, Dwight (painter of *The Vikings*), 144
French, the, 103
French delegation, 91–92
Freydis, 50; expedition to Vínland (1011), 50
Frogner Park, Norway, 95–96
Fücher, Carlo, Mrs., 172
Furuseth, Andrew, 21

Gaa Paa (Strike Forth, Norwegian-American newspaper), 109
Gade, F. G., ix
Gade, F. Herman (Norwegian consul), 93
Garborg, Arne (Norwegian nationalist author), 88
Garborg, Hulda (wife of Arne Garborg), 88

German Americans, 117, 156
German immigrants, 8, 107, 111
German invasion of Norway, 189, 191, 194–95
German occupation of Norway, xii, xx, 160, 189
German prisoners, viii, 199
Germans, 2, 94, 103, 156, 189–90, 194; German nationalism, 94
Germany, viii, 47, 155, 167, 183, 189, 208, 214
Ghosts (Ibsen), 165
Giants in the Earth (Rølvaag), 122, 131
Gierløff, Christian, 77, 142, 150–51
Gjerdrum, Jørgen, 30
Gjerset, Knut, 50, 133; *History of the Norwegian People* (1915), 50
Glimt fra Amerika (Glimpes from America) (Hambro), 150
God, 59, 64, 137, 140, 170, 203
Golden Gate Exhibition, 182
Goodhue County, Minnesota, 18
Gosse, Sir Edmund, 166
Gramsci, Antonio, 221
Grand Central Hotel (Chicago), 62
Grand Forks, North Dakota, 201
Grant, Madison, 112, 119
Grant, Ulysses (president and general of the United States), 62, 137
Great Depression, 11, 23, 164
Greater Norway, viii–xvi, xviii, xx–xxi, 116, 150–51, 154–55, 158–89, 191–92, 199–200, 202, 204–9, 211–24; America and Norway reciprocate love to Norwegian Americans, 209; benefits Norway's self-image, 162, 222–24; both territorial and extraterritorial, 221; building bridges between Norway and Norwegian America, 160–64, 169, 191–93, 204–6, 208–9; celebrations of the

homeland, 159, 192–93; commemorating and reinventing Norway, 212; communities of ethnic Norwegians outside Norway, 159, 213; diaspora dynamic, 220, 222; "ethno-symbolic reconstruction" of Norway's national identity, 219–20; genesis, ix, 116–17, 138, 150–51; homeland Norway, 159, 162–64, 206, 209, 213; honoring Norway's legacy, 160, 204–6, 208–9; idealized landscapes, 212–13; imagined community, 212–13, 224; key to Norway's future, 209; leaders, 159–60; Leif Erikson as symbol, 154–55, 204–6; modern Vikings, 206; more than an abstraction, 160, 224; non-Norwegian contributions, 213–14; Norway's greatness extends beyond its borders, 150–51, 154–55, 159, 192–93, 208–9, 212, 223–24; Norwegian Americans are first line of defense of Norwegian cultural values, 209; Norwegian Americans are loyal citizens of the Norwegian nation, 116–17, 160–61, 199–200, 209, 219, 222–23; Norwegian-American contributions are major factor in Norway's liberation, 209, 223–24; realized through ties of friendship, family, and love, 213; real national community, 213, 224; recognition of Norwegian contributions, 159, 199–200, 204–5; restoration of Norwegian-American legacy, 163–64, 223–24; sacrifice required, 160, 213, 221–22; shedding of blood, 213, 220–21; successful in Norway and America, 164, 204–9, 212–13, 223–24; ties Norway's national prestige to powerful America, 164, 205–6, 223; transnational celebrations, xii, xx, 154–55, 160, 165–88, 219; transnationalism, viii, xviii, 217–19; transnational Norway, 159–60, 162–64, 199–200, 205, 208–9, 214–15, 218–20, 223–24; transnational spaces, 160–61, 212–13, 219, 221–24; validation, xii, 208–9, 221, 223; vital strategy for defeating Hitler and Nazi Germany, 191, 193, 204–5, 223–24

Greater Norway, A (Et større Norge), 159, 161

Greater Poland, 162. *See also* Polonia

Great Transformation *(den store hamskiftet)*, 4

Greece, 91

Greeks, 103

Green Bay, Wisconsin, 15

Greenland, vii, 43, 151

Grevstad, Nicolay A., 102, 171

Groth, Selmer (mayor of Mayville, North Dakota), 183

Grundtvig, Nikolai F. S., 33, 44

Gudrid (wife of one of first Norwegian settlers in the New World), 143

Gustav Adolf (crown prince of Sweden), 179

Haakon VII, king of Norway, vii, xi, 79, 95, 145, 147, 153, 165–66, 169, 177, 189, 193–94, 199, 202–4, 206–8; endorsement of Norwegian-American self-image, 145, 177; May 17 and Norway's liberation from Germany's slave state, 204; President Roosevelt's "Look to Norway" speech, 202–3; returns home to Norway, vii, 199, 208; sends telegram to President Franklin Roosevelt on 1935 Leif Erikson Day, 177; seventieth birthday honored,

202; symbol of modern Norway, vii, 193, 199, 202–4
Haas Park, 59–60
Hagen, H. J. (chair of the Rollo Committee), 91
Hague, The, 151
Halland, John G. (professor at North Dakota Agricultural College), 85, 87
Halvorsen, Reverend H., 64
Hamar, Norway, 190
Hambro, Carl J., 96, 141, 147, 150, 152, 157, 165–66, 169, 201, 204; refutes Nazi takeover of Nordmanns-Forbundet, 201; sharp critique of the Quota Law, 157
Hammer, Borgny (opera singer), 144
Hamsun, Knut, 36, 66, 129
Hande, Hallvard, 109
Handel og Sjøfartstidende (Norwegian newspaper), 141
Hanna, L. B. (governor of North Dakota), 96
Hansa, Beret, 131
Hansa, Per, 131
Hansen, Carl G. O., 110, 112, 123, 153, 167
Hansen, Hans, 52
Hansen, Howard (colonel), 183
Hansen, Marcus Lee, 155, 216
Harald Fairhair (king of Norway), 46, 59–60, 193
Harding, William (governor of Iowa), 117
Harrison, Carter (mayor of Chicago), 69
H. Aschehoug and Company (Norwegian publisher), 159
Hatton, North Dakota, 184
Hauge, Hans Nielsen, 4, 84, 88; Haugeanism, 4, 88; Haugeans, 15; picture of monument, 89; statue dedicated, 84–85, 88

Hauge, Hans Nielsen (pastor from Norway and grandson of Hans Nielsen Hauge), 88
Haugen, Einar, 198–99
Haugen, Ole, 36. *See also* Foss, Hans A.
Haugesund, Norway, 60
Hauke, E. B. (president of the Sons of Norway), 203–4
Haymarket Riot, 109
Heg, Hans Christian (colonel), xi–xii, xvi, 54–55, 137–38, 143, 152, 180; death at Battle of Chickamauga, 54–55, 137–39; opposition to slavery, 137; proof of Norwegian sacrifice to America, 55; statue in America unveiled, 139, 152; statue in Norway unveiled, 152; symbol of the greater Norway, 138, 152
Heimland, xiv
Hendrichsen, Peter, 28–29
Hendricksdatter, Anne, 52
Hippodrome (St. Paul), 184
historians, 141
History of the Norwegian People in America (1925), 140
Hitler, Adolf, 189, 191, 195
Hjelm-Hansen, Paul, 8
Hobe, F. H. (consul of Norway), 185
Hoiland (minister for the Norwegian Seamen's Church), 170
Holand, Hjalmar Rued, 48, 50, 52, 56; Norwegian firsts in the New World, 48–49, 52, 72
Holden, Sigvald, 181
Holmes, Oliver Wendell, 62
Holstad, S. H., 133
Holt, Henry (lieutenant governor of North Dakota), 201; printing firm publishes *Nordmanns-Forbundet*, 201
Homestead Act (1862), 19
Hordaland (province of Norway), 12

Hornby, Dr. Charles, 79
Hotel Spalding (Duluth, Minnesota), 153
Hougen, J. O. (Norwegian pastor), 87
House of Representatives, U.S., 134
Houston County, Minnesota, 18
Høverstad, Torstein (Norwegian scholar), 209
Hovland, Gjert G., 13
Høyre ("the Right") Party (conservative political party in Norway), 151
Hudson River, 52
Hudson's Bay, 52

Ibsen, Henrik, xv, 35, 37, 83–84, 87, 129, 164–68; bust dedicated, 83–84, 86, 91; centennial of his birth (1928), 165–68; criticism of Norwegian society, 167; exemplar of truth and freedom, 167; personification of Norwegian character, 88, 129, 167; social realism, 37, 167; support of progressive reforms, 167; universal appeal, 167
Iceland, 39, 43–44, 46, 49, 147, 193; colonized by Norwegians, 44, 147
Icelanders, vii
idealized (racial) standard, 103, 107
Illinois, 17–18, 23, 54, 77, 90, 120, 143–44, 174, 194
Illinois State Historical Society, 174
immigrant groups, xii, 8, 27, 42–43, 54, 55, 72, 75, 80, 111, 117, 131, 214; Catholic immigrants, 49; claims as the best Americans, 111; claims of being American prior to immigration, 131; differ from national groups, 214–15; importance of constructed history, 42–43; importance of cultural heroes, 54; loyalty to American values, 43, 51; need to impress Anglo-Americans, 42, 51, 117; World War I changes their status, 117
immigrants, 19, 22–23, 102–3, 106, 112, 118, 130; English-speaking children, 130; restriction legislation, 22–23, 115, 118
Immigrants, The (Bojer), 150
immigration, xx, 18, 118, 214–17; theories, xii–xiii, 21, 80, 214–17
Immigration Restriction Act (1924). *See* Johnson-Reed Immigration Act
Indians (Native Americans), 74
Inntrykk fra Amerika (Impressions from America) (Taranger), 141
International Court of Arbitration, 151
Iowa, 1, 15, 17–18, 90, 117
Ireland, x, 2, 155–57
Irish, the, 2, 103
Irish immigrants, 8, 28–29, 80
Island Park (Fargo, North Dakota), 184
Isle of Man, 201
Italian Americans, 176–77
Italian immigrants, 8, 49, 76, 100
Italians, 2, 76, 103, 118, 156
Italy, 49

Jaabæk, Søren, 35
Jamaica, 156
Janson, Kristofer, 33–34, 36, 63; *Amerikanske Fantasier* (American Fantasies), 33–34
jarl (earl), 61
Jefferson Prairie, Wisconsin, 15–16
Jersey City, New Jersey, 52
Jewish immigrants, 80, 100, 111
Jews, the, 103, 118
Jews in Norway, 87
Johnson, Albert, 119
Johnson, John A., 27, 54; history on the Scandinavian Regiment, 27, 54

Johnson, J. S., 96, 110, 112
Johnson, Ole C., 8
Johnson, Robert Underwood, 165–66
Johnson, Simon, 53, 80
Johnson, Thomas, 52
Johnson-Reed Immigration Act (Immigration Restriction Act), xi, 11, 118–19, 155; northern European bias, 118, 155
Jorgenson, Theodore (professor at St. Olaf College), 176, 181
Judeo-Christianity, 63
Jul i Vesterheim (Christmas in the Western World), 132

Kalberlahn, Dr. Johan M., 52
Kaldahl, Reverend, 53
Kallen, Horace, 120
Kandiyohi County, Minnesota, 18
Karl XIV Johan (king of Sweden-Norway), 3
Karl Johans Avenue (Oslo), 166
Karlsefni, Thorfinn, 50
Keilau, Wilhelm, 164
Kendall County, New York, 12, 54
Kenosha, Wisconsin, 109
Kensington Rune Stone (1898), 50
Keyser, Rudolf (Norwegian historian), 44
Kielland, Alexander, 35
Kildal, Arne (general secretary for Nordmands-Forbundet), 149–50, 154, 161–63, 175, 202; *De gjorde Norge større* (They Made Norway Greater), 202; promotes greater Norway concept, 161–62, 175; speeches on Leif Erikson Day in Norway, 154–55
Klaveness, Thoralv, 72, 96, 102, 108, 120, 142
Koht, Halvdan, xii, 108, 151, 165, 200

Kolderup, Thomas H. (Norway's consul in Seattle), 143
Kolstad, Thor, 39. See also Boyesen, Hjalmar Hjorth
Kolstad, Tollef, 39. See also Boyesen, Hjalmar Hjorth
Kongen (The King), 35
Kraabel, A. L., 90
Kristiania (Christiania, capital of Norway), ix, xi, 12, 79, 95. See also Oslo
Kristiania intelligentsia, 214
Krogh, Christian, 69, 175, 214
Krogh, Per (son of Christian Krogh), 175–76
Krohn, Fred, 166
Ku Klux Klan, 157
Kvale, Ole J. (congressman from Minnesota), 134, 142
Kvartalskrift (journal of the Norwegian Society of America), 104
Kystens norske Sangerforbund (the Coast's Norwegian Singing Association), 143

laborers, 3, 7, 19, 20
Labor government (Norway), 11
Labor (Arbeider) party (Norway), 11, 142, 149
labor unions (Norway), 11
LaGuardia, Fiorello (mayor of New York), 186
Laing, Samuel, 43, 214
Lake Mills, Iowa, 1
Lake Telemark, New Jersey, 170
Land of the Midnight Sun (1881) (du Chaillu), 102
landscapes, 80, 161
Langlie, Arthur B. (mayor of Seattle), 183
Latin contributions to humanity, 44

Latter-day Vikings. *See* Vikings: modern
Leif Eiriksson Lodge (Seattle), 142
Leif Erikson (replica Viking ship), 152–53
Leif Erikson Memorial Association of America, 175
Leif Erikson Park (New York), 153, 176
Leif Erikson Square (Brooklyn, New York), 154, 179, 204
Leira, Norway, 212
Leiv Eiriksson aar 1000 (Leif Erikson 1,000 Years) parade, 142
"Leiv Eiriksson Review" *(Nordisk Tidende)*, 177
lendemand (feudal lord), 61
Liberal (Venstre) party (Norway), 11, 33, 36, 61
Lie, Tryggve (Norway's minister of foreign affairs), 193–94
Lier, Norway, 152
Life magazine, 189
Lincoln, Abraham (president of the United States), 46, 96, 137, 163–64, 184
Lindesnes, Norway, 208
Lofoten Islands, Norway, 195
London, England, 192, 199
Longfellow, Henry Wadsworth, 43, 62
Los Angeles, California, 182, 194
Lossing, Benson John, 101
Lund, Einar, 164
Lunde, Johan P. (bishop of Norway), 141–42
Lunde, Signe (Norwegian pianist), 143
Lutheran faith, 29, 49, 118, 124; Lutheran synods, 118
Luther College (Decorah, Iowa), 34, 96, 174, 180
Luther College Band, 143, 174
Lyceum (Minneapolis), 166
Lysaker Circle, the, 214

Madison, Wisconsin, 173
Malmin, R. (professor at Augsburg Seminary), 170
Markoe, Abraham, 52
Märtha (crown princess of Norway), 175, 179, 181, 183, 187–89, 191, 203, 208, 223; responds to President Roosevelt's "Look to Norway" speech, 203; returns home to Norway, 208; takes up residence in America, 189, 191; visit to America (1939), 175–89, 223. *See also* Norway's royal couple
Martin, Clarence D. (governor of Washington), 183
Marxist socialist and labor movement, 108, 149
Massachusetts, 62
Maud (queen of Norway), 79
Mauras, G. (secretary of the French embassy), 87
May 17 (Norway's Constitution Day), xv, 58–61, 82–83, 85–86, 91, 94, 100, 102, 108, 161–62, 182, 189, 193, 195, 203–4, 206; becomes shared symbol of Norway and America, 204, 206–7; children's processions, 60–61, 86, 91, 94, 204, 206; proclaimed as "America Day" by American government, 204
Mayville, North Dakota, 84, 86, 183
Meany Hall, 167
Mediterranean race, 103
Melbye, Johan E., 22
Melting Pot, The (1908) (play by Israel Zangwill), 106
melting pot concept, 106, 119
Melting Pot Mistake, The (1926), 119
Mengshoel, Emil Lauritz, 109
Meslo, Engel, 211
Michelsen, Christian, ix
Michigan, 17

Michigan Avenue (Chicago), 173–74
Midnight Sun, 45
migration memories, xiv–xv
Milwaukee, Wisconsin, 20, 94, 173
Minneapolis Daglig Tidende (*Minneapolis Tidende,* Norwegian-American newspaper), 79, 110, 140, 143, 153, 156, 161, 166–67, 172
Minnesota Democratic Party, 133
Minneapolis Journal, 70
Minneapolis–St. Paul, Minnesota (Twin Cities), 18, 52, 57, 60, 63, 72, 82–83, 85, 87, 95, 97, 102, 108–9, 135, 137, 141–42, 144, 149, 152, 165–67, 169–71, 173, 179, 184–85, 192–93, 195, 206; capital of Norwegian America, 91
Minnesota, 1, 15, 17–18, 72, 77, 80, 90–91, 117, 133, 144, 172
Minnesota (1914) (program of the Minnesota–Norway 1914 Centennial), 72, 96, 110
Minnesota–Norway 1914 Centennial, 72, 110
Minnesota–Norway 1914 Centennial Exposition Association, 110
Minnesota State Fairgrounds, 137
Mitchell County, Iowa, 18
Moderne Vikinger (Modern Vikings) (Stenholt), 71
Moe, Jørgen, 33
Moe, Moltke, ix
Moen, N. T., 133
monuments, 92
Moon Is Down, The (Steinbeck), 205
Moorhead, Minnesota, 84, 184
Moravian colony, 15
Morgenbladet (Norwegian newspaper), 48, 157
Morgenstierne, Wilhelm, 98, 143, 146–48, 159, 161, 163, 170, 175, 184, 191, 199, 206; promotes a greater Norway, 161, 163, 170, 175, 178, 199–200
"Mormon Lands," 77
Morton, John, 42
Moscow, Russia, 142
Moses, John (governor of North Dakota), 182–84
Mother Norway, 73
Mower County, Minnesota, 18
Mowinckel, Johan Ludwig (prime minister of Norway), 82, 145–46
Munch, P. A. (Norwegian historian), 44
Municipal Pier (Chicago), 142
Munk, Jens (captain), 52
Munthe, Gerhard, 214
myths, x; foundation myths, x, 48; hegemony myths, x, xx, 32, 216; homemaking myths, 42–43, 111, 214–15; ideology myths, 48; legacy myths, xi, xii, 32, 116, 216, 222; myth-making, 32; origin (creation) myths, x, xix, 25–26, 32, 216; right for place in America, 32

Nansen, Fridtjof, 74, 170, 214
Napoleonic Wars, 3
Nasjonal Samling (National Gathering, Norwegian fascist party), 189, 201
nation, 31, 214, 217–18, 221; ethnic origins, 218–19; great, 31; hybrid, 31; nation-building, 214
national identity theories, 217–21
nationalism, xiii, 37, 95, 186, 217–21; flexibility, 221; rooted in local symbols, 95; theories, xiii–xvi, 95, 186, 217–21
national myths, xiv, 213–14
National Origins Act (1927), 116, 155–56, 223. *See also* Origins Proviso and Quota Law

national romanticism, xviii, 3, 5, 32–33, 37, 57, 61, 64
National Socialism, 189, 195
National Theater (Oslo), 165–66
National Women's Party, 133
Nationen (Norwegian newspaper), 146, 161–62, 187, 208
Native Americans, 15
Native-stock Americans. *See* Anglo-Americans
Nattestad, Ansten, 14–16
Nattestad, Ole, 15–16
Nazis, vii–vii, 189, 193, 195, 198, 200–202, 205, 222; appropriation of Norway's Viking-age symbols, 195–98, 202; censorship of Norway's press, 201; Norway's romantic peasant past appropriated, 202
Nebraska, 117
Negroes, 156
Nelson, Knute (U.S. senator and governor), 54, 72–73, 117, 180, 184
Neuman, W. (minister of Norwegian diplomatic corps), 204
Neumann, Jacob (bishop of the Archdiocese of Bergen, Norway), 14
New Amsterdam, 52
New England, 47, 51, 62
Newfoundland, 47
New Normandy (Normandy in America), 80, 90, 92; colonized by Norwegian immigrants, 80, 90–91
Newport Tower, 32, 50
newspapermen's tour of Norway, 152
newspapers in America, 20
New Sweden, 51
New World, x, 1–2, 12, 25, 28, 43, 46, 50–51, 62, 69, 75, 86, 107, 123, 134, 147, 171, 193, 198, 202, 209, 222
New York (city), 18, 20, 23, 30, 38, 52, 54, 61, 69, 109, 144, 161, 170–71, 176–77, 179, 185–86, 189–90, 194, 200, 204, 206–7
New York (state), 4, 52, 198
New York Armory, 144
New York Philharmonic Orchestra, 144, 207
New York's World Fair (1939), 179–80, 182
New York Times, 205
Nicoll, Claus, 108
Nidaros Cathedral (Trondheim, Norway), 169–70
Nilsson, Svein, 28, 43, 48, 56
Ninety-ninth Battalion, vii–viii, xii; honor guard, vii; symbol of Norway, vii–viii. *See also* Viking Battalion
Nobel Prize, 66
Nora Society, 59
Norbeck, Peter (senator of South Dakota), 143, 156
Norborg, Sverre, 204
Nord-Aurdal, Norway, 212
Norden (The North, Norwegian journal), 28
Norden (The North, Norwegian-American newspaper), 109
Nordhordalland bygdelag, 141
Nordic home, 27, 78
Nordic race, 63, 103, 112, 136, 151, 156, 174, 189;
Nordisk Tidende (Norwegian-American newspaper), 134, 141, 144, 157, 168–69, 172, 174, 176–77, 179, 195–98, 203–5, 208; editorial responds to President Roosevelt's "Look to Norway" speech, 203
Nordkapp, Norway, 208
Nordlandslaget, 153
Nordmændenes opdagelse af Amerika (The Norwegians' Discovery of America) (Stenholt), 71

Nordmændenes Sangforening. *See* Norwegian Singing Association

Nordmands-Forbundet (Nordmanns-Forbundet), ix, xi, 92–93, 95–96, 126, 150–53, 155, 159, 161–62, 173, 188, 191, 200–202, 204, 222; American version promotes the greater Norway concept, 202; building bridges with Norwegian America, 155, 161, 173, 188; establishes Leif Erikson Day in Norway, 153; importance of business and professional elite to its founding, 151; "Janus-faced years," 201; promotes Norwegian-American identity, 151, 153; refuses to endorse "Normannafolket," 201

Nordmands-Forbundet (Nordmanns-Forbundet, journal of Nordmands-Forbundet), 93, 148, 150, 201

Nordraak Twin Cities Males Singers' Association, 172

"Norge i Amerika" (Norway in America), 77

Norge i Amerika (Norway in America) (Stenholt), 76, 98, 100

Norgeposten (Norwegian-American newspaper), 156

Norgesbygning (Norway's Building at 1915 Panama Exhibition), 93

"Norge, vaar mor" (Norway, Our Mother), 171

Norlie, Olaf M., 58, 139–40, 144

Norman-American Congress, 91

Normanden (Norwegian-American newspaper), 92

Normandy, xix, 44, 46, 72, 90, 147, 193; Norwegian colonization, 44, 46, 72

Normandy settlement, Texas, 15

"Normannafolket" (The Norman People, Norwegian Nazi exhibition in Oslo), 201

Normanna Mandskor (Northmen's Male Chorus), 153

Normans, 92

Normennenes Klubhus (Norwegians' Club House), 174

Norse-American Centennial (1925), xi–xii, xvi, xx, 57, 116, 120, 133–37, 139–42, 144, 146–49, 152, 216, 223; challenges Anglo-American superiority, 139; commemorative stamps, 134–35; modeled on 1914 Eidsvold Centennial, 137; Norse-American Centennial Inc. (committee), 133–34; scholars view as last hurrah of the immigrant community, 216; silver coin medallion, 134–35

Norse-American Centennial (Stavanger, Norway), 147, 152

Norse-American Centennial of Illinois, 143–44

Norse-American Centennial of the Pacific Northwest, 142, 146

Norseland, 70

Norsemen, 43, 45, 90, 101, 103

Norsemen's Singing Society (Chicago), 62

Norse pioneers, 90

"Norse Spirit of Old on the March to Victory, The" (cartoon), 195, 198

Norsk-Amerikanernes festskrift (Norwegian-American Literary Celebration) (1914), 109–10

Norske Venner av Amerika. *See* Norwegian Friends of America

"Norske vikinger i det 19de aarhundrede," (Norwegian Vikings in the Nineteenth Century) (Nelson), 73–74

Norsk Fylkings (Norwegian Counties) Free Norway Festival, 207

"Norskheten i Amerika" (Norwegian identity in America), 150
Norsk Jægerskvadron (Norwegian Hunter Squadron), 194
Norsk læsebok (Norwegian reader) (ed. Rølvaag), 121, 123
North Dakota, 1, 18–19, 83–86, 90, 96, 117, 182
North Dakota Agricultural College, 85–87, 90, 184
North Dakota State School of Science, 86
Northerly Island, 173
Northfield, Minnesota, 2, 121, 173, 179–80
Northmen, 101
North Peoria Street (Chicago), 59
Northumberland, 147
Northwest, the, 141
Nortun Lodge, 153
Norway, vii–xii, xv–xvi, xviii–xxi, 1–15, 18–20, 22–23, 25, 27, 29–33, 35–40, 46, 51, 54, 56, 60–62, 67, 69, 71–80, 82, 84–88, 90, 92–96, 98–102, 104, 108–10, 113, 116–17, 120–21, 123, 125–26, 129, 132–35, 137, 140–55, 157, 159–95, 199–200, 202–9, 211–15, 217–24; anti-emigration literature, 33–35; art, 33; ceremonies in both Norway and America, xii, xx, 96, 147, 160, 165–88, 219; Christianity, 137, 168–70, 208; cities, 10, 20, 59–60, 137; compared to the Holy Land, 152; constitution, xi, xvi, 14, 59, 93, 161, 168, 193–94, 202–4, 214; constitution as symbol of modern Norway, 193–94, 202–4; cultural nationalism, 32, 218–19; declares independence from Sweden (June 7, 1905), 78–79, 222; decline in international position, 157; defiance during World War II earns America's admiration, 202–5; "discovers" Norwegian America, 188; dynastic union with Sweden, 3, 78, 208, 222; economic transformation, 8–9; economy, 4, 8; fights for true democracy and freedom, 200, 202–5; government, xvi, 22, 35–36, 79, 92–94, 141, 143, 145–46, 152–53, 157, 178, 185, 189–90, 192, 194, 206, 208; government endorsement of Norwegian-American self-image, 145, 152, 154–55, 161, 175, 177–78; history, 32, 37, 100, 147, 169–71, 175, 181, 199, 202–4, 218; homeland, 2, 20, 33–34, 77–78, 92, 117, 140, 142, 146–47, 149–50, 159, 168, 186, 188, 195, 208, 211, 217, 219, 222; image-makers, 31, 98, 160–61; individualism, 192, 200, 204; landscapes, 33, 124, 161, 170, 211–12; Leif Erikson Day, 153–54, 176–77, 205; liberal ideas, 37; "little Norways," 18; lower classes (labor), 5, 142; Lutheran churches, 141–42; made greater and richer by Norwegian Americans, 145–46, 185–88; merchant marine, 189, 194; military contributions of Norwegian Americans, 199–200, 202; modern and progressive nation, 113, 125–26, 151, 183, 193, 204, 214; modern economy, 11, 151; modernization, 32, 37; modern Vikings, 74, 100, 113, 147, 173, 176, 191, 193, 199, 204–5; more egalitarian and democratic than America, 108; more freedom than America, 120; musicians, 3; nation, viii–ix, xv–xvi, xviii, xxi, 3, 86, 93, 186, 190, 203–4, 206, 214, 213; "the National Breakthrough," 32–33; national identity, xx, 3, 27, 32, 40,

47, 64, 65–66, 86, 137, 145, 149–51, 153, 158–59, 169, 202–5, 218–19; nationalism, xv–xvi, 32–33, 47, 66, 87, 109–10, 113, 133, 135–36, 145–46, 149, 151, 166, 179, 185, 202–5, 215; national mythmakers, 31; national prestige tied to powerful America, 164, 178, 182, 185, 202–4; nation building, 32; navy, 213; Norwegian Americans essential to winning World War II, 191, 202, 224; Norwegian race, 147, 151, 176, 178, 189, 205; official language, 35; official presence at Norwegian-American events, 193; peaceful nation, 176, 182–83, 193, 203–4; peasant influences, 101, 143; positive view of emigrated Norwegians, 116, 145, 147–48, 150–51, 154–55; President Roosevelt's "Look to Norway" speech, 202–3, 207; professionals, 3, 141; pure Norwegian nation, 3; quotas in America criticized, 157; reactionary and backward, 36; responsible for restoring Norwegian-American legacy, 163, 223; return migration, 10–11, 14–15, 22; romanticized view, 101, 211, 213–14, 222; shared values with America, xii, 72, 87, 120, 178, 192, 202–5, 223–24; shipping industry, 8–10, 109, 151; social legislation, 183; societal divisions, 168; takes lead in promoting Norwegian-American identity, 161, 163–64, 179, 219, 223; ties to Norwegian America, xx, 3, 71, 86, 92, 98, 142, 145–46, 150, 161, 165–88, 193, 199, 203–4, 223–24; unique role in promoting success of its emigrants, 162; universities, 141; Viking legacy, 60–61, 71–72, 102, 169, 174–76, 178, 195–99, 204–5;

world's model of democracy, 126; youthfulness, 180
"Norway, a Fighting Ally" (exhibition), 194
Norway, Wisconsin, 54
Norway Day, 165, 173, 182, 195
Norway Grove Church, Wisconsin, 38
"Norway i Amerika" (Norway in America, article in *Aftenposten*), 146
Norway in America, x, xvi, 75–76, 79–80, 82, 97–98, 100, 113, 141, 146
Norway Lake, Minnesota, 74
Norway: Neutral and Invaded (Koht), 200
Norway's national anthem, 60, 86, 93, 135, 169, 171, 183
Norway's pavilion at the New York's World Fair (1939), 179–80, 186
Norway's pavilion at the World's Columbian Exposition in Chicago (1893), 69
Norway's royal couple, 179–82, 186; visit to America, 179–80, 182–83, 185–86, 192
Norwegian America, xii, 19, 21, 36–37, 40, 87, 92, 107, 109, 116, 148–50, 166–69, 171, 174, 176, 178–79, 187–88, 195, 202, 208, 216; greatness, 148; nation, 68; wartime service to Norway, 202
Norwegian-American Centennial, 1825–1925 (New York), 144, 146
Norwegian-American Centennial Festival (Chicago), 142
Norwegian-American churches, xviii, 30, 63, 76–77, 123, 141, 211
Norwegian-American civil war veterans, 25
Norwegian (American) communities, xiv, 7, 12, 15, 17–18, 20, 26, 31, 58, 71,

85–87, 96, 101, 108, 115, 134, 165, 167, 170, 177–78, 188–91, 194–95, 203, 209
Norwegian-American culture, 115, 119
Norwegian-American farmers, 17, 55–58, 71, 77
Norwegian-American golden age, 112
Norwegian-American heroes, xii, 42, 44, 58, 74, 137–38, 160, 183–84
Norwegian-American historians, 41–58; constructed history, 41–57; creating a colonial Norwegian presence, 51–52; first Europeans to discover the New World, 41; importance of the Viking age, 50–51; Norwegians as the creators of American values, 41, 48–51; romanticized view of Norwegian-American farmer, 57
Norwegian-American Historical Association (NAHA), 58, 174, 216; creation of legacy myths, 216
Norwegian-American identity (self-image), ix–xii, xix–xx, 2, 14, 18, 24, 27–28, 30–31, 38, 40–41, 45–46, 51, 56, 59–61, 65–67, 71–72, 75–76, 81–83, 87–88, 91–94, 96, 98, 100, 102–4, 106, 109–10, 112, 115–16, 120–21, 123–28, 130–31, 134–50, 152–57, 160–64, 166–88, 191–92, 195–96, 199, 202–9, 211, 216–19, 222–24; agents of civilization, 137; America and Norway reciprocate love of Norwegian Americans, 209; American Civil War, x, 25–27, 100, 102, 110–11, 137, 222; American government validation, 175–79, 202–3, 205, 209; becoming American, 25–26, 28–29, 78, 102, 104, 124–25, 134–36; benefits to America, 120, 125, 127, 136, 138, 145; best Americans, 101–4, 107, 111, 136, 147; best immigrant group, 32, 73, 76, 91, 102, 222; bound to Norway's national identity, ix–x, 25, 44, 71, 74–76, 87, 109, 159–61, 175–88, 205, 209; brothers with homeland Norwegians, 191, 205–6; built America into world's greatest nation, 145, 147, 177–78; colonists from Norway, 55–56, 75, 77, 141, 150, 178; complementary identity, 148, 184; conflicts with American values, 18; constructed history, 41–58, 150; countering Nazi appropriations of Viking-age symbols, 195–96; descendants of Odin and Thor, 60, 136; desire for America to recognize Norwegian contributions, 126–27, 154, 203; ethnic enclaves, 2, 18, 83; foundation myths, 55; generosity, 185; genesis, xix, 25–26; hegemony myths, 32, 107, 112, 222; homeland Norwegians learn extent of Norwegian-American relief during the war, 208; homemaking myths, 46, 55; honesty, 56, 110–11, 140, 177; hybrid identity, 40, 59, 92, 104, 113; ideology, 27, 31–32, 55; immigration restrictions, 156; individualism, 183; justice, 180; "kings of the prairie," 76; landscape, 211; law abiding, 128, 140; legacy myths, 102, 116, 121, 123, 132–33, 148, 199, 216; loss of Norwegian traditions, 30, 38, 106, 129–30; love of freedom and democracy, 112, 128–29, 136, 180, 205; loyalty to America, 148, 180, 183, 185, 205; loyalty to Norway and its traditions, 180, 184–85, 202–5; Lutheran orientation, 29, 88, 103, 140; modern Vikings, 71–75, 100, 131–32, 153, 174, 183, 191, 195–96, 199, 205; more Protestant than

Anglo-Americans, 107, 112; myths, x; nationalism, 95, 113, 145, 149, 158, 166, 168, 179, 185, 190; need to maintain Norwegian traditions, 88, 104, 124, 128, 131, 139, 141–43, 146, 163; Norway's independence, 202, 205, 208; Norwegian-American youth, 88, 134; Norwegian blood in English and Americans, 46, 139; Norwegians are greatest people in the world, 136–37; Norwegians as creators of American values, 41, 44–48, 104, 106–7; origin myths, 26, 32, 107, 222; peasant influences, 94, 112–13; pioneers in America, 28, 72–74, 76–77, 110, 142, 144, 146, 175, 177; positive image compared to Irish Americans, 28–29; positive publicity from Leif Erikson proclamation, 177–79, 205; progressive (modern) image, 96, 110, 112, 123–24, 139, 167, 180, 183, 185; proto identity, 27; proud of the fatherland, 76–77, 142–43, 146; racial purity, 157; racial ties to Anglo-Americans, 55, 70, 101, 134, 139, 178; regional identity, 84, 87; reorient Norwegian-American identity in Norway, 126, 160; restoring the Norwegian-American self-image, 160–61, 175–76; Rølvaag's characteristics of Norwegian Americans, 128–30, 180; rural versus urban, 83, 94–95, 222–23; sacrifice to America, 25–27, 42, 55, 100, 110, 123, 137, 144; shared American values, xi, xix–xx, 25–26, 44, 57, 72, 87, 100, 104, 107, 116, 128–29, 133–34, 180, 186, 205, 222; "spirit of Norway," 182, 206; strong religious character, 123, 132, 140, 142, 145, 147, 180; success of Norwegian Americans bolsters Norwegian national image, 146–48, 168, 187, 205–6; superiority to Anglo-Americans, xix, 28, 100, 104, 107, 112, 121, 130, 133, 139–40, 148; superiority to Catholic groups, 91; symbolic affirmation, 135; tarnished, 157; transatlantic (transnational) identity, 24, 60, 87, 92, 145, 150, 155, 166–88, 204–5, 209, 223–24; triangulation with American and Norwegian identities, 30–31, 41, 43–45, 59, 66–67, 75–76, 87–88, 90, 113, 133, 141–47, 155, 186; validation, 135, 155, 162, 164, 175, 179–80, 187–88, 203, 209; vanguard of civilization, 55–57, 140, 144; Viking legacy, 51, 61, 71–72, 75, 94, 100–101, 110, 174, 176, 183, 195–96, 199, 205; "Vikings on the Prairie," 72, 131, 209; wartime service to Norway, 202, 205–6

Norwegian-American leaders, x–xi, xix–xx, 3, 25–26, 29–32, 36, 40, 43, 49, 59, 67, 71–72, 74–75, 81, 83–84, 87, 90–92, 100, 103, 107, 109, 111–12, 115–16, 120, 124–26, 129, 133–34, 143, 148, 158, 160, 168, 174–76, 191, 194, 200, 209; businessmen, 93; challenges to Anglo-American authority, 111–12, 120; Leif Erikson, 176; hegemony myths, 91, 112; identity makers, 31, 43, 48–49, 103, 113, 121, 132; ideology, 32; image-makers, xix, 25, 31, 40, 43, 72, 75, 116, 148, 160, 186; legacy myths, 32; myth-makers, 32; Norwegian-American elite, 26, 29–30, 59, 67, 81–82, 85–86, 109; secure financial support for Norway, 191

Norwegian-American Line (1911), 93

Norwegian-American literature, 101, 126

Norwegian-American male choirs, 144–45
Norwegian-American newspapers (press), 19–20, 70, 76–77, 117–19, 125, 136, 141, 152, 161, 171, 187–88; coverage of royal couple's visit to America (1939), 187–88
Norwegian-American pavilion (1914), xi
Norwegian-American pioneer museum (Vesterheim, in Decorah, Iowa), 133, 216
Norwegian Americans, ix–xi, xv–xvi, xviii–xix, 2, 8, 10, 19, 21–23, 26, 29, 31–32, 36, 41, 45, 47, 49–50, 53–54, 56, 62, 71–72, 74–80, 82, 84–88, 91–94, 98–101, 103–4, 106, 108–9, 111–12, 115–17, 120–27, 134–36, 138–39, 141–45, 147–50, 152–53, 161, 163, 166, 169, 176–77, 179, 182–83, 185, 190, 192, 194, 199, 202–3, 206, 208–9, 211, 214–15, 218, 217, 224; active organizational life, 150; best immigrant group, 26, 32, 91, 104, 108; best traits of Norway and America, 148, 169; builders of America, 121, 123–25, 127, 136, 138, 141, 177, 185; commonalities with Norway, 149, 169; complementary identity, 41, 72, 104, 113, 148; contributions to America, 53–54, 82, 109–10, 127, 136, 145, 147; counteroffensive, 133; deep religious values, 145; defenders of American values, 125–26, 128, 132; feel betrayed by homeland Norwegians in World War II, 190–91; hard workers, 142; involvement in American Civil War, 26; love of liberty, 88; loyalty to America, 116, 121, 123, 134, 148, 183; loyalty to Norway, 79, 86–87, 141, 143, 150, 161; Lutheran orientation, 117, 124; material assistance provided to Norway, 192–95, 202, 208; modern Vikings, 71–72, 74–75, 153, 183, 199; more Protestant than Anglo-Americans, 107; Norway's greatest export, 150; preserve Norwegian traditions, 77, 87–88, 104, 107–8, 110, 139, 141–43; race, 124, 139; return to Norway, 22; self-reliance, 142; share in Norway's legacy, 169, 203, 206; success bolsters Norway's national identity, 100, 116, 120, 145–48, 205–6, 209; trailblazers, 56; transnational identity, 122, 138, 150, 161, 163, 169, 209; wartime service to Norway, 202, 206, 208–9
Norwegian-American schoolchildren, 135
Norwegian-American schools, 76–77
Norwegian-American settlements, 55, 76
Norwegian-American singers, 173
Norwegian-American societies, 96
Norwegian-American studies, 127
Norwegian-American World's Exposition Committee, 173
Norwegian Arctic explorers, 74
Norwegian Bakery Workers Union (Norway), 108
Norwegian blood sacrifice, 25–26, 55
Norwegian Chamber of Commerce, 183
Norwegian Christianity, 129
Norwegian Club (New York), 82
Norwegian colonies, 143–44
Norwegian conservatives, 22
Norwegian consular service (separate), 78
Norwegian culture, xviii, 3, 26, 55, 83, 93, 104, 106, 120–21, 126, 129–30, 168, 217; compatibility with American

values, 26, 104, 106; superior to American culture, 130
Norwegian customs (traditions), 2, 87
Norwegian-Danish chapter of the Socialist Party of America, 109
Norwegian diaspora, 19, 220–21
Norwegian emigrants, xvi, 11, 19, 21, 35, 54, 80, 90, 92–93, 95–96, 98, 100–101, 145–47, 149–50, 154, 162, 171, 202, 214, 217, 222; could remain members of Norway, 80; earned respect in new homelands, 146–47; King Haakon VII's pride for them, 147; least desirable elements in Norway, 21; Leif Erikson Day in Norway their day, 154; love for Norway, 90, 145; opportunities in America, 19; recognition by Norway, 95–96; sacrificed for America, 90; symbols for the greatness of Norway, 101, 149; theme in Norway's history, 171; unity among homeland and emigrated Norwegians, 93, 98, 100
Norwegian emigration, 1, 4, 6, 8–11, 20–22, 33–35, 116, 127, 150–51, 159, 164, 175, 187, 215; causes, 6–11; conservative motivations, 10–11; ignored by Norwegian historians, 151; makes the greater Norway possible, 159, 215; Norwegian authors, 33–36; part of worldwide transformation, 20; reform efforts, 22; strategies, 35–36; value of return migrants to Norway, 22
Norwegian ethnicity, xviii, xvi, xviii, 37, 61, 87, 101, 124–25, 185, 214; ethnic character differences between immigrant group and national group, 214–15
Norwegian farmers, 87

Norwegian flag(s), 59, 79, 86, 135–37, 166–67, 175, 180, 184, 204, 207–8; living Norwegian flag, 135
Norwegian folk dancers, 144
Norwegian Friends of America, 178
Norwegian-German supernationalism, 201–2
Norwegian Glee Club, 166
Norwegian historical school, 33, 44, 47
Norwegian heroes, 44, 84, 87, 160, 170, 214; statues, 85
Norwegian identity (national), xiii–ix, xi–xii, xx, 31–33, 37, 39–40, 48, 58–67, 71, 74, 80, 83, 86–86, 88, 92–93, 100–101, 110, 116, 121, 125, 129, 137, 140–41, 145–51, 153–55, 157, 159, 162–88, 191–93, 199–200, 202–9, 212–15, 217–24; business and professional elite, 151, 221, 223; Christian heritage, 169–70, 172, 207–8; constitutional government, 219; construction, 151, 204, 218; enhanced by greater Norway concept, 162, 170–71, 178–79, 201–4, 208–9, 212, 221–22; first Europeans to discover the New World, 102, 134; generosity, 185; glorification of peasant culture, 32–33, 37, 93; heritage, xii, 70–71, 83, 95, 107, 204, 208–9; human dignity, 207–8; inclusion of Leif Erikson, 48, 71, 153–55, 176, 178–79, 204–6; individualism, 192, 200; international promotion, 179, 186–87, 202–3, 209; justice, 167, 207–8, 221; love of democracy, 100, 163–64, 175, 185–86, 200, 203–4, 207; love of liberty (freedom), 88, 100, 167, 177, 182, 185–86, 193, 200, 202–5, 207–8, 219; May 17 as modern symbol, 204; modern saga, 147, 193; modern

Vikings, 74, 100, 113, 147, 150, 153–55, 173–74, 176, 178, 191, 193, 199, 204–6, 209; mutually intertwined with Norwegian-American identity, 116, 121, 141, 145–48, 153–55, 157–58, 162–88, 191, 193, 202–4, 208, 218, 222, 224; *norskhet* ("Norwegianness"), xi, 120–21, 160, 212; Norwegian historians, 151, 178; Norwegian race, 8, 106–7, 150–51, 171, 176, 178; origins of American democracy, 175; peaceful nation, 177, 182, 203–4; positive image of emigrated Norwegians, 145–48, 150, 202–3, 205, 208, 215; positive international reputation for Norway, 147, 179, 187, 202–9; pre-Christian traits, 33, 70–71, 74, 93; President Roosevelt's "Look to Norway" speech, 202–3; progressive and modern nature of Norway, 71, 94, 116, 125, 151, 167, 183–86, 193, 203–4, 207, 214; rebirth of the nation, 86; resistance to Nazi tyranny, 205; rural versus urban, 83, 94–95; shared values with America, 163–64, 178, 186–87, 192, 203–5; society based on tolerance, 208; success of Norwegian emigrants bolsters Norway's image, 148, 150, 177, 179, 187, 206, 209; superior national traits, 150, 202–9; superior Norwegian culture, 129; traditional view of Norway, 214, 218–20; transnational identity, 80, 92, 117, 140, 147, 150, 154–55, 159–60, 163–88, 191–92, 199–200, 204–5, 207–8, 212–15, 217–20, 222–23; validation of Norwegian-American identity, 157–58, 163, 179, 185–88, 202–3, 205–6, 208–9; Vikings reveal best characteristics of Norwegians, 74, 93, 100, 150, 168–71,174, 204–6, 223; virtue, 39–40, 202–4, 207–8; vitality and youth, 180, 207; world travelers, 171

Norwegian Immigrant Contributions to America's Making (ed. Sundby-Hansen), 125

Norwegian immigrants, xv, xviii, 1– 3, 12–18, 20–21, 23–28, 30, 36, 38, 42, 73–74, 77–78, 88, 93–94, 100, 102, 107, 120, 123, 125, 127, 130–31, 133, 137, 142–43, 146, 148, 156, 160–61, 175, 209, 217, 219; agents of civilization, 28; America as a modern nation, 36; best Americans, 102, 130; best immigrant group, 102; contributions to America, 107, 125, 127; integration into American life, 24, 90, 127; law-abiding, 28; local identity, 93–94; loss of Norwegian traditions, 38; maintain Norwegian traditions, 77–78; modern Vikings, 131; moral citizens, 28, 30; Norway's greatest colonists, 148; numbers reduced, 156; opportunities in America, 13–19, 36; pioneers in America, 28, 143, 146; professional-class training, 23–24; prosperous, 30; religious character, 88, 100, 123; sacrifice to America, 25–27, 100, 102; shared values with America, 120; success bolsters Norway's national image, 146, 148, 209; tamers of the American frontier (pioneers), 42, 74, 77, 100, 123, 127, 142; traits inherited from Norway, 73–74; transformation into good Americans, 130; women, 21–23. *See also* Norway in America; Norwegian America; Norwegian Americans

Norwegian immigration, xviii, 1, 12, 15, 19, 22–23, 101, 126, 142
Norwegian independence, 3
Norwegian intellectuals, xviii, 3, 75, 108
Norwegian islands, 147
Norwegian labor movement, 108–9
Norwegian landscapes, 80–81
Norwegian language, xi, xviii, 1, 32, 35, 55, 59, 76, 88, 104, 106, 117–18, 121, 126, 128, 131, 148, 150, 162, 167, 181–82, 184, 188, 222–24; concerns about it dying off, 115, 118, 126, 139, 148, 222; declining usage, 150, 162, 188, 223–24; Landsmaal, 35, 170, 214; need to preserve in America, 104, 106–7; Riksmaal (Dano-Norwegian), 35
Norwegian leaders, xix–xx, 3, 32–33, 47, 82, 92, 112, 116, 151, 158, 160–61, 163–64, 218; cultural elite, 32–33, 35, 47, 67, 75, 82, 92, 22, 2231; greatness of the Norwegian race, 151; image-makers, 160–61, 179; promote a greater Norway, 161, 218–21
Norwegian liberals, 21, 35, 37. *See also* Liberal (Venstre) party, Norway
Norwegian Liberation Rally, 195
Norwegian literature, 90
Norwegian Lutheran Church Council, 141
Norwegian Lutheran Church in America, 115, 140, 150, 169, 184
Norwegian Lutheran clergy, 59, 82, 144
Norwegian Lutheranism, 84, 88; congregations, 88, 117–18
Norwegian Memorial Church, 169
Norwegian Migration to America (Blegen), 200
Norwegian movement and strength, viii–ix, 123
Norwegian National League, 153, 166, 169, 172, 175

Norwegian National Theater (retinue), 60
Norwegian Nazis, 201
Norwegian newspapers (press), 19, 149, 153–54, 161, 177, 186–87, 201, 211; coverage of royal couple's visit to America (1939), 186–87; under Nazi censorship, 201
Norwegian peasantry, xviii, 3–4, 14–15, 19–21, 32–33, 35, 44, 46, 94–95, 167, 202, 214, 222; becoming Americans, 29; desire to own land, 19; foundation of Norwegian nationalism, 32–33; Nazi appropriation of romantic peasant past, 202; political activity, 21–22, 35; pure-blooded Norwegians, 44, 46; rural way of life, 11; sense of self-worth, 5; struggle in Norway compare to struggle against the Confederacy, 27; true Norwegian culture, 32–33, 214
Norwegian professionals, 20–21, 23, 57
Norwegian Relief, Inc. (American Relief for Norway), 194
Norwegian royal family, xi, 79, 160, 179
Norwegians, vii–viii, x, xvi, xviii–xxi, 1–4, 7, 9, 15, 17–18, 20–21, 24, 26–29, 31–36, 39–40, 43, 48–49, 51, 53–54, 56–57, 62–63, 69, 71–72, 74–75, 77–79, 83–85, 87–88, 91–93, 96, 100–102, 107–11, 120–22, 125, 132, 134, 136, 139–47, 150, 153, 156–57, 160–63, 166–70, 172, 178, 185–86, 189–90, 199–201, 203–7, 211; Christian orientation, 132, 172, 207; contributions in the Middle Ages, 144; contributions of significant individuals, 53–54, 121; creators of American values, 26, 43–44, 75; discovered America, 77, 102, 121, 134, 153–54, 203–4; elite, 142; emi-

grated Norwegians are best proof of Norway's greatness, 147, 208–9; homeland, 32, 78–79, 87, 92–93, 107–8, 146, 161–62, 206; inventors, 144; love of liberty, 50–51, 69, 88, 205; migration, viii, 1, 4, 7; mistaken for Swedes, 186; modern Vikings, 40, 44–49, 69, 71–72, 74–75, 199; Norman conquests, 26; pure and unblemished race, 157; purest Nordics, 151, 157; sacrifice their lives for America and Norway, 24, 160, 205–6; settlement of England, 26; struggle to get Norwegian discovery of America recognized, 154; success as proof of Norway's greatness, 168, 205–6; superiority, 136; traitors, 190; transnational identity, 143, 159–60, 168, 163, 205–6; Viking traits, 71–72, 75, 168, 204–6
Norwegian sailors and seamen, 160, 173, 201
Norwegian school system, xvi, 98
Norwegian Seamen's Church, 170
Norwegian Seamen's Mission, 190
Norwegian settlements in America, 26, 29, 62–63, 72, 75, 91
Norwegian settlers, 15, 17, 123, 143
Norwegian Shipping and Trade Mission (Nortraships), 190
Norwegian Singing Association, 166–67, 170, 206
Norwegian singing societies, 86, 166, 182
Norwegians most racially pure Nordics, 44
Norwegian society, 3, 11, 21, 35
Norwegian Society, 85, 152
Norwegian Society of America, 82–83
Norwegian Society of Minneapolis, 82
Norwegian songs, 86, 144
Norwegian's Seamen Home, 69

Norwegian State Lutheran Church, 4, 15, 87
Norwegian student singing societies, 102
Norwegian-Swedish union, 72, 78–79, 92
Norwegian symbols, 30, 61, 82, 86, 94, 168–69, 174, 193, 202; modern-day, 202
Norwegian Synod, 28, 63, 96
Norwegian travelers, 75–77
Norwegian wedding, traditional, 86
Nova Dania, 52
Numedal, Norway, 15
Nygaardsvold, Johan (prime minister of Norway), 177, 193, 204, 206, 208; auctions old hat for war bonds, 206; comments on one hundredth thirtieth anniversary of Norway's constitution, 204; Leif Erikson Day speech (1935), 177; May 17 speech in Minneapolis, 193; returns home to Norway, 208
nyt Rige, I et (From Fjord to Prairie, or In the New Kingdom) (Johnson), 80
"Nytt lys over Leif Eiriksson" (New Light over Leif Erikson, editorial), 198

Oftedal, Sven (pastor), 64
Olaf Haraldsson (Olav Haraldsson, king of Norway). *See* St. Olaf
Olav (crown prince of Norway), xii, xvi, 79, 165–66, 175, 179–81, 183–89, 191–92, 208, 223; lecture tour of America during World War II, 192; returns home to Norway, 208; visits Lincoln's home, 186; visit to America (1939), xvi, 175, 179–89, 223. *See also* Norway's royal couple

Olav, Hans (Norwegian press attaché), 181, 183
Olav Trygvason Choir, 183
Old Norse sagas, 43, 193
Oleana (colony in Pennsylvania), 7
Olner, Pastor, 213
Olson, Floyd Bjørnstjerne (governor of Minnesota), 172
Olson, Julius E. (professor at University of Wisconsin), 87–88, 91–92, 126
"Om at bevare vort modersmaal" (Preserving our Mother Tongue), 104
One Hundred Percent American campaign, 117, 157
"Open Letter to the Unconquerable Norwegians, An" (Auslander), 205
Order of Cincinnati, 52
Order of the Knights of the White Cross, Nora Lodge, 59
Oregon, 19, 77
Origins Proviso (1929), xi. *See also* National Origins Act
Orkneys, the, 201
Oskar (king of Norway and Sweden), 83
Osland, Birger, 93, 174
Oslo (capital of Norway), vii, 154, 165–66, 171, 189–90, 199, 201, 208, 212–13. *See also* Kristiania
Oslo fjord, 212
Oslo-Ibsen Committee, 166
Oslo Philharmonic Orchestra, 165
Other, the, 27
Ottawa, Illinois, 143–44
"Our Norwegian Ally" *(New York Times)*, 205
Our Savior's Cemetery (Oslo), 166

Pacific Coast, 17, 77, 179
Pacific Northwest, 20, 61, 183
Pageant of the Northmen, The, 137
Palmer, Thomas W., 69
Panama Exhibition (1915), 93
Pan-Scandinavianism, 60
Parades, 137
Passing of the Great Race, The (Grant), 112
Pearl Harbor, Hawaii, 192
Pedersen, C. O. (pastor of the Norwegian Seamen's Mission), 190; "Bridge Building—a Warning," 190
Peder Victorious, 131
Peer Gynt (Ibsen), 167
Peer Gynt Lodge (Los Angeles), 182
Peerson, Cleng, 7, 12–13, 54, 72, 74, 137, 143, 174; compared to Leif Erikson, 74 "father of Norwegian emigration," 12; monument dedicated, 174–75; "Peer Gynt on the Prairie," 12
Pennsylvania Amish, 119
Person, Johan, 31
Petersen, C. J. P. (pastor), 60
Petersen, Franklin, 157
Petersen, J. C. (bishop of Norway), 145
Peterson, Carl Fredrik, 31
Philadelphia, Pennsylvania, 52
Philippines, the, 80
Poland, 162
Polish immigrants, 8, 80, 162
Polonia, 162. *See also* Greater Poland
Polonians, 162
Pook's Hill, Maryland, 191
Pope County, Minnesota, 18
Presbyterian Scots, 103
Prestgard, Kristian, 152, 187
Preus, Herman A. (president of the Norwegian Synod), 28
Princeton, New Jersey, 201
Prohibition, 119
"Prophets, The," 64
Protestants, 103, 111
public celebrations, 58–59, 75

INDEX

pull factors, 1, 12–21
Puritans, 46, 53, 112
push factors, 1, 12, 118

Quakers, 4, 15
Quisling, Vidkun, 189, 195–96, 201–2; cartoon showing Hitler pinning medal on Quisling *(Nordisk Tidende)*, 196
Quota Board, 155
Quota Law, 156–57. *See also* National Origins Act (1927)

racial ideology, 102, 119
Racine, Wisconsin, 174
Ræder, Ole Munch, 27
Rafn, Carl C., 43
railroads, 9, 19
Red Hook (Brooklyn), New York, 17
Red River Valley (Minnesota and North Dakota), 84–87, 91, 92
Reed Amendment, 155
Reierson, Johan R., 15
Reistad, Ole (major in Norwegian Royal Air Force), 190–91
religious pietism, 6–7
Restaurationen (The Restoration), xi, 4–5, 12, 45, 54, 134, 154; Sloopers, 4, 12, 137, 143–44, 147
return migration, 10. *See also* Norway
Return to the Future (Undset), 200
Revolutionary War (America), 52, 78, 144
Rice County, Minnesota, 18
Riket grundlægges (Founding the Kingdom), 131
Ring, Frederick (Norwegian-American Methodist pastor), 147
Ristad, D. G. (pastor), 80
Rogaland (province of Norway), 12
Rolfsen, Nordahl, 74, 98, 100

Rollo (aka Gange-Rolf, "Rolf the Walker"), 72, 83–84, 86–88, 91; plants seeds of liberty, 91; statue dedicated, 83–88, 91; statue dedicated at Rouen, France, 91
Rollo Statue Committee, 92
Rome, Italy, 91
Rølvaag, Ole E., xix–xx, 53, 119, 121–25, 128–31, 139, 150–51, 165; need to preserve Norwegian traditions, 121–25, 129–30, 139; seven characteristics of Norwegians, 128–30
Roosevelt, Franklin D., 54, 175, 177, 179, 187, 189, 191, 202–3, 205, 223; Leif Erikson Day proclamation (October 9, 1935), 54, 175, 177, 223; Leif Erikson Day proclamation (October 9, 1944), 205; "Look to Norway" speech, 202–3; Norway represents the truest ideals of democracy and freedom, 191, 202–3; Norwegians as fellow fighters in sacred cause of democracy, 205; ties together the two halves of the Norwegian people, 205–6
Roosevelt, Theodore, ix, 78, 83, 107–8
Rosseland, Guri Endresen, 74
Rouen, France, 91
Rove, Olaf I. (Norwegian consul in Milwaukee), 95
Royal Air Force (Britain), 194
Royal Norwegian Palace (Slottet), 166, 208
Russia, 3
Russians, 156
Russo-Japanese War, 78
Ruud, Martin B. (professor of philosophy and English at the University of Minnesota), 167, 172
Rygg, A. N., 194
Rynning, Ole, 7, 14–15

sacred feminine principle, 86
sagas, Norwegian, 44, 193
Sagene Church, Norway, 213
Samtiden (Norwegian journal), 72–73
San Francisco, California, 17, 20–21, 93, 182, 194, 206
Saturday Evening Post, 205
Scandia Hall (Chicago), 70
Scandinavia, 79, 88, 102–3; Teutonic spirit found there, 88
Scandinavian Americans, 50, 72, 107, 117
Scandinavian countries, 155, 173
Scandinavian Element in the United States, The (Babcock), 111
Scandinavian girls: domestic employment, 21
Scandinavian heritage, 83
Scandinavian immigration, 118
Scandinavian languages, 74
Scandinavian Regiment (Fifteenth Wisconsin), 27, 29, 54. *See also* Fifteenth Wisconsin Regiment; Johnson, John A.; Schøyen, David Monrad
Scandinavians, 27–28, 52, 57, 61, 63, 72, 92, 103, 111–12, 156, 174
Schøyen, David Monrad, 29
Scotland, 157, 201
Seaman's Hotel, 190
Seattle, Washington, 18, 20, 142–43, 146, 167, 171, 173, 183, 194–95, 206
Seland, Hans, 77, 102, 142
Semmingsen, Ingrid, 200
Senate, U.S., 157
Seventy-first Regiment, 145
Shakespeare, William, 167
Shame of the Cities (1904), 111
Shetlands, the, 201
shipping industry (America), 17, 19–20
Sigurd Jorsalfar Suite, 183
Sinding, John W. (president of the Norwegian-American World's Exposition Committee), 173
Sioux Falls, South Dakota, 173
Skandinaven (Norwegian-American newspaper), 29, 70, 79, 102, 156, 187
Skandinavisk Socialist Forening for Chicago med Omegn (Scandinavian Socialist Association of Chicago and Vicinity), 108
Skard, Sigmund, 200
Skatmester (tax master), 61
"Skogen som klædde fjeldet" (The Forest That Clothed the Mountain), 124
slaves, 15
slekt (family ties), 19
Smestad, Norway, 213
Smith, Joshua T., 43
Social Darwinism, 50, 64, 119, 222
Socialist Labor Party, 109
Socialist Party of America, 108
socialists, 109
Societas Scandinaviensis, 52
Sogn county, Norway, 18
Sollid, A., 76
Solum, Reidar (consul of Norway), 206
sommer i Norge, En (A Summer in Norway) (Prestgard), 152
Sons of Norway, 81, 83, 86, 93, 95–96, 110, 142, 153, 175, 182, 189, 203, 206
"Sons of Norway" as a derogatory term, 190
Sophocles, 167
Sørland (the Southland), Norway, 22
Sørlandet (the Southland, Norwegian training ship), 173–74
South America, xiv
South Dakota, 18, 90
Southerners, 156
Søyland, Carl (editor of *Nordisk Tidende*), 179

Spain, 49, 69
Spanish-American War (1898), 80
Spanish immigrants, 49
"Spirit of the Vikings, The" (radio broadcast), 195
Spitsbergen, 151
Springfield, Illinois, 186
S. S. *Paducah*, 152
Stahlberg, A., 79
Stallare, Bjørn (member of Norwegian underground), 206
Stang-Andersen, Christian (vice consul of Norway), 183, 206
"Star-Spangled Banner" (America's national anthem), 135, 169
Stassen, Harold (governor of Minnesota), 184
Statuary Hall (U.S. Capitol Building), 176
Stavanger, Norway, xii, 147
stave church, 69
steamships, 9–10, 19; companies, 20
Steffen, Lincoln, 111
Stegner, George, 1
Stegner, Hilda, 1
Stegner, Wallace, 1
Steinbeck, John, 205
Stenholt, Lars, 71, 76, 102
Stevens Hotel, 173
stevnes (meetings organized around a specific *bygd*), 94
St. George's Hotel (New York), 145
Stiklestad, Battle of, 168, 170
Stoddard, Luther, 151
St. Olaf (Olaf Haraldsson, king of Norway), 137, 168–72; established Christianity in Norway, 137; linked with Fridtjof Nansen, 171; St. Olav celebration (nine-hundredth anniversary of his death), 168–72
St. Olaf Choir, 169

St. Olaf College (Northfield, Minnesota), 121, 132, 173, 176, 180–81
St. Olaf College Band, 166
St. Olav (Olav Haraldsson). *See* St. Olaf
Storlie, Caroline, 133
Storm, Gustav, 47
større Norge, Et (A Greater Norway) (Nordmanns-Forbundet), 159, 161
Storting (Norwegian national assembly), ix, 4, 79, 82, 95–96, 141, 145, 153, 157, 165, 168–69, 193, 202, 204; debate on America's quota law, 157; dissolution of the Swedish-Norwegian dynastic union, ix, 78–79; symbol of modern Norway, 193, 202, 204
Stowe, Leland (American journalist), 189–90; Norwegians offer little resistance against Germans, 189–90
Stub, Hans G., 96
Sundby-Hansen, Harry, 125–26
Superior, Wisconsin, 20, 185
Svalbard, 151
Svendsen, Johan (composer), 207
Sverdrup, Johan, 36
Svensk-amerikansk studier (Swedish-American studies), 31
Sweden, xv, 3, 61, 70, 117, 208, 214; Swedish influences, 32, 51, 60, 78–79, 92; views of Norway, 214
Swedes, 15, 44, 72, 149, 156, 186
Swedish-American identity, 31
Swedish-American leaders, 107
Swedish-American press, 155
Swedish Americans (Swedes in America), 31, 42, 50, 61, 78, 111, 117, 128, 149, 179; Norway's rebellion compared to Southern states, 78; tercentenary celebration, 179
Swedish immigrants, 42, 111

Sweet, W. D. (mayor of Fargo, North Dakota), 92
Swenson, Laurits S. (American minister to Norway), 147, 165
Swiss, the, 103
Synnøve Solbakken (Bjørnson), 33

Tacoma, Washington, 87
Takla, Knut, 22, 108
Talle, H. O., 180
Tangjerd, Peder, 123
Tank, Nils Otto, 15
Taranger, Absalom, 141
Taylor, Bayard, 214
Telemark (province of Norway), 15, 18
Tennyson, B. G., 85, 87
Teutonic race, 90, 140
Texas, 54
Their Fathers' God (Rølvaag), 53, 131
Thompson, J. Jørgen (dean of St. Olaf College), 181
Thorps family, 62
Thrane, Marcus, 5, 35
Tideman, Adolph, 33
Tidens Tegn (Norwegian newspaper), 177–78
"To Norway," (Nelson), 73
"To Norway's Fighting Forces" (cartoon), 195, 197
Torshov, Norway, 212
Torshov Church, Norway, 212
Trædel, Nils (Norwegian cabinet minister), 173
Tranmæl, Martin, 108
transatlantic celebrations, xii, 59–60, 96, 165–88, 219. *See also* Norway: ceremonies in both Norway and America; transnationalism: celebrations
transnationalism, xii–xiii, xvi–xvii, xx, 25, 80, 87, 92, 138, 154, 159–60, 169, 217–18, 220–21; celebrations, xvi, xx, 96, 154; radio broadcast, xii, 154, 169, 182, 184–85; theory, xvii, 217–18, 220–21
transnational spaces, 160, 217–21
Trollness (fictional Norwegian village), 205
Trønderlaget, 153
Trondhjem (Trondheim), Norway, 79, 88, 207
Trovaten, A. A., 85
Tullos, Rees Edgar (president of the United Lutheran Council), 207
Tusen norske skip (A Thousand Norwegian Ships), 194
two Norways, 44

Ueland, Ole G., 21
Ullman, Viggo, 82
Ulvestad, Martin, 48–50, 53
Ulvik, Norway, 1
Undset, Sigrid, xii, 200, 207; promotes the greater Norway, 200
Ungdomssrørsla (Rural Youth Movement), Norway, 214
unions (Norway), 9
United Lutheran Council, 207
University of Iowa, 52
University of Minnesota, 127, 153, 167, 172, 184
University of Oslo, 166, 171
University of Washington, 167
University of Wisconsin, 44
Upper Midwest, 15, 18–19, 62–63, 76, 182, 208
"Upon the Death of Abraham Lincoln" (Ibsen), 164
Upsi, Erik (bishop), 50

Vaar egen tid (Our Own Times) (Keilau), 164

Valdres, Norway, 18
Van der Bilt, Jan Arentszen, 52
Vang, Minnesota, 18
Veblen, A. A. (leader of the Valdres bygdelag), 109
Veblen, Thorsten, 24
Veien mot Vest (The Way to the West) (Semmingsen), 200
Vesterheim (Norwegian-American museum). *See* Norwegian-American Pioneer Museum
Vesterheim (Western Home), x, xiv, 124, 211
Vicker, E. J., 167
Vigeland, Gustav, 84
Viking (magazine of the Viking Battalion), 199
Viking (replica ship), 69–71, 77, 102, 153, 173–74
Viking age, xix, 29, 32, 43, 50, 53, 69, 74–75, 101, 123, 137, 150, 169, 174, 195, 200, 202, 214, 222; freedom and individualism, 200; history, 32, 43–44, 48, 75, 132, 137, 141, 150, 169, 195, 200; Norse presence in America, 43–44, 50, 123
Viking ancestors and descendants (blood), xix, 42, 51, 70–75, 104, 222; connection to American values, 72–73, 75, 104, 222
Viking Battalion, viii, xii, 160, 199, 212–13; American Forces Day (Oslo), 199, 212–13; guarded German prisoners, 199; modern Vikings, viii, xii, 199, 212; several men of the battalion marry homeland Norwegian women, 199; "sons of Norway," viii. *See also* Ninety-ninth Battalion
Vikingfærden: En illustreret beskrivelse af "Vikings" reise (An Illustrated Description of the *Viking's* Journey) (Andersen), 71
Viking race, 51, 55
Viking regalia, 59
Vikings, vii–x, xii, 26, 32, 40, 44–50, 55, 57, 60–61, 69–75, 92, 94–95, 100–101, 110, 128, 134–35, 139, 137, 147, 150, 153, 168, 175, 186, 190, 193, 195, 199–200, 212, 222; anti-Nazi cartoons, 195; battlelust, 110; eternal Vikings, viii–ix; first American pioneers, 199; first European discoverers of America, 26, 41–44, 150; heritage, xix, 32, 71, 74, 94, 101, 128, 190, 200; individual freedom, 129, 193, 200; modern Vikings, viii, xii, 39–40, 47–49, 69–72, 74–75, 100, 173, 199, 212; Norwegian Vikings, 101; symbols appropriated by the Nazis, 195; Viking blood in the Anglo-Saxon race, 70, 101; Viking traits, 39–40, 49, 55, 71–75, 92, 100, 128–29
Vikings, The (painting) (Franklin), 144
Viking ship, vii, 69–71, 77, 102, 144, 152–53, 173–74, 184, 199
"Vikings of the Midwest" (Risley), 132
Viking spirit, 39–40, 74, 91, 132, 174, 195; ability to succeed in modern society, 39–40, 74; links to Christianity, 132; National Socialism appropriation, 195
Viking warrior (Fall River, Massachusetts), 43, 50
Viking window, the, 132
Vinge, John, 52
Vinje, Aasmund Olavson, 35–36
Vínland (Vinland), vii, 50, 62, 154, 169, 171, 198
Vi vil vine (We Will Win) slogan, 204

Vogt, Nils Collett, 149–50; Norwegian Americans and homeland Norwegians diverged too much to be part of same nation, 149–50
Voice of Norway, The (Koht and Skard), 200
Voss, Norway, 18
Vossings, 17

Wahpeton, North Dakota, 83, 86, 91
Wales, 157
Walker, Colonel (commander of the Viking Battalion), 199
Wallem, Fredrik M., 29
Washington (state), 19, 77, 120
Washington, D.C., 79, 184, 192
Washington, George, 52–53
Washington Evening Star (American newspaper), 176
Washington Posten (Norwegian-American newspaper), 171, 182–83, 195, 203, 206
Wass, Denmark, 53
Waterford, Wisconsin, 54
Wefring, Carl Wilhelm (president of upper chamber of Norway's parliament), 145
Welles, Albert, 53
Werenskiold, Erik, 214
Wergeland, Agnes Mathilde, 23
Wergeland, Henrik, xv, 3, 32–33, 82, 84–88, 102; personification of Norwegian character, 87–88; statue erected, 82, 84–87, 96, 102, 107–8
Werner, August, 183, 206
West Coast (America), 93, 182–83
Westerners, 156

West Indies, 156
White race, 112
Whittier, John Greenleaf, 43
Wild Duck, The (Ibsen), 166
Williamsen, A. E., 153
William the Conqueror, 46
Wilson, Woodrow (president of the United States), 117
Windingstad, Ole (director of New York Philharmonic Orchestra), 144, 170
Winnebago County, Iowa, 18
Winneshiek County, Iowa, 18
Wisconsin, 15, 17–18, 29, 54, 77, 90, 117, 144, 189
Wist, Johannes B., 96–97, 109, 112, 118
world economic system, xix
world labor market, 1
World's Columbian Exposition (1893), 69, 76, 82, 102, 173
World's Fair in Philadelphia (1926), 152
World War I, xi, xx, 10–11, 48, 55, 76, 83, 90, 112, 115, 117–19, 121, 123, 139, 149, 168, 175, 189
World War II, viii, xii, xviii, xx, 23, 118, 160, 165, 175, 188–89, 208–9, 220, 223–24
Worst, J. H. (president of the North Dakota Agricultural College), 87, 90

Yankee Americans, 56, 77, 101, 106, 120. *See also* Anglo-Americans
Yankee system, 20

Zangwill, Israel, 106

DARON W. OLSON is assistant professor of history at Indiana University East in Richmond, Indiana.

DEC 2 4 2012